The Paradox of Progress

THE PARADOX OF PROGRESS

ECONOMIC CHANGE, INDIVIDUAL ENTERPRISE, AND POLITICAL CULTURE IN MICHIGAN, 1837-1878

Martin J. Hershock

OHIO UNIVERSITY PRESS
Athens

Ohio University Press, Athens, Ohio 45701
© 2003 by Ohio University Press

Printed in the United States of America
All rights reserved

Ohio University Press books are printed on acid-free paper ∞

11 10 09 08 07 06 05 04 03   5 4 3 2 1

Jacket and title page art: "Au Sable and Northwestern train,"
E.C. Photograph Collection, Bentley Historical Library, University of Michigan

Library of Congress Cataloging-in-Publication Data

Hershock, Martin J., 1962–
    The paradox of progress : economic change, individual enterprise, and political culture in
Michigan, 1837–1878 / Martin J. Hershock.
        p. cm.
    Includes bibliographical references and index.
    ISBN 0-8214-1513-1 (cloth : alk. paper)
        1. Republican Party (U.S. : 1854–)—History—19th century. 2. Michigan—Politics and
government—1837-1950. 3. Michigan—Economic conditions. I. Title.

JK2356.H47 2003
977.4'02—dc21

                                                                    2003044201

CONTENTS

ACKNOWLEDGMENTS

In more ways than I can ever acknowledge, this book has been a collaborative undertaking. I hasten to add, however, that those who have aided me in this endeavor bear none of the responsibility for any of its faults or shortcomings.

My first debt of gratitude is owed to Gillian Berchowitz and the wonderful editors and staff of the Ohio University Press. Their immediate and continued enthusiasm for this project and their efficient and congenial replies to my tiresome inquiries have been greatly appreciated. Many thanks are also owed to the staff of the Bentley Library at the University of Michigan. One could not ask for a friendlier place to work. I would also like to acknowledge the financial support of the Bentley Library through the award of two Mark C. Stevens Researcher Travel Fellowships and of the Horace H. Rackham School of Graduate Studies of the University of Michigan. Chapters 2 and 6 include materials that appear in slightly different form in my articles "To Shield a Bleeding Humanity: Conflict and Consensus in Mid-Nineteenth Century Michigan Political Culture," *Mid-America* (Winter 1995), and "Copperheads and Radicals: Michigan Partisan Politics during the Civil War Era, 1860–1865," *Michigan Historical Review* (Spring 1992). I would like to thank the editors of *Mid-America* and the *Michigan Historical Review* for permission to reprint these works. The maps in this book were graciously prepared by Kyle Rearick and Karl Longstreth, curator of the Map Library at the University of Michigan.

Over the course of my professional training, I have had the great fortune to have been guided and nurtured by a number of talented and truly gifted individuals. In particular, I wish to thank Donald Proctor, Peter Amann, Seth Wigderson, Marc Kruman, Sandra VanBurkleo, and Phil Mason for introducing me to the field of history and for instilling within me the desire to share my love of history with others. I am extremely appreciative of the support, constructive criticism, and often needed encouragement provided me by Maris Vinovskis, Gerry Moran, Fran Blouin, and Bruce Pietrykowski, my colleagues at

Hobart and William Smith Colleges and the University of Michigan–Dearborn, Harry Watson, and the anonymous readers for the Ohio University Press. To my historical mentor, J. Mills Thornton III, I owe a special debt—both personal and intellectual. His friendly, heartening manner and boundless intellect opened an entirely new world for me. It remains my greatest hope that I might someday change a student's life in the manner that he has changed mine. As a counselor and an adviser, he is unsurpassed. His enduring faith in me and this project has served as a constant source of comfort and inspiration. I thank him for everything.

To the hundreds of students who have passed through my life over the years and especially to those with whom I remain close, I extend my heartfelt gratitude. Their warm response to my teaching, their eagerness to learn, and their numerous insights have proven to me, time and time again, that I have made the right career choice. What I have taught them all pales in comparison with what they have taught me (about history, about teaching, and about myself) in return.

On a personal level, I wish to thank the many friends that have had to endure my constant whining and incessant pleas for sympathy and assistance: Cam Amin, Bill Atwell, Katie Barnes-Kerrigan, Suzanne Bergeron, Kevin Boyle, Dan Clark, Elaine Clark, Greg Field, Maureen Flynn, Liette Gidlow, Judy Mahoney, John Shovlin, Gebru Tareke, and Kevin Thornton. Thanks, too, to Cara Shelly, who unselfishly gave of herself so that this book might see the light of day. I consider myself most fortunate to have Bil Kerrigan in my corner. His never ending support, empathy, and sense of humor and his incredible insight mean the world to me. I only wish that everyone had such a friend and consider myself truly blessed to have him as mine.

I am also grateful for the encouragement provided by my family members. It was an ongoing source of solace to know that they had faith in me and in my ability to see this project through to its completion.

Undeniably, my greatest debt is owed to my wife, Kathy. For twenty years, her love and friendship have buoyed my spirits and lifted my heart. The many sacrifices that she has made to allow this dream to become a reality, though infrequently acknowledged, are much appreciated. I thank her for giving my life meaning and purpose and for inspiring me to do more than I thought possible. It is to her that this work is dedicated. Finally, I would like to thank my daughters, Rebecca and Rachel, for filling my life with love and laughter. The time that I have spent with them is my most cherished treasure, and I apologize for sometimes losing sight of that. I love them both more than they could ever know.

INTRODUCTION

American historians have long recognized the central importance of the nineteenth-century Republican Party in preserving the Union, ending slavery, and opening the way for industrial capitalism and the rise of big business in the Gilded Age. We now know that the party of Abraham Lincoln grew ideologically out of the "free-labor" ethos of America's yeoman farmers, the opportunity that free soil opened for their social and economic mobility, and the danger that slavery in the territories posed for the future and the liberty of these individuals and their families. Indeed, one need look no further than Lincoln himself—specifically, to his father's decision to move his family, including young Abraham, from proslavery Kentucky across the Ohio River to free-soil Indiana, thus allegedly paving the way for Abraham's rise to middle-class respectability and eventually to the White House—to find tangible representation of the power of the free-soil ideal and the antebellum Republican paradigm of individual enterprise. What is perhaps more puzzling, however, is how the party that supported the antislavery movement, free soil, free labor, and "Lincoln the Rail-Splitter" evolved into the party of Mark Hanna, J. P. Morgan, and William McKinley, a party that conflated the virtues of individual enterprise and big business.[1]

This work examines that transformation by exploring a deep, though sadly neglected, contradiction that lay at the heart of the supremely influential ideology of the early Republican Party. The party's celebration of free labor had deep roots in the anticapitalist culture of the Democratic Party that had emerged from Americans' struggles with railroads, the Bank of the United States, and various forms of threatened monopoly in the Jacksonian decades. It also drew heavily on the promarket commitments of the early Whig Party and the Whigs' celebration of progress, enterprise, and economic and cultural improvement. Torn between the competing tendencies of these contrary values, Republicans of the Civil War era struggled to resolve their ideological dilemma with a formula that would enable them not only to win popular elections but also to model America's acceptance of Gilded Age capitalism. Nowhere was this process more obvious or more absorbing than in mid-nineteenth-century Michigan, the birthplace of the Republican Party.

For the generation of Americans who came of age during the middle decades of the nineteenth century, rampant change was an inescapable part of life. Within this relatively short span of years, they confronted the social, economic, and cultural upheaval engendered by the ongoing development of a market economy, renewed the national debate over slavery's expansion as the nation added new western territories, and experienced the demise of the Jacksonian party system and the creation of a new and more sectionally oriented party system in its stead. Americans desperately hoped that this new party system would help them cope with and direct or curb the onslaught of change and that it would provide them with a modicum of stability in a tumultuous world. Their hopes, however, were rapidly dashed, and they were forced to face yet another, even more unsettling ordeal: four bloody years of civil war, followed by another twelve years spent reconstructing their divided nation.

Arguably, no change affected antebellum Americans more profoundly than the market revolution. Driven by a burgeoning and mobile population and aided by the improvement and expansion of the nation's transportation and communications networks, the market economy emerged full blown in the United States during the first half of the nineteenth century and quickly began to penetrate even the most remote corners of the nation. Many Americans, enticed by the opportunity to get ahead and increasingly connected to the world beyond their immediate neighborhoods, turned their backs on the personal, face-to-face traditions of self-provisioning agriculture or abandoned customary methods of artisanal manufacturing and began producing specifically for the market, dragging others along with them. The changes wrought by this commercial metamorphosis were far reaching and, for many, mind numbing.[2]

During the mid-nineteenth century, few states in the Union experienced the disruptive effects of this transformation in as short a span of time as did Michigan. By 1850, after thirteen years of statehood, Michigan and its citizens were just beginning (due to the lingering effects of the panic of 1837) to feel the full impact of the encroaching world of the cash nexus. Over the ensuing decade, thanks in large measure to a railroad boom, the state came to occupy a central location in the nation's transportation network, serving as a crossroads between the East and West and becoming a center of market activity. To say that this transition came off without a hitch, however, would be extremely misleading.

Reactions to the market in Michigan ran the gamut from outright resistance to partial accommodation to the complete abandonment of traditional subsistence axioms and an embrace of the world of cash exchange. The ambivalence evident among Michigan residents, though perhaps more pronounced than that of citizens elsewhere due to the rapidity and timing of change in the state, was shared, to some degree, by all Americans. Unpredictable cycles of boom and bust, the intangible operations of the law of supply and demand, the requirements of competition, the uncertainties of international trade, and the total disruption of the nation's traditional cooperative and community-oriented social order led a great many Americans to question whether active participation in the market was worth the risk to their security and independence. Made uneasy by the speed and scope of social and economic change, many worried that their society was spinning out of control. This feeling of vertigo induced anxiety-laden Americans to seek sources of solace and stability in a world in which they felt adrift.[3]

This work attempts to develop a better understanding of this ambivalence toward change and its implications by exploring the expectations and attitudes—which gave rise to well-defined social and economic precepts and a correlative political culture—of mid-nineteenth-century Michiganians as they confronted this transformation. To understand more fully the implications of this ambivalence, the volume concentrates upon one of its most tangible and influential manifestations—the state's political culture, a manifestation constantly redefined in the face of ongoing change. Michigan's two constitutional conventions in this period, one in 1850 and the other in 1867, and the state's position as the birthplace of the Republican Party offer ready means through which to examine America's mid-nineteenth-century political culture and, in the process, reveal much about how antebellum northerners dealt with the myriad changes reordering their lives.

Though focused on political culture and political action, this work does not rely upon the sort of systematic quantitative analysis of voter behavior employed by many political and social historians. On a practical level, as noted by numerous social scientists, the use of aggregate-level data to make inferences about individual voting behaviors (the standard methodological trope utilized in such works) is problematic and often produces distorted and flawed conclusions. Beyond such theoretical concerns, however, this book refrains from employing statistical methods because it seeks to describe a frame of mind, or ethic, that engendered the formulation of a set of coherent standards of moral, political, and economic judgment that, in turn, shaped human relationships; quantitative methodologies are ill suited for this approach. Put simply, this book explores, to borrow a term made famous by historian E. P. Thompson, the *moral economy* of mid-nineteenth-century Michigan.[4]

Michigan, of course, did not exist in a vacuum. In fact, the reactions of Michiganians to this period of intense change were similar to those of other Americans living in disparate parts of the nation, and although those reactions reflected local and regional circumstances, they nonetheless have far-reaching implications for the study of American history.

Michigan's midcentury political culture mirrored that of the nation at large. Shaped by a traditional republican fear of power and a strong democratic impulse, the political culture of Jacksonian America gave voice to the citizenry's fears of "enslavement" in a rapidly changing and increasingly individualistic society. But the focus of such fears (and antipodal hopes) varied with the population's differing perceptions of the notion of liberty and the best means of protecting it. A fundamental dichotomy in these perceptions served as the catalyst for the political conflict of the era and as a point of reference for the Democratic and Whig Parties that evolved in response to—and provided direction for—this conflict.[5]

The driving force behind this political culture was an internal tug-of-war that tormented Americans of all classes. In essence, antebellum Americans found themselves simultaneously attracted to the enticements of the new world of the market and repulsed by its excess and instability. The outcome of these visceral struggles, of course, was determined by personal character traits and individual experience. As they worked their way through this internal conflict and as they themselves continued to reshape their world, Americans turned to institutions that had given form to their hopes and fears and provided them comfort in the past. For many antebellum Americans, that meant the political system. Those individuals who embraced the modern world of the market—people who, as Lawrence Kohl described them, were "comfortable with rational, self-interested human relations" and who "expressed great confidence that both [they] and the country were destined to prosper"—tended to become Whigs. By contrast, those who believed that modernity had unleashed an impersonal and aggressive, predatory tide upon innocent Americans and who felt that they were the chief victims and casualties of such a society chose instead to join the ranks of the Democratic Party. Ironically, for both Whigs and Democrats, attraction to the social order of their political opponents played a major role in shaping partisan principles. Whigs, though excited by the individualistic world of the market and active in promoting its growth and development, lamented the loss of community and therefore sought to re-create the communal world of their political opponents. And Democrats, though disdainful of the self-interest and greed of the market, evinced a strong attraction to this new social order by emphasizing the need to preserve the individual in the face of a smothering community.[6]

Within the context of rapid social change, this ambivalence manifested itself in a pervasive sense of anxiety and uneasiness among the American electorate. Having organized the citizenry to defend their particular conception of just what America should be, Whig and Democratic leaders faced the task of identifying the root cause of this discomfort. What they unearthed was an organized conspiracy of power arrayed against American liberty. While agreeing that liberty was in danger, however, Whigs and Democrats differed on precisely what liberty meant and what threatened its survival. For Democrats, fearful of market forces and the alteration of traditional society, liberty represented individual autonomy—the ability of individuals and their families to live independently and to make it on their own. Consequently, Democrats identified and struck out against concentrations of power that seemed to threaten the ability of individuals to direct their own lives. Whigs, in contrast, embraced the emerging market economy and its self-oriented social order, viewing it as an emancipatory force that expanded individual liberty by providing Americans with opportunities for social mobility. Hence, they organized in order to unleash enslaved human potential by identifying and destroying those things that kept Americans from achieving all that they might achieve. Because neither Whigs nor Democrats realized that they did not attach the same definitions to liberty, they developed a fundamental mistrust of their opponents and their claims about how to safeguard freedom. This clearly articulated political culture spawned close party competition throughout the nation and effectively drew the electorate to the polls in very large numbers by convincing people that through the simple act of voting, they were helping to protect the Republic and American liberty. "This country is divided into two parties," the editor of a Democratic Detroit newspaper noted in 1850; "they are impelled by opposing motives, the one, by a desire to maintain liberty and equality; the other is impelled by the passion for power and privilege. The principle of the first is democracy; the second is aristocracy, or federalism, at present known as whiggery." Midcentury Michiganians viewed their changing world through the lens of this turbulent political culture.[7]

Many Michigan residents, of course, eagerly welcomed the new spirit of capitalism and feverishly worked to further its reach, promoting the expansion of the banking and rail systems, launching new commercial ventures, and creating a climate conducive to business and commercial investment. But others (notwithstanding many scholars' assertions to the contrary) felt differently. Like their counterparts throughout the nation, these individuals did not fully embrace the changes that accompanied the transition to market capitalism. Indeed, many midcentury residents of the Wolverine State seem to have been particularly leery of ongoing change and its related societal disorder. In 1850, having been conditioned to cringe at the mere thought of an expansive commercial economy by the panic of 1837 and the severe depression that followed, Michiganians struck out at the potential threat of unbridled economic and social change by erecting constitutional barriers against the market, by making state government more responsive to the will of the people, and, in the extreme, by physically attacking the most tangible manifestation of that change—the railroad.[8]

Despite the best efforts of Michigan's tradition-bound Democratic majority, the state's market revolution raced forward in the 1850s. The manner in which residents reacted to their changing world offers a number of important lessons. Most obviously, Michigan's mid-nineteenth-century history clearly indicates that by conceptualizing the American market revolution as a static entity—a conceptual framework that largely relegates its occurrence to the period before 1840—historians have missed what are arguably the most important ramifications of that transformation. For as Michigan's experience reveals, the market revolution, interpreted through the prism of the state's Jacksonian political culture, was a major contributor to the collapse of the second American party system, to the subsequent rise of the sectionally divided third American party system, and, as a result, to the coming of the Civil War. Accustomed to viewing the expanding commercial economy as either a threat to, or a promoter of, liberty, Michiganians felt extremely uneasy about the changes sweeping their state. For some, the pace of change was too fast; for others, it was not fast enough. Yet in the early 1850s, most state residents agreed that their freedom was imperiled and that the existing political parties no longer seemed capable of or interested in protecting them or the Republic. This widespread ambivalence about change and its relationship to American liberty brought on the collapse of the Jacksonian party system in Michigan.[9]

But the collapse of that system did not mean the collapse of the political culture that had spawned it. In fact, just the opposite was true. As the old party structure crashed to the ground around them, Michiganians clung to the familiar political culture. Although they felt adrift and vulnerable, their political training told them what needed to be done: threats to American freedom had to be positively identified and destroyed, and those forces that stood in opposition had to be removed.

In the minds of state residents, caught up in the dizzying socioeconomic transformation of the 1850s, there was no shortage of potential threats to their freedom. Numerous political movements emerged to vie for the loyalties of former Whig and Democratic voters by giving voice to the electorate's hopes and fears. To date, historians have focused upon political antislavery in Michigan and ethnocultural issues such as nativism and temperance as the most salient of these new movements. This study suggests, however, that, in reality, concerns over slavery and ethnocultural divisions merely masked a more profound cleavage in antebellum America. That is, ethnocultural conflicts and concerns about the preservation of free soil in the face of an organized "Slave Power" were deeply rooted in the cultural and ideological tensions surrounding the extraordinary change that accompanied the market revolution. Because antislavery and ethnocultural issues spoke in some manner to this deep-seated apprehensiveness, they resonated with the American electorate. To their credit, the founders of Michigan's Republican Party seem to have recognized this reality, a recognition that allowed them to carry these concerns into public life and debate and to fashion a broad-based political coalition in 1854. This coalition captured the state in its first electoral bid.[10]

The Republican Party's early appeal in Michigan had much to do with its ability to seamlessly and earnestly embrace differing attitudes toward the predominant issue of the day as viewed through the eyes of the residents: where would the state's ongoing transformation lead, and what effect would this change have upon the liberties of Michiganians? Through their endorsement of nativism, temperance, and a general railroad law for the state and, most important, through the free-soil issue (with its contention that an organized slave power posed a threat to freedom), Republicans successfully melded the competing understandings of freedom that had long divided state voters into hostile partisan camps. They endorsed free-soil doctrines with their attendant claim that the slave power threatened freedom, and they allowed party members with disparate political pedigrees to articulate their own positions on what exactly freedom meant. In this way, Michigan's Republican organization smoothed over long-standing differences by intermingling elements from both anticapitalist and prodevelopment traditions and thus gave the appearance of defending both of the contemporary understandings of freedom simultaneously. A similar course was pursued by the party in reference to its endorsement of a general railroad law in Michigan. In its final form, the bill appeared prodevelopmental by opening the field to all comers and antidevelopmental by imposing a series of regulations upon state railroad corporations. In short, by defining itself as the protector of American liberty and all that that concept represented to the electorate, the party positioned itself in a way that enabled it to be everything to everybody. This strategy paid large political dividends in Michigan and allowed the Republicans to quickly grab control of state politics. Throughout the remainder of the 1850s and continuing through the crisis of war and into the early Reconstruction period, the fundamental divisions inherent within the Jacksonian political culture, though they surfaced from time to time, remained effectively submerged within the free-soil debate. Only by understanding Republicanism in this light can we begin to make sense of the movement's appeal to members of a broader northern electorate, many of whom found themselves confronting similar unsettling change.

With the military defeat of the slave power in 1865 and its political defeat as symbolized by the repudiation of President Andrew Johnson's plan of Reconstruction and the massive Republican electoral victory in 1866, the free-soil issue rapidly retreated into the shadows. When it did, Michigan's postbellum Republican leadership, eager to fuse the ethos of individual enterprise and the ideology of industrial capitalism, promoted a political agenda characterized by unbridled devotion to economic change (most identifiably through the party's failed efforts to reverse the antidevelopment tendencies of the state constitution through proposed revisions in 1867 and 1870 and through its repeated efforts to champion local aid for railroad construction). Undaunted and completely misinterpreting the public backlash against their efforts, Michigan's Republican leaders blatantly disregarded the concerns and fears of the party's diverse and sometimes contradictory constituency and obliviously forged ahead with their crusade. Such behavior, made more ominous in the eyes of many by the panic of 1873 and the deepening agricultural crisis, produced widespread disaffection from the party and exposed a still deeply divided electorate and the contested ideological and cultural fault line within it. The reemergence of this largely dormant and suddenly intensifying rift, in turn, further threatened and occasionally disrupted the Republicans' political hegemony and ideological evolution in the state in the latter decades of the century. Throughout the protracted debate that ensued, however, the same tension between conflicting and contradictory ideals and attitudes, as relevant in 1878 and beyond as they had been in 1850, continued to chart the state's—and the nation's—course.[11]

The Paradox of Progress

Map 1. Route of Michigan Central Railroad c. 1850. County boundaries are modern.

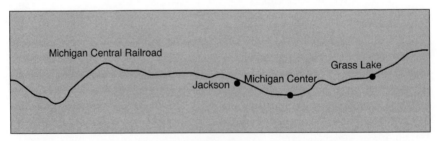

Map 2. Jackson County c. 1850. Site of the Michigan Railroad Conspiracy.

"We Were then, as it were, Still in Our Knickerbockers"

Michigan's Growing Pains

As UNPRECEDENTED socioeconomic change reshaped the nation and as the nascent political culture of the Jacksonian era was gaining its legs, Michigan entered the Union as the twenty-sixth state in 1837. Buoyed by the booming national economy and teeming with emigrants from the East stricken with "Michigan fever," the state was immediately caught up in the speculative frenzy of the day. Land was rapidly surveyed and put on the market, where it sold quickly, increased in value, and sold again. Proposed town sites, "portrayed with bewitching minuteness for the delectation of the ordinary observer," were platted, and their lots rapidly sold. Banks (most of which were woefully undercapitalized) were created at dizzying speed under Michigan's liberal banking law, and their dubious currencies flooded the state. Moreover, the state government, desirous of replicating other states' successful endeavors to create a network of internal improvements, borrowed heavily and embarked upon an ambitious and unwarranted plan to crisscross the state with railroads, canals, and roads. Unfortunately for Michigan, however, it joined the Union as the nation's economy entered a period of prolonged decline and stagnation.[1]

Although Michigan miraculously avoided the initial downturn brought on by the panic of 1837, its luck did not hold. By 1839, severe economic hardship arrived. Virtually overnight, the speculative bubble burst. Land prices plummeted, and property reverted to the state for nonpayment of taxes. Paper boomtowns, never built, remained no more than ghostly ink stains, fading into historical memory. The state's "wildcat" banks—including the ill-fated Bank of Michigan, designated the state's fiscal agent by the Whig legislature of 1841—closed their doors as quickly as they had opened them, leaving behind thousands of dollars in worthless, unredeemable banknotes. As mortgages were foreclosed, currencies collapsed, farm prices fell, and loans were called in, many Michiganians faced the very real threat of losing everything they had. To make matters worse, Michigan itself teetered on the brink of insolvency, unable to meet its loan obligations. As a result, the state was forced to abandon its quixotic general internal improvement plan and to concentrate its efforts on completing only the most promising of its projects, notably the Michigan Central and Michigan Southern Railroads.[2]

Politically, Michigan spent most of its first decade as a state atoning for its ill fortune and economic naïveté. The 1840s began with Whigs in control of both houses of the state legislature and of the governor's seat—a feat they would never replicate. Sensing an opportunity for victory in 1839, state Whigs, after a great deal of internal bickering, had finally agreed upon the conservative Springwells attorney William Woodbridge as their nominee for governor. Blessed with Woodbridge's impeccable credentials and long résumé of political service to the state and running on a platform calling for "Woodbridge . . . and reform," Michigan Whigs used the state's financial woes to oust their Democratic opponents in a closely fought contest.[3]

Once in power, the Whigs worked to meet the economic crisis. Tax deadlines were extended, government spending was slashed by cutting salaries and abolishing some offices, and the state's commissioners of internal improvements were forbidden to enter into any further construction contracts. In addition, recognizing the need to create a stable currency with which to pay taxes and move crops, Whig legislators passed a currency act in 1840 which authorized the state to issue drafts that would serve as the basis for loans from solvent banks so that the government could meet its payments to contractors. In return for accepting the drafts, banks were allowed to suspend specie payment and to increase their note issues.[4]

Sustained tenure in office, however, proved elusive for Michigan Whigs. As the election of 1841 neared, their party suffered a number of crushing setbacks. The death of William Henry Harrison and the apostasy of John Tyler shook state Whigs, as did the failure of the Bank of Michigan in 1841.

Reeling, they found themselves without the leadership of the popular Woodbridge, who had resigned as governor in December 1840 to accept a seat in the U.S. Senate. Not surprisingly, internal party divisions rapidly resurfaced, disrupting an always tenuous party unity and producing widespread disaffection among partisans—a disaffection enhanced by the gubernatorial nomination of a little-known Adrian banker and railroad executive, Philo C. Fuller.[5]

Watching their wounded opponents and echoing the Whigs' cry of "retrenchment and reform," Michigan Democrats moved in for the kill. Putting aside their own internal disputes, they agreed upon the popular Constantine merchant John S. Barry as their nominee for governor. Led by Barry, a fiscally conservative, antibank westerner, the Democrats easily dispatched their Whig rivals and regained control of both houses of the state legislature and of the governor's seat—a control the party would not relinquish until defeated by the upstart Republican Party in 1854.

Throughout Barry's first two terms in office, Michigan's Democrats remained true to their word, directing their efforts toward dealing with the devastating economic crisis paralyzing the state. Barry himself offered an example of economy in government by refusing the services of a state-employed secretary; in a later term, he went as far as selling the hay from the lawn of the capitol building and using the proceeds to help defray the costs of the constitutional convention of 1850. More important, Barry wasted little time in rallying his forces against what he perceived to be the true cause of the state's economic woes—the banking system. Within their first year in office, Democrats passed a series of laws aimed at destroying Michigan's remaining banks. Refusal to redeem banknotes in specie was made the test of insolvency, and the charters of banks not redeeming notes were repealed, the corporate rights of banks established under the state's free banking law were abolished, and the charter of the never organized state bank was negated. In 1844, the Democratic supreme court dealt the deathblow to Michigan's banks when it declared the state's 1837 general banking law unconstitutional.[6]

Democratic retrenchment did not stop with banks. One of the most pressing matters facing Barry and the Democrats was the $5 million debt accrued by the state as the result of its internal improvement mania. In 1838, unable to sell the bonds to support its ambitious infrastructure scheme locally, the state had turned to the New Jersey–based Morris Canal and Banking Company to serve as its selling agent. The Morris Company bought one-quarter of the bonds, and the remainder were purchased by the Pennsylvania branch of the

Bank of the United States. But in 1840, the Morris Company collapsed, followed by the Pennsylvania bank one year later. Having received a mere $2.6 million from the sale of its bonds and unable to recover the unsold bonds (which had been used as collateral by the defunct institutions), Michigan was left holding the bag. In 1843, despite the vehement protests of the Whigs, Michigan's Democrats successfully repudiated a portion of the state's outstanding debt by enacting the Butler Bill, which authorized the government to contest the payment of interest and principal on that portion of the outstanding bonds for which it had received no compensation. In the same year, legislators voted to halt construction on the state's two remaining internal improvements projects. Construction on the Michigan Southern Railroad, running westward from Monroe through the state's southern tier of counties, would cease immediately at Hillsdale. The Michigan Central, which ran westward from Detroit through the central tier of counties, would be pushed forward only as far as Kalamazoo. All told, Barry and his fellow Democrats cut state expenses by one-quarter in their first term alone. Nevertheless, hard times continued in Michigan, and the state remained economically distressed.[7]

Barry's successor, Alpheus Felch, an antibank lawyer from Ann Arbor, continued his predecessor's economy-minded ways. When he assumed office in January 1846, Felch found the state still $4.1 million in debt. To complicate matters, the state's railroads, the Michigan Southern and the Michigan Central, though profitable, were already antiquated and in disrepair and required a substantial infusion of cash if they were to continue operating. As things stood, however, neither road would generate enough income for the needed repairs or the necessary funds to enable the state to meet its loan obligations. Michiganians therefore faced a steep but constitutionally mandated property tax increase. Intent upon burdening the public no further, Felch determined to take drastic action and asked the legislature to sell the state's railroads. The act authorizing the sale, signed on March 28, 1846, netted the state $2.5 million.[8]

Although the state debt was reduced by the sale of the railroads, and economic prosperity—spurred by a swelling tide of immigrants from the East and a mineral rush in the Upper Peninsula facilitated by the sale of land by local Chippewa tribes through the Treaty of LaPointe in 1842—was slowly returning to Michigan, state Democrats remained wary. This caution was readily apparent as the new governor, Epaphroditus Ransom of Kalamazoo, assumed his seat in January 1848. Cognizant of the problems with which the state had been burdened as the result of its premature internal improvements scheme but equally aware of the needs of the growing western and northern sections of Michigan, Ransom and his Democratic legislative cohorts sought a way to promote a limited program of internal improvements without offending the popular will. The plan they adopted avoided the extravagant and grandiose projects of the past and focused instead upon the construction of plank roads—a plan that made sense in terms of the state's vast timber resources and was consistent with popular opinion. Hoping to avoid the mistakes of the past, the legislature refused to provide direct grants of money for such projects. Rather, plank-road companies would be granted tracts of land by the state. This land could, in turn, be sold by the companies, thereby providing the capital needed for the construction of the roads. Moreover, in keeping with the Democrats' traditional emphasis on equal access/equal rights, the legislature made it easier for plank-road companies to organize by enacting a general plank road law during its 1848 session. No longer hampered by the necessity of obtaining individual charters from the legislature, plank-road companies could organize freely as long as they met minimum legal requirements.[9]

The state legislative session of 1848 provided further evidence of the widespread ambivalence about the apparent return of economic prosperity to Michigan. Democrats, aware of the popular suspicion of the market economy and its unpredictability, passed a homestead exemption bill. By exempting a forty-acre rural homestead or an urban homestead of one lot from forced sale on execution for any debt growing out of a contract entered into after July 3, 1848, these legislators were convinced that they would enable the state's citizenry to avoid the hard times of the recent past.[10]

The year 1848, however, marked a momentary interruption of Democratic Party cohesion in Michigan as the issue of slavery's extension, thrust into the national spotlight by the Mexican War and the actions of a Democratic congressman from Pennsylvania named David Wilmot, temporarily eclipsed the economic issues around which state Democrats had so readily united. As it did in the rest of the nation, the issue of territorial expansion proved very popular in Michigan. In 1844, led by favorite son Lewis Cass (who had barely lost the Democratic Party's nomination for president), Michigan gave its solid support to James K. Polk's expansionist platform calling for the acquisition of all of Texas and all of Oregon. And though disappointed by Polk's willingness to go to war over Texas while compromising on the Oregon boundary, Michigan Democrats, with Cass now in the U.S. Senate, remained firmly on the side of territorial expansion—that is, until Wilmot introduced his famous proviso attempting to preserve the territories gained as a result of the Mexican War as free soil. The question of free soil in the territories quickly achieved what years of Whig attacks, internal bickering, and sectional animosity in the state could not: a divided Democratic Party in Michigan.[11]

Wilmot's Proviso set partisan brother against partisan brother. The party's more "radical" wing, led by freshman congressman and future Republican governor and U.S. senator Kinsley Scott Bingham of Green Oak Township and the Monroe lawyer and future Republican senator Isaac P. Christiancy, readily embraced the proviso. Meanwhile, antiproviso "conservatives" fell in line behind Lewis Cass. In the immediate afterglow of Wilmot's proposal in August 1846, Cass had stood ready to vote to stop slavery's extension into the territories (in large part due to his determination to secure passage of the $2 million war appropriations bill to which it was appended). But the congressional session ended before such a vote could take place, and after further deliberation, Cass spoke openly against the proviso in December. Desirous of maintaining national unity during wartime, he implored all Americans to set aside debate over the fate of newly acquired territories until they were safely in American hands and the war was won. The proviso debate, he warned, threatened the one thing that all Americans agreed upon—the desirability of territorial expansion.[12]

Though at odds over the proviso, Michigan Democrats—bolstered by Cass's patriotic plea for unity during the war, his firm control over the state party apparatus, and partisan agreement upon local economic issues—managed to hold their party together throughout 1847 and well into 1848. The fall election of 1848, however, threatened to destroy the party for good.

Conscious of his status as the Democratic Party's front-runner for the presidency in 1848 and eager to avoid the vexatious question of slavery's expansion into the territories, Cass articulated a compromise solution to the territorial issue in a December 1847 letter to Tennessean Alfred O. P. Nicholson. In this letter, though he avoided taking a definitive stance on the question of congressional authority over slavery in the federal territories, Cass urged that such authority be "limited to the creation of popular governments and the necessary provision for their eventual admission into the Union; leaving it in the meantime to the people inhabiting them to regulate their own internal concerns in their own way." Designed to undercut the popularity of Wilmot's divisive proviso, Cass's policy of popular sovereignty appealed to Americans' sense of fairness and avoided the moral debate over slavery. More important, the plan sought to appease both northerners and southerners by remaining vague about when the residents of a territory could make their determination about slavery's future. Northern proponents of the plan argued that territorial residents could make such a determination at once, while southern advocates of popular sovereignty contended that only when a territory applied for statehood could it exclude slavery from within its boundaries. For northern Democrats, including those in Michigan, the line had been drawn: either they endorsed Cass and popular sovereignty or they stood outside the party and supported Wilmot's Proviso.[13]

In Michigan, Cass's candidacy worked to minimize such a polarization, as Democrats of all stripes rallied to their favorite son. Not all state Democrats, however, were willing to abandon their antislavery principles and stand upon Cass's popular sovereignty platform. Fortunately for these self-proclaimed Free-Soil Democrats, partisan bickering in New York provided them with a means by which to express and advance their concerns—the Free-Soil Party, organized in August 1848 at Buffalo. Echoing the new party's call for "Free Soil, Free Speech, Free Labor, and Free Men," Michigan's Free-Soilers gathered in Ann Arbor in September to plot their strategy. Devoutly committed to their cause yet fully aware of their numerical weakness, the delegates determined to form coalitions with either the Whigs or the Democrats in each of the state's three congressional districts so as to work for the election of proviso men to Congress.[14]

The election results were mixed. Cass, failing in his bid for the presidency, had won the state but with only a plurality of the vote. And the Free-Soilers' coalition strategy succeeded in two of the three congressional races. The electoral victories of the Free-Soil Whig William Sprague in the Second District and the militant Free-Soil Democrat Kinsley Bingham in the Third District devastated state Democrats and ensured that Michigan's congressional delegation would be controlled by proviso men. Moreover, although the newly elected state legislature was controlled by the Democrats, the potential for intraparty strife increased because proviso men within their party's ranks, elected with the help of the Free-Soilers, now held the balance of power.[15]

Almost immediately, the Democratic fault line began to rumble as party factions organized for the upcoming struggle over the election of a U.S. senator to fill the seat that Lewis Cass had given up in his failed bid for the presidency. Cass, hoping to regain the confidence of his party and determined to do his part to dispose of the divisive issue of slavery in the territories, let it be known that he would readily accept the nomination. He would not, however, be the only aspirant for the office. Western Michigan Democrats, distraught over being habitually ignored when it came time to elect senators, rallied behind the candidacy of Governor Epaphroditus Ransom. Seizing the opportunity and knowing that he needed to expand his base of support if he hoped to defeat Cass, Ransom denounced popular sovereignty and spoke out forcefully for the proviso in his annual state of the state message. With the battle lines drawn, Michigan's Democratic Party faced a true test.[16]

As the election neared, Cass used his control of the state Democratic organization to reinforce party loyalty among the legislators. In the end, partisanship prevailed, and the legislature returned Cass to the Senate by the thin margin of six votes. Having paid their party debt, however, proviso Democrats, with the aid of the Free-Soilers and Whigs, proceeded to handcuff Cass with a set of Free-Soil resolutions. In these resolutions, the legislature asserted that Congress had the power and the duty to exclude slavery from the territories. The resolutions also instructed Michigan's senators—and requested its representatives—"to use all honorable means" to assist Congress in achieving this end.[17]

Disheartened by their inability to defeat Cass yet at the same time congratulating themselves for successfully restricting his actions, Michigan's Free-Soilers eagerly awaited the fall 1849 elections. Victory in November would afford proviso men another opportunity to unseat Cass, whose term expired in March 1851. To achieve this victory, the Free-Soilers concluded, they had to redirect their strategy of coalition building so as to construct a statewide Whig–Free-Soil coalition.[18]

Though they had been relegated to minority status over the preceding eight years, Michigan Whigs remained divided over the efficacy and desirability of such a coalition. One group of Whig legislators, encouraged by the success of the Whig–Free-Soil coalition that had elected William Sprague to Congress, pushed for an expanded alliance. Other Whigs, led by the titular party head and U.S. attorney for Michigan Jacob M. Howard, reminded their partisan brethren that a Whig administration—led by Zachary Taylor—was now in power in Washington and that the true Whig course was "to remain united and firm, upholding with vigor and activity the national administration and maintaining a tone of perfect self-reliance." Howard feared, furthermore, that a proviso candidate and platform would alienate the state party from the national administration, which, after all, was run by a slaveholder, and that such a pattern—if pursued throughout the North—would lead to the irrevocable division of the party.[19]

Despite Howard's urging, the Whig State Central Committee authorized a concurrent convention with the Free-Soilers at Ann Arbor in June. There, however, Howard's old-line Whigs gained control of their convention and refused to make joint nominations. Instead, they nominated the absent Townsend E. Gidley, a conservative Jackson County farmer, as their candidate for governor. With coalition now improbable, the Free-Soilers made their own nomination for the governorship—Flavius Littlejohn of Allegan County. Littlejohn, a Jacksonian Democrat at heart, immediately diminished the chances for future cooperation by beginning his campaign with a fervid attack upon the Whigs on Democratic, not Free-Soil, grounds.[20]

After Gidley, whose name was put into nomination without consent, withdrew from the race in early September, the Whigs called for a new convention. Free-Soilers, sensing another opportunity for coalition, worked behind the scenes to get the inflammatory Littlejohn to relinquish his nomination. But at the behest of friends who believed that he would receive the Whig nomination, Littlejohn refused. His friends proved to be good prognosticators. They did not, however, foresee that old-line Whigs would refuse to acquiesce in Littlejohn's nomination and bolt the convention, thereby squelching any chance for a Whig–Free-Soil coalition.[21]

While the Whigs and Free-Soilers wrestled with coalition, Michigan's Democrats made strides toward reunifying their party. Greatly disturbed by the infighting surrounding the recent senatorial contest, they agreed that their party quarrels had gone too far and that a rapprochement was in order. Directed by Cass, who realized that the vocal proviso sentiment within his party had to be quelled if he had any hope of leading the party through the quagmire in which it had become trapped, Michigan's Democrats sought a means of standing behind popular sovereignty without alienating the Free-Soil wing of the party.

As Democrats gathered in convention on September 19, Cass worked behind the scenes to defeat the Free-Soil faction's efforts to have the former Monroe congressman Robert McClelland named as the party's nominee for governor. Having reasserted his control over the party, Cass worked with his allies and managed to capture the gubernatorial nomination for the popular Cass Democrat and former governor John Barry. Barry was a staunch Jacksonian and party man, yet he was personally opposed to slavery's extension into the territories; his nomination therefore offered something to Democrats of every stripe. To ease tensions further, the Democrats adopted a platform that remained silent on the issue of extending slavery. Michigan Democrats were united in the cause of their party, and they worked tirelessly for Barry's election and proved to be too much for the unstable Whig–Free-Soil coalition. Bolstered by the open support of many of the disaffected Old Line Whigs, Barry easily defeated the abrasive Littlejohn and garnered 54.2 percent of the popular vote. Democratic unity paid large dividends in local elections as well, as the Democrats managed to win fourteen of twenty-one state senate seats and forty-five of the sixty-five seats in the house.[22]

The postelection revelry was cut short for Michigan Democrats as events in Washington once again thrust the issue of extending slavery onto the national stage. Confronted with a mushrooming population in California and the lack of an organized government in the region, President Zachary Taylor made up his mind to avoid the slavery extension debate altogether by advocating admitting California directly into the Union as a free state, thus circumventing the vexatious question of congressional authority over the territories. Taylor's proposal was met with a firestorm of protest from the Congress. Unlike the situation in the past, however, renewed debate over the territories did not rend Michigan's Democratic Party. Rather, faced with a very real threat to their party's existence and, more important, a threat to the Republic itself, state Democrats cast aside intraparty differences and united in defense of their principles and the nation—concepts that were one and the same in their minds.

Lewis Cass assumed command of this partisan charge by becoming one of the earliest and most vocal supporters of Henry Clay's proposed compromise. Relying upon his control over the state party organization and intent upon saving the nation that he so deeply loved, Cass threatened to resign his Senate seat unless the Michigan legislature untied his hands and rescinded its 1849 proviso resolutions. In the face of the strong Free-Soil predilections of many of their fellow party members, Michigan Democrats struggled throughout the legislative session to accommodate Cass. In the end, partisan fealty proved too strong for the Free-Soilers. On April 2, 1850, in a very close vote, the Michigan legislature rescinded its pro-Wilmot resolutions. Cass had succeeded.[23]

Michigan's Democratic Party was whole once again, standing shoulder to shoulder behind Lewis Cass and the compromise. Moreover, with the troublesome national issue of slavery's extension about to be settled, relieved state Democrats could once more direct their attention inward, focusing on meeting the needs of their own constituents. Among those needs, according to a majority of the voters (who had approved an 1849 proposal to scrap the state's 1835 constitution by a vote of 33,193 to 4,095), was revision of Michigan's constitution. The state's rocky beginning and the devastating and lingering effects of the panic of 1837 remained foremost in the minds of the residents of the peninsular state. Constitutional reform was thus imperative to ensure that the liberties and freedoms of the citizenry would be protected from similar threats in the future. "It is for the convention," the *Grand Rapids Enquirer* reminded its readers, "to lay the cornerstone, and indeed the whole foundation of our state government, with such solidity and firmness, that it shall not crumble and drop from under us, before we arrive at majority as a political community." Unified and refocused, Democrats eagerly awaited the fast-approaching constitutional convention. Nonetheless, they still faced a potentially strong challenge from the Whigs, who hoped to leave their own imprint upon the new constitution. Partisans in both camps thus set to work to guarantee that the delegates elected to the upcoming convention were steadfast party men deeply devoted to "correct" principles, for as a letter to the *Detroit Free Press* noted, "by its [the convention's] action, our lives, our liberty, our property, and social relations—all that concerns man's temporal interests and prosperity, will be immeasurably affected for good or evil."[24]

"Because the People are, by the Grace of God, Free and Independent"

Jacksonian Political Culture in Michigan, 1850

THROUGHOUT THE sweltering Michigan summer of 1850, a hundred delegates met in convention at the newly created capital of Lansing, in an area that was, until very recently, an unbroken expanse of hardwood forest "where the howl of wolves and the hissing of missaugas [*sic*], and the groans of bullfrogs resound[ed] to the hammer of the woodpecker and the solitary note of the nightingale." The purpose of their meeting was the creation of a new state constitution—a constitution meant to give form to a host political culture steeped in fears of "enslavement" and determined to preserve American liberty. Simultaneously, in the rolling farmland of Jackson County forty miles southeast of Lansing, a group of exasperated farmers carried out a clandestine nightly offensive against the Michigan Central Railroad—an offensive that, like the convention, was intended to stave off enslavement and to preserve liberty. Indeed, these seemingly unrelated and disparate actions were inextricably linked and expressive of a body of thought and belief shared by most contemporary Americans. This shared political culture, albeit rooted in the Country Whig ideals of the founding fathers, was the distinct product of a more democratic era characterized by rapid social, economic, and political change.[1]

With only one week remaining until the election of delegates to the constitutional convention, the conservative Whig organ, the *Detroit Advertiser,* reminded its readers that in order to draft a constitution that embodied the reform measures demanded by the people, "it is necessary that prudent, patriotic, and strong men should be sent to the Convention. Men . . . who are conservative enough in their views to save the body from the dangers of extreme radicalism. Men from the bone and sinew of the Whig party . . . , practical men who rely upon support, who do not look to office as a means of profit, but who accept it at the call of their fellow citizens, and at the call of duty." Michigan's Whigs saw themselves as public-spirited statesmen motivated by the greater good and serving at the behest of their neighbors. Their Democratic opponents, by contrast, were considered mere politicians, demagogues who sought office and pandered to special interests so as to line their own pockets. A gathering as important as a convention to revise the constitution required the election of statesmen and the defeat of politicians if the long-term interests of the state and all of its citizens were to be served.[2]

Naturally, Michigan Whigs believed that the long-term interests of the state and its citizenry would best be provided for by a strict adherence to Whig principles. Foremost among these principles was the necessity of protecting and expanding American liberty in the face of the machinations of Democratic politicians. In its election-day call to arms, the *Detroit Advertiser* again reminded the electorate that

> the measures which will come before the convention . . . are measures which will affect your interests and those of your class [men dependent upon their own industry and enterprise], for all time. The evils which that convention is looked to to correct, are those of excessive taxation, excessive legislation, inefficient, uncertain and expensive administration of the laws—just the evils which weigh, and always have weighed, most heavily upon the mechanic, the merchant, and the business man. If you believe as we do that the cure of these overgrown evils are [*sic*] more safely to be entrusted to honest, upright, and able citizens, than to professed hackneyed politicians, we call upon you to go to the polls this morning and vote the Whig ticket.

Another paper, the *Grand River Eagle,* warned that without a strong Whig turnout, the convention would fall under the control of the "drones and leeches of the people—office seeking politicians." By voting for Whigs, Michiganians would be protecting their freedom by liberating themselves from the weight of those forces that kept them from reaching their fullest potential. A Whig convention was imperative if Michigan was to remain a free and progressive society.[3]

Michigan's Democrats vehemently disagreed. Understanding themselves to be the true purveyors of the public good and the guardians of liberty, they rallied to thwart the designs of their scheming, self-interested Whig opponents and to uphold their own party doctrines.

On April 16, the state organ of the Democratic Party, the *Detroit Free Press,* published a letter from a former Presbyterian minister and onetime state representative from Mackinac, William Norman MacLeod. In his open letter entitled "The Constitutional Convention: Who Should Be Its Members," MacLeod clearly articulated the duty of Michigan Democrats in the upcoming election. For the convention to reverse the evils of Michigan's old political system, MacLeod began, each delegate had to "be a crafts-master in his calling. He should possess a wide and thorough knowledge of moral philosophy, . . . be versed in the propositions of political economy, [and] in the principles of governmental polity." In addition, he continued, the "constitutional craftsman" should also be a public speaker. Most important, however, "the delegate should be a party man." Fully aware of the deep-seated suspicions that many of his contemporaries had regarding the desirability of organized political parties, he clarified his point. By a party man, he wrote, "we mean one who, in addition to his love of country, his wishes to conserve her interests and sustain her institutions, honor and integrity, shall also have settled convictions of the powers of government, the immunities of subjects, the policy of administrative measures, and, with these convictions, shall have entered into an organized union to give them efficacy and success. Party is as necessary to principle, as is the body to display the manifestations of the soul." Party allegiance, therefore, did not mean blind submission and obedience but rather involved selfless dedication to the cause of principle. Indeed, MacLeod affirmed, "the ark that held the sacred testament of the Hebrews, was scarcely less held in reverence than the holy covenant it contained. And the practical Patriot, while he bows to the principles of his creed, will uphold his party as the ark in which his covenant is enshrined." He concluded by reminding state Democrats, "Be Thou Eternal" and urging them to do their duty by electing Democrats to the constitutional convention. MacLeod's warning was well heeded. State Democrats succeeded beyond their wildest dreams, electing seventy-nine of the one hundred delegates to the convention.[4]

Even before the first gavel sounded on June 3, the new state constitution was well formed in the minds of many delegates. Not surprisingly, representatives of both parties endeavored to create a document that would reflect the democratic spirit of the age. "The present constitution of this State was framed at an unfavorable time in its history," the *Michigan State Journal* noted, "when wrong views of State policy and what a state should be were universally prevalent." "It should not be strange, then," the paper continued, "when a truer sense of the objects of a state had become settled policy, that some of its retinue could be dispensed without injury to the public interest." Indeed, as one prominent historian of the state has astutely noted, it was the "ferment of Jacksonian democracy" that drove Michiganians to demand a new constitution in 1849 and that determined the actual shape the document would assume. In addition, state Democrats, who controlled the convention, sought to codify their party doctrines in the new constitution and thus preserve the liberty of Michigan's citizens by removing state government from the economy, cutting government expenses, and protecting the polity from banks and other privileged institutions. The document that emerged from the Lansing constitutional convention succeeded both in making state and local government more accessible and responsive to voters and in embodying a full articulation of the Democratic Party's political creed. The new constitution marked the apex of Democratic power in the state.[5]

Of the myriad suggestions for constitutional reform put forth in the months prior to the opening of the convention—and throughout much of the convention itself—none were more popular with the citizens of Michigan, be they Democrats or Whigs, than the call to replace the state's annual legislative session with a limited, biennial session and the move to adopt the single-district system of representation. Indeed, newspapers in every corner of the state always included these two measures when proposing constitutional reforms. These proposals were so popular, the *Free Press* declared, that "we shall consider the convention a failure, if the[se] reforms are not adopted by it; and in our opinion, the adaptation of these alone would amply pay for holding the convention."[6]

Under Michigan's original state constitution, representation was tied to the number of organized counties. Each of the existing counties as of 1835 received at least one representative. Additional representation was given to the most heavily populated counties (which were concentrated in the southeastern corner of the state). Counties organized after 1835 would not receive their own representatives until reaching a set population plateau. The system of representation in the upper house—which would have one-third as many members as the lower house—was slightly different. The state was divided into districts (the constitution stipulated that there were to be no more than eight), and the electors in each district would then elect multiple members to the state senate. Critics argued that this system of representation left large portions of the state (mainly the newly settled areas in northern and western Michigan) without a political voice; promoted sectionalism, abuse of power, and selfishness; retarded the state's overall development; and, when combined with annual legislative sessions, would lead to frequent (and often poorly envisaged) changes and modifications of existing legislation and excessive governmental expenditures.

At the heart of the electorate's insistence upon limited biennial sessions and the single-district plan lay a deeply held conviction that Michigan's past problems stemmed directly from a legislature lacking sufficient controls and limitations. Among the political evils now fettering the people, the Whig *Detroit Advertiser* complained, was "that of too much private legislation." In fact, the paper concluded, "we are governed almost to death in this particular." A Democratic correspondent to the *Free Press* agreed. Because "the people are called upon to vote for men living at a distance from them, having no knowledge of, or sympathy with their wants and wishes," the inevitable consequence was the "violation of promises and pledges, great misrepresentation of the wishes of the constituency, and abuse of power for personal and selfish ends." Lamentably, the *Grand Rapids Enquirer* moaned, the old legislative structure had allowed political factions (in both parties) and sectional interests to establish a "tyranny" in the state. Only the adoption of single legislative districts, it asserted, "would break up those arrangements and scatter the capital, which trading Politicians have brought into the game."[7]

All of these observers shared a firm belief that state government had fallen into the hands of demagogues, politicians, and lobbyists—men who disregarded the commonweal and used their positions to benefit private interests. "The monster that consumes the public patience and public purse," wrote one state Democrat, "is BUNCOMBE; and all the efforts of the framers of the Legislative article of the Constitution should be exerted toward his destruction." The present constitution, a delegate wrote, "with its super annusted [*sic*] ethics, its imbecile obligations, its unpregnant and irreducible generalities, imposes no sufficient restraint upon the exuberance of juvenile power; and hence the capricious posturizings—the grand and lofty tumblings of a harlequin legislation." This perception was pervasive in Michigan, and even those who doubted the malevolence of the legislators conceded that the state suffered from an "excess and perhaps an abuse of legislation." At the very least, skeptics implied, because the legislature was filled with young and ambitious men eager to distinguish themselves, the state was burdened by ill-conceived and poorly formulated laws, the product of "crude ideas" that entered the "heated brains" of such men. What was needed to counteract the machinations of these politicians, demagogues, and misguided ideologues were single districts and a limited biennial legislative session.[8]

With the demand for reform of the legislature clearly stated in the state's press and at local partisan meetings, the constitutional convention immediately set to work to accommodate the citizens of Michigan. On the convention's first day of substantive business, Dewitt C. Walker, a Democratic delegate from Macomb County, called for biennial sessions because he believed "the frequent changes, modifications and alterations in the laws to be a great evil." Walker's plea had been anticipated and already acted upon by the Committee on the Legislative Department. On June 11, the chair of that committee, Democrat Robert McClelland of Monroe, presented his committee's report to the convention. It included articles providing for biennial legislative sessions of no longer than forty days and the election of state representatives by single districts.[9]

But not everyone agreed that such reforms were necessary or desirable. Citing Thomas Jefferson's famous dictum "where annual sessions end, tyranny begins," critics argued that biennial sessions did not make government more responsive to the citizens of Michigan but rather had just the opposite effect, leaving the legislators to pass whatever type of laws they wanted without fear of immediate reprisal. Indeed, Charles P. Bush, a Democrat from Ingham County, reminded the convention, "It is conceded by everyone, that when power returns more frequently into the hands of the people, it is least liable to abuse." "Power that is delegated for a long period," he asserted, "is universally abused." To make matters worse, Bush continued in the best Country Whig tradition, biennial sessions limited "the action and lessen[ed] the efficiency of a department the least likely to abuse [the legislature], and close[d] from the public eye . . . the transactions of a department [the executive] most likely to abuse their power."[10]

Proponents of reform, however, were undeterred by such attacks; they remained convinced that biennial sessions would foster economy in government, end excessive legislation and demagoguery, and create a more responsive and representative state legislature. "We have yet to hear of the first complaint against biennial sessions from the people of any of the states that have them," one state paper observed. "And the fact that the changes have all been from annual to biennial, and none from biennial to annual sessions, shows that biennial sessions work well in practice." Moreover, a Democrat asserted, limited biennial sessions would not only enhance the "prosperity, stability, and respectability" of the state but also "add greatly to the prudence, wisdom, and honesty with which our public affairs are conducted." This improvement would occur, he believed, because the dignity and responsibility of the legislative office would be elevated, which, in turn, would ensure that "there will be more competition for the office of Legislator . . . among the very men whom it is most for the interest of the people to elect—the honest, the intelligent, the steadfast." Finally, this observer affirmed, biennial sessions would allow "the people [to] WATCH the Legislature" by eliminating the annual "diluted and extended" reports of the legislature's proceedings— reports that "passed by with little interest to the great mass of readers," thereby allowing imprudent legislation to slip through unnoticed.[11]

The single-district system encountered even greater resistance. In the early days of the convention, Joseph H. Bagg, a Democratic delegate from Detroit (which stood to lose some of its influence if the change was enacted), delivered a diatribe against having the single-district system considered by the Committee on the Legislative Department. This innovation, Bagg argued, was not only unnecessary but also "contrary to the spirit and genius of our institutions, and calculated to injure the masses." Single districts, he alleged, ran counter to the republican credo that placed the good of the whole before that of its component parts. By "breaking us up," he warned, the convention would be creating minute distinctions and would "give the cent/per cent men—the almighty dollar . . . , which has always been against the intellect, . . . undue power." Other voices echoed Bagg's concerns. "Take a small community," said Democrat Alfred H. Hanscom, a delegate from Oakland County, "among whom there may be an aristocratic nabob with his millions. Hundreds of persons may be dependent on him for employment. He, sir, will have absolute control in his district." Thus, Hanscom argued, single districts would act to "localize so as to bring the power into the hands of an individual, rather than the people." Single districts, he added, would "reduce the character of our Legislature [with] men of less ability and less integrity . . . elected from your counties." Such critics sought to protect the autonomy of the electorate by preventing the concentration of power and influence in the hands of a moneyed interest that would be able to control district nominations and promote its own agenda without any regard for the greater good.[12]

Still other delegates, led by Robert McClelland, conceded that the single-district system was fine for the state house but implored their cohorts not to apply single districts to the state senate. "The object in creating a Senate," claimed St. Clair County farmer John Clark, "was to make it a conservative body, so that it should operate as a check on the hasty and immature legislation of the more popular branch. That object was proposed to be accomplished by electing the members for a longer time, and making them the representatives of more general interests. By making the Senate a more numerous body, by electing in single districts and for a shorter period, the object for which the Senate was created would be lost." Legislators had to make a senator "responsible to a large extent of territory," McClelland added, so that, "although he may reside in the midst of the popular excitement, yet he will generally survey the whole district, and act in accordance with the desires and interests of all. Representatives have charge of particular localities; but Senators should have their attention directed to large districts, and to the interests of the whole state." These men and others of a like mind sought a senate composed of "statesmen," men with foresight, men who were able to look to the broader implications of an issue, men whose actions were motivated by concern for the good of the wider community—in sum, men like themselves. Single districts, they concluded, would only aggravate the evil that Michiganians so desperately hoped to end.[13]

Despite such objections, however, few delegates were willing to disregard the public demand for the single-district system. Consequently, that system was readily adopted for both houses of the state legislature. This measure, along with biennial sessions, became the framework around which the new state constitution would be constructed. Most delegates believed that, with these reforms in place, the door had been barred against pandering demagogues, so the state could rest safely.

But who exactly were the demagogic and self-interested politicians who threatened to destroy republican government in Michigan? The debates and proceedings of the 1850 constitutional convention surrounding the single-district system offer some revealing answers.

The delegates to Michigan's 1850 constitutional convention saw a host of potential threats to the liberties of the state's citizenry; numerous sources of greed, self-interest, power, and demagoguery were readily identifiable. For partisans of a Democratic bent, Whigs—with their selfish and destructive probank, market-oriented policies—posed an obvious threat to liberty. Conversely, for the handful of Whig delegates at the convention, the rapacious and constraining policies of the Democrats loomed ominously over the state. As a result, Democrats and Whigs alike continued to flail away at their partisan foes for the duration of the convention. That is not to say, however, that they did so without hesitation.

Imbued with the distrust of organized political parties endemic to the era, party newspapers in both camps called for the abandonment of partisanship during the convention. "We cannot readily see how party lines will be drawn in the Convention," the editor of the *Grand Rapids Enquirer* stated, "and we rejoice on this account; because all of its members will be free, removed from the influence of such a pressure, to co-operate freely in the best plans and measures of amendment." Such entreaties were in vain, however, given the delegates' convictions that their particular partisan principles were best suited to promote the welfare and protect the liberty of the state and the nation. "If a man believes that the good of the country depends upon such a particular form of government," one Democratic delegate queried, "should he not direct his attention in the Convention, as well as elsewhere, to that class of measures which will keep in ascendancy a particular political party?" The answer for the assembled delegates was an unqualified yes. Divisions in the convention along party lines, the result of the very different worldviews held by Democrats and Whigs, were unavoidable and naturally resulted in mutual denunciation and reproach.[14]

Such mistrust of his partisan opponents and their intentions led the convention president, Judge Daniel Goodwin, a Wayne County Democrat, to appoint the Whig convention delegates to "the tail end of the several committees," as Whig delegate Hezekiah G. Wells of Kalamazoo County later recalled. But Whigs were also unwilling to abandon their party tenets and remained leery of the motivations of their political foes.[15]

Convinced that the election of state senators via single districts would increase their party's numbers in the legislature while destroying the most grasping demagogues (who, of course, were assumed to be from the Democratic ranks), Whig delegates to the Lansing convention delivered a flurry of speeches in favor of the proposition. Democrat Joseph Bagg responded by claiming that

> our Whig and free soil friends anticipate a good time, and it will come. Those gentlemen have been still; and why? Because Democrats are doing the business themselves. We are getting into the meshes of the net while playing at blind Harry—but now they are afraid we cannot any longer be hoodwinked, and that the double system will prevail; hence you see the gentleman with the double principle, who represents the triangle, begins to have apprehensions that the double district system will go.

If the single-district system prevailed, Bagg warned, "we all know that the very first moment you get into this system, one-half [of the legislators elected from Wayne County] will come here Whigs." "Is it right and proper," he asked, "standing in relation as 80 to 20, to make a law, and say the masses shall not have their rights? To bind them hand and foot, and not have the advantage of union?" In short, Bagg argued, the proposed single-district system was nothing more than a ploy by the Whigs to promote their selfish agenda in the face of an overwhelmingly Democratic citizenry.[16]

This partisan spirit did not subside once the issue of single districts for the senate had been determined. It continued unabated throughout the convention and persisted well into the ensuing months and beyond. Commenting on the proceedings of the convention, a Lansing correspondent for the *Free Press* noted that "there is not a great amount of time spent in making speeches, but considerable time is taken up proposing amendments, which are intended for 'Buncomb.'" The originators of these amendments were not hard to identify, the correspondent affirmed. Members of the Whig minority,

> feeling little or no responsibility, are not backward when an opportunity offers to make a little thunder for home consumption. . . . They appear to act in concert, and examine and weigh the effect of this and that proposition, on the whig party of the state. I think they look to paract [*sic*] more in concert. This is to be expected, where the responsibility is not felt by the minority, as it should be. A whig leader will make a proposition for instance, and threaten that, if it is rejected, he will oppose the adoption of the Constitution at the polls. The whigs will fall in, and make the same threat. In this way, many things are inserted by consent of the majority, rather than encounter the organized opposition of the whig party, when in truth the twenty whigs in the convention could not influence two hundred votes, in the State.

The constitutional reforms demanded by the citizens of Michigan were being undermined by self-serving politicians—the "Whig descendants of the Hartford Conventionists." It was therefore incumbent upon the Democratic majority, the correspondent concluded, to "make such a Constitution as will meet the favor of their constituents, regardless of the demagogues."[17]

Whigs expressed some strikingly similar fears about what was transpiring in Lansing. "It is obvious," the *Advertiser* lamented, "that the leading measures of reform for which the convention was called, are to be mainly overlooked and disregarded," adding, "the truth is, the people of the state have arrived at the conclusion that the doings of the convention, so far as the needs and wishes of the people are concerned, are of very little consequence." Disgusted by the protracted convention and by partisan attacks upon the Whig delegation, the Lansing correspondent to the *Advertiser,* "Boots" (Whig delegate Nathan Pierce of Calhoun County), pointed to "a scramble among certain leading locofocos for political capital to build upon hereafter" and to the "eagerness and jealousy of each other" exhibited by these same men as the source of the problem. "I can account for this attack . . . upon the Whig minority in convention, in no other way," Pierce continued, "than a desire on the part of leading democrats to divert the public eye from their blunders in convention." Indeed, another correspondent affirmed, "political tricksters seem to be numerous enough to defeat almost anything they chose. And let me here say that political aims are the mainspring of action to at least a dozen of the chief fuglemen among the majority of the convention." As things looked, the *Advertiser* moaned as the convention stretched into August, "the demagogues," by tacking on "innumerable objectionable provisions, expecting to carry them with the people on the popularity of a few measures of reform which were loudly called for," had ensured that the new constitution would be universally abhorred by the citizens of Michigan. This belief led the *Advertiser* to comment as the convention closed, "Our own opinion is, that this Convention has been the greatest humbug that the people of this state—notwithstanding the general reign of Locofocoism—have ever been called upon to pay the expenses of." Though the convention "contained some good men . . . men whose actions were controlled only by the best interests of their constituents . . . such [men] have been outmatched in numbers, and therefore overruled by the veeriest [*sic*] demagogues that ever sucked the life-blood of a free people."[18]

Partisan confrontations, however, represented but one source of concern. The Lansing delegates also identified and struck out at a number of other concentrations of self-interested power that seemed to impede liberty in Michigan. Residents of western and northern Michigan, for example, resentful of the power of the lower tiers of counties, believed that sectional politicians threatened the state and its interests as much as, if not more than, partisan rivalry. On July 13, in the midst of the debate on single senatorial districts, John Bartow, a Democratic delegate from Genesee County, reintroduced a previous proposal to provide the state's new counties with immediate representation in the house. Commenting on the proposal, Ionia County Whig Cyrus Lovell noted that many delegates had "told us how the old counties love the new ones," but he added that "words are cheap—actions only tell." "The new portions of the state," he contended, "are in the power of two

tiers of counties." "Look at the five million dollar loan," he implored, referring to the funds granted to launch the state's internal improvement program in 1837: "Whose votes divided it? The two southern tiers of counties."
Conceding that "to a statesmanlike mind, there is [not] any real rivalry between parts of this State, save a generous competition in progress and improvement," Kent County Democrat Thomas B. Church went on to argue
that, nonetheless, "such language is used, and oftentimes such a course pursued as indicates a rivalry between districts." A new county, Church concluded, "cannot depend upon the Representative from other counties to
take care of her. A man from herself, and full of regard for home and home
interests, must be had." As long as politicians promoted local interests in lieu
of the commonweal, outstate Michigan needed its own representatives in
order to make its needs heard.[19]

Still other rivalries and divisions surfaced during the convention. One of
the principal reasons for the public demand for single districts, Robert Mc-
Clelland affirmed in a long speech on the subject, "is that the people in the
rural districts think that the politicians in your cities and villages, manage
your conventions, and too often outrage their feelings." Moreover, though
the evidence is tenuous, there does appear to have been some animosity between delegates from Detroit and those representing the city's hinterlands
and between towns that had been overlooked by the railroads and those that
had not. Clearer are the tensions between younger partisans and older,
"hunker" politicians, or "Young America" versus the "Old Fogies."[20]

"Old Hunkerism," the *Grand Rapids Enquirer* waxed angrily, "both Democratic and Whig, has so far controlled the policies of this state, aided in its
operation by a vicious social organization." This was not to say, the paper
was quick to add, that the "council of old men" was to be rejected. Still, the
Enquirer warned, "the old men can't do it [create a new constitution] alone."
The paper exclaimed, "Let the voice of the young democracy be heard"; by
so doing, "[we will] not have too much conservatism, nor too much reform;
but if possible, just enough of each." The time had come for the older generation of political leaders to give up some of their power, power that they
had too often exercised in complete disregard of the views of younger
people and newly settled regions of the state.[21]

No matter where one turned, the liberties of Michigan's citizens seemed
to be endangered by selfish, unscrupulous power brokers, be they Democrats, Whigs, representatives of sectional interests, urban dwellers, Detroiters, advocates from railroad towns, or hunker politicians. This overarching
fear of power had compelled Michiganians to demand revision of their state

constitution, and this same fear now drove convention delegates into battle to constrain and destroy, root and branch, the abusers of power, whomever they might be, through a system of biennial sessions and single-district representation. Nevertheless, a great many Michiganians remained convinced that these limited reforms did not go far enough in curtailing the power of the legislature.

One such person was the delegate from Mackinac County, William Norman MacLeod. MacLeod bemoaned the fact that Michigan had departed from the simple truths of political science when creating its constitution in 1835. Through that document, he argued, "the Governor was invested with extraordinary prerogatives." Worse yet,

> the Legislature was left to float on every passing wave, the sport of every popular wind; to roam wheresoever his errant will should guide him, and having no law, to become a law unto himself—a speculative freebooter and rover of the seas. The inhibitions of the constitution were so scant, general and easy to be avoided that they served for no other purpose than as so many beacon-lights to warn of the quicksand and the shoals, without imposing a single restraint upon the free-roaming of the sea.

As a result, MacLeod asserted, the legislature had been in session for four years, three months, and eight days out of the fifteen years of statehood and had burdened Michigan with over three thousand statutes, the majority of which related to private, not public, legislative matters.[22]

MacLeod chided his peers in the convention for arguing that biennial sessions would alleviate this problem. Surely, he acknowledged, limited biennial sessions "diminish our legislative harlequinades by one half," but, he asked rhetorically, "do they lay the axe to the root of the evil?" For MacLeod, the answer was a resounding no. "The power and the disposition" for evil remained. In fact, biennial sessions would actually harm the general interests of the state, as each legislator, representing "a specific interest in addition to the general interests which he represents in common with his fellows," would "force forward his peculiar weakness" so that not "until the horse-leech cry of each sectional interest shall have been heard [that] the interests of the common weal [would] be attended to. And then, as the period of adjournment hath drawn nigh, these great measures of public utility will be sacrificed or mutilated by precipitancy or neglect." The proper remedy, MacLeod concluded, was not biennial sessions (though he was willing to accede to them if they were demanded by the people) but circumscription of the powers and duties of the legislature. Only by limiting the range open to these lawmakers could Michigan hope to avoid the curse of excessive and irresponsible legislation. MacLeod's sentiments were widely shared.[23]

Throughout the early days of the convention, numerous proposals aimed at limiting the power of the state legislature were advanced. Future lieutenant governor Calvin Britain, a Berrien County Democrat, proposed that the speaker of the house be directly elected by the people in order to eliminate political horse-trading, factionalism, and the influence of the "third house" (lobbyists) and to ensure that the legislature promptly began its business. Macomb County's Dewitt C. Walker suggested that a two-thirds vote of all members of the legislature be required to alter, create, or amend any law. And in a move intended to avert a repetition of the legislative debacle that had bound the hands of Lewis Cass and threatened to destroy the Democratic Party in Michigan, Democrat Ebenezer Raynale of Oakland County offered a resolution requiring a two-thirds vote of the state legislature to instruct Michigan's federal representatives and senators. Though none of these specific measures found their way into the new constitution, they symbolized the desire to curb the power of government.[24]

Of greater importance were the many measures that did become part of the organic law of the state. Indeed, Michigan's 1850 constitution, as adopted, posed a direct challenge to the continued abuse of legislative power. As previously mentioned, limited biennial sessions and the single-district system were at the core of the constitution's legislative article. In addition, the convention placed responsibility for determining the boundaries of representative and senatorial districts beyond the grasp of the legislative branch and bestowed it upon the county supervisors. In an attempt to prevent pork barrel appropriations and private legislation, the new constitution dictated that "no law shall embrace more than one object, which shall be expressed in its title." Furthermore, no bill could be introduced in either house during the last three days of the session without the unanimous consent of the house in which it originated. The object was to ensure that political wire-pullers would be unable to sneak their pet projects through the legislature during the flurry of activity that often marked the closing days of a session.[25]

The members of the convention did not stop with these limitations. Approval of two-thirds of the members elected to each house was now required for the legislature to appropriate public money or property for local or private purposes. In addition, the legislature was prohibited from passing special acts of incorporation. Henceforth, corporations could be organized only under general laws. Finally, to avoid a recurrence of the hard times experienced in the past, the state debt was limited to no more than $50,000 and the state was prohibited from becoming a party in any work of internal improvement.[26]

The constitutional articles limiting the power of Michigan's state government—especially those measures relating to its legislative branch, the traditional voice of people—have often been misunderstood. If the intention of the assembled delegates was to democratize state government and make it more responsive to the demands of Michigan's polity, why would these same delegates turn upon the one branch of government best suited to that end? This apparent contradiction led one early historian of the constitutional convention to profess that the new constitution "exhibits the apparent paradox that while the rights of the people in the matter of elections of state officers and judges of all grades are much enlarged, the powers of the legislature are very strictly circumscribed and limited."[27]

For the delegates to the Lansing convention and for the citizens of Michigan, there was no such paradox. Limiting the powers of the legislative branch, as well as those of the executive and judicial branches, was entirely consistent with their desire to make government work for the common person. In fact, the actions of the convention delegates demonstrated that Michiganians firmly believed that a truly democratic government could not exist without such restrictions. Restraint was necessary to be sure that self-interest, greed, and ambition did not run roughshod over the public good. Thus, rather than limiting the power of the polity, measures aimed at curtailing the power of the legislative branch actually served to expand and protect liberty by averting shortsighted, specious, and self-serving legislation.

But the legislature was not the only branch of government from which people feared potential abuse of power. Indeed, as future supreme court justice James V. Campbell, a contemporary of the delegates assembled at Lansing, later noted in his political history of Michigan, the constitution of 1850 was a document "which intimates from first to last that no one is to be trusted." Firm in this conviction, the delegates also imposed limitations upon the executive branch. Uppermost in their minds was the need to make that branch accountable to the citizens of Michigan. The new constitution stripped the governor of much of his (or her) extensive patronage power by making state posts such as attorney general, secretary of state, and state treasurer, along with the regents of the state university, elective offices rather than appointive positions controlled by the governor. Furthermore, the governor was prohibited from holding any other office while serving as governor—a response to the previous loss of two seated governors to the U.S. Senate. And in order to avoid the mistakes of youthful inexperience (the alleged shortcoming of the state's first chief executive, the "boy" governor Stevens T. Mason), the new constitution required that future governors be at least thirty years old.[28]

The judicial branch, "the department of government, the operation of which is best seen by the people at large," was also the subject of a great deal of intense scrutiny. The question of revising the state's judicial branch touched off one of the most divisive and protracted debates of the convention, even though every delegate agreed on the need for reform. Agreement quickly dissipated as the delegates split into two competing factions and rallied, regardless of party affiliation, behind alternative plans of reorganization. Prior to the sequestered meeting of the Judiciary Committee, whose job it was to produce the judicial article of the new constitution, numerous delegates introduced resolutions meant to shape and influence the committee's proceedings. From the onset, two very different judicial plans jostled for supremacy—the independent supreme court plan and the circuit court plan (a revision of the existing system in which the judges of the circuit court served concurrently as justices of the high court). Proponents of both plans contended that their particular design would reduce expenses, hasten the legal process, and make the judicial branch more responsive to the citizens of Michigan.[29]

With the battle commenced, the state's newspapers rapidly joined the fray. Virtually every major paper in the state, whatever its political affiliation, endorsed the independent supreme court. "Judges of the tribunal of last resort ought not to be the same as those employed in the trial of cases in the several circuits," asserted the Whig *Grand River Eagle*. Such a system would undermine the appellate function of the court because "there is a delicacy felt by judges about reversing the decisions of each other; and when they get together as a court of review, as they now do, there is a disposition to mutual forbearance; a kind of pairing off—letting one error stand in consideration that another just as bad is undisturbed. A bench composed in this way is too much exposed to the logrolling temptation." The rival *Grand Rapids Enquirer* agreed, adding that an independent supreme court would, "better than any other, secure a cheap and speedy administration of the laws of the land." It would be folly, the paper insisted, to disregard previous experience and to adopt "a Judiciary system which has been already been tried and universally condemned."[30]

Supporters of the independent judiciary plan believed that the courts were as much to blame for Michigan's troubled adolescence as the legislature. The courts had not done their job—they had not applied the brake to a legislature propelling the state headlong toward the abyss of economic and political enslavement. "There [is] an impression among the people," argued Alfred Hanscom, the most vocal supporter of the independent court, "that, under the present system, inducements influencing the lower courts, entered into the supreme court, and gave undue influence to its decisions." The state needed an independent supreme court staffed by wise, public-spirited men.[31]

Though the independent supreme court plan attracted a great deal of attention in the press and from convention delegates, the commitments of those advocating the circuit court alternative had not been entirely over-whelmed. On the contrary, as members of the Judiciary Committee emerged from behind closed doors to report their recommendations, the extent of the rift between the two sides in the contest over the courts became abundantly clear. The supporters of the independent supreme court plan had succeeded in controlling the committee and reported in favor of that plan. The margin of victory, however, was razor thin—just one vote—and a minority report endorsing the circuit court system was quickly placed before the convention delegates. Certainly, the *Free Press* argued, the Judiciary Committee had settled upon the best plan that could be devised—an uncomplicated system of distinct courts with separate jurisdictions, a system capable of a rapid and economical dispatch of business. Advocates of the circuit court plan, however, quickly set to work to sway the undecided delegates.[32]

Opposed to an independent court, Volney Hascall, a Kalamazoo County Democrat, charged that such a court would "lose its practical character, and become abstract and metaphysical"; it would be detached from the people. "Are you prepared," he asked the assembled delegates, "to surrender your inalienable rights, your sovereign privileges, into the hands of a power thus removed from your resistance, thus elevated above you?" To make matters worse, Hascall continued, an independent court favored the powerful and wealthy. "The rich man, who has a contest with a poor man, although he (the rich man) may be clearly in the wrong, can deprive the poor man of his rights by requiring him to follow his cause to a court where he has not the pecuniary ability to go." Leading his audience down a familiar path, Hascall moved in for the kill: "I object to the system, because it originated with a view to political ends, and not to the public good. It is a scheme by which politicians are managing to increase the number of high offices in the state, for the purpose of enjoying them themselves, or of placing troublesome men therein to remove them from the path of political preferment."[33]

Seeing that the convention had reached an impasse on the judicial article, Robert McClelland, who believed that the state's paucity of trained lawyers undermined its ability to sustain an independent court, proposed a compromise measure. Under his plan, the circuit court system would be incorporated into the new constitution, but after six years, the state legislature could establish an independent supreme court. Despite the illness that was decimating the convention, the oppressive summer heat, and an overabundance of airborne dust (know locally as "free soil"), McClelland's proposal came to a vote on the afternoon of August 2. In a nonpartisan vote, the compromise passed with forty-two yeas to thirty-eight nays.[34]

Dismayed, the *Free Press* wondered why the compromise had not instead established an independent court for a trial period of six years and contended, "Could the choice between the Independent Supreme Court and the proposed Circuit System have been submitted to the direct vote of the people, a very large majority would have endorsed the former." The circuit court system, the *Grand Rapids Enquirer* complained, "will be just what it has been—a source of vexation and delay." Noting the defeat (by three votes this time) of a final effort to replace McClelland's compromise with an independent court, the *Pontiac Jacksonian* labeled the actions of the delegates "a direct and wanton violation of the people's wishes." "Had the step which has now been taken, been anticipated previous to the election in May last," the paper scolded, "not 20 delegates opposed to the independent supreme court would have occupied seats in the convention."[35]

Despite the best efforts of its enemies, the circuit court system became the centerpiece of the judiciary article of the 1850 constitution. According to its provisions, the state was divided into eight judicial circuits. The eight circuit judges would serve concurrently as justices of the state supreme court. The most striking feature of the 1850 judiciary article was its provision for the direct election of all state judges. Though not an entirely novel idea (a constitutional amendment providing for the popular election of judges had been ratified the previous November by the voters of Michigan), the provision was considered an important and vital improvement. The new judiciary article replaced the state's old at-large system of electing judges with a new system based upon electoral districts. Like their legislative counterparts and for the same reasons applied to that branch of government, Michigan's judges would also be elected by districts. The architects of the new state constitution had made their intentions crystal clear—government had to be made more responsive to the citizenry of Michigan.[36]

Confident that they had finally put to rest the political ghosts that had haunted their state for so long, delegates at the Democrat-controlled convention shifted their attention toward exorcizing from Michigan, once and for all, the demonic force that had been invoked by power-hungry individuals and the market economy. The enticements of a booming market, dangled like candy before the eyes of the infant state, had driven Michigan to enact a series of reckless and dangerous laws, many Democrats maintained. This same market, after shamelessly denying Michigan its anticipated rewards, had pushed the state and many of its citizens, dazed and confused about what had transpired, to the brink of economic, social, and political ruin. Over the preceding decade, Democratic delegates believed, their party had worked tirelessly to remove Michigan from danger. But the lessons of the hard economic times and the vagaries of the market economy, as well as the continued social dislocation that accompanied the market, convinced a great many residents of the state that they were not yet safe—nor would they ever be as long as the market threatened to dispossess them of everything that they had worked to create. Accordingly, the convention delegates determined to ease the fears and anxieties of their peers by assuring them that under a constitution that imposed the proper restraints upon the market, their liberties would be secured.

In this spirit, the Lansing delegates wove a number of specific provisions into the proposed constitution. The most important were aimed at severing the ties between the state and the world of the market, connections that had produced disastrous results in the past. Although begun with the best of intentions, early efforts to construct an extensive system of roads, canals, and railroads in order to tie the state into a growing national market had nearly bankrupted Michigan and its citizens. Moreover, the siren song of numerous internal improvements projects continued to entice Michigan in dangerous directions. To steer clear of the mistakes of the past, the delegates, as noted earlier, prohibited the state from becoming a party in any future internal improvements projects and limited the state debt to no more than $50,000.[37]

A more vile manifestation of the market economy, however, and the locus—according to the majority of delegates—of many of the evils that had befallen the young state was the traditional nemesis of the Democratic Party: banks. Virtually as soon as the convention commenced, the delegates made clear the course of debate upon the subject. On June 8, Joseph Bagg of Detroit, driven by the belief that "all banks were based on a doctrine of injustice and unequal rights," requested that the Committee on Banking and Other Corporations except Municipal inquire into the expediency of denying the legislature the power to grant any charters for banking purposes. But other delegates had different ideas. On the same day, Robert McClelland, a pro-bank Democrat, asked the committee to consider "a provision requiring all banking institutions to be established by general laws, and to be based on state stock securities, so as to make the bill-holder perfectly secure; and that such general laws, before they take effect, be submitted to a vote of the people." As this resolution shows, probank advocates such as McClelland had to balance their own proclivities and staunchly antibank public opinion by couching their proposals in moderate, cautious terms. The best that they could realistically expect was to establish the principle of a general banking law. At the very least, McClelland and his allies (many of whom were Whigs) hoped that, by including a proviso submitting a banking law to a vote of the people, they might persuade other delegates that their proposal was the most democratic means of deciding the issue.[38]

On July 25, the Committee on Banking and Other Corporations except Municipal reported its recommendations to a committee of the whole. The article that was reported, though slightly different from that desired by McClelland, marked a victory for the probank forces. Alfred Hanscom of Oakland County immediately spoke out against the proposal, questioning whether the convention should authorize "under any circumstances, the creation of such institutions in this state"—particularly "when all experience demonstrates that all [banking] systems are bad ones." Hanscom asked the convention to "concur with me in preventing for all coming time the creation of any banks in the state." Fellow Oakland County delegate J. Van Valkenburgh volunteered, "I am with my colleague. I would make war on all banks. Since President Jackson strangled the monster, public sentiment has endorsed it. With the California gold and mint drops, we can get along very well without banks." John D. Pierce of Calhoun County fervently agreed; banking, he thundered, "is a system adopted to rob labor of its reward, by enabling persons to bank on a debt and nothing but a debt." The power of banking corporations was said to be an affront to the liberties of the common person. Banks could not be tolerated, and it was the duty of the delegates to destroy them. "I consider that banks stand in the same relation to the financial world that ardent spirits do to the human system," asserted Joseph Bagg. "Give them one drink, they feel well; another, he is rich; another, he has property to sell; another, the whole world is at his control." He reminded his listeners, "Banks are a monopoly—corruption and fraud."[39]

The Whig *Detroit Advertiser* vehemently disagreed. "Every business man who knows anything about the commercial interests of the country," the paper had asserted well before the delegates assembled at Lansing, "every merchant . . . whose dealings are not confined to a little 'truck and dicker' trade" saw the absurdity of the Democrats' antibank policies. Rather than being a means of enslavement, banks were engines of progress and freedom. They provided needed capital, capital that, in turn, allowed its holders to buy more land, grow more wheat, produce more goods, build roads and railroads, and so forth. Historian Lawrence Kohl has argued that to Whigs, banking institutions were "not a form of fraud built on deception" but "a device to enhance the opportunities of the common man." Whig delegate Nathan Pierce affirmed, "I am in favor of having plenty of circulation, because I am a farmer. With a specie circulation we . . . get three or four dollars for an article which with a paper circulation we may get fifteen." The *Advertiser* charged that Hanscom clearly had foisted his antibank proposition upon the convention in spite of the fact that he "knew that even the business of his own constituents could not be conveniently carried on with an exclusive specie currency," let alone "the great commercial interests between the states" and of the nation as a whole. Unfortunately, the paper inferred, "the subject of banking, is one upon which demagogues will expect to manufacture an immense amount of [political] capital, because the people have been so outrageously swindled and humbugged by former legislation upon the subject." Still, the *Advertiser* found solace in the perception that the citizens of Michigan "are now beginning to understand that we can have safe banks."[40]

Sectional animosity once again arose as the contest over the banking issue grew more heated. Berrien County delegate Calvin Britain claimed that Hanscom's proposal put the convention in an awkward position, for if the delegates "voted with [Hanscom], they voted for giving Detroit a monopoly of banking for all time to come; and if they voted against his proposition, they would be branded by him as opposed to the democratic doctrine of opposition to banks." It was necessary, Britain contended, either to free the state of banks entirely or to permit "individual enterprise to make banks wherever business invites it to make them." Anything less, he resolved, "would be a great injustice to the balance of the state, as it would continue the whole produce business of the western portion of the state subject to the control of the city of Detroit." Swayed by Britian's logic, Hanscom amended his proposition so as to end all banking charters then in place by 1852. Unfortunately for him (and his staunchly antibank allies), however, McClelland's position proved more appealing to the bulk of the delegates and gained the final assent of the convention on July 31.[41]

Yet McClelland's victory should in no way be construed as a victory for probanking forces in Michigan. In fact, just the opposite was the case. As stated earlier, McClelland's amendment conceded much to the antibanking forces in Michigan. Moreover, although the legislature would be authorized to draft a general banking law and to submit it to the citizens of the state for their approval, antibanking forces made sure that any future banking corporations would have their powers severely curtailed. These antibank conservatives, for example, successfully imposed unlimited liability on bank officers and stockholders. In addition, banks were prohibited from suspending specie payments, the note holders of insolvent banks were given first preference in the distribution of corporate assets, and all banknotes circulated by Michigan banks were required to be registered with the state and secured "to the full amount of notes and bills so registered" by state and U.S. bonds bearing interest. Advocates of such measures insisted that Michigan must never again suffer at the hands of privileged banking corporations.[42]

Banking was, of course, just one of the numerous economic activities that induced capitalists to organize into corporations. Because of their potential power, corporations of all types—whether they were formed to mine copper or iron ore, to build a plank road or a railroad, or to manufacture woolen cloth—required restrictions similar to those imposed on banks in order to ensure that they did not become a threat to the liberties of the polity. Determined to protect Michigan from pillaging by rapacious corporations, the Committee on Banking and Other Corporations except Municipal, chaired by Hillsdale Democrat John Cook, reported a proposed amendment effectively granting legislators the power to control corporations by authorizing the 1880 state legislature to annul any existing corporate charter. "The people," Cook lectured the convention, "have not granted to Legislatures a power to grant irrepealable acts of incorporation. . . . I do not believe in any such doctrine. I believe the right is with the people. They cannot confine themselves in perpetuity and prospectively." Concurring in the opinion of his colleague, John Pierce angrily denounced those who sought to strike out the provision. "I . . . abhor the doctrine of vested rights," he roared, "a multitude of corporations and the State no control over them!" Attempting to highlight the stark absurdity of granting perpetual corporate rights, Pierce railed, "No matter how much evil they may induce, no matter how much mischief may follow in their train, they must continue to all time; their rights are permanent—they are vested rights." Beyond all else, proponents of this measure made clear, the commonweal was paramount over the vested rights of a soulless corporation. "Those vested rights," Pierce later unabashedly asserted, "created by charters, must yield, when they come into conflict with the supreme law—the public good."[43]

Sensing the coming storm, the Whig delegation had attempted in late June to head off any such interference with corporations by pushing for a clause prohibiting the legislature from obstructing vested rights. Excited by the prospect of obtaining such an amendment (a prospect that never reached fruition), the *Detroit Advertiser* encouraged the Whig delegates and reminded its readers, "That which has affected us more disastrously than anything else, is our legislative interference with the vested rights of private individuals." Such interference, the paper claimed, "has decreased the confidence of eastern capitalists, driven capital from our state, and rendered Michigan fidelity a bye word and reproach." Faced with the actuality that their greatest fears were about to be realized, the *Advertiser* condemned the action of the Committee on Banking and Other Corporations except Municipal as the "offspring of mere demagogueism, . . . designed to make capital for its instigators with a class of persons, upon whom empty promises of 'hatred of monopolies' have always had their influence." "We trust, however," the paper maintained, "that the honest and sound members of the convention—they who have still remaining in their hearts some sense of honor left, and some touch of regard for the good name of the state at home and abroad, will exert their influence in arresting the progress of a measure so eminently destructive of honor, prosperity, and good name." Because of such regressive, demagogic policies,

> our state is suffering . . . from the general unstable, reckless, and unprincipled character of her legislature. A war has been for years waged and carried on by Michigan against her best interests; and permanent sources of prosperity and wealth have been shoved from her shores, as though they contained within them the germs of her dissolution. Associated capital, which we need in this state, to develop our natural resources, to improve our water power, to manufacture our wool into cloth, to work our mines, to manufacture our copper and iron, and build our dry docks, has been deterred from attempting so hazardous and fearful experiment as that of trusting itself to the tender mercies of time-serving demagogues, and has found investment elsewhere. The emigrant and settler have for years passed our fair shores in crowds, frightened by unjust taxation. . . . The public domain . . . remains within our bounds to the extent of twenty-five million acres, a howling wilderness, given up to beasts of prey, and about, it would seem from recent indications, itself to become a prey to hungry politicians, a race more inexorable, more insatiable, and more deadly, than any which nature unassisted has ever reared.

In short, a Democratic legislature had shackled the state and its citizens, restraining them from achieving success and happiness.[44]

In spite of the warnings of their political opponents, Cook, Pierce, and their allies held their ground and continued to support the Committee on Banking and Other Corporations' proposed amendment while the document was before the committee of the whole. Though a measure granting the state the power to rescind corporate charters did not become part of the new constitution, a similar provision did. Under this proviso, no corporation (except those chartered for municipal purposes, railroads, canals, and plank-road companies) could be established for longer than thirty years. The delegates also ratified a number of other significant amendments limiting the power of corporations. As with banks, corporations were henceforth to be formed under general laws rather than through specific legislative charters. This measure was meant not only to eliminate the political wire-pulling power and influence of those seeking to establish corporate bodies but also to ensure that access to this form of organization would be open and available to all who could meet the stated requirements. In addition, the delegates, mindful of past legislative attempts to circumvent similar laws by chartering "associations," clearly defined the term *corporation*. Corporations were also prohibited from holding most real estate for longer than ten years. And finally, the stockholders of all corporations were made individually liable for "all labor" performed by the corporations.[45]

Although the monster had been chained and weakened, Michigan's Democrats remained uneasy. Could the monster regain its strength? If it did, would the constitutional chains be able to hold it? What would happen to the liberties of Michiganians if the chains were too weak and the monster once again set out to suck the lifeblood of the state? The answer was clear: Michigan and its citizens would once again find themselves slaves to the power of the market. This perception, shaped by an all-consuming fear of power, led the Democrat-controlled convention to create a buffer between the polity and the market, a kind of rudimentary safety net to catch the citizenry and protect it before it lost its grip and slid into the abyss. The measure proposed as a last barrier between liberty and enslavement was homestead exemption.

Homestead exemption was something of a national mania in the years preceding the Civil War. The principle of safeguarding enough land to guarantee a means of continued subsistence in the face of economic uncertainty found favor throughout the nation and led to the passage of such laws in virtually every state. The appeal of homestead exemption was that it went further than other interventions in the free market by "purport[ing] to offer permanent security, not just temporary relief from hard times" by shielding the family from total loss at the hands of creditors. The leading champion of Michigan's homestead exemption clause was the father of the state's 1848 exemption law, Democrat John Pierce.[46]

Pierce's unswerving devotion to the cause of homestead exemption had deep roots, roots that stretched back a lifetime. Born in 1797 in Chesterfield, New Hampshire, Pierce lost his father at the age of two. His widowed mother, unable to provide for her two children, sent young John to live with his grandfather. Though his mother soon remarried, her new husband already had a large number of children, and Pierce continued to live with his grandfather. When he was ten, his grandfather passed away, leaving him $100, which he would receive on his twenty-first birthday. John was then taken in by a nearby uncle, but the boy was considered a burden and an intruder by his aunt, already encumbered with several children of her own. Young John, though, retained his uncle's favor by doing chores and working on the family farm. At age eighteen, Pierce "experienced a 'conversion' that fired him with ambition to become a minister of the gospel." Recognizing that the two months of annual schooling that he had received each winter was inadequate for his new calling, he obtained his uncle's permission to go out to work for himself. For over two years, he toiled on a neighboring farm, managing to save $100. This sum, along with the equal amount left to him by his grandfather, provided Pierce with the means to obtain an education. Upon completion of his theological studies at Brown University in 1824, he was licensed to preach by the Congregational Society. From 1825 to 1829, he was pastor of a church in Oneida County, New York. But because he was a Freemason, Pierce was forced to leave when the "anti-Masonic furor descended upon his community." He then returned to the East and assumed the position of principal at the academy in Goshen, Connecticut, for a year. In 1831, he packed his bags and headed west to Michigan, settling in the town of Marshall.[47]

Although Pierce was successful as a preacher and a teacher in Michigan, his business ventures were marred by misfortune. Soon after arriving in Michigan, he and some other individuals built a mill that immediately proved unprofitable. Worse yet, the mill collapsed only a few years after it was built because of a poor foundation. Pierce also invested in a thousand-acre farm, along with a consortium of other men. Eager to take advantage of Michigan's growing wool trade and a believer in the superiority of thoroughbred stock, he imported a flock of merino sheep from New York. Again, Pierce miscalculated, and his wool experiment failed, "since all of the state's woolen mills had spindles for coarse wool only and his Merino sheep produced a fine wool."

The unfortunate Pierce next turned his attention to cattle raising and dairying. In these endeavors, he had seemingly found his calling, successfully raising a large herd and sending it to market in Buffalo, New York, under the care of one of his employees. But the employee disappeared with the proceeds, and Pierce was forced to settle the bills out of his own pocket. Undaunted and knowing that the Michigan Central Railroad was moving westward from Jackson, he put in eighty acres of wheat, expecting the railroad to reach Marshall by harvest time. But the railroad was not finished in time, and Pierce found himself with no market for his crop. To add insult to injury, he was forced to sell his land to offset the accumulated debt of the other syndicate members, a debt incurred without his knowledge.[48]

Pierce, in short, was well acquainted with the perils of the market. In fact, his life epitomized the hopes and fears that had led to the creation of the Democratic Party. Enticed into participation in the market by the lure of wealth and success, he had learned a hard lesson—the market could just as easily leave one with nothing. This lesson led Pierce to reevaluate his priorities and to value, above all else, his independence and autonomy in the face of the precarious world of the market. This conviction had motivated him when he championed the cause of homestead exemption during the 1847–1848 legislative sessions, and this same belief would lead him into the fray once more to promote that cause at the Lansing constitutional convention in 1850.

Pierce faced an uphill battle. Personally hostile to the principle of property exemption, convention president Daniel Goodwin had loaded the Committee on Exemptions and the Rights of Married Women with opponents of exemption, two of whom were Whigs. Not surprisingly, the majority report of the committee recommended that the topic be omitted from the constitution.[49]

Livid, Pierce took the floor and offered a minority report proposing the inclusion of a homestead exemption provision in the new constitution. The principle of exemption, he reminded his fellow delegates, was vital "because the people are, by the grace of God, free and independent." Homestead exemption, he continued, "is so accordant with the real spirit of progress, so just in itself, so wisely expedient in all exigencies to which families are liable, so alleviating when ill fortune bears them down, and so consonant with the popular sentiment and the principles of true Christian morality, that no power on earth can prevent its universal adoption." Sarcastically, Whig delegate Henry Backus of Wayne County noted that it was the obvious "will of the convention to abandon the credit system" and moved to destroy all laws for collection of debt.[50]

Pierce remained adamant. "The spirit of aggregated capital," he asserted, is aggressive. It has no limit, no bounds. Controlling legislation of the world, it has been resistless in its sway. It never tires, it never sleeps. Soulless, heartless, remorseless, conscienceless, it presses onward, regardless of the dying or the dead. It produces nothing, but watches with an eagle-eye all the products of labor. It taxes all classes. It watches the wheat grower, the wool grower, the cotton grower, the laborer, the spinner, and the washer-woman, and is never satisfied except with the lion's portion. Robbing labor of its reward, it reduces to, and leaves the man and his family in abject poverty; not satisfied, it takes his cot, and turns him, wife and children, out.

The home, Pierce insisted, "must be inviolate, or liberty is but a name, and freedom a mockery. . . . To deprive any man or any family of a home . . . under any pretense whatever, is downright tyranny." It was up to the state, the only entity powerful enough to stand up to accumulated capital, "to throw around every homestead, every fireside, every hearth-stone, the shield of its protection—to stay the proud waves of wealth, capital, and usury, from carrying over the homes of suffering, crushed, bleeding humanity." By these means alone could every citizen retain autonomy and could "sit every man under his vine and fig tree." Ultimately, Pierce's logic prevailed, and the assembled delegates incorporated the principle of homestead exemption into the new state constitution.[51]

With their work done, the convention delegates adjourned on August 15, leaving the fate of their final product in the hands of the citizens of Michigan. Endorsing the new constitution, the *Free Press* pronounced it "stringent, plain, [and] democratic." A Farmington Democrat agreed, stating that he was "fully satisfied that its adoption by the people is expedient and would be well calculated to serve our future prosperity and advancement as a State." The new constitution, the *Grand Rapids Enquirer* approvingly noted, "contains all of the old constitution that was worth preserving, and many new features which commend it to our favor." The *Adrian Watchtower* concluded, "As a whole, it is a document upon which the people of Michigan need not feel ashamed to set their seal of approbation." Even the state's Whig press endorsed the constitution. Despite a number of objectionable clauses, the *Jackson American Citizen* said, the document was "as near correct, and as plausible as anything we have seen originating as this did, in the midst of a locofoco quarrel." Not surprisingly, the paper attributed the saving features of the document to the Whigs, "who took advantage of the divisions in the locofoco delegation to insert something for the people, instead of the Democratic party." Indeed, the *Advertiser* added, because of "the integrity and firmness of some of the best men in the body, some objectionable measures sought to be retained, were defeated, and great improvements substituted."[52]

While their elected representatives at the Lansing convention grappled rhetorically with the threat menacing the liberties of Michigan, a number of Michiganians chose to engage the most tangible symbol of that threat—the railroads—in more direct combat, waging a desperate struggle to preserve their independence. Fighting a losing battle to maintain a constitutional amendment providing the state with a means of repealing corporate charters, John Pierce warned his fellow delegates, "Deny this right, and the people have no remedy; however inconsistent with the public good; however burdensome and oppressive, and productive of evil corporations may become, they are sacred, they are not to be touched." "No remedy is left," he intoned, "but the last resort of an oppressed people—revolution by physical force." By the summer of 1850, Michigan found itself on the brink of such a revolution.[53]

Widespread animosity toward the railroads in Michigan was a fairly new phenomenon in 1850, stemming primarily from the state's sale of its railroad assets four years earlier. Development of Michigan's railroads had been intended to promote the general welfare of the state by "democratiz[ing] the economy and expanding the sphere of individual enterprise." But by 1846, although the railroads were profitable, they were in desperate need of repair and modernization. Facing a mounting state debt and lacking the pecuniary means of improving and expanding its rail network, Michigan sold its two railroads, the 46-mile Michigan Southern and the 143-mile Michigan Central, to private investors.

Not everyone agreed that the sale would achieve positive results. Democratic state senator and future lieutenant governor William M. Fenton, for one, believed the sale meant that "principles will be sacrificed upon the altar of gain—the integrity of the people will be destroyed in an indiscriminate worship at the shrine of mammon. The wheels of government which should roll quietly on in an unimpeded track in their onward course toward civil, social, and political improvement—will be clogged by the crash of locomotives, and the strife of aspirants for the loaves and fishes which fall from the tables of those in power." Proponents of the sale, by contrast, remained convinced that the transaction would "increase [the railroads'] usefulness to the community." To ensure that the public interest was furthered by the sale, the state legislature required that the new owners adhere to a number of regulatory measures: differences between long-haul and short-haul rates were regulated, upper limits were set on charges for hauling basic agricultural products and necessities, grain and flour rates were limited to three-quarters of the fare previously charged by the state, rate discrimination was prohibited, and the companies were required to replace and extend the track to the Lake Michigan shoreline within three years. In return for agreeing to these restrictions, the companies were granted a monopoly that prohibited the construction of parallel routes within five miles of the existing roadbed, the Michigan Central was granted permission to alter its route west of Kalamazoo to the southwestern Michigan town of New Buffalo instead of the original destination of St. Joseph, and the companies were allowed to purchase the railroads with bonds and warrants issued by the state—bonds that circulated at a 25 percent discount on the open market.[54]

The Michigan Central, headed by Detroit attorney James F. Joy and New York civil engineer John W. Brooks, moved aggressively to meet its obligations. Spurred on by rapidly increasing revenues, the railroad reached New Buffalo, on the Michigan-Indiana border, in April 1849. From there, the company operated a line of steamers to Chicago, which allowed passengers from Detroit to reach that city within a day and a half. Moreover, the company modernized its holdings by replacing the state's oak and iron strap rails with newer, sixty-pound T-rails—an improvement that allowed the company to operate heavier equipment at a greater rate of speed. The lengthening reach of the railroad initiated a radical transformation of the state's farming economy. Enticed by the opportunity provided by quick and reliable market connections, many farmers residing near the rail lines began shifting in the direction of commercial farming, thus thrusting the state's central tier of counties into the world of the cash nexus. Virtually overnight, wheat production in the counties contiguous to the Michigan Central soared from 500,000 bushels in 1837 to over 1,618,000 bushels in 1850. Similarly, the value of flour produced by the same counties jumped from $303,000 to $1,038,000. In the five years between 1845 and 1850, the gross tonnage of goods passing over the Michigan Central's rails jumped over 415.4 percent, from 26,000 to 134,000. Increased speed and traffic on the railroad, however, exacted their toll.[55]

Traveling at the unheard-of speed of thirty miles per hour, the new engines of the Michigan Central were involved in a growing number of accidents with free-ranging livestock that wandered onto the unfenced track. Such accidents had, of course, happened when the road was under state ownership (though its trains traveled much more slowly). In those cases, out of political necessity and in keeping with local township and county ordinances that recognized livestock as free commoners, the state had paid farmers the full amount claimed for their livestock. But Superintendent Brooks, having no concern for the electorate and responsible only to the company's directors and stockholders, decided to make farmers face up to what he interpreted as their own negligence and cupidity by implementing a policy of paying only one-half the appraised value of any livestock killed by the railroad. In the minds of the farmers, Brooks's offer amounted to an admission of guilt, and bolstered by the state's open-range tradition, they continued to press the company for full restitution. When satisfaction was not forthcoming, tempers reached a flash point.[56]

To understand fully the depth of the farmers' anger, it is essential to recognize that the preservation of traditional communal rights represented by the principle of open-range grazing was a prominent concern for northern family farmers in the antebellum period. An 1876 memoir entitled *The Bark Covered House*, written by William Nowlin, illustrates the central role of the range in northern farm family subsistence. Shortly after the pioneer family's arrival in Dearborn, Michigan, in 1834, Nowlin's father purchased two oxen and one cow. Nowlin remembered that the family's free-ranging cattle fed on "cow-slips and leeks, which grew in abundance, also on little 'French-bogs'" that were green all winter; young Nowlin daily tracked these cattle across miles of timbered and newly broken farmland. The animals were the family's "main dependence" for many years and, in Nowlin's words, "our stand-by through thick and thin." As the family struggled to clear its land (employing the free-roaming oxen) and later as it worked to clear the farm from an encumbering mortgage, potatoes and milk and "thickened milk" (rolled lumps of salted, dampened flour boiled in milk) were staples in the Nowlins' diet for years.[57]

Such practices had been adhered to for generations in the East and thus made perfect sense to the tide of Yankee settlers flooding into Michigan in the middle decades of the nineteenth century. The daunting task of clearing heavily timbered land and the lack of a reliable transportation network throughout much of the era ensured that even the most commercially minded farmers would spend a substantial number of years in subsistence farming. Making use of unimproved, open land (for grazing, foraging, or hunting) was a fundamental element of that precapitalist subsistence strategy. While the extensive herding characteristic of the southern yeomanry may not have been common among northern self-provisioning farmers, reliance on small livestock herds that were grazed upon open lands most assuredly was. The diminished scale of such activities did not necessarily lessen their importance.[58]

Sadly, for far too long, scholars have generally ignored the enduring subsistence ethic among northern farmers and have overwhelmingly depicted them as eager, budding capitalists. Susan Gray's *Yankee West,* which focuses on the settlement and growth of Kalamazoo County, Michigan, during the 1830s, argues that the region's Yankee settlers sought "to create traditional communities of unlimited potential for economic growth." Market participation, neighborliness, and land purchase were, in Gray's estimation, viewed by Kalamazoo County's Yankee settlers as symbiotic instruments to promote a shared goal of capital accretion, financial reward, and profit. Although it is undeniably true that a great many of these folks openly embraced the opportunities provided by the emerging market economy (and thus became proponents of such things as fencing laws in order to protect their market crops from foraging livestock), it is equally certain, though widely overlooked, that many did not—or at least did so with much hesitancy and trepidation.[59]

Thus, while it might be tempting to assume that the farmers' sharp bargaining with the Michigan Central over livestock values represented, as historians Shawn Kantor and J. Morgan Kousser claimed in their study of the postbellum southern reaction to the closing of the range, "a calculating state of mind characteristic of capitalism," such a conclusion misses the mark. Participation in and cognizance of the market did not always mean complete acceptance of it. A good argument could be made, in fact, that the Michigan farmers' pricing savvy was adopted as a survival strategy in the face of an expanding cash nexus. Given their livestock's importance in their day-to-day lives, an awareness of the replacement cost of the animals would have been essential. This interpretation is further supported by the all too frequent claims made by the Michigan Central and its supporters that the farmers inflated the value of their animals or that they intentionally drove sick and feeble animals onto the tracks. Certainly, some farmers may have done so. Others, however, may have claimed seemingly exorbitant values for their livestock because, in their self-provisioning world, those animals represented an invaluable asset.[60]

Even if the railroad were removed from the picture, the fact that these farmers continued to operate on the "fencing-out" principle is a strong indication that they were still, in many respects, precapitalist. As historian Steven Hahn and others have demonstrated, proponents of laws (often referred to as stock laws) requiring the "fencing-in" of animals advocated such measures as a means of securing property rights. Morever, supporters of these laws argued that such measures would foster improved stock breeding, renew the fertility of land through pasturage, facilitate the intensification of agriculture, and free up capital and labor (required to maintain the extensive fences needed to enclose large fields) for more productive purposes—trends closely associated with a capitalist sensibility. It is inconceivable that they would have reacted with righteous rage to accidental railroad slaughter if they had already accepted the "fencing-in" notion that free-roaming stock was a threat to their market crops. Again, Nowlin's memoir offers a tangible illustration of this tension. After working diligently to clear a portion of his land and to construct brush fencing around his fields, Nowlin's father put in a small crop of wheat. But one day, the author recalled, "a neighbor's unruly ox broke into it." Young Nowlin was told by his father to retrieve the ox and to take it home. When he arrived at his neighbor's house with the animal, Nowlin told the neighbor "that his ox had been in our wheat and that father wished him to keep his ox away." The neighbor replied that the Nowlins "must make the fence better and he [the ox] wouldn't get in." The senior Nowlin's desire to protect his market commodity from the foraging ox (though wheat, of course, would also serve as a staple in a self-provisioning household) and the neighbor's insistence upon the continuation and acknowledgment of traditional open-range privileges nicely illustrate the parameters of the tensions spawned by encroaching capitalism—tensions brought to a head by the conflict between the Michigan Central Railroad and the farmers of Michigan.[61]

Up and down the rail line, the state's yeomanry reacted to the new challenge posed to their communities and to their way of life. Throughout the spring of 1849, protests flared along the road from Ann Arbor to Niles. Between Niles and Dowagiac, where it was reported that 160 animals had been killed on a twelve-mile stretch of the road, farmers retaliated against Brooks's half-pay offer by committing serious depredations, "going so far as to derail an engine by opening a switch." West of Kalamazoo, a group of angry farmers took their revenge on the railroad by greasing the tracks on the upgrades with the lard salvaged from the carcasses of their dead livestock. Near Ann Arbor, irate farmers actually tore up the tracks.[62]

From the perspective of many Michigan farmers, such violent reactions were completely justified. Their world and the rules by which it operated had changed suddenly, without their consent and in an unsettling manner. At every turn, they seemingly found their tradition of community-based, self-provisioning agriculture—exemplified most readily by the open range, with its presupposition of surplus time and resources—under attack by the impersonal forces of the market—embodied by the railroads, with their presupposition that both time and goods were in short supply. Faced with a choice between continuing their traditional practices or modifying or abandoning those practices to become individual producers for market consumption, many farmers remained ambivalent about which course to follow. A large number of these farmers—confronting the actions of the

Michigan Central Railroad Corporation, an obvious and alarming symbol of the market economy—opted to retain as much of their traditional life as possible and to avoid full-fledged involvement in the market. John Pierce, himself the victim of Brooks's half-pay policy, summed up the attitude of the rebellious farmers in a June 1849 letter to the *Marshall Democratic Expounder*. In that letter, Pierce alleged that

> the road has been for a long time, one gore of blood. No heathen altar ever smoked more continually with the blood of its victims. Horses and Oxen and cows and sheep and hogs—all free common-ers by law—the road not fenced, and yet we are told that the owners [of the livestock] are the trespassers. They [the company] force their way through our farms, leaving our fields and meadows and pastures all open as commons, and yet we are the trespassers if our stock pass over the road of their high-mightiness, and liable to them for damages. . . . I gave it as my opinion to Mr. Brooks, more than two years ago, that the company would find themselves precipitated upon such a state of things as now exists, if they changed from the policy of the state in paying for damage done. . . . The road must be fenced, in the meantime, something near the value of the property destroyed must be paid.

These sentiments drove scores of exasperated Michiganians to protect their livelihoods and liberties—and to reaffirm their commitment to their tradi-tional lifestyle—by personally attacking the railroad. Indeed, the use of per-sonal violence, even against inanimate objects such as train engines, further reflected their traditional ideal of personal dependencies and face-to-face relations and spoke to their determination to allow traditional community norms and dynamics to shape and direct their responses to the crisis they faced. For the agitated citizens of Michigan, more was at stake than a simple question of dead livestock.[63]

Other complaints were leveled by state farmers against the Michigan Central. Many resented the condemnation proceedings that had split their farms or given choice lands to the company. Others were offended by the company's refusal to cease running its trains on the Sabbath or by its notori-ously low wages for contract work such as building fences along the right-of-way. Still others, blaming the road's high shipping fees for the low prices they received for their goods, denounced the Michigan Central as a "shameful monopoly" and railed against its allegedly discriminatory rate schedule—a schedule that made it cheaper to ship goods from Niles to Detroit than over shorter distances.[64]

The Michigan Central, however, was not the only railroad in the state. Although often overlooked by historians, Michigan's other railroad corporations also felt the wrath of an aggrieved public. On the evening of December 12, 1849, for example, a group of Detroiters, angry after their complaints were ignored by the corporate officers of the Detroit and Pontiac Railroad Company and by their own Common Council, tore up the company's rails for several blocks along Gratiot Street because they claimed the tracks made the thoroughfare impassable. The following summer, those citizens met on the steps of the city hall to denounce the corporation. The disgruntled group stated that they had heard "of a proposition before the Common Council, to permit the Pontiac R. R. Co., to relay their track on said street, and to use said street—dedicated to the public use—for the benefit of a private corporation as a Railway." The use of Gratiot Street as a railroad, they protested, "does directly and materially impair the value of property . . . , drives business from it, and prevents its use as a great thoroughfare for public travel, and renders it an unpleasant and insecure section of the city for private residences." Furthermore, they complained, "the high sanctions of state law and state authority have been inadequate to protect either state or people" from the encroachments of the Detroit and Pontiac Railroad Corporation. The company "seems not only destitute of a soul, but if it was even a body, we have been unable to ascertain its local habitation—its evil consequences among us, being its only tangible features."[65]

The Michigan Southern Railroad Company also received its share of criticism in early 1850. Throughout the spring legislative session, the company employed all the resources at its disposal to persuade state legislators to alter its charter so as to allow the road, upon reaching the town of Coldwater, to veer southward into Indiana (the eventual goal being Chicago). The proposition released a tide of anger and resentment across the state. Already piqued by the company's use of Toledo rather than Monroe as its eastern hub, the *Centreville Western Chronicle* condemned the proposal for "depriving the southern counties of Michigan of a road originally intended for their benefit." Under a call alerting residents—"Our City and State in Danger"—public meetings were held in Detroit and Pontiac to protest the company's attempt to ignore the public good. If the road were allowed to alter its charter, participants in the Detroit meeting declared, "we believe . . . the interests of the whole state are to be seriously injured." Simply put, the question was "whether there shall be a great thoroughfare through our own State connecting with the west, or whether we shall be confined within the Peninsula—whether the legislature of Michigan shall grant the right . . . to a company which is striving to build up a great commercial city on Lake Erie, making it the market for the produce of the west in opposition to the best interests of this State?" Indeed, the *Free Press* exclaimed, "if this bill ever becomes law," the end result would be to "make our Peninsular [*sic*] a barren cone, whose base rests on Ohio and Indiana, and whose travel, trade, industry, and wealth, is to be drained into foreign channels and foreign pockets." The message was clear: the people were organizing in defense of liberty and equality against what they perceived to be the manifest arrogance of railroad power.[66]

Michigan's elected officials took note of the rising tide of animosity directed toward railroad corporations. During the same 1850 legislative session in which the Michigan Southern unleashed an army of lobbyists in order to obtain a revision of its charter, the chairman of the Senate Committee on Corporations, a Democrat from Jackson County named Michael Shoemaker, introduced a bill (the first of many) requiring railroad corporations to fence the right-of-way, to post warning signs and build cattle guards at crossings, and to put bells on locomotives. Although Shoemaker's bill passed the senate, it was defeated in the lower house by those who argued that such a measure was an infringement of vested rights.[67]

Later that year, in the summer heat of Lansing, the topic of railroad corporations once again surfaced as the constitutional convention debated limiting corporate charters to thirty years. Robert McClelland, a delegate from the railroad county of Monroe, asked to amend the provision so that it exempted railroad corporations. If, he argued, "we are to grant a charter to a rail road which will not run longer than thirty years, it will be very difficult to get the stock taken up." John Pierce answered quickly: the amendment had been designed with railroads in mind. Alarmed that the convention seemed to side with McClelland, he offered the delegates a number of reasons why railroads should be included in the article. Conceding that contracts were inviolable and that the state had sold the Michigan Central Railroad a permanent charter, Pierce insisted that the state "never intended to surrender the power of control" to the company. For that matter, he continued, even if that had been the state's intention, the convention was the proper body to return that power to its rightful holders—the people. In the end, Pierce's pleas fell upon deaf ears, and the convention adopted the amendment with an exemption for railroad corporations.[68]

The growing public outcry against the railroads received its fullest expression during the latter half of 1850 in a region of Jackson County thereafter known to the employees of the Michigan Central as "the badlands." Nowhere in the state was the opposition to the railroads (in this case, the Michigan Central) so "intensive and so sustained" as along the stretch of track between the eastern Jackson County communities of Grass Lake and Michigan Center. Though the loss of livestock in this region seems to have been no heavier than in other areas of the state, local resistance was catalyzed by the presence of two men dedicated to ensuring that justice was done—Abel F. Fitch, a successful Michigan Center farmer, and Benjamin F. Burnett, a country lawyer from Grass Lake who would later be the editor of the antirailroad *Grass Lake Public Sentiment*.[69]

By the spring of 1849, Fitch and Burnett had galvanized their community to act in response to the Michigan Central's refusal to pay the full damages claimed by local farmers for livestock killed by the locomotives. At numerous public meetings, both men called for Brooks to modify his policy; they also wrote to him with such requests. Brooks responded by offering to take a test case to the state supreme court to decide the question of liability, with all costs and fees up to $50 to be paid by the company. Suspicious of the power and influence of railroad money, Fitch denounced the scheme as a "perfect humbug."

Meanwhile, local farmers responded to Brooks's offer by commencing a nightly war upon the Michigan Central: placing obstructions on the tracks, burning woodpiles, stoning trains, and, in some cases, shooting at them. When one local resident warned an irate insurgent named William Corwin that innocent lives could be lost because of the attacks on the trains, Corwin allegedly replied, "Damn 'em, if they don't want to be shot let 'em pay for the cattle they have killed." In 1851, a correspondent of the *Jackson American Citizen* echoed Corwin's opinion. The writer claimed he had never yet seen "any argument any way satisfactory to my mind that a railroad company has any more right to kill my property that may be trespassing on the bank of their road, than I have to kill my neighbor's ox which I may find destroying my cornfield." "Deep will be the retribution," he warned, "when insulted freemen shall call them [the Michigan Central] to cancel the many insults that have been heaped upon them." Even the arrival of the state attorney general, George V. N. Lothrop, did not defuse the situation. Throughout the summer of 1849 and beginning again with the thawing of the lakes and the reopening of rail traffic in the spring of 1850, the trains of the Michigan Central came under constant attack as they proceeded through the badlands.[70]

By the summer of 1850, the attacks had become so frequent and so disruptive that the company was forced to run a handcar ahead of its trains to keep the tracks clear—a tactic that did not work very well, as the so-called conspirators simply waited for the passage of the car before beginning their handiwork. In August, while the delegates to the constitutional convention finished their business in Lansing, Jackson County farmers derailed an eastbound engine, the *Gazelle*. In September, trains bound for or returning from the state fair in Ann Arbor were subjected to nightly terrors. On the heels of lower than expected earnings in 1849 and contending with the declining passenger revenues that resulted from the wide press coverage of the attacks, Brooks took aggressive steps and inundated Jackson County with undercover operatives in order to gather the evidence needed to break the back of the rebellion. Matters began to come to a head on the evening of November 18, 1850, when the Michigan Central Depot in Detroit burned to the ground. Authorities quickly blamed the blaze on an incendiary device.[71]

Working throughout the winter, Brooks traced the alleged depot arson back to Fitch and the other conspirators in Jackson County. On April 19, 1851, convinced that he had a case, he dispatched the sheriff of Wayne County, along with sixty handpicked deputized employees of the railroad, to arrest the responsible parties. In all, some fifty individuals—primarily residents of Jackson County, including Fitch and Burnett—were arrested.

Who were these antirailroad activists, and what did they hope to achieve? A brief statistical profile of those arrested offers some interesting insights.[72]

Among the first things that are evident about the members of this group are their relatively young ages and their overwhelmingly Yankee origins. Of those arrested, 71.4 percent were under the age of forty. Most of these men (70 percent of the sample group and 50 percent of the overall total) were between twenty-five and forty years of age, and 40 percent were between thirty and thirty-nine. Moreover, 78.6 percent of them were born in New England or New York, with another 11.9 percent giving their state of origin as either Pennsylvania or New Jersey. Such findings suggest that these were individuals who had long exposure to the emerging market economy, having matured during its heyday prior to the panic of 1837 and having witnessed its transformation of the eastern United States. At the same time, these men were also well acquainted with the tradition of open-range grazing, coming as they did from states where, in many cases (New York being the most relevant example), such practices were still protected by law as late as 1860. Their economic awareness must have been further enhanced by the fact that they came of age politically at the height of the Jacksonian debates over banking, internal improvements, federal land policy, tariffs, and other economic concerns. Finally, this same group likely also felt the full effects of the panic of

1837 and may have thus found it increasingly difficult to assert their independence in the face of economic downturn. In other words, these men belonged to the generation of Americans that was intimately acquainted with socioeconomic change and its positive—and perhaps more important, its negative—ramifications.[73]

It is not surprising that the movement drew the bulk of its support from the more tradition-based segments of Michigan society. Of those arrested, twenty-seven (64.3 percent) were farmers, and another ten (23.8 percent) were artisans, figures in line with the state's overall occupation profile (farmers comprised 60.3 percent of the state profile, and artisans 16.4 percent). Interestingly, however, although 2.7 percent of the people in the state as a whole were engaged in commercial occupations, none of the arrested men were. It seems, then, that these men belonged to those segments in Michigan society that were most immediately reconfigured in the face of sweeping economic change.[74]

A breakdown of the mean value of real estate held by the sample group, when compared to the figures for the state as a whole, also yields some interesting results. The mean real estate value for the sample group was $1,062.76, a figure roughly comparable to the state figure of $1,048, but a bit below the Leoni Township (where most of the men lived) value of $1,299.59. When the sample figure is recalculated without the value attributed to Abel Fitch's farm ($8,000), the mean plummets to $893. Indeed, that figure is a more accurate reflection of the holdings of the arrested population, of which 40.5 percent either rented farms from others or resided on their parents' farms as dependents. As a group, these men generally had not fared as well as their neighbors or their peers throughout the state.[75]

Further indications that these men, though connected to the cash nexus, were somewhat less prosperous than many of their peers can be derived from data extracted from the Agricultural Census of 1850. The data show, for example, that the mean value of farms owned by the accused, $1,330.67 (again, with Fitch's farm excluded), was 10.6 percent lower than the mean for farms throughout the state, $1,488, and 15 percent lower than the Jackson County mean of $1,565.17—a difference made even more significant when one considers the direct access to markets available to these men due to their farms' prime location near the tracks of the Michigan Central. Furthermore, the alleged conspirators had farms with a lower mean number of improved acres (44.4) than did the rest of the state's farmers, whose average stood at 55.3 acres. More telling yet is the fact that this figure fell 32.4 percent short of the Jackson County mean of 65.72 acres. Consequently, these same farmers tended to produce much less marketable grain (wheat, corn, and oats) than did their statewide peer group—227.9 bushels compared to 356.7, or 5.14 bushels per improved acre (20 percent) less than a statewide figure of 6.4 bushels. Similarly, the mean value of their herds, $146.58, also fell short of their statewide cohort group's mean of $225, a possible indicator of the minimal market value placed upon their inferior-quality free-ranging stock. Finally, the average value of agricultural implements owned by the accused stood at $44.17, or 99.5 cents per improved acre, as opposed to the state average of $79, or $1.42 per improved acre.[76]

Clearly, such impressionistic evidence, though by no means indisputable, is suggestive. It strongly implies that those individuals involved in the ongoing resistence to the Michigan Central and the changes that it symbolized, though frequently connected to the market, shied away from a complete immersion in the emerging capitalist order. Why this was the case we can only speculate. Perhaps these men resented the loss of autonomy to the impersonal world of the market, a loss driven home by their inability to preserve their traditional way of life and established rights in the face of corporate power (a frame of mind consistent with the Democratic proclivities of many of the arrested). For others, such as Abel Fitch and the outspoken critic of the railroad John Pierce, traumatic experiences in the marketplace may have led them to reevaluate their priorities (Fitch endured losses as the result of bad investments and the panic of 1837, and Pierce, as mentioned previously, suffered a number of severe economic setbacks in commercial ventures). Younger activists and those who were not yet established as independent producers might have felt insecure about their prospects or may have considered themselves inadequate and incapable of meeting the social expectations imposed upon them by the emerging capitalist order. Others may have seen the issue as a simple matter of preserving the nation's republican heritage and traditional property rights. Benjamin Burnett, for one, felt that "an iron armoured slave-holding giant without any soul, is the owner and possessor of Michigan, and has the keeping of her fetters." "How often," he asked, "has this tyrant of a slave dealer, sought the destruction of freemen?" Whatever the reason for their activism, what is clear is that these men felt buffeted and threatened by the shifting world around them, and thus, they reacted by attacking those forces most closely identified with commercial expansion. Echoing this feeling of immediate peril, Fitch wrote his wife, Amanda, from his Detroit jail cell:

> If this railroad company must rule this state why the sooner we know
> it the better and perhaps I may as well be the first victim as the last

. . . why I never laid a straw in their way except to tell them openly and plainly that their policy was bad and to kill the poor man's last cow and leave families destitute was wrong. If this I say is all due in accordance with the principals [*sic*] of our government and the people of Michigan are willing to submit to it why I must of course suffer, but God only knows who's turn will come next.[77]

The trial of the alleged conspirators began in May 1851 and stretched into August. When all was said and done, twelve men were convicted of conspiring to destroy railroad property and imprisoned for terms varying from five to ten years. Fitch fulfilled his prophecy and became a martyr for his cause, dying while awaiting his day in court. He also proved correct in his assessment of the people of Michigan—they would not be willing to submit to railroad power. The conclusion of the railroad conspiracy trial in August 1851 did not end antirailroad feelings in the state. On the contrary, bitterness and animosity toward the railroads continued to simmer and eventually boiled. And through this critical period, diverse elements of the population were fused together under the pressures of the times in a movement that would ultimately result in the creation of the Republican Party in 1854.

This, then, was Michigan in 1850—a living testimony to the strength and pervasiveness of the political culture of Jacksonian America. Michigan was a young state, a state racked by growing pains, a state desperately trying to come to grips with itself and its relation to the wider world. For Michiganians, the political culture of the era warned of impending slavery and demanded eternal vigilance. Yet at the same time, they found within that culture a sense of direction and a path to follow through the turbulent times, looking to a future in which their state could mature and prosper. All of Michigan's citizens understood (though not in the same way) the perils that could ravage their adolescent commonwealth, and they stood ready and determined to help their state stay the course. Accordingly, on November 5, 1850, they rallied overwhelmingly to endorse the constitution produced by their chosen delegates. Meanwhile, the scattered voices of protest raised against the power of railroad corporations refused to be silenced and, in fact, would soon reach a crescendo. Michigan, however, reached its cognitive age as the Jacksonian party system was in decline and as a new wave of change swept across the United States. Over the next decade, the state found itself continuously lashed by massive and rapid social and economic changes, a pounding that threatened to rip to shreds the political garment that the young state had only recently donned.[78]

"This Age is Big With Importance"

Socioeconomic Change in Michigan, 1850–1860

RECOUNTING HIS nine-month sojourn in Jacksonian America between 1831 and 1832, the French aristocrat Alexis de Tocqueville noted in his *Democracy in America* that "the United States of America have only been emancipated for a half a century from the state of colonial dependence in which they stood to Great Britain. Yet no people in the world have made such rapid progress in trade and manufacturing as the Americans." As historian Charles Sellers's study of the era deftly illustrated, Tocqueville was correct: antebellum Americans found themselves in the throes of a market revolution—a revolution that transformed almost every facet of their lives. Change of such a sweeping nature inevitably exacts a toll. For Jacksonian Americans, that toll was a ubiquitous sense of anxiety and uneasiness about their shifting world, a pervasive discomfort and worry about where they and their nation were headed. Although this rampant anguish was expressed in innumerable ways, one of its most tangible manifestations was the creation of the Democratic and Whig Parties—organizations that sought to ease their supporters' minds by identifying and then eradicating the sources of their anxieties.[1]

The events of 1850 provided Michiganians with ample evidence of this strong political determination to calm the tempestuous seas that threatened to swallow Jacksonian society. In that year, the Democrat-controlled state constitutional convention identified and struck at concentrated and self-serving political power in an all-out effort to free state government from the clutches of grasping politicians, while at the same time making it more responsive to the needs of the citizenry. Moreover, still haunted by memories of Michigan's long bout with economic infirmity and egged on by the state's insurgent antirailroad farmers, the delegates worked to assuage people's fears by protecting the state and its inhabitants from the uncertainties of an encroaching market economy. The document that eventually emerged from the convention, a majority of the delegates and the electorate firmly believed, guaranteed that the evil forces that had disrupted their ideal social order and shattered their peace of mind would forever be restrained. Michigan's respite from anxiety, however, proved short-lived. Over the decade ahead, Michiganians were to endure a level of uneasiness that eclipsed all they had previously known as their state experienced a second economic boom, characterized by a series of rapid and far-reaching changes that irrevocably transformed Michigan from a subsistence-oriented frontier community into a center of market activity.

In many respects, Michigan was still in its infancy in 1850. Despite thirteen years of steady and sometimes spectacular growth and rapid population increase, vast areas of the state remained in their natural condition, "half smothered in luxuriant foliage." Nothing symbolized the state's incomplete emergence from the wilderness more aptly than its newly constructed capital at Lansing, where the "forests were standing within gunshot" and where, as one observer related, only one of the town's two hundred buildings, the capitol, "appeared to be finished." Two-thirds of Michigan's 397,654 inhabitants lived in the southernmost reaches of the state, one-third in the five southeastern counties of Wayne, Oakland, Macomb, Monroe, and Washtenaw. In 1850, even the most heavily populated county, Wayne, had more unimproved land within its borders than improved land.[2]

Certainly, market forces had made inroads into Michigan prior to that year, and many citizens had eagerly embraced them. Many others, however, made intimately aware of the perils involved in market production by the state's early economic woes and circumscribed by more limited access to market, steered clear of the world of cash exchange and clung to more traditional patterns of subsistence-oriented agriculture. "The majority [of farmers]," commercially minded Michigan farmer A. C. Glidden derisively recalled of the period, "were more interested in how to get a living, than in how to farm." Despite Glidden's disdain, farmers in 1850 Michigan remained committed to a safety-first, "self-sufficing diversified" type of agriculture in which "in so far as possible each farm and each community planned to produce those things which were needed for local consumption." A great many Michigan farmers succeeded in meeting this goal. On the farm of Simeon Owens, his great-granddaughter remembered, "everybody worked and all needs were met, with little money involved." Owens's farm stood as a paragon of self-sufficiency, with all of the family's necessities—from grain, dairy, and meat to shoes, candles, ice, maple sugar, and honey—procured from within its boundaries. Federal census data for 1850 indicate that Owens was not the only Michigan farmer concerned with home manufacturing. From June 1849 to June 1850, Michiganians produced $340,948 worth of home manufactures, or roughly $.84 per person or $10 per farm—a figure 199 percent higher than the $113,995 (or $.54 per person) recorded a decade earlier. As these figures suggest, the severity of the panic of 1837 in Michigan forced a great many residents to reassess their relationship to the market and to seek, in self-sufficiency, shelter from the economic storm.[3]

But self-sufficiency did not mean go-it-alone individualism. On the contrary, traditional subsistence farming and family self-sufficiency were, in reality, dependent upon a web of familial and interpersonal interactions and exchanges. Barn raisings, husking bees, and threshing gangs were only the most outward manifestations of this community interdependence. Much more common were the mutual exchanges and borrowing that occurred on a daily basis, a custom that prompted one female resident of the state, obviously unaccustomed to such practices, to complain: "Not only are all kitchen utensils as much your neighbors as your own, but bedsteads, beds, blankets, sheets, travel from house to house. . . . Sieves, smoothing irons, and churns run about as if they had legs; one brass kettle is enough for a whole neighborhood; and I could point to a cradle that has rocked half the babies in Montacute [a fictitious name used for Pinckney]." The manner in which items were borrowed was "straight-forward and honest, none of your hypocritical civility and servile gratitude! Your true Republican, when he finds that you possess anything which would contribute to his convenience, walks in with, 'Are you going to use your horse today?' if horses happen to be the thing he needs." Massive socioeconomic change, however, would soon unalterably disrupt the tradition-bound world of Michigan's self-provisioning farmers.[4]

The primary impetus for the state's coming of age was the continued development, improvement, and expansion of the transportation and communication networks. Without the means to move goods to market and while encumbered by frontier living conditions, Michiganians had little choice but to concentrate their efforts on subsistence farming and limited artisanal endeavors. In other words, safety-first agriculture, though a well-established pattern in midcentury Michigan, was not necessarily the ideal lifestyle for all of those involved in it. The development of roads, canals, and railroads, however, provided many of Michigan's farmers with a choice—a choice of whether to continue their traditional ways of doing things, to adopt some sort of middle way, or to abandon tradition and focus upon the production of goods and services for market consumption. Such decisions were largely determined by deep-seated and sometimes subconscious convictions based upon personal experience and influenced by circumstances. Still, without the requisite means of moving goods to market, even those predisposed to the world of the cash nexus could not act upon their predilections. At the same time, although a transportation network was a necessary precondition for market activity, such activity also served as an impetus for the development of transportation facilities. In short, Michigan's transportation boom had a symbiotic relationship with the state's developing market connections.

Michigan's unique geography provided its citizens with a vital and obvious means of moving goods and people—water. Directly linked to the Atlantic by the St. Lawrence River and the Erie Canal, the Great Lakes offered access deep into the heart of the continent. And as would later be the case with the state's developing East-West railroad network, Michigan lay at the gateway to the nation's interior. The state's farmers had long relied upon the lakes as an avenue of trade with the East. By midcentury, many of Michigan's interior farmers annually sent their produce down rivers such as the Grand, the St. Joseph, and the Kalamazoo to Great Lakes ports, where it was packed aboard lake steamers and transported eastward. To the north, Michigan's emerging lumber trade would come to rely upon a similar system of transporting its product to market, turning rivers such as the Saginaw, the Muskegon, and the Manistee into household names among contemporaries. As eastern and overseas demand for the products of the Midwest steadily increased and more and more of the region's land was brought under cultivation, traffic on the Great Lakes greatly increased. In Detroit alone, the number of vessels docking in the city rose from 2,341 (carrying a total of 671,545 tons) in 1850 to 3,351 (carrying 731,419 tons) in 1860.[5]

Although water transportation was crucial to Michigan's prosperity by midcentury, the state expended relatively little effort toward building canals. Canals had been a major component in the state's earlier internal improvements venture, until the panic of 1837 nearly bankrupted the state. From that point forward, Michigan hitched itself to the rising star on the transportation scene—the railroad. The one exception to this general rule was the state's repeated efforts to construct a canal around the rapids of the St. Mary's River at Sault Sainte Marie, a project rendered all the more important by the discovery of rich copper and iron-ore deposits in the far western reaches of the Upper Peninsula in the mid-1840s.

After the failure of Michigan's internal improvements program in the late 1830s, the state legislature immediately petitioned Congress for a grant of public land to aid in the construction of a canal around the falls of the St. Mary's River. The proposal, however, met with a great deal of resistance from those in Congress who shared Henry Clay's opinion that the canal would be "a work quite beyond the remotest settlement in the United States if not on the moon." Even the rush of prospectors, miners, and Boston dollars streaming into the region during the late 1840s failed to sway Congress, and Michigan would not receive its federal land grant until August 1852. The following year, the state granted the contract for the construction of the canal to the St. Mary's Falls Ship Canal Company. In return for 750,000 acres of land (much of which contained valuable mineral and timber resources), the company agreed to build a canal at least 100 feet wide and 12 feet deep with two locks 350 feet long and 70 feet wide. Completed on May 31, 1855 (less than two years after the start of work), the $1 million, 5,674-foot-long canal lifted its first steamer to the level of Lake Superior on June 18. Michigan's immense mineral stores could now reach their prospective market unimpeded. As copper and iron, along with other cargoes such as barrels of fish and maple sugar, began heading south through the locks, people, material, and money flowed northward.[6]

The railroad, however, would assume the dominant role in the development of the state's transportation facilities. By 1850, Michigan could boast 344 miles of railroad track within its borders, second only to Ohio among the western states. One decade later, in 1860, that amount had risen to nearly 800 miles, an increase of 133 percent. But while notable, the expansion of Michigan's railroad network during the 1850s paled in comparison to that of states to the north and west, and as a result, by 1860, Michigan had fallen to fifth among the Midwestern states in railroad mileage, with only Iowa and the newly admitted state of Minnesota claiming fewer miles of track. It must be noted, however, that the track laid in Michigan between 1850 and 1860, coupled with the railroads constructed in adjacent areas, had a far greater impact upon the state than Michigan's relatively modest expansion of rail mileage might suggest. The state's early development had been retarded, in comparison to other northwestern states, because of its distance from the Ohio River, the established East-West route into the region. By the 1850s, though, geographic location and the state's incomplete early effort to build railroads—once considered handicaps—came to be a boon to Michigan, placing it in an advantageous position at the crossroads of a new, more northerly, Great Lakes–oriented East-West transportation route, a position earlier imagined only by the state's most optimistic promoters.[7]

In 1850, Michigan's two major railroads, the Michigan Southern and particularly the Michigan Central, stood poised and ready to push the state onto the national stage. In that year, having met its obligation to the state to complete its road to Lake Michigan in 1849, the Michigan Central spanned the Lower Peninsula, stretching from Detroit westward through the central tier of counties to Kalamazoo and from there to New Buffalo on the Michigan-Indiana border. At both Detroit and New Buffalo, the company operated a fleet of steamships, which enabled it to conduct uninterrupted business between New York and the burgeoning city of Chicago and points west. Indeed, it was the growing importance of Chicago that had led the directors of the Michigan Central to petition the state for a variance from the company's original charter—a variance that allowed the railroad to terminate at New Buffalo, a mere seventy miles from Chicago, rather than at the state's intended terminus, St. Joseph, which lay much farther to the north.[8]

Chicago proved equally enticing to the directors of the state's other major railroad corporation, the Michigan Southern. At the beginning of 1850, the line ran from Monroe, on Lake Erie, westward to Jonesville, extending only ten miles farther than it had when it was originally sold by the state in 1846 (though the road had been surveyed and the track bed cleared as far west as Coldwater). Unlike its competitor to the north, the Michigan Southern expended little energy in meeting the terms of its obligations to the state. Rather, the Southern's directors, eager to reach Chicago as quickly as possible, used their influence to lobby the state legislature for permission to deviate from the company's original charter, which prohibited it from building southward into Indiana until its track reached the St. Joseph River. Optimistic about their success with the legislators, the directors concurrently worked to obtain controlling interests in other railroads in northern Indiana and Illinois so as to give their company a direct line into Chicago. At the same time, the Southern continued the construction of its road in a southwesterly direction, reaching the Michigan town of White Pigeon, four miles from the Indiana border, by 1851.[9]

However, the legislature was heavily lobbied by the Michigan Central in both 1850 and 1851, and it denied the Southern's request for a variance, in large part because the company had shifted its eastern terminus and port facilities for the railroad from Monroe to Toledo, Ohio; this transfer was made possible by the Southern's 1849 procurement of a perpetual lease for the thirty-mile-long Erie and Kalamazoo Railroad, which operated between Toledo and the Michigan town of Adrian on the Southern line. At loggerheads with the Michigan legislature, the Southern arranged to have a South Bend capitalist build a four-mile spur southward from White Pigeon across the Indiana state line. This spur line was then leased to the Michigan Southern, and the company's route to Chicago was clear.[10]

The race for Chicago remained close as the Michigan Central and the Michigan Southern fought it out in the Indiana and Illinois legislatures. In the end, the Southern prevailed (at least temporarily), its first train entering Chicago in February 1852, three months before the arrival of an engine owned by the Central. Now firmly connected to the nation's vast interior, both roads shifted their attention toward solidifying their links to the commercial mecca of the nation, New York City. As one early historian of Michigan's railroads noted, "the year 1852 . . . mark[ed] the dawning of a new period of railroad development in the state of Michigan"—a period characterized by the consolidation of diverse rail lines into an integrated railroad system.[11]

By 1852, both the Michigan Central and the Michigan Southern had well-established connections to New York City via their steamship lines and the Erie Canal. Unfortunately, dependence upon water transportation proved a major hindrance to business because the annual arrival of winter in the region severed such tenuous arteries of trade, bringing railroad operations in Michigan to a virtual standstill. Accordingly, both railroad corporations encouraged the building of eastern rail lines that would connect them directly with those roads already doing business with New York City, thereby allowing them to operate year-round. To accomplish this goal, the Southern (rechartered as the Michigan Southern and Northern Indiana in May 1855) concentrated its efforts on promoting the construction of connecting lines through northern Ohio and Pennsylvania, while the Central focused its attention on furthering the construction of the Great Western Railway across Ontario from Fort Erie, opposite Buffalo, to Windsor, opposite Detroit. Both efforts proved successful, and by 1855, Michigan became both the gateway to the West and the conduit by which the products of Michigan and the other northwestern states reached the East. In that year alone, the Michigan Southern did over $2.5 million in business (a figure well in excess of its reported earnings of $305,686 in 1851—an increase of 720 percent); the Michigan Central did over $2.6 million. Two years later, the two railroads combined carried 565,996 westbound passengers and 470,941 eastbound passengers—a figure that dwarfed the 80,000 passengers that the Michigan Central had carried just nine years earlier.[12]

In the remaining years of the decade, Michigan's position as the cross-roads of the North was further enhanced by the construction of yet another East-West transpeninsular railroad: the Detroit and Milwaukee. Completed in 1858, primarily with funds supplied by the Great Western, the Detroit and Milwaukee pushed northwestward from Detroit to the Lake Michigan port of Grand Haven. From Grand Haven, passengers and freight reached Milwaukee aboard one of the company's steamers. The Detroit and Milwaukee line was an immediate success and was quickly dubbed the "emigrant route" because many foreigners, especially Germans, used this railroad to reach Wisconsin. The construction of a spur line connecting Detroit with Monroe and Toledo to the south in July 1856 (a line leased to the Michigan Southern to allow it entrée into Detroit) and another joining Detroit and Port Huron to the north in 1859 (a road that tied Detroit to the recently completed Grand Trunk Railway at Sarnia across the St. Clair River from Port Huron) filled in the remaining gaps in Michigan's antebellum rail network.[13]

Within one decade, that network, envisioned by its original advocates as a means of opening the state to settlement and as a vehicle for servicing the state's hinterlands, had become something much more. Michigan's railroads now effected dynamic connections in a national transportation network, forming crucial links between the East and the West. Rather than merely serving the needs of the state, these roads had, by 1860, come to benefit the entire nation. They supplied the American hinterland, transported the nation's settlers into the western territories, and served as the route by which the rich agricultural yields and vast resources of the West were sent to eastern markets and beyond—a pattern that prompted Ralph Waldo Emerson to comment: "A clever fellow was acquainted with the expansive force of steam; he also saw the wealth of wheat and grass rotting in Michigan. Then he cunningly screws on the steam pipe to the wheat-crop. Puff now, O Steam! The steam puffs and expands as before, but this time it is dragging all Michigan at its back to hungry New York and hungry England."[14]

Railroads, of course, were not the only means of transportation available to mid-nineteenth-century Michiganians, nor were they the sole engine of Michigan's economic boom. Of far greater importance in the everyday lives of many people, especially those inhabiting areas removed from the state's rail lines, was the plank road. In fact, Michigan witnessed a "plank-road craze" during the mid-nineteenth century as entrepreneurs scrambled to keep up with the incessant public demand for these improvements. One noted historian of the state, Willis F. Dunbar, argued that this passion for plank roads inhibited railroad building in Michigan. Certainly, the state's midcentury railroad expansion paled in comparison to that of its neighbors in the Midwest. Dunbar failed to recognize, however, that Michigan's railroad companies did not seek primarily the further expansion of their lines but rather looked toward the development of a fully integrated railroad system linking the East and West—a goal they achieved. If anything, the development of Michigan's railroads served as an impetus for the building of plank roads by introducing the state to the enticements of the market economy. Dunbar unknowingly reached the same conclusion when he correctly noted that "the plank-roads served as feeders for existing rail lines." Without the railroads, there would have been far fewer plank roads.[15]

With abundant timber still standing in most parts of Michigan, plank-road companies were formed virtually everywhere. Prior to 1848, a legislative charter was required for the formation of each firm, but the passage of a general incorporation law for plank-road companies in that year opened the field to all comers as long as they agreed to build "good, smooth, permanent roads" a minimum of sixteen feet wide, eight feet of which was to be constructed of three-inch planks. In return, the companies were allowed to collect a toll of $.02 per mile for two-horse wagons and $.01 per mile for one-horse wagons. Numerous plank roads were built throughout the state, connecting places such as Grand Rapids, which had no rail connection until 1858, with Kalamazoo on the Michigan Central line or the thriving farming community of Howell, in Livingston County, with Detroit. Plank roads, like the railroads, extended the reach of the market economy far into the hinterlands of Michigan by affording, as the *Grand River Eagle* argued, "great advantages . . . in the transportation of merchandize and produce." These supposed advantages compelled state farmers to determine to what degree they would become involved in the impersonal world of the cash nexus.[16]

Faster, more reliable means of transportation also resulted in better communications for the residents of antebellum Michigan, as trips that once took weeks or days were now made in a matter of days or hours. In addition, the exchange of news and information, previously slowed by the onset of winter, now continued apace regardless of the weather. Extended rail and road networks also allowed for expanded mail delivery and provided the state's interior residents with better access to more newspapers.

Moreover, the railroad brought an ancillary communication technology to Michigan—the telegraph. The telegraph was first used in the state on November 30, 1847, when messages were exchanged between the Michigan Central cities of Detroit and Ypsilanti. By April of the following year, telegraphic messages were being transmitted between Detroit and Chicago and between Detroit and New York. Instantaneous communication by means of the telegraph was possible between most of Michigan's largest cities and the rest of the country by 1860.[17]

The brisk development of Michigan's transportation and communication facilities during the 1850s had an immediate and far-reaching impact upon farmers (the backbone of the state's economy) and rapidly "broke down many of the traits of self-sufficiency and isolation." Tied to the national market as never before, even those Michigan farmers who sought to avoid the impersonal world of the cash nexus increasingly found themselves forced into market activity to one degree or another as the traditional social and economic ties that had once served to ensure their subsistence disintegrated. No longer able to rely upon the help of neighbors, friends, and family, many of whom had abandoned the ideal of family self-sufficiency in favor of market production, more and more self-provisioning farmers, in need of cash to meet their family's needs, were driven into the sphere of market relations. Still other farmers cast eager glances at newly accessible markets and "became progressively more specialized in many of their major crop and livestock enterprises," ushering in what historian Richard Sewell described as a decade of "steady advance" in Michigan agriculture. This transition to specialized production, of course, was not limited to Michigan but took place throughout the nation during the mid-nineteenth century. Indeed, many agricultural historians concur that the era marked a turning point in "the transformation of agriculture in the United States from the family-oriented, self-sufficient farm to commercial agriculture serving distant consumers"—a transition that converted Michigan into one of "the agricultural leaders of the west" by 1860.[18]

Between 1850 and 1860, the number of farms in Michigan jumped from 34,089 to 62,422 (an increase of 83 percent), and Michigan farmers increased the amount of improved land in the state by over 77 percent, from 1,929,110 acres in 1850 to 3,149,861 acres in 1860. More important, the agricultural output throughout the decade testified to an escalating degree of specialization among Michigan farmers, which resulted in increased productivity. By 1860, corn production had skyrocketed to 12,444,676 bushels, a 115 percent increase over 1850 levels. Wheat production also rose, from slightly under 5,000,000 bushels in 1850 to 8,336,368 bushels, a 69 percent increase—a figure that placed Michigan as the nation's ninth largest wheat producer. Wool production underwent similar growth, pushing Michigan into the number four position nationally. In addition, Lake Michigan's moderating effect on the climate of the western portion of the state permitted farmers to develop a "fruit-growing district that by the Civil War was already attracting national attention."[19]

The transformation of Michigan's agricultural sector in the direction of commercial farming also contributed to the demise of home manufacturing in the state. In fact, the transition to the market was so rapid during the 1850s that the value of home manufactures decreased to only $142,756 in 1860 (a 58 percent decline since 1850), roughly $.19 per person or $2.29 per farm (a figure 77 percent lower than that recorded for 1850). As previously noted, the total number of farms in Michigan grew by 28,333 between 1850 and 1860. Accordingly, one would have anticipated that the value of home manufactures would also have increased. The fact that there was a sharp decline rather than an increase suggests that many state farmers had abandoned home manufacturing, choosing instead to purchase needed items in the marketplace. "The prosperity of the farmers is astonishing," wrote U.S. secretary of the interior Robert McClelland in 1854, describing a visit back to Michigan. "They are rapidly becoming opulent, and in a few years," he added, "the state will be one of the richest and most respectable in the union."[20]

The rapid encroachment of the market into Michigan, as noted earlier, was made possible by the state's enhanced connections with both eastern and western markets after 1852—a point not unnoticed by contemporaries. "Michigan is improving wonderfully," Marshall farmer Preston Mitchell wrote his brother in June 1852, "increasing in population rapidly and on the whole is in a very healthy condition." The state's prosperity, he acknowledged, was attributable to the fact that Michigan "has become very central, there is so many beyond and so much country and the facilities for traveling has become so rapid and cheap that we think our position a good one." "Not only that," he hastened to add, "but our soil produces so readily and so abundantly, all that is required to keep both man and beast in abundance, to sustain life, and make both comfortable and happy." Ties to outside markets brought a world of change and led the editor of the *Kalamazoo Gazette* to boast in 1851 that "one of the most gratifying symptoms in the business transactions in our village is that the unhallowed 'dicker' traffic is in great measure going out of use. There is scarcely any produce which the Farmer now brings to market, but that he can readily exchange it for cash. . . . There is not one evil which can afflict a community in a business point of view more calamitously than the 'swap and dicker' operations which have reigned among us for the last twelve years."[21]

A series of mid-1850s circulars, distributed by James D. Johnston of Detroit to gather information for a promotional pamphlet on state agriculture, provide further evidence of Michigan's brisk immersion into the world of the market. Above all else, the circulars give clear evidence of the farmers' ties to a broader market. Virtually every local official responding to the circular stated that his particular town's merchants purchased their goods from Detroit, New York, or Boston. Moreover, these informants indicated that many state farmers marketed their produce in Detroit and points east. Without exception, the returned circulars confirmed that local produce was marketed in towns along the state's rail lines and from there, one presumes, shipped to Detroit, Toledo, and other eastern markets. Clearly, Michigan was experiencing a dramatic and ongoing metamorphosis into a market society. Indeed, the acting governor, Andrew Parsons, astutely (though perhaps a bit arrogantly) noted in his annual message for 1855, "Michigan is rapidly increasing in population, and developing its rich resources; it is a gratification to me that its progress in the way of wealth and prosperity has never been more rapid than during the last two years."[22]

Transformation and development, however, were not limited to the state's rich agricultural sector. Enhanced transportation capabilities and access to new eastern, western, and overseas markets also spurred the development of Michigan's extractive industries and the harvest of the state's bountiful natural resources—resources in demand throughout the rest of the nation.

Among the most alluring of Michigan's assets was the untold mineral wealth lying beneath the rocky soil of the state's Upper Peninsula. For centuries, the northern peninsula had drawn explorers and adventurers (both native and European) with tales of pure copper boulders and precious metals. Yet not until 1841, with the publication of state geologist Douglass Houghton's report confirming the existence of abundant mineral reserves in the region (and the subsequent termination of native land claims in the area with the Treaty of LaPointe in 1842), were any sustained efforts made to exploit these resources. Word of Houghton's report spread so quickly that by 1846, a mineral rush was in full swing in Michigan's copper country, the Keweenaw Peninsula. Nevertheless, as contended by Angus Murdoch, an eminent historian of the Michigan copper industry, "the copper range [did not] shuck its swaddling clothes and exchange its pinafores for long pants" until the 1850s. During that decade, Murdoch asserted, "the district insisted, willy-nilly, on growing up. The dreams of the wide-eyed prospector and his prattle of solid copper mountains were relegated to the background by the practical visions and mature voice of finance. [And the] polysyllabic words—'production,' 'tonnage,' and 'concentrates'—entered the vocabulary of the range." Between 1846 and 1865, at least three hundred mining ventures were launched throughout the copper range, including ninety-four joint-stock corporations with an aggregate capitalization of $25 million. Two-thirds of these ventures produced little or no copper. Still, success stories such as the Cliff Mine, which produced over 1 million tons of copper in 1849 (the year of its first corporate dividend), encouraged continued investment in the region, as did the federal government's lowering of land prices to $1.25 per acre in the region in 1850.[23]

In that year, Michigan's output of copper totaled 1,281,000 pounds, 88 percent of the total production of the United States, and was valued at $280,000. Four years later, just prior to the opening of the Sault Canal in 1855, production had risen to over 4 million pounds (slightly over 80 percent of the U.S. total), valued at $900,000. The opening of the Sault Canal proved to be a bonanza for the state's copper mines. Capital and labor poured into the region: the number of workers in the copper mines grew from 706 in 1850 to 3,681 by 1860, helping to boost the population of Houghton County, the heart of the copper country, from 708 in 1850 to 9,234 in just ten years. Copper now flowed, uninterrupted, outward to the market. Throughout the remainder of the decade, the Keweenaw's mines expanded their production threefold, reaching an output of over 12 million pounds (valued at $2,690,000) by 1860, an increase of 842 percent over production figures for 1850. Though the discovery of new lodes and the formation of new producing companies accounted for much of this growth, a concurrent "trend toward [a] larger scale of production of the individual enterprises making up the industry" was also discernable in the years before the Civil War—further evidence of the degree to which market considerations had come to dominate the Michigan landscape by 1860.[24]

The state's developing iron-mining industry (centered near the present-day cities of Marquette, Negaunee, and Ishpeming) experienced similar growth during the decade. Discoveries of high-grade ores in the area of Teal Lake in 1845 induced a number of small-time bog iron producers from southern Michigan to form the Jackson Mining Company. Faced with a logistics nightmare brought about by the isolation of its claims and the lack of transportation facilities, the company quickly moved to build an iron forge on location at its mine and by 1848 had begun to produce iron. To facilitate the movement of its iron to the port at Marquette, eleven miles to the east where a dock was constructed in 1855, the company constructed the first railroad in the Upper Peninsula between 1852 and 1857. Again, however, it would be the opening of the Sault Canal in 1855 that would initiate a period of sustained growth for the industry. In that year, the Jackson Mining Company, along with the newly created Cleveland Iron Company, shipped a total of 1,449 tons of ore. The next year, the two companies' shipments stood at 36,000 tons. By the end of the decade, state iron-ore production reached 114,401 tons. The products of Michigan's mines were finding their way to national and international markets.[25]

Michigan's fisheries, supplying a lucrative market in the nation's burgeoning cities, drew attention at midcentury as well. In 1854, fishermen shipped over 24 million pounds of fish, primarily to eastern markets. Five years later, in 1859, incomplete figures set the value of the state's fish harvest at over $650,000 on a catch of more than 18 million pounds. During the same year, 4,359 barrels of fish passed southward through the Sault Canal, bound for the lower lakes. The 1860 census provided further evidence of the importance of the fisheries to the state. According to census data, 186 fishing companies were in operation throughout the state in that year, employing nearly 1,000 men and women. Mackinac County alone contained thirty-two such companies, employing 130 persons.[26]

Other natural resources were similarly converted to cash in the state's developing economy. As new settlers flooded into Michigan, the laborious process of clearing homesteads picked up pace. Acre upon acre of old-growth hardwood timber yielded to the ax, and farmers promptly converted the debris into a readily marketable item—ash. Sold to the state's growing number of asheries, where it was refined further into "black salts," or potash (a base ingredient in the manufacture of soap, glass, baking soda, and other commodities), the ash produced a much needed cash stream for new settlers, many of whom were unable to put in crops during their first season on their land. The ash trade furthered market activity in the state and expanded commercial ties between Michigan and external markets (the ash was a major commodity in the Buffalo and New York City markets). By 1850, fourteen large-scale asheries operated in the state. That number would continue to grow thereafter, mirroring the accelerating growth and development of Michigan, until reaching a peak of forty-three in 1884. The rapid pace of advancement in the state was further borne out by the fact that the state's two major rail lines (the Michigan Southern and the Michigan Central) noted annual increases in the amount of ash shipped over their tracks throughout the 1850s, 1860s, and 1870s.[27]

Of even greater consequence, however, was the expansion of the state's commercial lumber industry during this period. "Green gold" would prove to be more valuable to mid-nineteenth-century Michigan than any other natural resource. Covering approximately two-thirds of the state, Michigan's vast pine forests, dominated by the stately white pine, produced a timber that was compact, light, soft, straight-grained, and easily workable—a timber that "until its exhaustion . . . suffered no rival as the nation's building material."[28]

During Michigan's first thirteen years as a state, lumbering had played a central role in the development of the economy, providing residents with wood for building homes, barns, plank roads, railroads, and numerous other items. However, after 1845, as one detailed study of the industry demonstrated, lumbering underwent "a strong, steady expansion," which only "accelerated after 1850." Census data for the period support this assertion. In 1850, Michigan's lumber counties contained 193 mills producing just under 200 million board feet of lumber, placing Michigan within the nation's top five lumber-producing states. Just four years later, the number of mills in these counties had risen to 315, and production had increased to over 240 million feet. Mill employment in these counties experienced a similar growth, jumping from slightly over 1,500 people in 1850 to nearly 2,700 in 1854 (roughly an 80 percent rise). Statewide, 4,579 workers toiled in 889 mills in 1854. Six years later, 927 lumber mills were in operation in Michigan, employing 6,673 men and women. In that year, all but fourteen counties in the state reported the sawing of lumber as the chief industry outside of agriculture. Even in Wayne County, the industry ranked second to the manufacture of machinery. Nevertheless, by the fall of 1860, in spite of the best efforts of Michigan's lumber producers, "demand in both the east and the west exceeded supply."[29]

Once again, as with most economic change in midcentury Michigan, closer ties to the national market served as the major impetus for development of the state's lumber resources. In 1840, less than 5 percent of Michigan's lumber output found a market beyond state borders. By 1855, however, less than 15 percent of the lumber produced in the state was retained for domestic consumption; over 85 percent was shipped elsewhere in the United States—especially to Chicago. As the population of Chicago and the treeless prairies beyond increased during the late 1840s and early 1850s, so, too, did the need for lumber. More important, the completion of the Illinois and Michigan Canal in 1848 and the continued extension of rail lines westward and southward from Chicago in the 1850s provided that city with easy access to the Mississippi River and to the plains settlements. Overnight, Chicago became the major market for Michigan lumber, particularly lumber from the Grand and Muskegon River valleys, consuming a full 60 percent of the state's output by 1855.[30]

The lumbering industry found ready buyers in other markets as well. For example, in the 1850s, the Wisconsin lake ports became major purchasers, and as supplies of good pine from New York and Maine neared depletion during that decade, Michigan pine, principally that from the Saginaw Valley, was increasingly sought by buyers in the eastern cities of Cleveland, Buffalo, and Albany. The enhanced ability to reach this national market spurred Michigan's lumber industry to greater efforts and resulted in a statewide lumber boom. Moreover, the expansion of the industry spawned a parallel trend toward increased capitalization, vertical integration, and augmented marketing techniques—developments that, according to historian Barbara Benson, "increased after about 1850 in Michigan" and would make lumbering the most important industry in the state. Soon, Michigan was able to claim the title as the nation's leading lumber producer.[31]

Though lumbering dominated Michigan's manufacturing landscape by 1860, it was by no means the only industry in the state. Over the course of the decade preceding the census of 1860, Michigan began to build a diversified manufacturing base. In those ten years, the proportion of the state's working population listed as farmers decreased from 60 percent in 1849 to 53 percent in 1859. Conversely, the proportion of the state's workforce engaged in manufacturing increased from 1 percent in 1850, as estimated by Willis Dunbar, to nearly 10 percent, as reported by the census of 1860. The number of manufacturing establishments in the state rose by 70 percent over the decade, from 2,033 in 1850 to 3,488 in 1860, and the value of their products grew from slightly under $11 million to $32.7 million. Over the same ten-year period, per capita investment in manufacturing nearly doubled in Michigan, rising by 93 percent to $31.78 in 1859, while the value of per capita manufactured product jumped by $16, or 58 percent.[32]

By 1860, Wayne County and its county seat, Detroit, stood as the state's leading manufacturing center, with 368 establishments employing 3,710 workers. Though Detroit was not an industrial city in 1860 by any stretch of the imagination, "it is possible without too great a strain on the imagination or too liberal an interpretation of the facts," historian George Stark maintained, "to place the beginning of [the city's] amazing industrial development at about 1850." During the decade preceding the Civil War, Detroiters witnessed the construction of two railroad car–manufacturing plants, four iron blast furnaces, the mammoth Eureka Iron and Steel Works with the accompanying Wyandotte Rolling Mills, a brass foundry, a copper smelter, a dry dock for shipbuilding, a paint factory, a stove works, and numerous machine shops. The bulk of Detroit's industrial facilities, however, remained closely tied to agriculture, still the dominant force in the state's economy. In 1860, six flour mills operated in the city. In addition, Detroit counted among its factories thirty breweries and fifteen tanneries.[33]

The rapid development of an industrial base in Detroit and the increased influence of manufacturing were further demonstrated by the swift rise of Detroit industrialists into the ranks of the city's rich and powerful. Indeed, Alexandra McCoy's study of antebellum Detroit clearly indicated that between 1844 and 1860, members of Detroit's manufacturing class were increasingly represented among the city's economic elite. Yet despite its impressive midcentury industrial development, Detroit remained predominantly a commercial city in 1860. Warehouses and the offices of commission merchants lined the city's riverfront and main thoroughfares, Jefferson and Woodward Avenues. Detroit's agricultural commission business with the East and with the state's lumber and mineral regions proved extremely lucrative and was growing by leaps and bounds. In addition, the city's wholesale trade with the interior, especially that in groceries, ready-made clothing, and farm products, also experienced remarkable growth and allowed Detroit, by 1860, to become the chief commercial center for a region three hundred miles in radius.[34]

Besides the numerous and sometimes incomprehensible economic and social changes that accompanied Michigan's transformation into a market society, residents experienced more palpable changes as well. For instance, Michiganians could not have helped but notice the daily arrival of new settlers to their state. In the four years from 1850 to 1854, Michigan's population grew from 397,654 to 509,374. By 1860, the number stood at 749,113, an increase of 83 percent over the 1850 figure. The state's population density rose from 21.8 persons per square mile in 1850 to approximately 30 persons per square mile by 1860. This trend was exacerbated in the most heavily populated counties. Within the same ten-year period, Wayne County, the state's most populous county, grew from a population of 42,756 (about 40.3 persons per square mile) to 75,547 (71.2 persons per square mile). Furthermore, a greater proportion of Michigan's residents could be found living in the growing cities. In 1860, nearly 10 percent of the state's inhabitants lived in the five largest cities (Detroit, Grand Rapids, Adrian, Kalamazoo, and Ann Arbor), whose aggregate population reached 71,084, a figure twice that of 1850.[35]

Detroit, by far the largest of the state's cities, experienced explosive growth during the decade preceding the Civil War. In 1850, it was an overgrown town of 21,019. Within ten years, its population had swelled to 45,619, a growth of 117 percent. Detroit's burgeoning population, however, did not always stay in one place for long. In fact, as JoEllen Vinyard's study of Irish settlement in antebellum Detroit suggested, just the opposite was the case. Like many frontier settlements, the city served as a temporary refuge and staging point for a restless and highly mobile population. Only 46 percent of those individuals enumerated in the 1850 census as residents of Detroit still inhabited the city by 1860. This transient population, mainly composed of single young males, crowded the city's central wards, and by 1854, such individuals equaled the number of married men residing in these neighborhoods.[36]

A rising tide of foreign-born emigrants settled in or passed through Detroit in this period. In 1850, Michigan's foreign-born population stood at slightly over 54,000 and comprised nearly 14 percent of the state's total population. Over the ensuing decade, that number grew to 149,093, 20 percent of the state's 1860 population. Interestingly, as Ronald Formisano pointed out, "the image of foreigners concentrated in cities is erroneous for Michigan in 1860." Instead, Michigan's immigrants were dispersed in pockets throughout the state and could be found as readily in the mining, fishing, and lumbering counties of the north and the rich southern agricultural counties as in Michigan's cities. By 1860, 6,355 Dutch settlers had begun to concentrate in the western counties of Kent and Ottawa. Germans, numbering 38,787, lived in large numbers in rural Saginaw County and in Detroit and Ann Arbor. The state's 30,049 Irish people, though heavily concentrated in Detroit (where they comprised one-seventh of the city's population), could also be found in Adrian, in the fertile fishing grounds of northern Lake Michigan and the Straits of Mackinac, and in the mining communities of the Upper Peninsula. Also prominent among the early residents of the copper country were the Cornish, who began arriving in large numbers during the 1850s. Increasingly aware that their state contained an ever growing number of foreign-born residents (drawn by the booming economy and plentiful land), American-born residents began to look upon their new neighbors with growing suspicion.[37]

Beyond their strange customs, dress, and languages, many of Michigan's newest inhabitants also practiced what the state's New England– or New York–born Protestant majority considered a strange and potentially threatening religion: Catholicism. Certainly, given the state's French heritage, Catholicism was nothing new to Michigan. But prior to the late 1840s and early 1850s, adherents of the Catholic Church made up a small and shrinking minority of the state's population. The arrival of large numbers of Irish and

German Catholics reversed this trend, and Catholics became "a substantial minority" in the city of Detroit and a growing factor in state politics. Moreover, recognizing their minority status and hoping to preserve their religious and cultural customs, Michigan's Catholics quickly moved to establish not only their own churches but also separate schools (such as Holy Trinity and St. Mary's School for Girls in Detroit) and social institutions as well, a trend that angered many of Michigan's American-born majority, who interpreted such actions as a clannish preservation of a bizarre and threatening religion.[38]

Finally, the state population was further diversified by the arrival of a growing number of African Americans in the years prior to 1860. Michigan counted only 2,583 African Americans among its population in 1850, many of whom lived in Detroit (587) and rural Cass County (389). Within ten years, the total increased to 6,799. The growing commercial hub of Detroit continued to draw the plurality of the state's black population, with 1,402 black inhabitants, making up roughly 3 percent of the city's population; another 271 blacks lived elsewhere in Wayne County. Cass County was a close second to Wayne, with a population of 1,368 blacks. All in all, Michigan's 1860 population bore little resemblance to that of a decade earlier.[39]

In hindsight, it seems a simple task to describe and demarcate the socioeconomic changes that buffeted and reshaped mid-nineteenth-century Michigan as it experienced a speedy yet awkward transition from the tradition-bound world of the self-provisioning family farm to the competitive, individualistic world of the cash nexus. Undeniably, midcentury Michigan was a society in flux, offering little in the way of stability or permanence. For contemporary residents of the state, lacking the census data, statistical case studies, and extensive historical literature of the modern researcher, the rate of change and the degree to which that change had transformed their state were not quantifiable phenomena; nor was the state's metamorphosis widely understood. Nevertheless, Michiganians were very much aware that their world had been altered. "In the agricultural and mechanical world," state superintendent of public instruction Francis W. Shearman noted in 1853, "we seem to have commenced a new era." Ionia resident William Brown wrote that same year, "Michigan is yet in its infancy, . . . though her progress toward prosperity has been like the strides of a giant."[40]

It was difficult for these individuals to decipher their thoughts and feelings about the transformation that had occurred. The residents of antebellum Michigan exhibited mixed attitudes about their altered circumstances. Some welcomed the state's entry into the marketplace and the modified social relations that accompanied that entry as harbingers of progress and guarantors of future success. Conversely, many others looked upon the new world of cash exchange with disdain, longing for a return to what they perceived to be a less complicated time. Most found themselves, to varying degrees, both attracted and repulsed by the market, and they struggled to determine, according to their personal experiences, the extent of their involvement in the world of commercial exchange. Regardless of how they felt about these changes, however, Michiganians shared a pervasive sense of uneasiness—an anxiety triggered by the unsettling rapidity with which their world was being altered and by fears of what it might become. "This age is big with importance," schoolteacher Anson de Puy Van Buren conceded in 1854, "but there is much more bustle than brains often displayed."[41]

With the subsistence-oriented family farm besieged by market forces, with a rapidly expanding and transient population, with the looming prospect of industrial development, and with the continued dominance of its traditional New England–based cultural values in doubt, Michigan showed signs of the strain, experiencing what historian Sidney Glazer wrote off as "growing pains," a term that perhaps minimizes the extent of the pain and fear involved. Although the aggregate value of real and personal property in Michigan increased by 330 percent during the 1850s, the number of paupers in the state rose by an incredible 550 percent, from 1,619 (4 out of every 1,000 inhabitants) to 10,572 (14 out of every 1,000). The number of vagrants incarcerated in Detroit jails also rose dramatically, jumping from 1 of every 450 in 1848 to 1 in every 11 by 1863. Escalating poverty in Michigan contributed as well to a spiraling crime rate, with the number of people convicted of crimes in the state during 1859 being 32 percent higher than the number for 1849. Over the course of the 1850s, the number of inmates in the state prison at Jackson jumped by 219 percent. The suicide rate, a barometer of social distress, also showed an alarming increase, rising 112 percent from 1849 to 1859. Obviously, Michigan's embrace of the market did not occur without casualties.[42]

Augmented connections to the national market and the rising tide of commercialism in Michigan convinced many residents that principles had been abandoned for tangible results and that greed, self-centeredness, and covetousness had come to replace community, self-sufficiency, and the good of the whole. "Of all the causes which conspire to unhinge society," the *Hillsdale Gazette* warned, "that of individuals considering themselves superior to and more perfect than others . . . , is the worst and most to be lamented. It begets a spirit of disorder, sows the seeds of disorganization and ends in the ultimate loss of society itself." Writing to his cousin in 1856, Detroiter A. R.

Morgan complained, "Fred this world is all vanity, vanity. Every man for himself and the Devil take the hindmost." He implored, "Let us raise all the wind we can [and] emigrate to the west, [where] we should enjoy life a damned site more than slaverry [*sic*] in a city." Disgusted with what he perceived to be the materialistic spirit of the day, the editor of the *Grass Lake Public Sentiment* wrote,

> I have a neighbor who is so busy that he has no leisure to laugh; the whole business of his life is to get money, and more money, that he may still get more money. He is still drudging on, saying that Solomon says, "the diligent hand maketh rich." . . . It is true indeed; but he considers not that it is not in the power of riches to make a happy man. . . . We see but the outside of a rich man's happiness; few consider him to be like the silkworm that when she seems to play, is at the very same time spinning her own bowels and consumeing [*sic*] herself. And this may rich men do—loading themselves with corroding cares, to keep what they have already got. Let us therefore be thankful for health and competence, and above all for a quiet conscience.

Reflecting on his life, early settler John M. Norton expressed regret about the loss of community brought on by the arrival of the railroad, the paramount symbol of the market economy, in Oakland County. "I have sometimes felt," he noted, "that the railroad building has narrowed social limits to a local geographical extent not in accordance with the best and most conservative moral and social welfare of the people." "In pioneer times," he proudly reminded his readers, "the limits of a neighborhood covered miles in extent. Now intimate social relation is limited to a block in the cities, or to a rural four corners." Simply put, Norton and other like-minded Michiganians lamented the breakdown of community and the rampant individualism wrought by the state's immersion into the market.[43]

While confessing that Michigan was in a "most flourishing condition," Secretary of the Interior Robert McClelland, his ardor for unbridled commercialism blunted by Michigan's earlier cataclysmic economic collapse, warned Sen. Alpheus Felch in 1853 that "speculation is nearly as rife as it was in 1836 and a crisis may fairly be expected. Many are as crazy now as then, and reason does not appear to characterize their action. But we, who tested the fiery ordeal, will avoid the fire and not again burn our fingers." Such fears were widespread throughout Michigan. Denouncing the "host of hungry creditors of mercantile rapacity" who ensnared unsuspecting farmers in the web of the market, the *Centreville Western Chronicle* sadly reported that "the Constables are now busy securing the products of those farmers who have 'counted their chickens before they were hatched.'" Indeed, the *Hillsdale Gazette* reminded its readers, "as long as one half of the world tries to live on the other man's labor, so long somebody will see hard times." The way to avoid becoming a victim of the market, the paper concluded, was to "buy less—produce more." Returning to Michigan in 1858 after two years of teaching in the south, Anson de Puy Van Buren wrote an acquaintance that he felt "like a stranger" amidst the "turmoil of [Michigan's] busy practical life." "Because we are so practical and acquisitive," he continued, " . . . we count time money, and hence look upon leisure and the ease of a quiet life with indolence which is kith and kin to poverty."[44]

But others among Michigan's populace welcomed the new world of commercial relations. "My situation is a pleasant one," boasted Preston Mitchell, a commercial farmer from Marshall. "I am prospering in pecuniary matters as fast perhaps as is for the best—at least [I] am getting a good living." John Ball, a Grand Rapids entrepreneur and land speculator, commented that "what strikes the eastern man particularly" about the Grand River valley "is the . . . great progress made by the settlers in their improvements." "For it is almost uniformly found," he added, "that the industrious settler, in ten years can show an estate of as many thousands . . . as he began with hundreds." Fred B. Porter, a twenty-three-year-old student at the University of Michigan, spoke in even more glowing terms about the spirit of the times. "Ambition in some form or other is the lever of the world," he wrote in 1854, adding that

> it would be especially difficult now to find any man of eminence or even usefulness, in whom this quality is not *a* if not *the* leading motive. Selfishness is part and parcel of our nature. I venture to say it is recognized and sanctioned by the law of God. We are commanded to love our neighbors as we love ourselves—to do unto others as we would that they should do to us. We are not commanded to seek Heaven for the sake of our fellow men, nor for the glory of God: but the strongest motive presented is our own ultimate happiness.

Clearly, the opportunities offered by the new world of the market appealed to a great many residents. Given the "great activity and energy, [the] liberal public spirit, and [the] high order of intelligence" in Detroit, the *Tribune* bragged, "who can fix a limit to its growth and prosperity?"[45]

Yet even among those excited by Michigan's transformation into a market society, anxiety persisted—anxiety triggered by the rate at which their world was being recast and by fears about what their society might become. Some, such as James V. Campbell, feared that abundant resources, fertile land, and ready access to markets actually worked against the state. After visiting Mackinac Island and witnessing firsthand the ease with which the island's inhabitants obtained their living from the surrounding waters of the Straits of Mackinac, Campbell had nothing but disdain for the "laziness" and backward attitudes of the region's fishermen. Future U.S. senator and state supreme court justice Isaac P. Christiancy of Monroe exhibited a similar ambivalence about the market; he engaged in numerous market activities in which he was only marginally successful, yet he never, despite his continued fears, turned against the market economy. More common, however, was the uneasiness expressed in the *Albion Weekly Review*. Visiting Detroit in 1860 for the first time in fourteen years, the paper's editor marveled at the transformation of that city by what he labeled "the spirit of enterprise." Sadly, however, Detroit was destined to grow no further: "Her wealth," the paper complained, "is in the wrong hands, hands that hoard and live upon the interest of money; hands that will not encourage industry by launching out their coffers to the support of factories, which would give enterprise an impetus hardly credible. In a business point of view, Detroit is an auxillary [*sic*] . . . she is content to allow the looms and spinning jennies of the eastern world to make her clothes and modefy [*sic*] her markets." Detroit, the state, and, for many, the nation, although undergoing massive change, required additional alterations. These individuals perceived the market as a great liberating force, a force that allowed individuals to reach their full potential; many, as the preceding quotation suggests, worried that the advance of the market and the world of commerce had been stalled and, with it, the march of the state's residents toward fuller freedom.[46]

As one might expect, Michiganians dealt with their feelings of anxiety and anguish in many different ways. With the traditional subsistence-oriented family farm in a state of disarray and faced with the prospects of more limited access to land upon which to perpetuate that system, many families responded to the new realities of a market economy by limiting the number of children in the household. Others found a more public means of venting their anxieties, actively participating in a myriad of reform movements aimed at reordering and reforming themselves and their society. Some, such as the Strangite sect of the Mormon Church that settled on Beaver Island, withdrew from society and established utopian communes to serve as models of correct social organization. Still others sought solace and stability in somewhat less rigorous religions. Most important, however, Michigan's citizens—devoted to their nation's republican heritage and imbued with the democratic strictures of the Jacksonian political culture—once again turned to the institution upon which they had come to rely in voicing their hopes, fears, and concerns: the political system. From the start, the forces working to reshape Michigan and those that sought to resist that reshaping in the decade before the Civil War spilled over into state politics, as politicians actively tried to identify the sources of their supporters' hopes and uneasiness. Reaching a consensus regarding the roots of the electorate's anxiety, however, proved nothing short of impossible. As traditional partisan affiliations fell victim to bitter conflict, new political movements moved forward to gather the disenchanted. What eventually emerged, as the smoke of battle cleared, was a new national political party and a greatly altered political landscape.[47]

4

"Politics . . . have Undergone a Thorough Change"

The Crucible of the Republican Party

IN EARLY July 1854, over fifteen hundred politically discontented Michiganians flooded the southern Michigan community of Jackson, intent upon creating a new political party to give voice to their hopes, frustrations, and fears. Unable to find a facility in town large enough to accommodate the teeming throng, convention organizers moved their meeting to an oak grove on a nearby tract of land known as Morgan's Forty. There, "under the oaks," convention delegates successfully fused seemingly incongruous strains of political thought—nativism, temperance, antirailroad/antimonopoly hostility, and Free-Soilism—into a unified movement. From this meeting emerged a new state political party and, shortly thereafter, a new national party system. Over the ensuing six years, the Republican Party's rise was nothing short of meteoric—a rise that enabled the Republicans to capture the highest political office in the land in 1860. Oddly, many historians have come to see the birth of the Republican Party in Michigan as pure happenstance and have relegated discussion of Michigan politics to a few brief sentences or to footnotes, thereby creating an impression that the state's role in the creation of the third American party system was inconsequential. While it is true that the emergence in 1854 of political Free-Soilism as the leading element in Michigan's Republican organization was largely a matter of circumstance, the same cannot be said for the emergence of new political movements in the state during the early 1850s as a whole. Importantly, Michigan's rapid immersion in the market economy coincided with and contributed to the decomposition of the Jacksonian party system. Faced with socioeconomic change of an unparalleled magnitude and no longer confident in the ability of existing political parties to address their concerns or to ease their apprehensions, Michiganians abandoned the Democratic and particularly the Whig Parties in droves, readily joining new political movements that identified and attacked threats to American liberties. In the end, Michigan's Republican organization would provide these diverse movements with a home and a focused political orthodoxy.[1]

The transformation of the United States into a market society in the years prior to the Civil War is well documented, as is the importance of this transformation in shaping the Jacksonian party system. "The Age of Jackson," Harry Watson argued in his work *Liberty and Power,*

> was also the age of steam and iron, an age of complex developments in the economy and larger society. Many Americans looked upon these changes optimistically, confident that new technology and a new society would bring wealth to all and fulfillment of republican ambitions. Others were not so sure and wondered how their own liberties would survive in a world overshadowed by the power of distant institutions and monopolies. Competing visions of the future jostled uneasily in Jacksonian America. Citizens were acutely aware that government could lend a hand to the forces of change, or it could try its best to reverse the tide, and every election became an urgent referendum on the character of the future. "Jacksonian Democracy" and the political party system it inspired grew up in this atmosphere of social and economic confrontation.

Undeniably, conflict and confrontation shaped the political culture of the Jacksonian era. At the same time, however, historians have also identified a strong consensual thread in the politics of the period—a consensus based upon the nation's republican heritage and the belief that concentrated power threatened liberty. The republican inheritance provided Americans with a lens through which to examine the implications of the market revolution. The same ideology eventually convinced them to see those who disagreed about the desirability of the new world associated with the marketplace as constituting a threat to American liberty; it then enabled them to deal with that threat by organizing into political parties. In the end, consensus and conflict were two sides of the same coin, and the political culture that defined the age of Jackson, although in part rooted in the Country Whig ideals of the founding fathers, was the distinct product of a more democratic era characterized by swift social, economic, and political change.[2]

Despite the collapse of this party system in the early 1850s, Jacksonian political culture continued to prevail well into the decade—even, according to historian Charles Sellers, "surviv[ing] in considerable measure . . . the upheaval of civil war and reconstruction." Strangely, however, though historians such as Sellers recognize the longevity of Jacksonian political culture, they are not so eager to extend that recognition to the market forces that helped to generate the political culture. In his highly acclaimed synthesis of the Jacksonian era, Sellers mistakenly left his readers with the impression that the market revolution was over in the United States by about 1840. This impression could not be further from the truth. Rather, many of the western and southern states and, indeed, more remote regions in the more established states remained largely beyond the sprawl of the market well past 1840. In fact, not until the late 1840s and early 1850s did states such as Michigan and Alabama, to name but two, experience the throes of the market revolution. In short, the market revolution did not occur everywhere in the United States at once, nor did it transform particular regions into bustling commercial entrepôts overnight. Instead, the process of transforming the United States into a market society was a long, drawn-out, and haphazard process, affecting different areas at different times and proceeding at an uneven pace.[3]

Historians specializing in the collapse of the second party system have, in the main, similarly ignored the continuing economic transformation of the United States during the 1850s. Instead, scholars such as Michael Holt, William Gienapp, and Tyler Anbinder, three of the leading experts on the political crisis of the 1850s, attribute the decline of the Whig and Democratic Parties and the rise of new political movements such as the Republican and Know-Nothing Parties to a pervasive consensus between the two national parties on traditionally divisive issues and to a growing suspicion of politicians and their motivations among an American electorate that, both despite and because of years of partisan struggle, remained uneasy and anxious about the fate of the Republic. Unquestionably, many Americans felt restive at midcentury and had come to distrust their political leaders and the established parties. Indeed, many expressed a foreboding sense that self-interested politicians were running amok and that liberty and the American ideal of the commonweal had fallen by the wayside. What Holt, Gienapp, and Anbinder fail to acknowledge, however, is that much of this pervasive angst, which they attribute mainly to ethnocultural causes and antislavery concerns, stemmed from the upheaval that accompanied the continued transition of the nation into a market society—a transition that rapidly accelerated in many parts of the nation in the 1850s. One such place was Michigan.[4]

As previously described, Michiganians experienced a sweeping and unsettling introduction to the world of cash exchange during the late 1840s and especially during the early 1850s. For those residents who feared the market economy and who believed that they had, in 1850, successfully constructed a constitutional buffer against its further expansion and aggressions, the state's continued drift toward the cash nexus was nothing short of terrifying. What had gone wrong? Constitutional restrictions on market activity were now in place, yet commercialization raced onward, not merely unimpeded but at an accelerated pace. Clearly, many people seem to have concluded, something—or, more likely, someone—was actively engaged in circumventing the intentions of the state's new constitution. Ironically, among Michiganians who embraced the emerging commercial order, fear and suspicion were also prevalent. These folks undeniably welcomed most of the changes that were reshaping their state at midcentury. Their complaint was that Michigan's market revolution and the increased economic opportunity it brought, as well as its establishment of an ordered and moral social structure, were being actively impeded by the state's new constitution and by those exercising power in Lansing—the benighted Democrats.

Both of these groups shared a feeling that their ideal social order and thus American liberty were under immediate attack. As they had done in the months and years prior to the state's constitutional convention of 1850, Michiganians pointed an accusatory finger at the selfish, shortsighted politicians who held sway in their county seats, in Lansing, and in Washington as the root cause of their unhappiness and as the real threat to liberty. It only stood to reason that if self-interest and greed controlled the centers of government, myopic and specious laws would be the natural outcome. Anxiety and fear continued to plague Michigan and liberty remained endangered, residents concluded, because the true problems of the state and nation were being ignored and/or misconstrued by demagogic politicians. This situation led one denizen of Adrian to complain of "too much selfishness" among contemporary political figures. Howell resident E. M. Mason concurred. In a speech enclosed in a letter to a friend, Mason complained that "the offices of trust in our country, are not only now, but for a long time past, have been

filled by notorious political demagogues, and abandoned office seeking traitors to the cause of truth, humanity and justice. . . . So much dishonesty, hy-
pocrisy and evil as are tolerated in all political organizations, disgraces the
study of politics and those who engage in it." Nevertheless, despite the general perception of political decay alluded to in his speech, Mason remained
optimistic about the political system. The study of politics, he confirmed, "is
still a noble study, and one well worthy of attentions of us all; one which if it
has not, should engage the thought of the wisest and best in our land. And
one which should be freed from the corrupting influences, and evil practices,
now so prevalent in all political parties." What was needed, he concluded, was
an evaluation of existing political organizations and the abandonment of
those that failed to "stand for the preservation of the whole union, and the
constitution, in all the primeval purity which it possessed when first it left the
hands of its immortal framers, and started forth in its mission for the protection of mankind."[5]

Though Mason's intent was to attract Michiganians to the newly created
Republican Party, he nevertheless spoke for many state residents. People
across Michigan believed that the existing political parties no longer served
the purpose for which they had been created—the protection of American
liberty. Rather, they had become infested with demagogues and politicians
who disregarded the state's and the nation's problems and instead concentrated on lining their own pockets and promoting special interests. Mourning the passing of such "profound statesmen" as Andrew Jackson, John
Quincy Adams, Henry Clay, Daniel Webster, and John C. Calhoun, one resident expressed his fears plainly: "Where are other men, who can ever fill
their places? Not on this continent. . . . Of this, I have no doubt." This belief
led many Michiganians to abandon their traditional partisan fealties during
the 1850s and to join new political organizations—organizations that clearly
identified and sought to battle threats to liberty and that proposed new policies to ensure liberty's preservation.[6]

Although the varied causes and platforms championed by these nascent
political organizations predated the political crisis of the 1850s, they had
long been relegated to a minor place within Michigan's Jacksonian party system. As the public's attitude toward the existing political parties changed,
however, and as the Jacksonian party system collapsed, these political under-
currents quickly swelled into full-fledged political movements in their own
right. In Michigan, one of the strongest of these new political crusades
(though it is the least appreciated by historians) was formed in opposition to
the power of the state's railroad corporations.[7]

As mentioned earlier, hostility toward Michigan's railroad corporations was pervasive by 1850 and at times openly violent. Nevertheless, this hostility remained rather diffuse and unorganized, encompassing a spectrum of attitudes: some hated the railroads as representatives of market forces, while others hated them because of their monopoly status. In 1851, however, two important court cases involving railroads greatly altered this state of affairs. Ironically, although 1851 brought an end to the physical attacks upon railroad property with the arrest of the Jackson County conspirators in April, the state's railroad corporations, particularly the Michigan Central, faced a consolidated and increasingly vocal and broad-based antirailroad/antimonopoly movement by the end of that year.[8]

Of all the diverse sources sustaining antirailroad sentiment in Michigan, no single issue evoked the same degree of passion and emotion as did the destruction of livestock by locomotives and the related struggle to preserve traditional open-range prerogatives in the face of accelerating market encroachment. In its July 1851 session, the Michigan Supreme Court confronted this controversial issue in the case of *Williams v. Michigan Central Railroad Company*. The case involved the killing of a number of horses belonging to a Wayne County farmer, Edward Williams, by engines operated by the Michigan Central along the company's track near the town of Dearborn. Lawyers for the plaintiff argued that, according to township law, the horses were free commoners on unfenced land and that therefore the Michigan Central, which had not fenced its property to keep livestock off its tracks, was liable for damages. The court, however, did not agree.[9]

In its decision, written by Justice Abner Pratt of Marshall, the court argued that Williams's horses were not rightfully on the road. "The idea that because horses and cattle are free commoners, they have therefore the lawful right of trespassing on private property," Justice Pratt asserted unequivocally in his majority opinion, "is absurd—preposterous in the extreme." "What are free commoners? Where may they run?" he continued, "Surely not on individual property." "In legal contemplation," Pratt asserted, "the railroad is neither a *public common* nor a *public highway*." Accordingly, "the voters of the township of Dearborn could not, by any power vested in them by the Legislature, confer upon the plaintiff the right of grazing his cattle and horses on lands granted to the defendants, exclusively for the construction and use of their railroad." Concluding with a rhetorical flourish, Pratt asked if a railroad corporation should "be compelled to assume the guardianship of all the stray cattle, horses, and swine . . . found strolling along the track on their Railroad? Most certainly not. The owners are the only persons to look after them; and if they do not, it is but just that they alone should suffer the consequences of their own negligence and wrongful act—of their own want of care, in the protection and preservation of their own property." The court had affirmed the position taken just two years previously by John Brooks, the superintendent of the Michigan Central Railroad Company: the owners of the livestock killed along the railroad were culpable for their loss. The Michigan Central was free to continue, unabated, the dismantling of the traditional world of the state's self-provisioning yeomanry.[10]

Despite siding with the Michigan Central, Judge Pratt, a Democrat, suggested a method of redress to the state's antirailroad forces. He insisted that, according to the company's charter, the Michigan Central was not required to fence in its road for the protection of domestic animals; in short, Pratt was not saying that he necessarily agreed with the state legislature's actions on this matter. Nevertheless, he conceded, "whether their charter contains powers and privileges which were improvidently granted by the Legislature, is not a question to be considered here in deciding the case." By thus limiting the competence of the court, "he was suggesting," historian Charles Hirschfeld astutely noted, "that what the lawmakers had given, only the lawmakers could take away." In other words, in order for the state's antirailroad/antimonopoly forces to counter the power of railroad corporations, they would have to focus upon (1) a legislative initiative aimed at forcing concessions from the state's railroad companies when and if they sought amendments to their charters (a very plausible strategy, given the Michigan Southern and Michigan Central efforts to obtain variances allowing them to run their lines into Indiana and then on to Chicago), and (2) promoting the passage of a general incorporation law for future railroads under a system of public regulation.[11]

In short order, the opponents of the Michigan Central had this lesson driven home as the trial of the Jackson County conspirators neared its climax in Detroit. The trial garnered a great deal of public attention—"'tis the all absorbing thought of our city," wrote Detroit resident Elizabeth Stuart, the mother of Wayne County prosecutor David Stuart—and received widespread press coverage, most of which favored the railroad. But the public mood shifted perceptibly when Abel Fitch, the outspoken critic of the Michigan Central and alleged ringleader of the conspiracy, died in a Detroit hospital on August 24 without ever having had his day in court. The same day, his body was transported home to Michigan Center, and the following morning, a procession of carriages and teams nearly one-half mile long gathered to accompany Fitch's body to Jackson for the funeral. The Congregational Church of Jackson was filled to overflowing, with those unable to gain entry gathered outside the building's doors and windows. In his funeral sermon, the Reverend Gustavus L. Foster was careful not to portray Fitch as a saint, but he did describe him as a victim and heap blame for his death upon civil authorities and the Michigan Central. "It is well known," Foster affirmed to his receptive audience, "that heavy, moneyed corporations are not apt to be distinguished for their tender mercies, nor for their regard for justice, except it can contribute to pecuniary gain. *Corporations become corporate for the sake of the dollar.* Everything else is apt to be made subservient to its attainment. Somebody has recently said, 'Corporations have no souls.' How true! And no conscience—and no regard for God nor man—except so far as both God and man will subserve the interests for which they became corporate." In the end, historian Hirschfeld argued, "the death of Fitch, though it shook the defense, brought it fresh accessions of public support and sympathy."[12]

Leading the attack upon the Michigan Central was Charles V. DeLand, the editor of the *American Citizen,* a Jackson-based Whig sheet. Labeling Fitch as a victim "of the jealousy and malice of the Central Railroad monopoly," DeLand vociferously stepped up his attacks upon the company and the trial, declaring "a war as lasting as life . . . against [the Michigan Central's] despotism." DeLand's paper was not the only periodical expressing sympathy for Fitch and voicing doubts about his guilt. The *Detroit Tribune,* which had been among the most strident critics of the accused just four months earlier, reversed its course. This reversal, however, was not as surprising as it might appear at first blush. The *Tribune,* like the *American Citizen,* was a Free-Soil Whig paper. Battling desperately to advance their principles and to bolster their standing within their own party, both papers unflinchingly linked the interests of the Michigan Central with the political fortunes of the state's Democratic Party, the party that had originally granted the railroad its charter and was now handling the prosecution of the conspirators; the *American Citizen* referred to the corporation as a "locofoco bantling." "There is a conspiracy [afoot] on one side or the other," the *Tribune* concluded on August 15. Moneyed power had to be used prudently and "never to control public opinion, Courts, Juries, the Press, or [to] oppress the weak and the poor." In the end, however, the *Tribune* affirmed, justice would prevail because there was too much respect for justice in Detroit and "too much hatred of oppression and tyranny whether manifested by governments or corporations" to allow any other outcome.[13]

Clearly, given the Whig Party's traditional support for the market economy and the agents of commerce, the position taken relative to the Michigan Central by the *American Citizen* and the *Tribune* might seem rather contradictory. But as mentioned earlier, the Free-Soil wing of the Whig Party apparently

saw in the rapidly swelling antirailroad movement an opportunity to make political capital. More important, however, the traditionally Democratic position
promoted by DeLand and the ease with which Whigs and Democrats alike
were able to unite and cooperate in the fight against the Michigan Central suggest that partisan lines were blurring in Michigan well before the traditional
mid-1850s dates attributed by historians to the party realignment. In short, the
Free-Soil Whig position regarding the Michigan Central foreshadowed the
more thorough partisan melding that would be necessary to create the Republican Party in 1854. Not surprisingly, Charles DeLand would play a critical role
in the formation of that party.

The growing sympathy for the defendants in the conspiracy case, in conjunction with the recent judicial decision in *Williams v. Michigan Central Railroad Company,* breathed new life into an antirailroad movement that had
been devastated by the arrest and trial of Fitch and the other alleged Jackson
County conspirators. But this rejuvenated movement would differ greatly
from the one of the recent past in that it would be well organized, unified,
and led by a new and more respectable cadre of men. It is not surprising that
the locus of this movement was Jackson County, where a letter to DeLand's
American Citizen put the matter succinctly, asking whether "our hardy yeomanry stand ready 'to be humbled' at the beck or nod of the agents of a great
monied monopoly."[14]

The answer was a resounding no. Just four days after Fitch's death, out-
raged residents held an "indignation meeting"—a gathering of citizens organized to discuss or protest an unpopular action or event—at the courthouse
in Jackson. The speakers at the meeting maintained a temperate tone and
were careful to blame both the alleged conspirators and the Michigan Central for the current state of affairs, but the railroad representatives, they asserted, had been the "first aggressors." A series of resolutions were drawn up,
protesting the Central's unwillingness to reimburse farmers for livestock
killed by the railroad, the company's use of spies, the method of arrest employed by Wayne County officials, the excessive bail set for the defendants,
and the generally poor jail conditions in which the prisoners were being
held. Participants at the meeting went on to express their hope that future
opposition to the railroad would follow legal channels and would not devolve
into criminal violence. And in a telling statement, they urged that the right of
competition be upheld and that all means be employed to further that right.
Here was a departure from past practice and an opportunity to fuse two very
different agendas. By criticizing the Michigan Central for failing to pay farmers enough for their livestock, the residents of Jackson County were appeal-

ing to their fellow citizens who opposed railroads because they symbolized the loss of a traditional way of life. At the same time, however, by demanding open competition with the Michigan Central, participants in the Jackson meeting held out a hand to those individuals who eagerly embraced modern transportation and the socioeconomic changes that accompanied its expansion but had also been critical of the state's railroads, especially the Michigan Central, because their monopoly status impeded the construction of new lines. Finally, the meeting closed after a committee was selected to prepare for a larger mass assembly to be held on September 13.[15]

The September 13 meeting, lauded by DeLand's *American Citizen* as "5000 Freemen in Council," likewise condemned the authorities' handling of the trial. The assembled group bristled with excitement when William T. Howell, a former Democratic state senator who had opposed the sale of the Michigan Central by the state in 1846, denounced the actions of the railroad as "the curse of an insolent and overgrown monopoly on the people." Howell went on to warn that "[a] Revolution a mighty Revolution is destined to follow the movements of these monopolies." Inspired, the assembly unanimously decried the Central's use of "our laws and Government as a means of oppression, outrage, and injustice." Unlike the participants at the earlier meeting, however, this group tacitly endorsed the course of action implicitly suggested by Judge Pratt in his *Williams* decision—that is, they agreed that what Michiganians needed was a legislature that responded to *their* interests, not to those of a moneyed corporation. Thus, they proposed to keep the railroad under careful scrutiny, to elect only honest men to office, and to push forward a proposed branch road between Jackson and the Michigan Southern Railroad at Adrian—a road that the Michigan Southern was, indeed, obligated by its original charter to complete—in order to promote competition with the Michigan Central. In closing, the attendees vowed that they would "ever cherish the memory of the virtues of our lamented friend and fellow citizen, Abel F. Fitch, the victim of a foul conspiracy of unjust oppression and cruel wrong."[16]

Within this tumultuous milieu, the prosecution and defense in the conspiracy case began their closing arguments. A throng of nearly one thousand, their interest in the proceedings piqued by the death of Fitch and the growing public outcry against the Michigan Central, flocked to the courthouse to witness the trial's close. Seeking a venue large enough for the assembled crowd, city officials relocated the concluding sessions of the court to the great hall on the third floor of the newly constructed Fireman's Hall. In the flurry of oratory that followed, the prosecution chastised the defense for fanning the flames of public discord. "Have the prosecuting counsel run through the streets pledging their honors to the innocence or guilt of the prisoners?" prosecuting attorney James A. Van Dyke asked the jury. "Have they sought, day after day, to raise an influence that might be brought to bear on your deliberations? Have they sown distrust broadcast in the community, or gathered public meetings for the purpose of denouncing these judicial proceedings? Have they got up deathbed scenes . . . ? Have they published sermons of doubtful morality and perverted taste, for distribution?[17]

The defense responded as anticipated by railing both against the state for its handling of the arrest and trial of the accused and against the "monetary power" of the Michigan Central, "a power behind and above the government—a power that is seldom regulated by humane and just sentiments; that always seeks to crush those it cannot cajole." Indeed, star defense attorney William Seward warned the jury that "corporate wealth cannot long oppress the citizen in such a country and under such a government as this. Your verdict against these defendants, if it shall appear to be well grounded upon the evidence, will abate a rapidly rising popular commotion; but, if it shall not be sustained by the evidence, a people which make the wrongs of each one the common cause of all, will pick a strong matter of wrath out of the bloody finger ends of a successful conspiracy." Defense attorney Henry Frink, a recently departed resident of Jackson, then proceeded to play up the death of Fitch, reminding the jury that "God in his providence has permitted him to fall upon the altar of freedom—a victim of injustice and oppression."[18]

Appalled by what he perceived to be a blatant appeal to bend justice to the popular will, Van Dyke fired back. In so doing, he laid bare the very essence of the trial: Michiganians were really debating the merits of the market revolution. The *Williams* case and the trial of the Jackson County conspirators brought to the fore an ongoing debate that, until that point, had been quietly waged along Michigan's country lanes, in isolated frontier clearings, in village taverns and country stores, and beside the hearths of the state's numerous family farms. In these two highly publicized and extremely symbolic cases, the emerging capitalist order had its day in court.

The railroad and the broader changes that it represented, Van Dyke professed, had done nothing but good in Michigan. The sale of the Michigan Central by the state was a serendipitous event, for

where heaven's light was once shut out by dense forests, it [now] shines over fertile fields and rich luxuriant harvests . . . ; hope and energy sprung from their lethargic sleep, labor clapped her glad hands and shouted for joy; and Michigan, bent for the moment like a sapling by the fierceness of a passing tempest, relieved from the debts and burthens, rose erect, and in her youthful strength, stood proudly up among her sister states. . . . A detestable monopoly! These railroads built by united energies and capital are the great instruments in the hand of God to hasten onward the glorious mission of Religion and Civilization.

"Who shall stop this glorious work which is spreading blessings and prosperity around us," Van Dyke queried, "who shall dare to say 'thus far shalt thou go and no farther?'" Warming to the task, the prosecutor asserted that "beneath the beneficial influence of Companies like this, space is annihilated; weeks are reduced to the compass of days, and in spite of the wicked purposes of bad men, this and kindred Companies shall continue to spread and contribute to the greatness and prosperity of our country, until the earth vibrates with the pulse of her glory." The Jackson County conspirators had to be found guilty, he concluded, because

if these dangerous doctrines which produced the outrages we are considering, are to spread from the hamlet of Leoni, throughout the breadth of the land, and even to the jury box of our courts; if men animated by deep hate against a corporation, feel and think that they are justified in redressing their own real or fancied wrongs, in their own way . . . then indeed have evil days come upon us. Capital, virtue, peace and property will be trodden over, and crushed by mob violence and all the dire evils which follow in its train. . . . The first jury which renders a verdict, tainted by the unhallowed spirit of fear, or public opinion, or prejudiced by loud clamors against monopolies and tyrannical corporations, will have stricken a death blow at this country's honor and welfare.

The question facing the Detroit jury and the residents of Michigan was clear: which competing social vision would prevail—traditional open-range self-provisioning norms or the market's common law principle of unhindered personal property rights?[19]

On September 25, the case went to the jury. After nine hours of deliberation, the jurors returned with the verdict. Twelve of the defendants were found guilty as charged; twenty were released. The presiding judge, Warner Wing, sentenced the twelve to prison terms varying in length from five to ten years.[20]

The Central's opponents were stunned by the verdict. Not even "great legal talent," DeLand's *American Citizen* lamented, "could prevail against adverse public opinion backed by the . . . almighty power of a monied corporation." But the *Jonesville Telegraph* reminded its readers that the soundness of the verdict was not the only question at issue. "Another of far more importance is involved. It is the power and pretensions of a mighty corporation, aided by the use of an immense capital, on one side, over the high prerogatives of the people and the just attributes of sovereignty on the other—a war between the *creature* and the *creator*." Calling upon the state legislature to remedy the situation, the paper warned that "we are only in our infancy, and if we allow supinneness [*sic*] and inactivity to control us, we shall never, as a state arrive at manhood." With the trial now over, though, and with no opportunity for legislative assistance in its struggle against the Michigan Central until January of 1853, the antirailroad/antimonopoly movement temporarily withdrew into the shadows. One would be mistaken, however, in assuming that the movement was therefore inactive. On the contrary, antirailroad and antimonopoly forces continued to work and to plan for the upcoming legislative session, and from time to time, they stirred themselves and revealed their growing strength.[21]

Such an exhibition occurred in November 1851. In Michigan, 1851 was a gubernatorial election year, and as might have been expected, antirailroad animus became entwined with state politics in Jackson County during the campaign. Local prorailroad Whigs and Democrats charged the opposition's candidate with promising, if elected, to pardon the convicted conspirators. Antirailroad voters criticized the candidates for posing as railroad men in Wayne County and antirailroad men in Jackson County. In the end, although he lost the election to his Democratic rival Robert McClelland, the Whig candidate, Townsend E. Gidley, a Jackson County farmer, won his home county, as Charles Hirschfeld argued, "solely because the voters of Leoni and Grass Lake Townships, who had the year before given the Democrats small majorities, now turned on the railroad-dominated administration and gave large majorities to the Whigs."[22]

In late 1852, hatred of the Michigan Central again flared up in Jackson County when Henry Phelps, the Central's chief informer in the railroad conspiracy trial, made the mistake of visiting friends in Grass Lake. Phelps was immediately arrested on a warrant sworn out by a local lawyer and ardent antirailroad man, Benjamin Burnett, and charged with conspiracy to convict the men of Leoni. After Phelps's arrest, a Jackson County justice, also known as a "hot anti railroad man," set his bail at $5,000, which was immediately paid by the Michigan Central. Phelps then went before the county grand jury, where he was indicted. Trial was set for March 1853. Faced with this unexpected and undesirable turn of events, the Michigan Central applied all its resources to defend its employee. Phelps's company-hired lawyer managed to get a county judge to grant a change of venue to Washtenaw County. Then, the Jackson County prosecutor, Austin Blair, was persuaded by Moses A. McNaughton, a Free-Soil state senator from Jackson acting on behalf of the railroad, to drop the charges against Phelps. A free man, Henry Phelps quickly disappeared from Michigan.[23]

Later that same year, the congressional contest in the First District, which encompassed Wayne, Washtenaw, Jackson, and Livingston Counties, further riled the foes of the Michigan Central. It appears that the publicity surrounding the railroad conspiracy case and the deep rift in the district produced by that trial may have influenced the parties' selection of candidates— David A. Stuart, the Wayne County prosecutor who oversaw the case, for the Democrats and William A. Howard, one of the defense attorneys in the case and a strong advocate of Free-Soil principles, for the Whigs. For many district voters, the election undoubtedly represented an opportunity to voice their opinion about the trial's outcome.

In Jackson County, Stuart's candidacy faced widespread hostility. In a letter to one of Stuart's siblings, his mother, Elizabeth, wrote, "Dave is having hard times—Jackson, from where he expected a large majority, sware [*sic*] vengeance against him. This is the home, or nest, of the R.R. Conspirators. They say their comrades are suffering imprisonment unjustly—that they were put there on false oaths &c." Cognizant of his weak position in Jackson County, Stuart immediately set to work to overcome his handicap. According to the *American Citizen*, he offered large sums of money "to conciliate the opposition of certain prominent democrats in this county" to his candidacy. In addition, he and several prominent Jackson County residents signed a petition to Governor McClelland, requesting a pardon of some of the prisoners. To placate his opponents further, Stuart met privately with Benjamin F. Gleason, a prominent local Democrat and one of the acquitted conspirators. In a letter to the *American Citizen,* Gleason alleged that Stuart had asked for his support, had personally taken credit for the acquittal of some of the so-called conspirators, and had emphasized that he now sought pardons for the rest. In return for his support, Gleason further alleged, Stuart had promised him a job if elected. "After being rode and made a cripple by his lies," Gleason asserted, "I cant [*sic*] vote for him." Denouncing the trumped-up charges against the accused, he concluded by challenging Stuart: "If you are an honest man, you will come out and tell the truth. That we ask before we can vote for you." In the end, despite such vocal opposition, Stuart managed to win the election because of his strength in Wayne and Livingston Counties. To no one's surprise, Jackson County went to Whig candidate William Howard, even though the county gave Democrat Franklin Pierce a majority over Whig Winfield Scott in the presidential campaign. However, the defeat of the antirailroad forces at the district level would prove to be but a temporary one.[24]

After over a year of frustration and of constant reminders of their recent defeat and fueled by the rapidly expanding power of the Michigan Central, which had reached Chicago in the spring of 1852, opponents of the company launched a wide-ranging assault upon the railroad in 1853. The opening salvo in this clash was fired by the indomitable Grass Lake antirailroad zealot Benjamin Burnett. In January 1853, Burnett began publishing an antirailroad newspaper called the *Grass Lake Public Sentiment*. Convinced that justice had been "sacrificed under the iron heel of R.R. power," he pledged to keep the cause of the Jackson County conspirators before the people. His paper seethed with anger, suspicion, and vituperation:

> Oh! How we covet the pen of the ready writer, that we might broadcast all over Michigan, and the rest of mankind, the dooming deeds of oppression, of hireling editors, villanous [*sic*] lawyer[s] and other equally degraded gold stultified menials, who suck at the teats of this beast, which has with its golden barbed horns, gone pushing down the altars of justice, turning and overturning our Constitution, and tossing high and dry some of the members of our Legislature, and so deranging their moral and intellectual machinery, as to make it run only to the tune of railroad gold!

"Does '*Tuebor, si quaeris peninsulam amoenam circumspice,*' mean 'I swear to defend our beautiful peninsula,'" Burnett queried in a subsequent edition of his paper, "or does it mean to defend the Michigan Central Railroad Company?" Declaring railroad tyranny his uncompromising enemy, he swore to "take open ground on all questions involving the rights or liberties of freemen." "The freemen of Michigan," Burnett correctly surmised, would repudiate the tyranny of the Michigan Central "with a vengeance."[25]

With that end in mind, the opponents of the Michigan Central took their fight to the floor of the state legislature when it reconvened in January 1853. As the legislators arrived in Lansing, it became increasingly apparent that antirailroad rancor continued to fester in Michigan. Awaiting the newly seated legislators were numerous petitions, including those bearing the signatures of nearly one thousand legal voters from Oakland and Jackson Counties, demanding the pardon of the antirailroad conspirators. Indeed, a great many Michiganians, including Gov. Robert McClelland—who, historian Charles Hirschfeld argued, had decided that a pardon was necessary and who was merely awaiting the beginning of the new legislative session before acting—seem to have concluded that pardoning the alleged conspirators was the correct course for the state. Recognizing an opportunity when he saw one, Sen. Moses McNaughton from Jackson County urged James Joy, the Central's agent in Lansing, to procure pardons for four of the convicted men—Ebenezer Farnham, Erastus Champlin, Erastus Smith, and Andrew Freeland. "I speak of the thing merely and solely as a matter of policy," McNaughton wrote Joy. "The public generally believe, no matter what the facts may be," he continued,

> that these parties are not guilty of any serious obstruction being made by them or at their procurement, to your road. . . . I think it would not be amiss to institute an inquiry as to the present secret intentions of the . . . named parties toward your road, provided they could be pardoned. . . . Public feeling can neither be stifled nor forcibly turned backward in its channel, but may be directed, turned, changed, controlled, so as to subserve given interests. It is the part of wisdom to act wisely! It is neither for the interest, or the honor, of the Michigan Central Railroad or the county of Jackson to widen the break now between them. Let wisdom not passion, let providence not feeling, guide us.

Joy concurred with McNaughton "that such an act may be productive of much good," and after meeting with three of the previously mentioned men in the state penitentiary at Jackson, he urged Governor McClelland to pardon Champlin, Farnham, and Smith. At this point, however, as Hirschfeld noted, "progress bogged down in the political jockeying connected with the fight in the legislature between the Michigan Central and Michigan Southern forces."[26]

Inundated by petitions for pardons, the state house appointed a special committee to deal with the issue. Apparently controlled by friends of the Michigan Southern and enemies of the Michigan Central, the committee issued a report attacking the entire prosecution of the conspiracy trial and recommended the pardon of all the conspirators. A motion to adopt the report and the resolution passed the house by a vote of thirty-nine to twenty-three. After further debate and active lobbying by the Michigan Central, however, the house reversed itself and tabled the matter. Finally, on March 4, Governor McClelland, just prior to resigning his office to become the U.S. secretary of the interior, issued a pardon for Farnham, Champlin, and Smith.[27]

While efforts were under way to obtain the release of the alleged Jackson County conspirators, a related political tide—a movement to regulate the state's railroads—began to swell in Lansing. In the early days of the session, a regulatory bill found its way into the legislature once again; it had first been proposed in 1850 and then again in 1851 by a senator from Jackson County, Michael Shoemaker. The bill, which required railroad companies to fence their rights-of-way, to build cattle guards at crossings and post warning signs there, and to put bells on their locomotives, passed the house with only one dissenting vote but was voted down in the senate.[28]

But the bill's defeat did not end debate on the issue. The measure's regulatory features were integrated into a proposed general railroad bill designed to reform Michigan's socioeconomic order by simultaneously regulating the activities of railroad corporations and by facilitating the construction of new competing lines (which would theoretically promote responsible behavior) through democratizing the process of incorporation. Intended to tap both antirailroad and prodevelopment/antimonopoly hostility, the bill's broad scope offered something to everyone and thus enabled those with potentially contradictory views of the developing commercial economy to rally to the cause.

This movement's salience in the 1853 legislative session was largely the by-product of the heated and intense competition between the Michigan Southern Railroad and the Michigan Central. As noted earlier, the two rival railroads had entered Chicago within one month of each other in the spring of 1852 and were locked in a bitter struggle to dominate the burgeoning East-West through trade. As 1852 drew to a close, the directors of the Michigan Southern determined to seek an amendment to their company's charter, allowing them to extend their line northward from Monroe to Detroit. The intent of this proposal was clear: the Southern hoped to divert a portion of the Central's trade to its main trunk line. When the company presented its proposal to the state legislature in 1853, James Joy and the Michigan Central went on the attack and countered with a petition for an amendment to the company's charter, allowing it to build the proposed line. As deadlock set in, the Southern shifted its tactics and threw its support behind the growing effort to pass a general railroad bill. "Whatever projects you plan the Southern road may have, or whatever professions they make," a correspondent warned Joy, "I understand from revelations made that their great object now is to get a general railroad law, that they might organize under it . . . hoping that their connection thereafter can be sustained."[29]

The proposal to pass such a general incorporation law for railroads was nothing new in Michigan by 1853. On the contrary, the topic had garnered a great deal of attention during the 1851 state legislative session. At that time, as in 1853, a frustrated Michigan Southern—on that occasion, piqued by its failure to obtain a variance of its charter permitting the road to turn southward into Indiana and then on to Chicago—was the driving force behind the movement. The Michigan Southern had then found willing allies among the Jackson County delegates, who saw such a law as a means of diminishing the power of the Michigan Central. Among the most supportive of the Jackson County representatives was Michael Shoemaker, chairman pro tempore of the state senate and chair of its Committee on Corporations. Shoemaker reported out a general railroad bill from his committee, but Joy and the Michigan Central proved equal to the task of defeating it.[30]

Over the next two years, popular opinion in favor of a general railroad bill strengthened. On December 24, 1852, a large group of people in favor of the bill gathered in Marshall. Pursuant to the meeting's call for a general railroad law, the Democratic *Grand Rapids Enquirer* added its voice to the growing clamor in favor of the measure and insisted that all railroad improvements "be carried on under, and regulated by a general law; give them all, the benefit of Democratic equality." "Corporations are persons in law," the paper went on, "and we would apply to them the good old fashioned Jeffersonian doctrine; we would have them 'born free and equal,' not 'booted and spurred' to ride over each other or the people." Similarly, Governor McClelland, in his address to the state legislature, called for the passage of a general railroad law in order to meet the "growing necessities and increasing business of our state," adding that "I cannot perceive how the state can be injured by it."[31]

Despite bright prospects, however, the proponents of the general railroad law faced a tough battle against entrenched railroad interests. With the addition of the Michigan Southern and its lobby to their ranks, the advocates of the general law immediately set to work. On January 22, 1853, agents for the Michigan Southern staged a large rally in support of the law in Detroit. In their memorial to the legislature, the assembled citizens asserted, in reference to the proposed law, that "no portion of our own State, feeling the necessity of such an improvement, will long be content without it. . . . Nor is it consistent with their intelligence or independence of character to suppose that they will long remain indifferent to the apparent monopoly which now prevails in the State. Competition is not only the life of business, but it tends to remove and usually does remove all grounds of complaint or murmuring at the use of corporate privileges." But the Michigan Central did not take this attack lying down, emanating as it did from the railroad's own backyard. Rather, James Joy and other friends of the Central and opponents of the law addressed the Detroit meeting. Although they failed to stop participants at the meeting from sending a memorial in favor of the bill to Lansing on January 22, they were able to get them to reverse their course the following day and to adopt a resolution opposing the law.[32]

The debate over the merits of the law quickly spread throughout the state, and numerous public meetings were held in support of both positions. As the contest reached the state legislature, the *Jackson American Citizen* delineated the issue facing state residents: "Shall the people be benefitted, or shall the treasury bag of corporations only be legislated for? Shall the body politic be granted the privileges they wish, or shall a few men only be enriched?" Lobbying both on behalf of and against the proposed bill was intense, a situation that led Burnett's *Grass Lake Public Sentiment* to remark, "Our legislators (like some of our noble rivers, dammed up with floodwood) seem to be struggling amidst lobbies innumerable, to reach an end of their forty days." When the dust stirred by the contest settled in Lansing, the Michigan Central again emerged victorious: the general railroad law was buried in the shuffle of unfinished business at the end of the legislative session. The defeat of the bill, the Democratic *Spirit of the Times* in Saginaw reported, would have an immediate impact upon state politics, especially for the Democrats. It is "with surprise and regret," the paper's editor conceded,

> that we now witness several professing democratic papers, and democratic representatives of the people, in our halls of legislation, forsaking the golden principles of their party [Equal Laws and Equal Rights for all], . . . and [endorsing] the anti-democratic doctrine that it is for the present interest of Michigan to foster powerful monopolies and aristocratic establishments. This course on their part professing as they do to be representatives of the party, although [they] misrepresent its principles, is the unkindest thrust that could be given the cause of Democracy.

Only after the bill's defeat did the Michigan Southern opt to play its last card in this high-stakes game: it agreed to complete the forlorn Jackson branch railroad and to extend it to the Grand River valley as a means of tapping into the Michigan Central's traffic.[33]

As the general railroad bill was being buried in the state senate, Rep. Amos Root of Jackson succeeded in obtaining assurance from Elisha Litchfield, one of the Southern Railroad's directors, that his company would build the Jackson branch within three years. In return, however, Litchfield insisted that the Michigan Southern be given the right-of-way extending ten miles south of Jackson free of charge. Jackson County residents, long distrustful of the Michigan Central and the power it wielded over them and still angry about all that had recently transpired in relation to the company, willingly acceded to the Southern's demand. In short order, local promoters of the project began buying up the promised land, opened books for the sale of additional Michigan Southern stock to help finance the project, and advertised for bids on needed materials. In addition, several hundred men were put to work grading the right-of-way. As the local effort gained momentum, boosters, hoping to rally public support further and to raise badly needed capital, organized a mass meeting to be held in Jackson on August 22, 1853.[34]

As the appointed date neared, the *American Citizen* urged the assemblage to assume a reasoned and dispassionate tone. "The people of this State know, as well as we," the paper assured its readership, "the soulless character of the great Central monopoly. They know too, the dishonor it has wrought to us. They feel that in this struggle they have a direct interest. They sympathise [*sic*] with us in the matter of the Branch Railroad, for it is a stepping stone to break the gigantic power of this mammoth. If we can by honest or legal measures break the monopolies they hold, deliverance will come to others."[35]

On August 23, two thousand citizens gathered at the Jackson County courthouse. Again, the tenor of the meeting revealed a great deal about how far antirailroad/antimonopoly forces had come in creating a broad-based political movement. Speaker after speaker tailored his message to the diverse crowd; all of these speeches, although varied in their details and perspectives, emphasized the preservation of liberty in the face of all-consuming power. Following such a carefully plotted strategy allowed the meeting's speakers to unify a disparate group of people who disagreed about exactly what was threatening the liberties of Michiganians—or, for that matter, about what liberty itself meant—but who, at the same time, shared a deeply ingrained distrust of power. "Now, gentlemen, let us keep on our way," harangued W. T. Howell of Jonesville:

Build your road across this wall—batter it down—improve the heritage you have—watch this company. They boast their millions—
watch their money. Let it not barter away your rights. To save these,
lay aside political differences and all things else. This is called an
age of progress—if that means an age of sin and corruption, it is
true. In railroad progress it is true, for they progress over all our
rights and on the most sacred privileges of our people. They are
good servants, but outrageous masters. By keeping this corporation
where it belongs it will be a great blessing—such let us make it.

The remedy for this situation, the meeting resolved, was the immediate construction of the Jackson Branch and the passage of a general railroad law
(incorporating both regulatory and democratic features) by the state legislature. As a final means of keeping the issue before the people, a committee on
permanent organization was appointed.[36]

The Michigan Central reacted to this growing storm forcefully and decisively. Within a week of the Jackson meeting, the company filed suit in Wayne
County Circuit Court, contending that the proposed line to Jackson violated
the terms of the Central's charter and that it would tap the Central's business
and erode its profits. Lawyers for the Southern Railroad countered that their
corporation was only fulfilling the conditions of its own charter, which required it to complete the line between Adrian and Jackson. Judge Samuel
Douglass, however, determined that the proposed line was in conflict with
the Central's charter and granted an injunction against further construction. Thus, the Jackson branch was effectively killed and could now be resus-
citated only by the passage of a general railroad law.[37]

Although Jackson County was at the heart of the antirailroad/antimo-
nopoly movement, the sentiments of that movement were not purely local.
On the contrary, throughout the spring and summer of 1853 and with even
greater frequency after the Central's successful thwarting of the Jackson
Branch late that autumn, the public expressed its rancor against the Michigan Central in a number of well-attended meetings throughout the state. "I
find through the state," a Grand Rapids resident wrote to Joy, "that the general railroad law is yet in discussion and you may rely upon it an effort concerted and well arranged will be made to press it through the next session of
the legislature." Again and again—in Adrian, Birmingham, Detroit, Grand
Rapids, and elsewhere—the meetings resolved that a general railroad law
was essential to preserve the liberty of the state's citizenry and that some sort
of state regulation of railroad corporations was necessary.[38]

As 1853 drew to a close, the grassroots demand for a general railroad law reached a crescendo. The general railroad law, the *American Citizen* asserted, was a measure "of the people; politicians have nothing to do with [it]; party should be eschewed. . . . If monopolies or individuals undertake to ride down the people, and deprive them of their rights, the people must oppose; and thus we should act as regards a special session. *We all want it,—let us all unite in calling for it.*" Three very large meetings were held in December at Adrian, Detroit, and Jackson, with the aim of pressuring Gov. Andrew Parsons into calling a special session of the state legislature in order to enact the desired railroad law. In the end, Parsons resisted the mounting pressure. But as the well-attended meetings made clear, the antirailroad/antimonopoly movement had reached high tide and could no longer be restrained. As the *American Citizen* put it, "The [Jackson] Convention settled one fact—that hereafter the will of the people must be respected by our Legislature. The days of Corporation Monopoly bearing sway over the rights of citizens is at an end. Politicians and 'traders in stock' will find soon, like Othello, their 'Vocations gone'—that there is a race of men inhabiting this Peninsula, and they demand rights and attention." Editor DeLand's prophecy proved accurate: attention was quick in coming. The railroad issue had truly become, as historian Charles Hirschfeld wrote, "one of the ingredients in the bubbling political cauldron in the state."[39]

Not all Michiganians, of course, were spurred to action by hostility toward powerful railroads. Indeed, while thousands met to protest the actions of the Michigan Central, a great many others attempted to assuage their anxieties by organizing to deal with what was seen as an equally ominous threat to their state and to liberty (and one that could also be tied directly to the state's commercial growth)—the increasing number of immigrants, many of them Catholic, in Michigan.[40]

In 1850, Michigan's foreign-born population stood at 56,113, slightly over 14 percent of the state's total population. In Detroit, the city's 9,927 foreigners comprised over 47 percent of its population of 21,019. Michigan's ensuing development proved alluring to immigrants, and thousands more joined the stream of settlers headed to the state. By 1860, those of foreign birth (149,092) would make up over 20 percent of the state's population. Meanwhile, Detroit's immigrant population, although remaining a constant 47 percent of the total, jumped to 45,619. Of far greater significance for the state's native-born Protestant population was the rapid increase in the number of Catholics. In 1850, there were thirty-nine Catholic churches in Michigan. Within ten years, that number reached fifty-six. Detroit alone added three new churches between 1850 and 1862, raising the total number of Catholic churches in the city to five. By 1860, the *Catholic Almanac* was able to boast about a Catholic population of 85,000 in Michigan, out of a total state population of 749,113. Within the context of the rapid changes transforming Michigan and the pervasive fears about the very survival of American freedom, this burgeoning Catholic population would quickly become the target of a concerted Protestant backlash.[41]

In the minds of many native-born Protestants, particularly those of the Whig persuasion, Catholicism was equated with a host of evils. Above all else, it was considered to run counter to the republican heritage of the United States. Protestantism, the argument went, with its emphasis upon personal salvation, local congregational control, individual interpretation of the Bible, and equality in the eyes of God, defined and upheld American freedom and democracy. Catholicism, by contrast, with its entrenched hierarchy and feudal heritage, was autocratic, inhibited individual autonomy, and was based upon mysticism and ignorance. These characteristics supposedly marked Catholics as being long accustomed to subservience, as voting according to the dictates of church officials, and therefore as antithetical to the nation's republican institutions and to American freedom. This lack of independence, nativists contended, allowed the success of scheming politicians and pandering demagogues, who, in return for political favors, could always count on an ever growing and always solid bloc of Catholic votes. It did not help matters that Detroit's Catholic population was primarily composed of poor, unskilled, culturally distinct, largely illiterate, working-class Irish and Germans (many of whom worked in the state's emerging manufacturing/commercial sector), for whom a large number of native-born residents held nothing but disdain. Nor were native residents receptive to the increasingly assertive political behavior of this rapidly growing group. For many living in the turbulent milieu of midcentury Michigan, doing something about the "foreign problem" seemed like an obvious remedy for the unceasing sense of anxiety plaguing the state's citizenry.[42]

Nativism was certainly nothing new to Michigan in the 1850s. Throughout the late 1830s and early 1840s, nativism, predominantly within the ranks of the Whig Party, had been a staple in state politics. From 1843 to 1845, for example, Detroit's Catholic and Protestant communities battled over which translation of the Bible to use as a text in city schools. In February 1845, the school board compromised on the issue by allowing the reading of either the Protestant or the Catholic Bible by city teachers, a position that actually represented a victory for the Protestant community because most teachers were

Protestant. The same year, as this so-called Bible War drew to a close, a Native American ticket entered Detroit's city election, though it fared very poorly. The following year, a nativist newspaper, the *American,* briefly emerged in Ann Arbor. By the late 1840s, however, perhaps as the result of the emergence of the issue of slavery's extension, nativism died down in Michigan. With the presumed compromise settlement of that issue in 1850, nativism threatened to burst forth once again. But state Whigs, following the lead of the national party, largely abandoned nativism in a desperate attempt to boost the sagging fortunes of their party, and they openly courted foreign voters. In Detroit's mayoral election in 1851, the victorious Whig candidate for office, Zachariah Chandler, attended St. Patrick's Day celebrations, heaped praise upon the Irish for their role in the American Revolution, and joined a fund-raising drive for German liberty. Again in 1852, Chandler, this time in an unsuccessful bid for the governorship, and the unsuccessful Whig candidate for president, Winfield Scott, followed a similar strategy. As historian Ronald Formisano argued, "The humiliation of defeat sharpened the resentment of Whig nativists against foreigners and Catholics, and perhaps more than usual because the latter had spurned Whig offerings." The stage had thus been set for a revival of nativism in Michigan. That revival occurred in 1853.[43]

The initial spark that helped rekindle nativism emanated from a rather unexpected source: Detroit's Common Council. Confronted with the daily arrival of hundreds of newcomers and the bewildering and uncontrolled physical growth of the city, members of the council on January 3, 1853, proposed a number of amendments to the city's charter relating to public improvements. The amendments provided for street paving to be paid for by property taxes on adjacent land, the establishment of a city workhouse and almshouse, and the creation of a public waterworks and Board of Water Commissioners with the power to borrow up to $400,000 to replace the city's debt-ridden and outdated water system. Unexpectedly, a vocal opponent of the proposed measures quickly emerged—the bishop of the Catholic Diocese of Detroit, Peter Paul Lefevere.[44]

Lefevere's opposition to the proposed measures stemmed, in large part, from his church's ownership of vast tracts of property that, according to the amendments, would lose their tax-exempt status. In addition, Lefevere allegedly feared that the proposed almshouse would divert revenue away from the church's own charity hospital. Finally, the bishop charged that the new measures would burden Detroit's poor and that they were antirepublican. Clearly, Lefevere likely feared more than increased taxation and the loss of income. His subsequent actions suggest that he harbored apprehensions that the liberties of his church and its adherents were also in danger. Convinced that this was the case and bolstered by a belief that Catholics made up a majority of Detroit's population, Lefevere determined that the time had come for Catholics to make their stand.[45]

On January 5, a large assemblage of Detroiters gathered at the city hall to discuss the recent actions of the Common Council. Among the group were Lefevere and a large contingent of vocal followers. The opponents of the proposed charter amendments rapidly seized control of the meeting, howling down any who dared to speak in favor of the measures. Only Bishop Lefevere and other opponents of the measures were allowed to speak without interruption. Aware that a great opportunity was at hand, the bishop denounced the extravagance of city officials. Then—after railing against the burden of oppressive taxation that the city's poor, many of whom were Catholic, would have to shoulder as a result of the suggested improvements—he reminded his largely partisan audience of an even more abominable injustice imposed upon Catholics: being taxed for a public school system that they could not, in good conscience, use. To remedy that wrong, the prelate went on to demand a share of the state's school fund. Lefevere's speech exposed a raw nerve. In short order, the bishop's political assertiveness spawned an intense, nonpartisan, nativist backlash—a backlash that would have far-reaching political consequences. Catholics "have within the last week truly turned our city upside down," longtime Detroiter Elizabeth Stuart wrote her son from her Jefferson Avenue residence, "but they have begun too soon—In nothing do they shew [*sic*] their ignorance more than in their intire [*sic*] bewilderment in our Laws and People." "Our citizens, Dem[ocrat] and Whigg [*sic*], have come out nobly, . . ." she continued, "and now I believe, the great Battle has begun[;] all Europe is filled with it—and so shall we be." Nativism was about to wreak further havoc on Michigan's languishing political parties.[46]

After the January 5 meeting in Detroit, the school issue rapidly eclipsed the debate over city improvements and became the focal point around which ethnic conflict swirled. The crux of the problem for Detroit's Catholic community was, as "a Constitutional Catholic" wrote in a letter to the *Free Press,* that the state's common school system "is exclusive in its operation and that it is so designedly." In other words, Michigan Catholics were convinced that the state's public schools supported and espoused Protestant doctrines and that to accomplish this end, no stratagem would be overlooked. To make matters worse, as historian Leslie Tentler argued, "the poverty of most Catholics in this period meant that the attractions of state-supported free schools were considerable," a fact readily understood by Bishop Lefevere. The only fair remedy for the situation and the only way to ensure a proper education for the children of even the poorest of Catholics was for the state to turn over a portion of its school fund for the support of Catholic schools.[47]

To accomplish his goal, Lefevere launched simultaneous campaigns in Detroit, where an autonomous school system existed, and in Lansing. In Detroit, letters were written to the *Free Press,* and public meetings were held in an effort to disseminate the Catholic position. There is also some evidence to suggest that Detroit Catholics organized a boycott of the city's public schools. Of far greater consequence, however, was the battle waged in Lansing. Throughout the legislative session of 1853, state lawmakers were inundated with petitions signed by Catholic voters, requesting reform of the existing school law. Among the complaints articulated by one group of petitioners was that "notwithstanding [that] the constitution guarantees liberty of conscience to every citizen of our State, yet our Public school laws, compel us to violate our conscience, or deprive us unjustly of our share of the Public School funds, and also impose on us taxes for the support of schools, which, as a matter of conscience, we cannot allow our children to attend." Accordingly, they continued, "your petitioners . . . respectfully urge that the public school system for our State be based on [the] broad democratic principles of equal liberty to all, allowing freedom of conscience to the child, who also has a conscience, as well as to the instructor and parent." To guarantee a full airing of his views, Bishop Lefevere, together with a number of other prominent state Catholics, went to Lansing to lobby for the desired change and against the proposed revisions to Detroit's city charter.[48]

A great many residents were both disgusted and alarmed by the bishop's efforts. "The Catholics are giving us great trouble upon the school question," Elizabeth Stuart wrote to her daughter Kate "Bshp [*sic*] and Priests are all at Lansing." The elders and deacons of Stuart's congregation, the First Presbyterian Church of Detroit, also remonstrated against Lefevere's actions:

> We have received credible information and do veerily [*sic*] believe, that a project is entertained by the Romish priesthood in this State, acting doubtless, in obedience to the commands and suggestions of a foreign despotic sovereign, the object and interest whereof are none other but the subversion of the free system of schools which prevails in our State. . . . Indeed, so plain have the workings of the system made it [the alleged plot], that the tenets and discipline of that ambitious sect are at open war with all the ideas upon which

our Republican government is based; that the Managers of that sect
have found it necessary to direct their attacks at the very citadel of
Republican strength—the free education of youth and the conse-
quent independence of mind.

The common school system—the vehicle for disseminating and preserving
American values and traditions, the very cornerstone of the republic—was
under attack. As they had in the case of the Michigan Central Railroad, Michiganians had uncovered yet another new threat to their liberty and peace of
mind.[49]

On January 25, Jeremiah O'Callahan, a Catholic member of the state legislature from Detroit, introduced a bill granting relief to the Catholic petitioners. The bill was immediately referred to the Committee on Education,
where the majority of committee members opposed the measure. "Such
change," the committee's majority report asserted, "would interrupt the prosperity and progress of Primary Schools throughout the State, and would
introduce confusion and discord, in place of harmony and peace, and materially affect the interests of the rising generation." Disappointed, O'Callahan
offered a minority report in support of his bill. On February 12, a motion to
take up the bill was voted down, forty-eight to seventeen. "It was futile," stated
historian George Paré, "to prolong the contest against the dead-weight of misunderstanding and prejudice." Nevertheless, the school issue and the tensions that it had aroused persisted, especially in Detroit.[50]

Indeed, by late February and early March 1853, ethnic conflict had become so heated in Detroit that local partisan unity was no longer possible.
With a scapegoat for the anxiety plaguing state residents readily at hand, the
traditional partisan fealties of Detroiters fell by the wayside. Perceiving this
growing trend, Elizabeth Stuart presciently noted in a letter to her daughter, "Politics seem to be lost sight of, in the simple word Protestant." Hardest
hit by these shifting loyalties was Detroit's Democratic Party organization,
the traditional home of Detroit's Catholic community.[51]

On February 18, Detroit Democrats held their nominating convention
for the upcoming city election. Within a week's time, however, a number of
local Democrats, upset by the nominations of individuals from the regular
party machinery, put forward their own "independent" slate of candidates.
Decrying the fact that the regular party nominations were controlled by "enemies of city improvements and free schools," independents proclaimed
themselves "impelled by an imperative sense of duty, and a zealous devotion
to what we conceive to be the true interests of the city, and the true interests

of the democratic party [to nominate] on this ticket [only those] known to be decidedly in favor of city improvements and free schools." The Democratic split electrified city politics. "Our city is thrown into great excitement from the Bshp [sic] & Cath[olic] Priests having made a full nomination of men, pledged to them, to carry out their crusade against our Public Schools," Stuart wrote her son. Moreover, she continued,

> this has put Whiggery out of Michigan, & the cry now is Protestant-ism against Popery. The Whiggs [sic] say, you Dem[ocrats] put your best principled Men—Men who love our country & who value our institutions—we will bring all our support to elect your men. Politics & Pol[itical] Papers have undergone a thorough change—& I think for the better. How true, "God works in a mysterious way." He al-lowed these Cath[olics] to aid the Democracy, to so fully identify themselves with the most inveterate Anti-democratic body on Earth ... then confounded their council by giving them up, to work de-struction (we believe on themselves).

The timing of the school issue and the ensuing Democratic apostasy could not have been worse for the state's battered political organizations. Weak-ened by public distrust and apathy and fragmented by the nonpartisan anti-railroad/antimonopoly movement, Michigan's political structure was further disrupted by the groundswell of nativism in early 1853.[52]

As one might expect, Detroit Democrats desperately tried to minimize the tear in their party's fabric. Bemoaning the current state of affairs, a corre-spondent to the *Free Press* railed against the "independent" ticket and labeled it a "political monstrosity!" "Those disorganizers," the angry writer contin-ued, "will probably defeat a part, and the best part, of the democratic ticket." Accordingly, the *Free Press,* though in favor of city improvements and main-taining the current school system, announced that it would, "in good faith, support the regular democratic ticket." The paper did, however, acknowl-edge that a division existed, and it agreed to print both electoral tickets. For their part, supporters of the independent ticket justified their actions by pointing to the allegedly tyrannical designs of Bishop Lefevere and his overt attempt to manipulate and control the Democratic Party for his own malevo-lent purposes. "The democratic party proscribe no man for his country or re-ligion," a supporter of the independent cause reassured the readers of the *Free Press,* "but when a Catholic Bishop descends to the political arena, and undertakes to seize the machinery of the democratic party to carry out his measures, it is time for protest, and, if necessary, for rebellion against caucuses thus controlled, and especially is that the case, if . . . the Bishop is a whig." Indeed, for many independents, the approaching election assumed millennial importance. "Popery," lamented Elizabeth Stuart, "with all its bitter deadly animosity is arrayed against Protestantism."[53]

The municipal election on March 7, 1853, was a complete victory for the independent ticket. Only in Detroit's Irish Catholic stronghold, the Eighth Ward, did the regular ticket manage to obtain a majority. Yet even there, the Democratic majority "plummeted from its normal landslide proportions." Surveying the election results, the *Free Press* ruefully noted that "party trammels, in this election, were entirely broken over. Not less than two thousand democrats voted the independent city ticket. . . . Such widespread defection is not a result without a cause. . . . The democratic party is strong in this city, but with such work it will not take long to make it weak and powerless." Elizabeth Stuart, by contrast, reveled in the triumph and wrote her son, "Our election is over, & we have obtained a most triumphant Victory over Jesuitism. Our Free Schools & City improvements, & Americanism are yet ours, & No to the Man or party, who would dare weaken that which God has so manifestly sustained. Our majority was 1900!! We can begin to see the goodness of God in scattering or annihilating the Whig party. They came unitedly, strongly to sustain a Ticket whose every man was a Democrat—yet American in heart." Americanism and liberty had prevailed over partisanship.[54]

Although partisan walls had been assailed and breached and the broad-based independent movement had emerged victorious, nativist hostility did not dissipate after the election. On the contrary, those within the independent movement consciously sought to keep the Catholic threat before the electorate. "You are right in thinking the Catholic question an important one," Stuart wrote her daughter, "it is the only one, which should at this moment occupy the American mind. They for the last twenty years have been moving all their powers to enslave our beautiful Republic, but they have gone too fast. . . . Every Christian has to buckle on his Armour & keep it bright, the Battle of the Lord of Hosts has begun."[55]

There is also evidence to suggest that the ripples from Detroit's municipal election spread widely throughout the state. Newspaper discussions of the school issue, of the activities of Bishop Lefevere, and of the independent ticket were widespread. Many state papers, especially those of the Whig persuasion, celebrated the independent victory in Detroit as a triumph of light over darkness, of good over evil. And although they cannot be directly linked to the heavily nativist independent ticket in Detroit, a number of similar independent tickets emerged in local elections across the state in the spring of 1853.[56]

Michigan's Catholic community did not sit idly by as nativist attacks continued. In April 1853, a new newspaper, the *Detroit Catholic Vindicator*, began publication. The paper's express purpose was to counter the often biased and hostile reporting of other papers. Deeply concerned about the unsettled state of Michigan's politics and the burgeoning and overt anti-Catholicism rampant in the state, the *Vindicator* warned its readership that the creation of "a Protestant party is not altogether improbable. The disorganized Whigs are ready for anything. And the Democrats—the party to which the Catholic citizens have clung for years—they seem equally ready for the coalition against us." The *Vindicator* was not the only paper worried about such a scenario. "May Heaven preserve our State and country," the Democratic *Grand Rapids Enquirer* pleaded, "from the horrors which will darken our land when religious prejudices shall be the controlling element in our political strifes."[57]

Although nativism never became "the controlling element" in state politics, it—like the antirailroad/antimonopoly movement—did irreparable harm to the state's established political parties, and it would continue to disrupt and unsettle Michigan politics throughout the remainder of 1853 and into 1854.

The traditional partisan loyalties of Michiganians were further strained during these crucial years by yet another divisive political issue: temperance—an issue that was, in numerous respects, closely linked in the minds of many with the nativism simultaneously sweeping the state. Temperance was a deep-seated and ongoing concern for many residents of Michigan by mid-century. The movement did, however, gain new strength and political clout in the early 1850s; the rapid pace of change experienced by the citizenry during this period—along with a resurgent nativism, a development that emphasized a long-standing association between immigrants and intemperance—had much to do with that groundswell.

Proponents of temperance in antebellum Michigan, as in other states, were motivated by different concerns. For many among the state's large New England–New York Protestant population who were predisposed to a millennialist outlook, sin such as intemperance, with its associated social problems (poverty, neglect, abuse, disease, homelessness, prostitution, and crime), had to be eradicated in order to pave the way for Christ's Second Coming and the creation of his Kingdom of Peace. "The millennium," Lyman Beecher warned a meeting of the Detroit Temperance Society in 1845, "could never come while such an evil was in the world. . . . One of the signs [that] God yet intends to redeem the world is that the destruction of this very greatest evil that opposes the progress of the gospel has already commenced." Others were drawn to the temperance cause because of their benevolent desire to improve society by emancipating individual potential and facilitating personal fulfillment. America, it seemed to many, was witnessing an "epidemic of alcoholism." Indeed, the evidence shows that such fears were not completely unfounded. In 1830, Americans over the age of fourteen consumed an estimated 9.5 gallons of hard liquor per person and another 30.3 gallons of hard cider and other assorted intoxicants, bringing the total consumption of pure alcohol to 7.1 gallons per person. Taverns and bars proliferated. By 1860, Detroit (a city of roughly 45,000) housed 400 to 500 bars and saloons. Caught up in an environment characterized by tumultuous change and accompanying social dislocation, many Michiganians viewed alcohol as a tangible cause of their overriding sense of anxiety. Tangled within the skein of the varied motivations and concerns that propelled temperance activists was a nativist undercurrent that inextricably linked drinking and its associated social ills with the burgeoning foreign and increasingly Catholic (and largely working-class) population residing within the state.[58]

Although they all agreed that drinking needed to be curtailed, advocates of temperance did not always concur on either their ultimate goal or the most efficacious means of accomplishing their ends. What is clear is that, during the 1840s, temperance forces increasingly shifted away from a policy of moral suasion and instead turned to legislative mechanisms. In 1845, temperance advocates in Michigan succeeded in obtaining a local option law from the state legislature. Under the law, the people were permitted to determine by ballot at upcoming township or municipal elections whether licenses for the sale of liquor would be granted by their town or city. The measure, however, proved unenforceable (vendors simply continued to operate without licenses, as legal officials were powerless to impose penalties other than fines), and as a result, voter interest in the licensing question rapidly waned.[59]

In response to the clear failure of the state's licensing system to curb the consumption of alcohol in Michigan, protemperance delegates to the state's constitutional convention in 1850 brought the issue before the assemblage. Despite being inundated with petitions requesting a provision in the new constitution to prohibit the manufacture and sale of alcohol, the delegates opted merely to prohibit the legislature from passing any act authorizing the granting of licenses for the sale of liquor. The overall effect of this provision, as Ronald Formisano noted, was to "obfuscate . . . . the temperance drive for the next three years." The obfuscation resulted from the fact that some delegates to the convention clearly believed that no licensing meant no liquor, whereas others believed that it was an endorsement of the open sale of liquor. Within this clouded milieu, state political managers successfully kept the temperance issue out of the limelight until late 1852.[60]

The passage of the now famous prohibitionary Maine Law by the Pine Tree State in 1852 revived the flagging spirits of Michigan's temperance crusaders. Rapidly, a movement to implement a similar law in Michigan gained momentum. A circular addressed to the "Friends of Temperance" stated the case succinctly:

> We regard such a law, in its theory and operation, "holy and just," and will be an instrument in our hands in which we may smite with a deadly blow the monster intemperance, and forever rid the community from its ravages. . . . Let such a law be enacted and faithfully executed in this State, and every department of industry, trade and commerce, will be benefitted. All classes especially the poor laboring classes will feel its salutary effects. Our taxes will be reduced. Pauperism, crime, and the various forms of misery will be greatly lessened. . . . Life will be more effectually protected. Every other moral enterprise will receive fresh stimulous [sic] and encouragement from success in this. The good order of society, reverence for the law, the hopes of humanity, and the interest of religion will be advanced, and in short, almost innumerable blessings will flow from it.

Petitions on behalf of such a law crisscrossed the state in anticipation of the upcoming 1853 legislative session. And in his annual address to the legislature, Democratic governor Robert McClelland added his support to the cause by acknowledging that "the existing law has not answered the expectations of its advocates, and is generally not enforced" and by urging the legislators to consult public opinion and to adopt a "well matured" law "adapted to the condition of the state."[61]

The petition drive proved to be extraordinarily effective. By January 20, petitions bearing some seventy thousand signatures arrived in Lansing. This concerted effort did not go unheeded. Oakland County representative Orrin Poppleton, a Democrat, noted to his colleagues, "The strongest argument which can be presented for prompt and decisive action by this legislature, is the enormous array of names here presented by the petitions." Although the state legislature followed Poppleton's advice and took prompt action on the matter, passing a Michigan variant of the Maine Law prohibiting the manufacture and sale of alcohol in the state by a vote of 57 to 12 in the house and

23 to 9 in the senate, it did not act decisively. In a blatant attempt to scuttle the proposed prohibition bill, opponents attached to it a provision requiring that the measure be submitted to a popular referendum in June. If approved by the voters, the law would go into effect in December; if defeated, the law was to take effect in 1870. "I regret," complained a Lansing correspondent for the *Free Press*, " . . . that the Arabian alchemists, who in their search for gold, are supposed to have discovered the mode by which ardent spirits are to be procured by distillation, had not fathomed the depth of man's appetite, and the true secret by which his ingenuity might be limited. As the bill now stands, it is clearly unconstitutional." "The action of the Legislature on this question," the *Jackson American Citizen* sadly pronounced, "is the veeriest [*sic*] anomaly, in legislation, shown to an intelligent people."[62]

Historians have gone to great lengths to cast the legislative vote on the law as a partisan struggle between Whigs (who generally voted in favor of the bill) and Democrats (who tended to oppose it). This assessment, however, fails to take into account the muddled nature of the proposed law. It is likely, for instance, that many who supported the temperance cause voted against the bill because of its questionable constitutionality. The act's unconstitutionality allegedly stemmed from two sources: first, a provision in the act that authorized township boards to grant a permit to one individual sanctioning the sale of alcohol for medicinal and mechanical purposes (a stipulation that many believed ran counter to the 1850 constitution's restriction against the state's passage of laws authorizing the granting of licenses for the sale of ardent spirits), and second, the mandate that the measure be submitted to a popular vote, which was construed as an unconstitutional delegation of legislative authority to the people. Moreover, the act of voting for the bill did not necessarily represent a clear statement on temperance. Some supporters obviously believed that they were voting to prohibit alcohol, whereas others sought merely to strike the pose of promoting a popular cause while really intending to undermine it. Given this situation, it is impossible to draw any firm conclusions about the legislative vote.[63]

In spite of (or perhaps because of) the law's shortcomings, the measure found widespread support on both ends of the political spectrum—further evidence of the porous condition of Michigan's political parties by 1853. Throughout the spring of that year, supporters of the law waged a vigorous campaign to ensure a victory for their cause at the polls in June. "Who cometh to the rescue?" asked the *Grass Lake Public Sentiment*, "armed with a little weapon, harmless and inoffensive in itself, but mighty in the ballot box, to effect the destruction of this beast." "Come ye then to the rescue!" the paper urged its readers, "and let the twentieth day of June, be a day of conquest; and as the sun, on that day shall go down . . . the lightening's [*sic*] trail-way shall shake from its wings of fire, the glorious news that Michigan is redeemed, purified, saved! that the people with the majesty of Deity, have spoken, let there be a Maine Law." Not everyone, of course, agreed with the *Public Sentiment*. In a letter to the *Free Press*, someone identified as "a Washtenaw Farmer" wrote that the law "is anti-republican and unconstitutional." Even the despotic governments of Europe, the correspondent argued, had "never been carried to the extent of dictating to men what they shall eat or drink." Such opinions, however, appear to have been in the minority. Far more common were the attitudes expressed in the following resolutions endorsed by the delegates to a temperance meeting in the Kent County settlement of Vergennes: "Whereas, we believe that the traffic in intoxicating liquor as a beverage, is the greatest evil that is now endured by the Free States, therefore . . . Resolved, that we heartily approve of the general principles of the Michigan Maine Law, and that we will use our utmost endeavors to secure its sanction at the upcoming election."[64]

Despite the issue's obvious importance to the state's residents, discussion of the Maine Law did not completely "dominate . . . Michigan politics and newspapers," as contended by historians Bruce Tap and Ronald Formisano. Other concerns, such as railroad matters and the school debate, often competed with the Maine Law for attention, and, in many cases, they succeeded in supplanting it as the predominant topic of the day. "We are all . . . in a hubbub," wrote Elizabeth Stuart, "about Main [*sic*] Liquor Laws—General R.R. Laws—and selling old Pres[byterian] Ch[urch]."[65]

On June 20, Michiganians went to the polls and overwhelmingly endorsed the Maine Law and its early implementation by a vote of 40,449 to 23,054, with only two of the thirty-six counties for which returns are available voting against the law. While the totals clearly represented an overwhelming victory for the measure, one must nevertheless proceed cautiously when evaluating the election results. Arguably, most of those who cast their votes in favor of the measure did so in the belief that they were voting for immediate prohibition in Michigan. Still, it is possible, given the law's questionable constitutionality, that some individuals voted for it as a means of blunting an obviously popular and increasingly effective temperance movement. Likewise, dissenting votes cannot simply be construed as antitemperance votes. It seems logical to conclude that some protemperance individuals voted against the statute for the same reason—its doubtful constitutionality. Further, statewide voter turnout numbers suggest there was a measure of confusion in reference to the law. Only 63,503 Michiganians bothered to cast their ballots in the special election. That figure was nearly 25 percent lower less than the 82,939 who voted in the 1852 presidential election—an election in which slightly fewer than 75 percent of those eligible actually participated—suggesting that the all-consuming interest in the election described by Formisano and others has been exaggerated. Even more interesting are the local returns. In Washtenaw County, for instance, in the heart of the state's so-called burned-over district, turnout was only 84 percent of the 1852 county vote. Perhaps Washtenaw County voters were so certain of the law's passage—over two-thirds of the votes cast were in favor of the measure—that they did not bother to go to the polls. Yet another possibility is that confusion over the law kept people at home. By contrast, residents of Detroit, the site of recent nativist-tinged elections and the home of the anti–Maine Law *Free Press,* turned out in force for the election, casting 94.4 percent of the number of votes tallied in the 1852 election.[66]

In spite of their electoral success, temperance advocates were not content to rest upon their laurels. Painfully aware of the ineffectiveness of earlier temperance laws in the state, they organized local vigilance committees, known as the Carson League, throughout the summer and fall of 1853. In each local chapter, membership dues were to be used to defray the costs of prosecuting those who broke the new liquor law. By December, Detroit's Carson League was ready to enforce the measure. When a local Democratic justice named B. Rush Bagg declared the law invalid on the grounds that it conflicted with the state constitution's restrictions against the delegation of legislative power and those barring the passage of licensing laws authorizing the sale of alcohol, the stage was set for a showdown. Confrontation was avoided, however, because of the actions of the state supreme court.[67]

On February 1, 1854, in the case of *People v. Collins,* the court split evenly over the constitutionality of the state's Maine Law. As many had anticipated, four justices—Warner Wing, Abner Pratt, Joseph Copeland, and Samuel Douglass—ruled that the June referendum had been a delegation of legislative power to the people and was therefore unconstitutional. Among the most interesting opinions delivered (and by far the most extensive) was that of Democratic justice Pratt. The result of allowing the citizenry the final say on statutes, he argued, would subvert republican government and replace it with a "collective democracy, the most uncertain and dangerous of all governments." He went further than the other dissenting justices in attacking the law, ruling the act's provision prohibiting the manufacture of liquor void. It was a "disgraceful" and "damnable doctrine," Pratt complained, to prevent the manufacture of intoxicants merely because the product might be abused. Even a tyrannical English Parliament, he chided, had never "committed such an outrage on private property." But Pratt saved his worst invective for the reformers who had pushed for such a law. The law, he wrote,

> is the mere thunder of canting hypocrites and political demagogues; the most detestable of all beings that ever infested a civil government. The world has never, at any stage of it, been reformed by oppressive penal laws, which are destructive of liberty and the right of property. And a legislative body might just as well undertake, by a despotic penal enactment, to chain down the winds of heaven to prevent their blowing, as to compel the American people, by such enactments, to be sober, moral, or religious.

This decision—along with two others by the court, *People v. Hoffman* and *People v. Hawley*, in which the court seemed to approve the law—left the "status of the law murky." The *Collins* case, which fell under the category of "questions reserved," was then referred back to Judge Douglass of the Wayne County Circuit Court, who held the state law to be unconstitutional. The *Collins* ruling, the *Adrian Watchtower* complained, was nothing better than a "studied fizzle decision." Its advocates now thoroughly frustrated, the "temperance enthusiasm," as Ronald Formisano wrote, "came together with other impulses in early 1854" to reorder state politics forever.[68]

Of all the political impulses coursing through mid-nineteenth-century Michigan, political antislavery has long garnered the lion's share of attention from historians. According to these scholars, the passage of the Kansas-Nebraska Act (with its explicit abrogation of the Missouri Compromise of 1820 and its prohibition of slavery in the region) in early 1854 loosed a tidal wave of antislavery repugnance among a citizenry already indignant about the passage of the Fugitive Slave Act of 1850. This antislavery hostility, the argument goes, rent traditional political loyalties asunder and led directly to the creation of the Republican Party at Jackson on July 6, 1854. Ironically, however, although assuming that this antipathy to slavery had a constant presence in antebellum Michigan, proponents of this traditional interpretation telescope time and avoid discussing the period between 1851 and the passage of the Kansas-Nebraska Act in 1854. This oversight occurs for a very obvious reason. Between 1851 and 1853, antislavery activity virtually disappeared from the state, and issues such as the general railroad law, temperance, and nativism came to the fore. As a result, as discussed previously, the state's political parties were in disarray and decay even before the Kansas-Nebraska Act, and antislavery became an issue with state voters. The resurgent antislavery movement of 1854, though undoubtedly very strong, was merely one of a number of diverse political movements operating in Michigan on the eve of the state's political realignment.[69]

Even more problematic for the purveyors of this traditional view of antebellum Michigan politics is their tendency to overemphasize opposition to slavery on moral grounds and their failure to differentiate between abolitionist sentiment and antislavery/antisouthernism. The evidence does, indeed, suggest that unadulterated moral hostility to slavery seems to have been more prevalent in Michigan than in many other northern states. For instance, many prominent Michigan politicians—a number of whom would assume leadership roles within the radical faction of the newly formed Republican Party, including Austin Blair, Zachariah Chandler, and Jacob M. Howard—were known as outspoken critics of the institution of slavery on moral grounds. Moreover, as historian John Quist pointed out, "notwithstanding their defeats at the polls [under the guise of the Liberty Party], political abolitionists in Michigan obtained a higher percentage of the vote than did their counterparts in any state outside of New England." Nevertheless, abolitionism always remained a minority position within the state. Even Michigan's Libertyites, Quist mentioned elsewhere, recognized the limited appeal of abolitionism and thus incorporated antislavery extension and anti–Slave Power doctrines into their political discourse in order to enhance their voter base. As in the remainder of the North, antislavery/antisouthern hostilities, or Free-Soil ideology, assumed much greater importance among the voters of Michigan than did moral aversion to slavery.[70]

Simply put, the Free-Soil argument held that northern society offered Americans unlimited opportunity for political democracy, social mobility, and economic security. Proponents of this view credited free labor for the growth and prosperity of the North. Free-Soil theorists further believed that the founding fathers had also understood the differences between free-labor society and slave-labor society and that they had intended, through the U.S. Constitution, to separate the national government from the institution of slavery and to prevent the institution's spread; now, however, the machinations of an organized conspiracy of slave owners were obstructing the original intent of the founders. In the Free-Soil imagination—one shaped by the popular literature of the day, such as *Uncle Tom's Cabin*, which was published in 1852—this Slave Power or Slaveocracy headed an aristocratic, backward, un-American society whose reliance on slavery degraded labor's value and perpetuated ignorance, stagnation, and social immobility for most southern whites. "The Slave States, all, have territory not occupied by Slaves but by poor whites," former Libertyite candidate for president and Michigan resident James G. Birney wrote to Horace Mann. Sadly, he continued, "these whites are generally the poorest of the poor—the most ignorant of the ignorant. The Slaveholders . . . get into the Legislature and all public offices; [and as a result] the *Legislature* is for *slaves* and not for advancing the improvement of *freemen*." Even more worrisome, Free-Soilers asserted, the Slave Power was now orchestrating plans to control national politics and to ensure slavery's expansion into the territories. If slavery were allowed to expand into the territories, the Free-Soil argument ran, free labor would necessarily be excluded; thus, the nation's future development would replicate that of the stagnant, aristocratic South, and the Slaveocracy's national political might would swell as new slave states ultimately formed and joined the Union. To protect the nation from such a fate, proponents of this view sought to stop slavery's spread into the territories, to preserve free soil, and thus to prevent the North's enslavement at the hands of the Slave Power. A call to arms issued by Michigan's Free Democrats, the official name by which the state's Free-Soilers were known, at the end of 1852 put the matter plainly: "We cordially invite the co-operation . . . of all who believe that the time has fully come when slavery is to be resisted; and the Slave Power shorn of all its influence in the National councils; When the doctrine that Freedom is the NATIONAL sentiment, and slavery the sectional, should be as fully recognized as it was by the fathers of our country and the framers of our Constitution."[71]

At the heart of this Free-Soil ideology stood the concept of free labor. Indeed, in the end, the appeal of free labor would prove invaluable in attracting a politically and socially diverse populace to the Free-Soil platform of the Republican Party. Among the farmers, small entrepreneurs, and craftspeople drawn to the Free-Soil argument, historians such as Eric Foner have discerned "an inordinate desire to improve." These individuals allegedly valued social mobility, opportunity, and economic independence above all else and believed that only in a free society, one unencumbered by slavery, was such freedom possible. Although generally correct in these assertions, Foner and others tend to assume a promarket, commercial mentality among Free-Soil constituents. But such a broad assumption in relation to antebellum Michigan, the birthplace of the Republican Party, is perilously fallacious. To his credit, Foner has since reached a similar conclusion, confessing in a new introduction for his book *Free Soil, Free Labor, Free Men* that "'free labor,' . . . was presented as a straightforward, unitary concept, with little sense of how different Americans might have infused it with substantially different meanings." It was precisely this ability to invoke different meanings from the shared experience of not being enslaved that gave free labor its power as a political symbol in Michigan—a power that allowed such diverse individuals as former Democrat Kinsley Bingham, former Whigs Zachariah Chandler and Jacob Howard, and former Free-Soilers Isaac Christiancy and Austin Blair to find common ground in 1854.[72]

That Michiganians of many political stripes, pounded as they were by ongoing socioeconomic transformation and uncertainty, could find solace in the Free-Soil argument cannot be denied. For instance, in June 1849, the Whig state convention, meeting in Ann Arbor, adopted the following resolution aimed at preserving liberty in the United States: "Let the soil of our extensive domain be ever kept free for the hardy pioneers of our land, and the oppressed and banished of other lands, seeking homes of comfort and fields of enterprise in the New World." Republican congressman and former Whig William Howard later echoed this refrain in an 1858 speech before the Philomanthesian Society of Middlebury College. "Our public domain," Howard insisted, "constitutes at once a vast fund for public improvement and a boundless field for individual effort. It invites to intelligent labor; and in return for that high estate of cultivation which freemen alone can produce, promises to yield a bountiful support for a thousand millions of happy people. But to do this it must be worked not skimmed; neither must it be poisoned by the tread of any slave nor bedewed by the reluctant sweat and scalding tears of unrequited toil." Similarly, in an 1850 speech in the U.S. House of Representatives defending the admission of California as a free state, freshman congressman Kinsley Bingham spoke on behalf of the liberties of his constituents. "Coming, as I do, from the laboring classes," he asserted, "I should have failed to discharge my duty if I had not spoken and acted when I thought their interests in jeopardy." Bingham continued, "As a Representative of free white laboring men, I mean to defend their rights . . . the free soil of the country must be preserved as the inheritance of the free laborer and his children." Though the Whig convention, William Howard, and the Democratic Bingham all vowed to defend the freedoms of Michigan's citizenry, it is clear that the preceding statements reflect very different understandings of what freedom meant. The Whig pronouncements, with their emphasis upon the need to preserve free soil as an arena for "enterprise" and as a "boundless field for individual effort," hinted at a worldview in which freedom was equated with liberation and opportunity for mobility—a worldview very much akin to the one originally attributed to free-labor theorists by Foner.

Bingham's speech, however, is suggestive of a dissimilar understanding of freedom. Kinsley Bingham had made a name for himself in Michigan as a successful pioneer farmer in Livingston County's Green Oak Township and as a staunch antibank/antimonopoly Democratic state legislator. For Bingham, the western territories represented a reserve of land upon which future generations of American farmers could build the kind of independent lifestyle he had known in Michigan; only by keeping the western territories free could freedom—that is, an autonomous, independent way of life—be maintained. Despite their disagreement over the exact meaning of freedom, however, both Bingham and his Whig counterparts recognized that free soil was essential if freedom was to survive in the United States. Endowed, like the other political movements discussed earlier in this chapter, with an all-inclusive and nonpartisan message, the Free-Soil movement further eroded Michigan's traditional party structure.[73]

Throughout late 1852 and 1853, however, the Free-Soil issue virtually disappeared from the state political scene. In fact, not until Congress began debating the proposed Kansas-Nebraska Bill in January 1854 would Free-Soilism emerge as a major political force in Michigan. As news reached the state that a revised version of the bill would repeal the Missouri Compromise of 1820 and its almost sacred demarcation between slave and free territory, a groundswell of public indignation rapidly surfaced among the state's already agitated citizenry. The *Detroit Daily Democrat* laid the issue plainly before the people: "Will the North quietly submit to be tricked and wheedled out of this free territory? Are the compromises only to be regarded when they advance the interests of slavery?" The answer had already been provided. On February 13, the citizens of Albion staged an anti-Nebraska rally. Five days later, a similar rally was held in Detroit. Other gatherings quickly followed in Kalamazoo, Dexter, Jackson, Leoni, Pontiac, and another in Detroit on June 7. The March 3 Pontiac meeting was typical. If the proposed bill became law, the assembled citizens declared, "a vast domain, solemnly dedicated to Freedom and free labor will be opened to and cursed by human slavery." The meeting then proceeded to denounce "as Traitors to Freedom those Northern Senators who voted for the Nebraska Bill." Finally, the assemblage concluded by warning that "as the slave holding states of this Union have thrown down the gauntlet by uniting and making common cause against freedom and Free labor, we accept the challenge and henceforth we will wage unceasing war against slavery in all climes, in all forms, without respect to the color of its victims." After adopting a set of like resolutions, the Jackson gathering, also held on March 3, added the following evocative pronouncement: "We do now here without distinction of party, as one man, utter and record what we mean to be an indignant and emphatic protest against the passage of this bill."[74]

Notwithstanding the widespread and vocal opposition to the Kansas-Nebraska Bill, Free-Soil agitation remained merely one part of the broader political current flowing through Michigan in early 1854. The public outcry for a general railroad law maintained its vigor and continued unabated into the new year. Not surprisingly, the *Grass Lake Public Sentiment* continued to promote the cause. The action of the Michigan Central in the conspiracy case, the paper intoned, was "a swindle in its character, more criminal in its consequences more destructive to the happiness of those against whom it was practiced, than that of the celebrated and much talked of Nebraska swindle, according to the most desperate, hair-brained [*sic*] conception of the most wild, hot-headed, passion-steeped Free Soiler in the state of Michigan." And as mentioned already, agitation over temperance came to a head in the early months of 1854, culminating in the February 1854 debate surrounding the state supreme court's subversion of Michigan's attempt to enact the Maine Law. Moreover, nativism also continued to stir the passions of voters, especially in Detroit. On February 28, Jacob Howard delivered a critical lecture on Jesuitism before a large and appreciative crowd at Detroit's Young Men's Hall. After tracing the history of the Jesuit order, he demonstrated, according to one enthralled listener, "that their entire spirit was utterly incompatible with civil or religious liberty." Elizabeth Stuart, for one, had no problem reconciling her nativism with her anti-Nebraska feelings, writing to her son, "I believe it [the Kansas-Nebraska Bill] is designed for this dreadful swarm of foreign Catholics which have come in among us."[75]

That these new political movements adversely affected Michigan's Whig and Democratic organizations is indisputable. Indeed, party disruption was so rampant that as early as September 1852, Battle Creek resident A. D. P. Van Buren confidently asserted in a letter to a friend, "Nothing in particular left of the old parties—they have disbanded." "Old party lines [are] forgotten," the *Niles Republican* similarly maintained in April 1854; " . . . whigs [war] against whigs, and democrats against democrats." The net effect of this disaffection was the creation of a highly fluid and volatile political environment in the state. "I see men joining hands at this time," Asa Whitney noted in a letter to Sen. Alpheus Felch, "who have been political opponents for years, and on the other hand giving the cold shoulder to others who have placed them in the position they now occupy." Obviously bothered by this trend, Whitney added that "such associations cannot be lasting as there is too much selfishness in their composition. Time, however, will devolve all, and I look with some little anxiety for the result." Clearly, then, by early 1854, suspicion and political disillusionment in Michigan were at flood tide, as residents desperately cast about for something solid to which to anchor themselves. Michiganians everywhere increasingly concluded that the existing political parties were no longer dependable moorings during this tempestuous time.[76]

5

"Misfortunes Make Strange Bedfellows"

The Creation and Consolidation of the
Republican Coalition in Michigan, 1854–1860

BY THE beginning of 1854, Michigan's Jacksonian party system strained under the weight of voter apathy and mistrust. The times, the *Lapeer County Democrat* lamented, were marked by "sham Democracy, sham Christianity, sham humanity, sham benevolence, sham delicacy, sham virtue, and sham everything else." These were days, the paper continued, typified by "time serving, fawning, creeping, [and] crouching." In spite of such disenchantment, however, Michigan's Democratic and Whig Parties limped forward, desperately struggling to retain the loyalty of their partisans. Faced with a party system that no longer served their needs—one that had seemingly left American freedom exposed to the ravages of corruption, avarice, and grasping power—and requiring the reassurance that political conflict imparted, Michiganians abandoned, in ever growing numbers and for increasingly prolonged periods of time, both the Whig and Democratic Parties and converged upon the profusion of long ignored or newly created political movements emerging throughout the state. "In a republican government," the indomitable Free-Soiler Kinsley Bingham argued, "agitation is as necessary as tranquility is dangerous. . . . To keep alive the patriotic feelings and pure motives which actuated the founders of this republic, the minds of men must be led

118

to excitement and the necessary commotions naturally arising result in party spirit and political strife. . . . It is the life blood of our country penetrating and perforating her every part, giving vigor to her strength and momentum to her advancement." That was not to say, Bingham hastened to add, that party systems were to remain static. On the contrary, "questions which at one time may have [been] leading topics the issues of which may have threatened some dire calamity to the nation, may give place to other and more essential subjects or have been forgotten in the hum of political excitement. Without this soul-moving power to drain the dregs of corruption which would otherwise clog the machinery of our government, we might like many other nations before us, have a melancholy history." All too many Michigan residents believed the nation would face just such a melancholy future if something was not immediately done to reinvigorate the political system by reorienting it toward new issues. "Agitate the waters of the political Bethsady [*sic*]," the *Lapeer County Democrat* strenuously urged its readership, "until they shall again possess healing virtues."[1]

Although political agitation was certainly on the increase by 1853 and into 1854, the participants in the various political movements sweeping the state recognized that the diffuse nature of these movements was an impediment to accomplishing their true goal: the preservation of American liberty in a rapidly changing and unpredictable world. Accordingly, prominent individuals within the various movements, many of whom were active in more than one, began working to fuse these disparate efforts into broader-based and more effective political coalitions.

Given the parochial roots of many of the emerging political issues, most of these fusion efforts, such as the one described earlier between Detroit's Whig and Democratic nativists in 1853, were undertaken primarily at the local level. This trend continued into the spring elections of 1854, which were marked by numerous local fusion initiatives. In Detroit, for instance, the Independent coalition of the previous year, goaded further by the supreme court's recent anti–Maine Law decision, succeeded in electing its mayoral candidate. Noticeably absent from the debates surrounding that contest was any discussion of the Kansas-Nebraska Act. Similarly, in Ann Arbor, a ticket of anti-Democratic "fusionists" dedicated to the Maine Law and to free schools emerged victorious. Fusion movements of this type achieved success in Berrien County, in the town of Constantine in St. Joseph County, and in Grand Rapids.[2]

Despite such local successes, however, many Michiganians clearly recognized that statewide fusion was imperative. Indeed, the experiences of those engaged in the antirailroad/antimonopoly, nativist, and temperance movements taught them that their problems went well beyond local control and that only a concerted statewide effort could succeed in dislodging the self-interested and destructive demagogues in Lansing from their entrenched positions. For Free-Soilers, statewide efforts were indispensable if there was to be any hope of counteracting the machinations of the Slave Power. Presented as they were in early 1854 with a political climate that afforded an unprecedented opportunity for furthering their agendas, many of the leaders of these various crusades stood poised to embrace some form of statewide organization that would enable them to accomplish their distinct goals. Two questions, however, remained unanswered. Who would take the lead in creating this fusion movement? And to what degree would the new organization promote the diffuse political agendas of its constituent base?

The first tentative steps toward creating this fusion movement were taken, as might have been expected, by the state's Free Democrats, the official name by which the state's Free-Soilers were known. Ever since their inception as a party in 1848, Michigan's Free-Soilers had focused upon coalition building, occasionally with great success, as a means of electing men committed to Free-Soil ideals. Fusion was therefore a proven political strategy for the movement, and Free-Soil leaders had become quite experienced at coalition building. Beyond such practical considerations, however, there was yet another reason why Free-Soilers took the lead in creating a fusion movement: the Free-Soil issue was the only matter broad enough for all of Michigan's disenchanted voters to rally around. Nativism, though clearly an important subject in many portions of the state, resonated primarily with Michigan's Whigs and, in most cases, drew little support from those of Democratic proclivities. Similarly, support for temperance, although the cause was more nonpartisan than nativism, was strongest among Whig constituencies. The same could not be said of the antirailroad/antimonopoly movement. Here was an issue that clearly cut across party lines and around which one might construct an anti-Democratic coalition. Such, however, would not be the case. Despite intense public interest in the issue and despite its nonpartisan appeal, it, too, proved to be an inadequate framework for a fusion movement. From the perspective of those advocating fusion, the problem was that, because of widespread popular hostility toward monopolistic railroad corporations and popular sentiment in favor of a general railroad law, state Democratic leaders had begun to make overtures toward the antirailroad/antimonopoly constituency—pardoning the Jackson County alleged conspirators, calling for the passage of a general railroad law, and so forth—thus rendering the movement ineffective as a means of maximizing anti-Democratic hostility.[3]

The Free-Soil issue suffered from no such handicaps. As in the case of antirailroad/antimonopoly sentiment, Free-Soilism, with its determination to protect freedom from the onslaught of the Slave Power, transcended partisan boundaries, appealing to both former Whigs and Democrats (though for very different reasons, as discussed elsewhere). Additionally, Free-Soil doctrines already drew a great deal of support from the same constituency that provided the bulk of the support for temperance and nativism—the Whigs. And because it spoke to the same broad concern as that expressed by antirailroad/antimonopoly forces—the protection of freedom—Free-Soilism would likely appeal to most of those involved in that movement as well. What is more, the Free-Soil doctrine seemingly stood in clear opposition to Democratic policy in reference to the territories. The Democrats were the party of the Kansas-Nebraska Act, the party that had repealed the Missouri Compromise, the party that exposed a region of the country once reserved for free labor to the evils of slavery. Most important, state Democrats, led by Lewis Cass, were now making support of the Kansas-Nebraska Act a test of party loyalty. By so doing, they had irrevocably sheared off a portion of their constituency. If those disgruntled Democrats could be united with the former members of the Whig and Free Democratic Parties, a viable anti-Democratic coalition could be built in Michigan.[4]

Armed with this knowledge, the state's Free Democrats readied themselves to begin their fusion effort. Almost immediately, however, the initiative was nearly scuttled by a division within the movement over tactics. The Free Democrats were principled men—men who, above all else, desired victory for their beliefs. All Free Democrats could agree upon that end. But in early 1854, the means by which that end might be accomplished were a source of much debate within the movement's ranks. Many Free-Soilers, such as Hovey Clarke and Kinsley Bingham, were stung by what they viewed as the audacity of the Slave Power and its sycophantic northern supporters; aware that state Whigs no longer had a party, they hoped to harness the popular outcry against the Kansas-Nebraska Act to build a fusion movement under the aegis of the Free Democratic Party. Others, most notably Isaac Christiancy and the Free-Soil Whig editors Charles DeLand of the *Jackson American Citizen* and Joseph Warren of the *Detroit Tribune,* hoped to create a fusion organization independent of existing party structures. Writing thirty years after the event, Christiancy outlined his thinking on the matter:

I felt that cordial union of this kind [under the Free Democratic banner] could never be effected under a call issued by any party organization *as such;* that, though we might thus obtain larger accessions to our party, we should not obtain enough to carry the State, the prejudice of party and attachment to party organizations being too strong. But I also felt sure that if a movement for a mass convention should be initiated by individuals of all parties agreeing in the object, the pride of party associations would be overcome and all could unite with us without laying themselves open to the charge of having gone over to the free-soilers.

The majority of the party's State Central Committee, however, apparently disagreed with Christiancy's logic, and on January 12, 1854, just eight days after the introduction of the Kansas-Nebraska Bill in Congress, the Free Democrats of Michigan issued a call for a party nominating convention to be held on February 22 in Jackson.[5]

On the evening preceding the appointed convention date, a meeting of six Free-Soil Whig newspaper editors (of the eight who had been invited) and a number of Free Democratic leaders, called together by Joseph Warren, met at the law office of Austin Blair in Jackson. Among those in attendance were Henry Barnes (Warren's colleague at the *Detroit Tribune*), Charles V. Deland, George A. Fitch of the *Kalamazoo Telegraph,* Harvey B. Rowlson of the *Hillsdale Standard,* Zephaniah B. Knight of the *Pontiac Gazette,* and Isaac Christiancy. The meeting had been called in a last-ditch effort to keep the Free Democrats from placing a ticket in the field for the fall state elections. To the chagrin of Christiancy, Warren, DeLand, and the other editors, the Free Democratic leaders determined to go ahead with their nominations. They did, however, agree to appoint a committee that would call a mass convention for the purpose of withdrawing their ticket if a practical plan of fusion was forthcoming. Disappointed, the Whig editors nevertheless agreed to continue their efforts and created the Committee of Correspondence to further their work.[6]

The following day, over three hundred people crowded the convention hall. By day's end, a full slate of candidates—five Free Democrats (Kinsley Bingham and, ironically, Isaac Christiancy among them) and three Whigs— had been nominated. It would be wrong, however, to assume that because the Free Democrats insisted upon putting their own ticket in the field, they eschewed any attempt to build a fusion movement. Just the opposite was the case. As demonstrated by the party's ticket, nominations were made in such a manner that voters of all stripes could find someone with whom they felt comfortable. Even better evidence of this desire for fusion is provided by the platform adopted by the convention. In an obvious attempt to reach out to the diffuse political movements operating throughout the state, the convention's plank on state affairs called for the passage of a prohibition law, the preservation of free schools, and the adoption of a general railroad law.[7]

As the Kansas-Nebraska Bill worked its way through Congress, Michiganians continued to vent their anger against the politicians in Washington. In addition, many in the state continued to plead for the creation of a new political alliance powerful enough to sweep the alliance of demagogues from office. Participants in a Pontiac meeting declared that they would "forget party ties and preconceived political feelings, and unite together in a solemn covenant to do, act, and suffer all things to destroy American slavery." Similarly, a Calhoun County meeting resolved to drop all party ties and unite with the "friends of freedom."[8]

On May 22, the House of Representatives passed the Kansas-Nebraska Bill. The next day, the State Central Committee of the Free Democratic Party issued a call for a mass protest meeting to be held in Kalamazoo on June 21. Also keeping a watchful eye on events in Washington was Isaac Christiancy. In the aftermath of the congressional affirmation of the bill, he renewed his efforts to form an independent anti-Democratic coalition by bombarding the Free Democratic candidates and party leadership, as well as sympathetic Whigs and Democrats, with correspondence. With the aid of Warren, he also arranged for a series of meetings in late May and early June at the offices of the *Tribune* and the *Free Democrat* in Detroit to discuss his proposal. Converts to the independent course, however, initially proved elusive. "Nebraska or anti-Nebraska is now the test," the prominent Whig Zachariah Chandler, a participant in the meetings, wrote to James Joy on May 30. Nevertheless, Chandler continued somberly, "whether we shall be able to coalesce with the Free Soilers or not I cannot say. *They now insist* upon our mounting their platform and taking their nominations *just as they are*. If we attempt to transfer the Whig to the Free Soil party in this way, I fear we shall fail. We don't ask *anything* but an independent nomination . . . to carry the party, the nomination must not be Free Soil. If it is we shall *slip up* on the votes. We are trying now for a fusion."[9]

Christiancy and his supporters would not be deterred. After seemingly endless discussion on the proposal, Bingham and the other Free Democrats yielded, attaching only one nonnegotiable condition to their plans: the Free Democratic Party would disband and withdraw its slate of candidates only after a mass convention had met and had adopted a platform embodying Free-Soil principles. "We shall unite with Free Soilers," rejoiced Zachariah Chandler.

"They agree to withdraw their ticket and go into mass convention if we declaim our sentiments in said mass convention." To avoid alienating potential supporters, Christiancy astutely recommended drawing up a call to the convention to be signed by those who approved of Free-Soil principles. Copies of the call would be circulated throughout the state, and the signed documents would then be collected, tabulated, and published. "This," Christiancy later recalled, "was to prevent the force of party discipline in the democratic party and among those of the whig party who still clung with tenacity to their organization, from being brought to bear to prevent their members from . . . joining in our movement." All who were in attendance agreed with the plan, and the date and location for the convention were set: July 6 in Jackson.[10]

The call itself embodied the essence of the state's Jacksonian political culture. "A great wrong has been perpetrated . . . Liberty is trampled under foot," the document read. "The safety of the Union," the manuscript continued, "the rights of the North—the interests of free labor . . . are involved in the issue forced upon the country by the slave power and its plastic Northern tools." Accordingly, the call concluded, "we invite all our fellow citizens, without reference to former political associations, who think that the time has arrived for the Union at the North, to protect liberty from being overthrown and downtrodden, to assemble in mass convention."[11]

With the wheels now set in motion, those previously inclined toward fusion increased their agitation. Joseph Warren, in the columns of his *Tribune,* immediately threw his support behind the fusion movement:

> If the Whigs are honest we are confident that they will not let their love for an empty name—a name under which they have suffered defeat of the most overwhelming and hopeless character for the last 14 years, each year growing smaller and weaker and more dispirited—for a moment stand in the way of their desires. That the Whig party will be disgracefully defeated at the next election if they "adhere" to their old organization and "stand by their time-honored banner" no sensible and well-informed Whig will deny. Indeed, this is frankly admitted by the shrewdest and most intelligent Whigs in the state. What then shall we have gained by adhering to our organization? Why simply a glorious defeat, and the preservation of our worthless name, at the expense of our principles.

George Fitch of the *Kalamazoo Telegraph* promoted the movement in even more strident terms:

We cannot look to any movements of the old parties in reference to the Nebraska bill and questions touching slavery that bring any promise of success, nor to any class of broken-winded, broken-down politicians; but we may look with a strong hope to see these measures consummated by the honorable and active young men of this state, those who have not trimmed their sails to catch every breeze which has swept across every political sea; those who have not acted for years as the mere weather cocks of public opinion, but active and untiring young men who shall enter with assurance and vigor into the field, those capable of grasping the questions of the time and bringing from them their meanings. We therefore advise the holding of a young men's Independent State Convention, irrespective of party.

From across the state, petitions endorsing the Jackson meeting, bearing the signatures of over ten thousand voters, flooded in. Popular interest in the movement steadily mounted.[12]

The expectant mood surrounding the widely anticipated Jackson convention ensured that the June 21 Free Democratic meeting at Kalamazoo would be sparsely attended. In point of fact, those assembled at Kalamazoo merely sought to offer some guidance to the upcoming convention. Beyond the standard resolutions seeking to rally the state's electorate in defense of imperiled liberty and denouncing the Slave Power and the repeal of the Missouri Compromise, the Free Democrats once again resolved formally to withdraw their nominations if the impending fusion convention at Jackson adopted a proper platform. "The Free Democracy of Michigan," the convention's final resolution proclaimed confidently, " . . . are conscious that the deeply-aroused feeling of the masses in this state will seek a suitable expression in a convention springing from themselves, irrespective of any political organization." Moreover, the resolution continued, "if such a movement shall be animated and guided by the principles expressed in the resolutions of this convention and shall contemplate an efficient organization to give effect to our principles in this state, we shall willingly surrender our distinctive organization, and with it the ticket for state officers nominated at Jackson on the 22nd of February last." The meeting closed by electing a new state committee of sixteen, of which Isaac Christiancy was elected chair; its purpose was to evaluate the suitability of the platform ratified by the Jackson convention.[13]

Certainly, it would be incorrect to describe the emerging fusion movement as a purely "spontaneous," grass-roots movement spawned entirely by the citizenry of Michigan—as presented in many traditional accounts of the origins of the Republican Party and as the platform of the Jackson Republican convention itself claimed. As demonstrated, it was largely because of the efforts of professional politicians and political insiders that the fusion movement even got off the ground. Still, it is important to point out, as historian Ronald Seavoy noted, that although the fusion movement may not have been spontaneous, "it *was* popular." In fact, given the political climate of the day, the movement could not have succeeded had it been seen as originating in the minds of politicians rather than springing from the people themselves. What is more, because it sought to ameliorate widespread uneasiness among the electorate and to unite a diverse body of people involved in disparate political movements (many of which did spring directly from the masses), the fusion drive did, after a fashion, become a grass-roots movement. The men most involved in the effort implicitly understood this and thus acted in a manner consistent with the expectations and desires of state residents: planning to form their new party at a mass convention, circulating the call for the convention throughout the state in order to obtain signatures endorsing that action, choosing as their candidates for office political outsiders and men of diverse political backgrounds, and so forth. In every respect, the Republican movement fully embodied the Jacksonian political culture then pervading Michigan.[14]

Conversely, that same political culture led some Michiganians to look upon the fusion effort with continued distrust and suspicion. The *Grass Lake Public Sentiment,* for example, wryly told its readers that "Jackson County is to be the stamping ground of one great grand menagerie—grand and lofty tumbling among the men; showing of teeth and other performances by the animals." "July 6th, is to come off at Jackson, the great throat trial, at which, three thousand politicians are going to swallow seven thousand," the paper continued; "if this fails, there is to be a great melting process" that would fuse together "all sorts and sizes, all shapes and colors; the one-eyed, the wind-broken, . . . the ring-boned, the stiff-kneed, the limber-kneed, the pole eviled and the evil poled; the slick-sided racer and the rock-ribbed plough horse." The undeniable purpose behind this effort, the journal asserted, was to make "one great political animal swift enough to outrun everything and anything that may be fitted against him, and strong enough to draw all his particular friends close up to the public crib, where they may 'wax fat and kick' at their pleasure."[15]

In spite of such open enmity and an environment laden with apprehension, an estimated fifteen hundred people flooded into Jackson on July 6. At

10:30 A.M., the temporary chairman of the meeting, Levi Baxter, a Free Democrat from Jonesville, opened the proceedings at Jackson's Bronson Hall. It immediately became apparent to Baxter that the hall's meager space was entirely incapable of holding all those interested in participating. He therefore called for an adjournment until 1:00, at which time the meeting was to reconvene in a nearby oak grove. The first order of business before the reassembled meeting was the selection of a convention president. In a move clearly aimed at attracting conservative Whig support, David S. Walbridge of Kalamazoo was elected to that position. The convention delegates, divided into four groups representing the state's four congressional districts, then selected the members of the Committees on Resolutions and Nominations and of the State Central Committee. The chairmanship of the important Committee on Resolutions went to Jacob Howard of Detroit. Howard was the perfect choice. Beyond his ties to both the conservative and Free-Soil wings of the Whig Party, he was also an ardent prohibitionist and a friend of nativism; it was Howard who had delivered the anti-Jesuit address in Detroit just a few months prior to the convention. Beyond that, he was well respected within antirailroad/antimonopoly circles. He had participated in a number of public antirailroad meetings and had openly avowed the necessity of a general railroad law. Moreover, in 1851, he had resigned from the prosecution in the midst of the railroad conspiracy trial after changing his mind about the guilt of the accused—a move that earned him the nickname "Honest Jake." If any one individual personified the goals of the Jackson meeting, it was Jacob Howard.[16]

As the members of the Committee on Resolutions withdrew to the edge of the grove to conduct their business, leading orators of all parties addressed the crowd. Among them was Zachariah Chandler. "Misfortunes," the Detroit Whig bellowed from the rostrum, "make strange bedfellows. I see before me Whigs, Democrats, and Free Soilers, all mingling together to rebuke a great national wrong." "I was born a Whig," he reminded his audience, "I have always lived a Whig and I hope to die fighting for some of the good Whig doctrines. But I do not stand here as a Whig. I have laid aside party to rebuke treachery." The large crowd, moved by the declaration, broke into an extended ovation.[17]

After its deliberations, the Committee on Resolutions reported a platform, drafted almost entirely by Howard, to the convention. As one might expect, the resolutions were thoroughly Free-Soil in character. Howard and the convention squarely blamed the Democrats for the injection of the slavery issue into national discourse, asserting that the Kansas-Nebraska Act was "an undisguised and unmanly contempt of the pledge given to the country . . . at the National Convention in 1852, not to 'agitate the subject of Slavery in or out of Congress.'" Furthermore, the platform resolved, the act was "greatly injurious to the free states, and to the territories themselves, tending to retard the settlement and to prevent the improvement of the country by means of free labor." Vowing not to let the North become a "mere province of a few slave holding oligarchs," the platform called for an end to slavery's extension, the repeal of the Fugitive Slave Act, and the abolition of slavery in the nation's capital. The platform concluded by asserting that "in view of the necessity of battling for the first principles of republican government, and against the schemes of aristocracy the most revolting and oppressive with which the earth was ever cursed . . . we will co-operate and be known as *Republicans* until the contest be terminated." The platform received unanimous approval.[18]

The convention was then addressed by the Jackson Free-Soiler Austin Blair, also a member of the Committee on Resolutions, who read a minority report that included planks on state affairs. Among other things, Blair's resolutions called for a "more economical administration of the government and a more rigid accountability of the public officers," goals very much compatible with the current public mood. More important, however, Blair also proposed the following: "Resolved, That in our opinion the commercial wants require the enactment of a general railroad law, which, while it shall secure the investment and encourage the enterprise of stockholders, shall also guard and protect the rights of the public and of individuals, and that the preparation of such a measure requires the first talents of the State." Convention president David Walbridge, considered by many to be a shill for the Michigan Central Railroad, refused to put the question of inclusion to a vote and unceremoniously left his chair. A number of angry delegates pursued him and forced him to return and submit the question to a vote. The convention voted for inclusion by a large majority. With the party's platform now fully articulated, Christiancy mounted the platform and officially withdrew the Free Democratic nominations from the field. The path for a full-fledged independent fusion movement was now clear. The delegates adjourned until the nominating committee could select a slate of Republican candidates for state and national office.[19]

An examination of the Republican platform reveals a number of interesting things, through its omissions as well as its inclusions. For example, the platform completely ignored any mention of nativism or temperance. As will be shown later, it would be wrong to assume that these issues were of no relevance to the delegates because they were omitted. On the contrary, they were matters of great importance. As discussed earlier, however, they also tended to be divisive issues and to draw support mainly from former Whigs. This group of voters was considered safe, or at least convention delegates thought that they were being placated in another manner; thus, no explicit plank touching upon these issues was thought necessary to bind these voters to the Republican cause. In addition, it is also possible that some sort of implicit understanding regarding these issues had been reached among fusion leaders who preferred to cope quietly with internally controversial topics.

The same concerns and tactics did not apply in regard to members of the antirailroad/antimonopoly constituency. Theirs was a cause that a majority of the convention's delegates believed deserved explicit inclusion in the party's platform. It seems improbable, though certainly not impossible, that those in attendance deemed this issue of far greater significance than either temperance or nativism. A more likely explanation is that the convention hoped to head off any possible defections on the basis of this particular issue. This fear was completely rational. Traditionally, the Democrats had stood in opposition to the expansion of market forces, symbolized by the railroad, in Michigan. Moreover, opposition to monopoly power was a Democratic staple. Thus, to maintain the loyalty of a group of voters who were largely (though by no means exclusively) predisposed to Democratic ideals and given that party's recent attempts to capitalize on this issue, the Republicans had no choice but to embrace this crusade.[20]

At 7:00 in the evening, the convention delegates once again reconvened, this time in Jackson's public square. As the names of the various candidates for office were read, great roars of approbation emanated from the crowd, culminating in thunderous applause as the name of Kinsley Bingham was announced as the Republican nominee for governor. The party's slate of candidates consisted of five former Whigs, two ex-Democrats, and three former Free Democrats. Beyond their diverse partisan affiliations, the Republican candidates also, as Ronald Formisano observed, "individually and collectively appealed to several 'reform' elements." Jacob Howard, the party's candidate for attorney general, appealed to many diverse constituencies. The same could be said of Bingham, the former Democrat and Free-Soiler, and of the ardent proponent of temperance and vocal Detroit Free-Soiler Silas M. Holmes, the Republican candidate for state treasurer. Such diffuse antecedents allowed Republicans a great deal of leeway in shaping the images of their party's candidates. With its work now complete, the convention adjourned, and Republicans set to work to build support for their new organization.[21]

Reaction to the Jackson convention was naturally mixed and generally set the tone for the upcoming fall election. Free Democrat and Free-Soil Whig newspapers universally embraced the new Republican movement. "The pressure of current events," the Whig *Hillsdale Standard* opined on the heels of the convention, "constrains us to lay aside, for the moment, party preferences, and take sides in an issue that brings into immediate conflict the opposing elements of Freedom and Despotism." "We support it as the People's ticket," the *Constantine Mercury* affirmed, "a ticket called for by the exigencies of the times, and not a Whig ticket by any means." The *Marshall Statesman* added, "We are much pleased with the name of the new party, and have no doubt all those who wish to battle against the most revolting schemes of aristocracy that ever cursed a nation, will rally under the broad banner of Republicanism."[22]

Not every Michigan Whig, however, responded positively to the new fusion movement. In fact, a great many of the state's "old-line," or conservative, Whigs proved extremely reluctant to abandon their party organization. The mouthpiece for this faction, the *Detroit Advertiser*, argued that the Republican Party was nothing more than a ruse meant to conceal the machinations of the Free Democrats. Nonplussed by some Whigs' rush to join the movement, the *Advertiser* strenuously insisted that the old party organization should be maintained. "Under these circumstances," the paper queried,

> are Whigs going to endorse the proceedings of the convention and support its nominees? Some may, but we do not believe the great body of them will. At any rate, we shall oppose uncompromisingly with whatever ability we possess, the ticket which has been nominated; and we call upon all good and true Whigs to do the same. Do this for the maintenance of the very principles upon which this Republican party rests, and for the preservation of the principles of your party, and that conservative influence which it has exerted so beneficially in the country; and do it to prevent the disbanding of your party by those seeking its destruction.

A group of Grand River valley Whigs agreed, stating that they could not "find it consistent either with their views of political duty and responsibility . . . , or with the obligations of an enlightened and enlarged patriotism, to sustain the action of the convention recently assembled at Jackson." To pursue such a course, the manifesto continued, would lead to the "creation of geographical party lines and distinctions, the engendering of sectional feuds and dissention [*sic*], denationalization, disunion, civil war and anarchy." The old

Whig organization had to be maintained, these individuals argued, in order to preserve the Union and American liberty.[23]

Throughout the summer of 1854, conservative Whigs managed to hold their band of supporters together. In September, Michigan's old-line Whigs successfully forced the chair of the Whig State Central Committee, William Howard (who had been in attendance at Jackson in an unofficial capacity and who personally supported the new Republican Party), to issue a call for a Whig state convention to meet on October 4 at Marshall. Very quickly, pro-fusion Whigs moved to control the upcoming event. Whig conventions in Berrien and Oakland Counties instructed their delegates to oppose the nomination of a Whig state ticket. Calhoun County Whigs went a step further and instructed their delegates to work to obtain the endorsement of the Republican ticket. The efforts of the fusion Whigs paid off. When the convention assembled on October 4, a great many Republicans, including Joseph Warren of the *Tribune*, were in attendance—so many, in fact, that one of their own, Rufus Hosmer, was elected president of the convention. In the end, the chair of the Committee on Resolutions, James Van Dyke of Detroit, declared that the party would retain its party organization but, at the same time, would make no nominations. The fusionists had succeeded in eliminating the possibility of a rump party behind which conservatives could rally. Without nominees of their own, fusionists reasoned, conservatives would have no choice but to support the Republican ticket.[24]

Ultimately, their conclusion would prove to be a sound one generally, but state Republicans were not entirely correct in assuming that old-line Whigs would have nowhere else to go but to the Republican Party. At least a few joined the ranks of the Democrats. A great many more conservative Whigs, including the editor of the *Detroit Advertiser*, concluded that the state's emerging but still shadowy nativist movement—a movement to which these same folks had given birth the previous year—offered a more appealing alternative. "The present period," the *Advertiser* argued in the aftermath of the fall election, "is favorable to the formation of a great conservative party which would exert a controlling influence on the government. Planting itself on true American principles that embrace the whole country, it would seek to protect what we have, to improve and adorn; to defend our institutions against internal enemies as well as external." Expressing such desires was one thing, but acting upon them seems to have been quite another matter. Michigan Know-Nothings, although allegedly having organized on a state basis on June 2, placed no candidates openly in the field in 1854. "Rather," historian Ronald Formisano maintained, "they caucused secretly and independently and supported Fusionists or Democrats to their liking. For the most part they chose Fusionists." This loose alliance between Know-Nothings and Republicans was natural, given the tacit approval that the Republican Party had given to the nativist cause through its inclusion of such noted nativists as Joseph Warren and its nomination of the anti-Catholic and protemperance Jacob Howard. The ties between these two movements were so strong, the Democratic press alleged, that the state Know-Nothing convention, meeting in Detroit on October 1, passed a resolution making the Republican candidates on the state, congressional, and county tickets second-degree members of their organization. What is clear is that even those old-line Whigs who refused to surrender their partisan identity and to meld with the Republican Party in 1854 still found that party's candidates more sympathetic to their principles than the Know-Nothings and thus cast their votes for the Republican ticket.[25]

The state Democratic Party naturally looked askance at fusion. "You will see by the papers," Robert McClelland wrote to Alpheus Felch, "that a fusion has been attempted in our state of the free-soilers, Whigs and sore headed Democrats." "The Nebraska bill," he continued, "has estranged many of our party, and there are many disappointed office hunters and both together make up a respectable number that might give us difficulty, if they would unite with the enemy." Being the good party man that he was, McClelland remained confident that the Democrats could prevail over this collection of demagogues and political hacks in the upcoming election. "If our friends are judicious," he wrote, "we have nothing to fear."[26]

Other state Democrats, encouraged by the ardent nationalist and titular leader of their party, Lewis Cass, saw the fusion movement as nothing more than a mask for antislavery zealots. "The only issue that can now be involved in the agitation of the slavery question," the *Grand Rapids Enquirer* flatly insisted, "is Dissolution." Cass, of course, was very eager to paint the fusionists as fanatics bent on civil war. Many believed that Cass, who was closely identified with the concept of popular sovereignty, was partly responsible for the passage of the Kansas-Nebraska Act, which substituted that principle for the ban on slavery in the northern Louisiana Purchase that had been imposed by the Missouri Compromise of 1820. Indeed, despite his expressed consternation over the abrogation of the Missouri Compromise, Cass nevertheless endorsed the Kansas-Nebraska Act because of its popular sovereignty provisions. As historian Frank Woodford aptly put it, the act was "a bastard child, mothered by Popular Sovereignty and deposited on his [Cass's] doorstep. He was forced to admit paternity." In addition, Cass and other Democratic leaders quickly moved to make support of the Kansas-Nebraska Act a test of party loyalty. Recognizing the uproar in the North over the act, Cass set immediately to work. In a speech given on the floor of the U.S. Senate on February 20, he asserted that slavery was a national misfortune. It was his greatest hope, he continued, that the institution would come to an end peaceably and justly. But he warned that the final decision on the matter had to be left up to those involved; no external influence should be applied because it would only aggravate the situation. Moreover, Cass reassured northerners, slavery would not spread to Kansas and Nebraska for two reasons: first, the region was not suited to slave labor, and second, popular sovereignty would, in fact, work to keep slavery out of those territories. "I am aware that the measure has excited a good deal of opposition in our State," Cass confided to J. H. Cleveland, "but I believe that the more it is examined and becomes known, the more favor it will meet from reasonable men of both parties."[27]

Michigan's Democratic partisans quickly followed Cass's lead. "The Nebraska Bill," the *Detroit Free Press* confidently exclaimed, "was a proposition in favor of freedom." In some measure anticipating Stephen Douglas's Freeport Doctrine, the paper later wrote, "Slavery is a creature of municipal law. IT CAN NO WHERE EXIST EXCEPT BY POSITIVE ENACTMENT. Until laws are passed in Nebraska and Kansas establishing slavery, every man there becomes a free man the moment he steps upon the soil." Such logic led the delegates to the Democratic congressional convention for the Third District to resolve, "We heartily approve of the late act of Congress organizing the Territories of Nebraska and Kansas upon the principle of popular sovereignty, subjecting the people of those Territories to the constitution and laws of the United States, but free to regulate their domestic institutions in such manner as they may think conducive to their happiness and prosperity."[28]

With their campaign strategy determined, Democrats turned to the unfinished business remaining before them—the selection of a slate of candidates and a platform. Like its Jackson counterpart, the state Democratic convention in Detroit revealed a great deal about the changing political currents in the state in 1854. The Democrats' campaign strategy was chiefly aimed at allaying the fears of the party's Free-Soil faction so as to head off mass desertions. At the same time, state Democrats saw before them an unprecedented opportunity to increase their strength among disaffected old-line Whigs. Given the current political situation, the Democratic convention set a middle course. Hoping to avoid the irksome issue of the Kansas-Nebraska Act as much as possible and lacking a viable Free-Soil Democratic candidate for governor after Robert McClelland was promoted to the post of

U.S. secretary of the interior, convention delegates, operating under the watchful eye of Lewis Cass, settled upon three-term former governor and known conservative John Barry as their candidate for governor. The platform adopted by the convention was short and to the point, consisting of only three planks: a call for a general railroad law, an affirmation of the principles embodied in the Democratic Party's Baltimore platform of 1852, and an endorsement of the principle of "Congressional non-intervention in the domestic legislation of the States and Territories."[29]

As the election neared, Michiganians of all political persuasions made it known that they believed that nothing less than the preservation of American freedom hung in the balance. The "real issue" facing the citizenry, the Republican *Jackson American Citizen* proclaimed to its readers, was whether "the Government of this free, enlightened and Christian nation [shall] become a great propagandist of Human Slavery?" The answer, the paper continued, was clear: "the people, without distinction of party—the people who love their country and its interests and the cause of freedom more than they love any party—have risen in their might, and are calling not only the perpetrators of, but the apologists for, and defenders of this scheme to an account, which promises to be as fearful to the leaders of sham democracy as it will be acceptable to all who love the right and are willing to sustain it." The Slave Power and its Democratic lackeys had to be defeated. "Remember," the *Detroit Daily Democrat* reminded Republicans, "this is a struggle between Slavery and freedom, and you vote for freedom."[30]

Democrats issued similar appeals to their voters. "This is the day of battle," the *Detroit Free Press* wrote on the morning of the election. "The issues are all made up," the paper stated: "it is now for every voter to determine on which side of them he will stand—whether he will cast his influence and his vote for POPULAR SOVEREIGNTY AND POPULAR RIGHTS *or* for CONGRESSIONAL DICTATION AND FEDERAL OPPRESSION." The *Grand Rapids Enquirer* implored,

> Put on your armour and prepare for the contest which is now close upon us. The enemies of Democratic principles, of the Constitution and the Union are in the field, prepared to battle again with the recklessness of desperation for the overthrow of the Democracy and the establishment of their odious principles and measures. Faction is doing its worst to divide the democratic party and lure democrats from the path of duty. Sectionalism is rearing its snaky crest, and would fasten its deadly fangs upon our revered constitution, and destroy the harmony of our glorious Union.

Continued devotion to the Democratic standard was deemed necessary for American freedom to be preserved.[31]

On election day, a political revolution occurred in Michigan. In a stunning reversal of political fortune, the fledgling Republican Party handily defeated its Democratic opponents. The Republican candidate for governor, Kinsley Bingham, easily outpolled his rival, John Barry, capturing 43,652 votes (53 percent of the votes cast) to Barry's 38,675 (47 percent). Moreover, Republican candidates emerged victorious in three out of the four congressional races, and the party attained control of the state legislature, winning twenty-two of thirty-one Senate seats and forty-three of the sixty-nine seats in the state house. Voter interest in the contest was high; for the first time since 1841, the number of voters in a state election and the number of voters participating in the preceding presidential election were nearly the same: only 612 fewer votes were cast in 1854 than in 1852. Further analysis of the election results suggests an interesting trend. As Floyd Streeter indicated, the bulk of the Republican vote came from the interior counties in the two southern tiers. These counties were primarily inhabited by small farmers who, as previously demonstrated, were experiencing the full impact of the market revolution by the early 1850s. It appears that the upheaval surrounding the market revolution produced a hospitable political climate in which Republicanism, with its diffuse political agenda, could take hold. Ironically, historian Dale Prentiss concluded, this pattern reveals that many of those who were attracted to the Republican Party, which he saw as a home for modern or progressive forces, were voters who did not share such goals. In reality, support of the Republican Party by more traditionally minded Michiganians was not incongruous at all. It is certainly true that Republicans tended to embrace the promarket and activist attitudes previously held by the Whigs. However, as noted earlier, the party's ideas and platform also had real appeal for those who remained leery of the emerging economic and social order. Anti-Democratic fusion had clearly succeeded. "Party harness," wrote Democrat Robert McClelland in the aftermath of the election, "did not fit very tightly, and was readily abandoned."[32]

With victory in hand, Republican Party leaders wasted no time in further cementing those who had voted for fusion to the new party organization. In his inaugural address, delivered on January 4, 1855, Governor Bingham spelled out the new party's diverse agenda. The bulk of his message was devoted to the issue of slavery. The Slave Power, he insisted, had ensconced itself in Washington, where it had tried to guarantee its permanent ascendancy through the passage of the Kansas-Nebraska Act, "a stupendous scheme . . . to nationalize slavery . . . and to sectionalize freedom." To un-seat the Slave Power and "denationalize" slavery, Bingham put forth a com-prehensive legislative plan: "There should be no slavery in the District of Columbia—none in national Territories—no slave catching under national law—no slave trade in American vessels, allowed or regulated by acts of Con-gress—no slave auction under process, out of Federal courts."[33]

But the inaugural speech did not focus entirely upon slavery. Bingham also addressed a great many of the other concerns shared by his varied con-stituency. The new governor endorsed a general railroad law that would protect the public interest and encourage capital investment. He reiterated the need for a new prohibition law in the state. In addition, he called for the establishment of an agricultural school in Michigan, a new general banking law, a national homestead law, and federal aid for the completion of the canal at Sault Sainte Marie.[34]

Among the first items of business for the new Republican legislature was consideration of a general railroad law. In a revealing letter to Governor Bing-ham, Isaac Christiancy presented the importance of such a measure plainly:

> What contributed to the unpopularity of the last legislature more than anything else was the impression among the people that they had been too much influenced by Railroad companies and ne-glected matters of general interest to the people. I notice that the Southern RR Co. are applying again for special favor and the Cen-tral Road through Van Dyke are endeavoring to throw obstacles in the way of an efficient general RR law, which to be general ought to allow companies to build roads wherever they can get the funds to build them.
>
> Now unless our legislators set their faces like flint against all these special favors to incorporated companies our Republican tri-umph . . . is at once blown to the winds. . . . The lobbies ought to be made to understand that the best thing they can do for their em-ployers is to go home on the shortest possible route.

Others of lesser renown echoed Christiancy's plea. In reference to problems with the Michigan Southern Railroad, a resident of Jonesville wrote that "we want some legislation to make them behave right. A law ought to be passed preventing trains going through the village at a greater speed than 5 miles an hour." This correspondent continued, "Another great cause of complaint, is because a Rail Road Co never settles any damages. . . . If you have any claim against the Co you must go to the head office in NY, Toledo or Chicago to get it settled. A law should be passed making it imperative to settle it where the property is deliverable to the consignee."[35]

The management of the general railroad bill was eagerly assumed by Austin Blair, the Jackson lawyer then serving as majority leader in the senate, who introduced the bill early in the legislative session. As anticipated, the Michigan Central lobby, headed by James Van Dyke, immediately swung into action against the bill. In a memorial presented to the senate, Van Dyke argued that the proposed law violated the company's charter by allowing competing railroads to be built. The Michigan Central, he maintained, had paid $2 million to the state for what it believed to be monopoly privileges. If the state was dissatisfied with the contract into which it had entered, it could simply repurchase the railroad according to the terms laid out in the charter. Such a law, another employee of the Michigan Central wrote in a letter to Governor Bingham, "is so manifestly unjust, inequitable and I think illegal and unconstitutional . . . that I think such an act would make the Republican party a stench in the nostrils of all honorable men." As it had in the past, the Michigan Central lobby proved to be up to the task and smothered the proposed bill.[36]

In late January, however, the Central lobby reversed its course, thereby clearing the way for the law's passage. The railroad's sudden reversal did not signify a surrender. In fact, the Michigan Central and the Michigan Southern had reached a tentative understanding in January 1855 that would result in a pooling agreement—not illegal in Michigan at the time—two years later, thus minimizing the threat of competition between the two lines. In addition, the nature of the proposed law itself helped alleviate the Central's fears. As Ronald Seavoy observed, "The only substantial limitation on railroads was a prohibition of mergers between parallel lines within the state." By contrast, the law encouraged the merger of other railroads so as to form trunk lines. The law did open the door for the creation of new railroad corporations (and thus placated antimonopoly activists); however, it also contained many prohibitory stipulations as well, stipulations that addressed the concerns of a very different group of Republican voters. All new railroads organized under the act were required to install upon their locomotives bells and steam whistles to be sounded before all grade crossings, to post warning signs at crossings, to fence the right-of-way, and to install special farm crossings with cattle guards where needed. The law also fixed maximum passenger rates and gave the legislature the power to reduce rates in the future, though to no lower an amount than that required to provide a 15 percent annual return on capital stock paid in. By passing the law, the Republicans had lived up to a very important political promise and had reassured Michiganians that their freedom was once again safe. Republican legislators further assuaged the Jacksonian wing of their party by cutting the state's property tax rate, thereby reducing the burden (and the need for ready cash) of state farmers.[37]

Yet even after this victory, a number of other vital political concerns still had to be addressed. As anticipated, support for the Republican ticket among the state's temperance forces was very strong. Although the new party had adopted no formal plank dealing with this issue during the campaign, the Republican-dominated legislature did not neglect its antiliquor proponents. On January 24, a bill to prohibit all persons from selling or manufacturing intoxicating beverages in Michigan passed the house by a vote of fifty-one to twenty-one. Eight days later it, was unanimously endorsed by the senate.[38]

Republicans also took care not to ignore their nativist supporters. Indeed, the 1855 legislative session produced some blatantly nativist enactments. In February, the legislature passed a church property bill that essentially affirmed "the precedence of state law over any common or canon law in governing relations between trustees, congregations, and clergy," thereby enhancing the power of trustees relative to that of parish priests. That same month, the legislature considered a bill to regulate Roman Catholic convents and schools and to provide for state visits to these institutions. Though the measure did not become law, its intent was indisputable.[39]

Banking was yet another issue of great concern for the new legislature. With the state fully caught up in a new period of sustained growth and development, questions of banking and currency weighed heavily on many minds. As previously mentioned, Governor Bingham favored a general banking law containing certain regulatory features. Other banking advocates pointed out that such a law was necessary to offset the deleterious effects of the profusion of banknotes from neighboring states, most of them of dubious reliability, that continually flowed into Michigan. A good many residents, as mentioned, remained very suspicious of banking institutions. This general ambivalence toward banks showed itself in the actions of the legislature. A general banking bill was first rejected by the legislature and then passed on the last day of the session. With the bill upon his desk and well aware that his party could ill afford to antagonize public opinion—which, according to the 1850 state constitution, would have to be consulted via a referendum if the measure should pass—Governor Bingham, despite his earlier endorsement of such a measure, vetoed it.[40]

Having proven itself a trustworthy steward of the varied political tenden-

cies drawn to its fledgling party, the Republican legislature turned its attention to the primary issue around which the party had been constructed—the
preservation of free soil. Both houses easily passed a joint resolution instructing Michigan's U.S. senators and requesting the state's congressmen to support all measures restricting slavery (the vote was twenty-three to five in the
senate and forty-eight to twenty-three in the house). The resolution went on
to denounce the Kansas-Nebraska Act as a "violation of a mutual covenant
between the free states and the slave-holding states," to call for a law preventing the extension of slavery into the territories, and to demand the repeal of
the Fugitive Slave Law of 1850. Unwilling to trust that such a repeal would be
forthcoming, Erastus Hussey, the former Libertyite and Free Democrat now
serving in the state senate, introduced a "personal liberty" bill. The proposed
measure required the prosecuting attorneys in each county to protect and
defend all persons claimed as fugitive slaves, extended the right of habeas
corpus and trial by jury to fugitive slaves, prohibited the imprisonment of any
person arrested as a fugitive in any state or local jail or prison, and required
the testimony of two credible witnesses to prove that a person was a fugitive
slave. The bill passed the senate on February 9 by a vote of eighteen to nine
and the house by a vote of forty to twenty-eight just three days later. Patting
itself on the back for having accomplished so much over the short span of its
busy session, the legislature adjourned.[41]

From their party's inception, Republican leaders, deeply devoted to the
principle of Free-Soilism, necessarily embraced a national perspective. But
that is not to say that state and local issues were insignificant to Republicans;
in fact, as their actions clearly demonstrated, just the opposite was true. Nevertheless, state and local issues did not always successfully transcend parochial
boundaries. Free-Soilism, however, clearly did. This was the issue upon which
people of very different political backgrounds and with very different economic and social outlooks could find common ground. Moreover, given what
seemed to them the Slave Power's entrenched dominance within the federal
government and its ever more obvious use of its sway to force its will upon the
American people, a national orientation was considered imperative if the
blessings of free labor and American liberty were to survive and be enjoyed by
future generations. Accordingly, in the immediate aftermath of the 1855 legislative session, Michigan Republicans set out to strengthen their infant party
in preparation for the upcoming state and national elections in the next year.
The broadly attractive appeal of Free-Soilism could help them promote and
solidify their organization beyond the state and local levels, thereby enabling
them to create an effective organization to challenge the Democratic Party

and, before 1856, the Know-Nothing Party—both of which had already developed extensive national structures. Fortunately for the Republicans, national events helped to promote their cause. One such event was the disruption of the American Party at its national convention in June 1855.

Concerned about the rising tide of sectionalism surging through the nation and worried about its impact upon their own party, delegates to the American Party convention, meeting in Philadelphia, attempted to skirt the problem by proposing that the issue of slavery's extension be avoided altogether by the party. Radical southerners and militant antislavery northerners, however, scuttled the effort, thereby exposing a sectional rift in the party. The dissatisfied northern Americans—or Know-Somethings, as they referred to themselves—withdrew from the convention, denouncing the Slave Power and its northern doughface supporters. Reassembling in Cleveland on June 14, the Know-Somethings declared the Slave Power the most ominous threat facing the nation and vowed to work against the further spread of slavery. The door was now open for a complete fusion between Republicans and Know-Nothings in Michigan.[42]

Concurrently, Michigan Republicans were busily attempting to create a national organization for their party. On August 1, the Republican State Central Committee issued a call for a meeting to be held on September 12 in Kalamazoo. The call made the purpose of the meeting clear:

> The friends of human liberty and the opponents of the further extension of slavery met together at Jackson, and casting behind them all previous party ties, struck hands together in mutual alliance. . . . In this independent organization, Michigan took the lead of all other states, and originated the work of a revolution and reorganization of the parties.
>
> Other sovereign states have, one after another, acknowledged before the world that their first political obligation is due to human freedom, and have taken upon themselves the Republican name and organization, as an outward emblem of their faith. Ohio, Illinois, Indiana, Iowa, Wisconsin, New Hampshire, Vermont, Massachusetts, and Maine have thrown aside the vain trappings of mock warfare, and stand upon the arena, girt with power for a death struggle upon a living issue.

The time had come to consolidate their party further and to plan a national campaign for the 1856 election. "We repeat the recommendation made at the Jackson convention, of July 6, 1854," the Kalamazoo delegates resolved, "for a general convention, of the Republican party of the free states and of such of the other states as may see fit to be there represented, with a view to the adoption of more extended and effectual measures in resistance of the encroachments of slavery; and that a committee of five persons be appointed to correspond and co-operate with our friends in other states on the subject." The efforts of Michigan Republicans and those in other states bore fruit, and on February 22, 1856, a preliminary Republican national convention convened in Pittsburgh and issued a call for a mass convention to be held in Philadelphia on June 17.[43]

In the meantime, throughout 1855 and into 1856, events in Kansas and Washington continued to fix northern attention upon the emerging Republican Party. In March 1855, proslavery Kansans, with the assistance of armed Missouri "border ruffians," elected a proslavery territorial legislature. Free-Soil Kansans quickly denounced the elections as fraudulent and organized a separate antislavery territorial legislature at Topeka. Very rapidly, the war of words between the two sides degenerated into violence on the plains of "Bleeding Kansas," culminating in the sack of the Free-Soil town of Lawrence by proslavery forces and the retaliatory massacre of proslavery settlers on Pottawatomie Creek by the abolitionist John Brown in May 1856. In the same month, the violence also spilled over into the halls of Congress when, on May 21, Congressman Preston Brooks of South Carolina severely caned Republican senator Charles Sumner of Massachusetts after Sumner delivered a scathing speech entitled "The Crime against Kansas."

"Bleeding Kansas and Bleeding Sumner," along with the South's canonization of Brooks, galvanized northern public opinion and sent droves of northern voters into the Republican Party. "If these Kansas outrages don't unite the north," Republican H. J. Alvord wrote to a friend in Michigan, "nothing will." Writing to Secretary of the Interior Robert McClelland as the violence in Kansas began to intensify, Michigan's attorney general, Jacob Howard, wrote, "If you give us war there will be great activity on this frontier. We are ready for it." "A little blood," he concluded, "would be palatable just now!" Seymour Treadwell asserted in a letter to Governor Bingham, "While the liberties of the friends of freedom in Kansas, and of free speech in Congress, are being struck down by the ruthless hand of slaveholding and border ruffianism, it is a question of expediency only whether we should longer forbear, or at once, at any hazard, meet force with force." Another Michigan resident, writing to Republican congressman Henry C. Waldron, noted that "the Lieutenant Governor thinks we'll have to send bullies there [to Washington] to offset the ruffians and Joe Clarke . . . swears that every northern man ought to sit in your house, or the Senate . . . armed and equipped a la brigand." At an indignation meeting held in Detroit on May 30, Zachariah Chandler harangued Brooks as a "cowardly assassin." "This assault," he roared, "is upon the entire North. So long have craven doughface representatives sat in her place in Congress that the South has come to doubt our manhood. . . . We should uphold the hands of our representatives, and tell them that an indignity offered to them is an indignity offered to us." "The political cauldron begins to boil. We shall have one of the fiercest contests that ever was known," Austin Blair had written in April 1856, adding, "We shall beat the northern Democracy in a great majority of the northern states, and before another four years rolls around the Republican party will be able to beat all its adversaries."[44]

Electrified by recent events, the Republican delegates gathered in convention in Philadelphia on June 12. The Michigan delegation—Chandler, Bingham, and Jacob Howard among them—favored the nomination of William Seward as their party's candidate for president, but after he declined to run, they cast their ballots for John C. Frémont, the "Great Pathfinder." Within a month's time, the Republican state convention, meeting in Marshall, endorsed Frémont and renominated the current state Republican administration as the party's candidates for the fall election. Soon thereafter, the Democrats held their national convention and settled upon James Buchanan for president, a man known for signing the Ostend Manifesto endorsing the U.S. acquisition of Cuba (a slave-based colony controlled by Spain) and for his absence from the country during the escalating debate over slavery in the territories. Following suit, Michigan Democrats named the former senator Alpheus Felch, who had spent the previous years settling land claims in California, as their candidate for governor.[45]

The Republicans' campaign in Michigan was intense. Every effort was expended to win converts to the new party and to get out the vote. The party's best orators stumped the state while others of more national renown, such as Abraham Lincoln, were brought to Michigan to argue the Free-Soil cause. In an August 27 speech at Kalamazoo, where he shared the stage with Lincoln and Jacob Howard, Zachariah Chandler aptly summed up his party's campaign theme:

> The Republicans of Michigan stand by the constitution, and when their defamers proclaim that they are a disunion party, as they do so often, they publish what they know to be a falsehood. . . . We are determined to stand by the constitution in all its parts,

and, more than that to make our adversaries stand by it in all and every part. . . .
There are but two candidates for the Presidency and but two platforms. The issue—the only issue—is: Shall slavery be national? Shall it be under our protection, or shall it be under the protection of the slave states only?

Elated by his party's growing strength, Jacob Howard gleefully wrote a friend, "Buchanan falls like dead weight about here. None but P. M.s [postmasters], etc., can even smile and with them it seems ghastly."[46]

State Democrats countered, as Chandler predicted they would, by painting their opponents as dangerous radicals bent on the dissolution of the Union. "Fellow citizens," the Democratic warhorse Lewis Cass began in a September campaign address, "did this government ever injure any of you?" The partisan crowd responded with cries of "No! No!" "Then why are you discontented," Cass queried, "why would you dissolve the Union?" Cass confided to fellow Democrat John P. Cook of Hillsdale, "I am tired of it all. I am tired of this everlasting harping upon slavery and this hazarding the freest and happiest government on the face of the globe, running the risk of sacrificing it to sectional divisions." McClelland warned a group of Democrats that the Republicans were nothing more than "the old Whig party gone daft on the abolition question . . . allied [with] a few stray democrats won over by the trumped up story of bleeding Kansas." The contest was on.[47]

Although unsuccessful in their first attempt to gain the presidency, the Republicans made a strong showing throughout the North, capturing over one-third of the popular vote and 114 electoral votes. In Michigan, the party's success was even more pronounced. Voter turnout in Michigan jumped 52.5 percent over that in the presidential election of 1852, with an estimated 85.4 percent of eligible voters participating. Frémont swept the state, garnering 71,762 votes to Buchanan's 52,136 and Millard Fillmore's paltry 1,660. Moreover, the Republicans enhanced their hold on state government, reelecting Bingham by 71,402 votes to Felch's 54,085 and capturing 29 of 32 state senate seats, 63 of 81 seats in the state house, and all 4 of the state's congressional seats. The Republican victory in Michigan was so overwhelming that not even the defeat of Frémont at the national level could lower the spirits of Michigan's Republican partisans. "It seems 'Buck and Breck' are elected but I think the Republicans fought a good fight," one Republican boasted, "and although defeated, [we] are not discouraged." To cap their triumph, on January 10, 1857, the newly elected Republican legislature of

Michigan repudiated the state's leading Democrat, the long-serving U.S. senator Lewis Cass, and elected in his stead one of their own, Zachariah Chandler, by a vote of 106 to 16.[48]

Chandler's election to the Senate did not come off without a hitch, however. The votes cast during the Republican legislative caucus on January 8 and 9, 1857, reveal something of a rift within the party's ranks. In each of the caucus's four informal ballots, Chandler was the clear favorite, but some Republican supporters of the Bingham administration made a concerted effort to rally support for the governor's close friend and political confidant Isaac Christiancy. In the end, however, the effort to derail Chandler's candidacy failed, and he received the legislative caucus's nomination. This scenario led Republican congressman Henry C. Waldron to comment,

> I am so well satisfied with the condemnation of Cass that I am easily reconciled to the choice of his successor, provided he be a Republican. My preferences were for Christiancy from motives of partizan policy—our Senators have heretofore all been from the Centre or the North, and furthermore I think the Democratic wing of the party should have had the Senator as the four Representatives are from the Whig side of the House—but if our Republican legislature has decided for Zack, I am bound to believe that it is all right.

Most state Republicans, it appears, concurred. The new Republican senator, the *Marshall Statesman* crowed, "will never bow the knee to the behests of the slave power, will never cringe to the threats of Southern fire-eaters, will never brook the sneers and insults of slavedom's bullies, but true to the memory of his Revolutionary Sires, he will battle for the right and prove an able champion of the guarantees of constitutional liberty."[49]

Although Free-Soil attitudes such as those articulated by the *Statesman* assumed great importance among Michigan's Republican legislators during their 1857 session, other issues also garnered much of their attention. In his January 7 address to the new state legislature, Governor Bingham identified a broad range of issues requiring that body's attention. In particular, he implored them to consider carefully the disposition of nearly 4 million acres of land granted the state by the federal government in 1856 to promote the construction of railroads into the state's hinterlands, the passage of a general banking law, the establishment of an independent state supreme court (an action permissible after 1856 under the state constitution of 1850), the need for a "just" system of property taxes to meet the expenses of state government and to pay the interest on the state's debt, and an appropriate response to the deepening crisis in Kansas.[50]

Among the first orders of business for the assembled legislators was devising a plan for allocating the federal land grants among the myriad railroad companies vying to construct the newly designated lines. Having seemingly placated those Michiganians who had been attracted to the Republican banner because of their hostility to the state's existing railroad corporations through the enactment of a general railroad law in 1855, the state legislature eagerly took up the distribution question. But the *Detroit Free Press* warned the body against undue haste. "There will not be a more important subject of legislation at Lansing this winter," the paper cautioned, "than that of the construction of certain railroads in pursuance of land grants by Congress at the last session." "The grand object the legislature should have in view is," the paper continued, "to place the construction of the roads in the hands of competent companies—companies of adequate means and composed of men of highest probity and honor." As the legislative deliberations continued into late January and the lobbying efforts of the interested parties increased, the Democratic sheet grew even more suspicious of Republican motives and denounced what it saw as the "plunder schemes" to "despoil the State and enrich a corporation" being promoted by the "black Republican" legislature in Lansing.[51]

By session's end, the legislature passed a bill, signed into law by Governor Bingham, that awarded land grants to nine separate railroad corporations, only one of which—the Detroit and Milwaukee—was an active carrier at that time. Under the law's provisions, the corporations were granted alternate sections of land on each side of their tracks to be located within a distance of six miles of the projected lines. The land, however, would not be turned over all at once to the railroad companies. Instead, title to the land would be transferred to the companies only as building progressed. Each company was required to complete at least twenty miles of track every year and to complete its entire line within seven years. In return for the land grants, the state required the roads to pay, in lieu of all other taxes, an annual 1 percent tax on the cost of construction and equipment; the state also reserved the right to impose a 2 percent tax on gross earnings after a period of ten years. A final stipulation provided for the creation of a six-member board of control, appointed by the governor and confirmed by the senate, to administer the grants. By passing this important measure, Michigan's Republican legislature undoubtedly hoped to bring to fruition the promise it had made to a very important voting bloc—the state's antirailroad/antimonopoly forces—in 1854 and 1855: that competition among railroad companies, operating under the watchful eye of the state, would ensure that all state residents would benefit from these corporate entities and that these corporations would be unable to abuse their power.[52]

Other economic considerations also loomed large for state legislators in 1857. As described earlier, Republicans attempted to pass a general banking law on the closing day of the 1855 session, only to see their efforts rejected by a worried Governor Bingham. Not surprisingly, the banking issue quickly reappeared in the 1857 legislative session. Anticipating such an occurrence, Bingham warned that body in his annual address that "you will undoubtedly be told that the business wants of many localities in this State require the establishment of banks, and will be urged to pass a bill to authorize them to go into operation. If so, I trust you will concur with me in the propriety of providing such safeguards as will secure the community against bankruptcy and fraud. In this most important matter, they have a right to look to you for protection." Isaac Christiancy agreed. "I have always been opposed to Banking as a system," he asserted in a letter to Bingham, "but while other states on our borders adopt that policy I do not see how we are to get along without banks." "Southern Michigan, having no banks is constantly flooded with the Illinois and Indiana banknotes of which the people know little and over which our state and our courts have no control, and I have no doubt," he concluded, "it would be better for the people to have a bank among themselves with proper safeguards."[53]

Among the most frequent claims made by Republicans in the legislature as they worked to draft a banking bill was that the state constitutional requirement that bank issues be backed by state stocks would sufficiently safeguard the state. Pointing out that similar provisions were in effect in both Indiana and Illinois and that the banking systems in those states were on the brink of collapse, the *Free Press* dismissively queried, "Is it possible that the bank experiences of the present, to say nothing of the experiences of the past, here and elsewhere, will be disregarded by the Legislature at Lansing as worthless? Is it worthless? Does it teach no lesson? Does it furnish no warning?" Stock security did not work in Illinois or Indiana, the paper continued, and "it will be no better in Michigan." "Those states have sown the wind; their harvest is the whirlwind," the *Free Press* warned; "the same seed in Michigan will provide none other than the same harvest."[54]

Republican legislators apparently disagreed with the *Free Press*'s gloomy forecast, however, and handily passed a general banking statute. The bill that emerged from the state legislature was very closely modeled after New York's free banking statute of 1838 and established relatively meager capital requirements—$25,000—for prospective banking corporations. Persuaded that the legislature had heeded his warnings, Bingham signed the bill as the legislature adjourned. As mandated under the constitution of 1850—which required that any such law be put before the electorate in a general election—the bill was then scheduled to be placed before Michigan voters in November 1858, at which time it was overwhelmingly approved.[55]

In spite of their attention to the railroad and banking issues, one matter remained paramount in the minds of a great many of Michigan's Republican legislators: the preservation of free soil in the face of renewed aggressions by the Slave Power. Once again, Kinsley Bingham set the tone for the legislative session in his annual address. Denouncing the last Congress for its "strenuous efforts . . . to extend the area and influence of slavery" and for its repeal of the Missouri Compromise, Bingham hastened to alert his fellow party members, "We have no ground to presume that this scheme will be abandoned." More to the point, he continued, "the contest between free labor and slave labor, between free society and slave society, will not probably terminate with the struggle in Kansas, whatever may be the result there. History teaches us that *privilege* never restrains its ambition to rule, nor abates a whit of its pretensions; and so long as in our country, it can surround itself with flatterers and parasites, it will continue to struggle for enlargement and preponderance." The Republican Party had to remain vigilant and had to devote its energies to unseating the Slave Power and its retainers in Washington. In the interim, Bingham implored the state legislature to do what it could to resist the aggression of the Slave Power and to relieve the suffering of the free-soil settlers in Kansas who had been its most recent victims.[56]

Michigan's Republican legislators wasted little time in following their governor's lead. As early as January 16, a joint resolution was introduced into the state senate, instructing Michigan's U.S. senators and requesting its congressional delegation "to resist to the utmost the admission of any more slave states into the Union; and to use their best exertions to secure the immediate admission of Kansas as a free state, the repeal of the fugitive slave law of 1850, and the prohibition by law of slavery in all the Territories and in the District of Columbia." In a slightly modified form, the resolution passed both houses of the state legislature and received the approval of Governor Bingham on February 4. Six days later, a second joint resolution, this one urging the state's congressmen and senators to work for the passage of an act declaring the Kansas slave code, a draconian measure passed by the territory's fraudulent pro-slavery legislature, null and void, also secured Bingham's blessing.

In addition, the state legislature appropriated $10,000 for the aid and relief of immigrants in Kansas from Michigan.[58]

Angered by the legislature's attention to the slavery issue, "an institution that does not exist in this State, and for the existence of which elsewhere this State is in no wise responsible," the *Free Press* denounced the introduction of what it labeled "Nigger Resolutions." "There is much home legislation wanted badly, which may be had," the paper argued, "if a week or two of the session shall not be thrown away upon 'Kansas.'" As the prospect of a state appropriation for settlers in Kansas grew, the Democratic mouthpiece offered the legislature the following advice: "[It is] better . . . that money be appropriated to misery within our own boundaries than that we should place some thousands of dollars in the hands of somebody appointed to seek misery a thousand miles away." Indeed, this strategy of criticizing the Republicans' handling of state finances quickly became the centerpiece of the state Democratic Party's campaign strategy for the 1858 election.[58]

As the 1857 legislative session drew to a close, the *Free Press* noted that "the distinguishing feature of the session will be found to be, the magnitude of the appropriations made from the treasury." In many respects, the *Free Press* was correct. The Democratic legislature of 1853 had appropriated approximately $125,000, of which $65,000 was earmarked for salaries and state governmental expenses. Their 1857 Republican counterparts, by contrast, giving voice to their Whiggish proclivities, made appropriations in excess of $300,000, much of which went toward funding institutions such as the state prison, state asylums, the new Michigan Agricultural College, and the state Normal School in Ypsilanti, not to mention the $10,000 sent to Kansas. All told, state expenditures between 1855 and 1860 rose over 19 percent (an increase all the more dramatic in light of the rampant deflation and the fact that the expense of running the state government and of paying salaries remained essentially unchanged from 1853). To meet its increased pecuniary needs, the state legislature levied a tax of four-tenths of a mill on all taxable property.[59]

Noticeably absent from the 1857 legislative session were the types of ethnocultural measures that had figured prominently in the Republican legislative agenda for 1855. This was not, however, due to any lack of interest on the part of many Michigan Republicans. Indeed, throughout its term, the legislature was inundated with petitions from temperance advocates requesting that that body do something to shore up the state's porous Maine Law. At first blush, one would expect that these petitions would have received a sympathetic hearing, for the law had been passed by a Republican-dominated legislature—which contained many of the same members—only two years earlier, but such was not the case. Governor Bingham tactfully ignored the divisive topic in his legislative address, and the state legislature squelched discussion of the issue. This inconsistency regarding temperance did not go unnoticed in the Democratic press. "There can be no more ample confession than this silence," the *Free Press* chided in an editorial, "[a] confession that black republicanism embraced the Maine law, not as a genuine temperance measure, but as a temporary element of popular strength, without regard to its consequences for temperance."[60]

One piece of alcohol-related legislation did make its way through this gauntlet of silence. On the closing day of the session, the legislature passed a bill, subsequently signed by Governor Bingham, permitting the sale of beer in Michigan. This apparent duplicity was attributable to the important role played by German voters in the Republican electoral victory in Michigan in 1856. German voters in Detroit and, more important, in the Saginaw Valley had, many party leaders believed, played a vital role in their party's 1856 triumph. To cement the Republican loyalties of these voters—many of whom undoubtedly shared the opinion of the recently arrived William Seyfferdt that "our choice in politics leaves much to be desired, slavery on the one side, the temperance humbug on the other"—Republican leaders eased up on temperance and nativism; they were "content," as historian Ronald Formisano stated, "to rest on early victories and symbolism." In concentrating more heavily upon the rallying cry of Free-Soilism and on banking, Republicans were also relying on the belief that temperance advocates and nativists would have nowhere else to turn. This strategy, as the party would learn the following year, was not without its risks.[61]

Unfortunately for state Republicans, Michigan's mid-nineteenth-century economic surge lurched to an abrupt halt with the panic of 1857. In the state's northern frontier counties, the *Port Huron Observer* wrote in May 1857, "there is much suffering from want of provisions. All kinds of provisions . . . are unusually high and very scarce throughout the northern regions. Instances of great suffering and almost starvation, in particular neighborhoods are reported." By September, the panic had paralyzed the state's economy, bankrupting the Bank of Tecumseh and forcing the two remaining banking institutions in the state to close their doors. "The crash that is now taking place in the business world is absolutely awful," the *Kalamazoo Gazette* moaned, and "every day the press and the telegraph wires teem with accounts of broken banks and fallen business houses. It is dangerous to have a bank bill in hands over night; and the downfall of the best firms throughout the country is destroying confidence to such an extent that business in many places is almost entirely suspended." Unemployment mounted in the state. The Michigan Central laid off 500, the Detroit Locomotive Works cut 100, and the Detroit Car Manufactory let its entire workforce go. "They say such dismal times were never seen as now exists [*sic*] in Detroit," longtime resident Elizabeth Stuart wrote in late May, "the streets seem as if a pestilence were raging—the pressure for money is terrible." In the state's Upper Peninsula, currency was so scarce that local mining companies began issuing their own drafts, known locally as "iron money," in payment for labor and materials. By October 1857, the value of land advertised for sale by the state for delinquent taxes reached $187,502. The same month, the *Grand Rapids Enquirer and Herald* reported that Michigan state stocks were selling for a mere 62.5 cents on the dollar. The *Detroit Advertiser* grieved, "The city is full of men and women who have no prospect before them but that of a winter, near at hand, threatening hunger, cold, and deprivation." As the crime rate increased in Detroit, the same paper wrote, "it becomes needful that every man should effectually arm himself, both at home and abroad, for his own protection, and that of those who are dependent upon him."[62]

At first, the state's Republican press did its best to downplay the severity of the panic. As late as the end of August, in fact, even the *Advertiser,* which later became more pessimistic, was confidently boasting that "so far as we have been able to observe, the stoppages and failures have produced but little uneasiness in this city." As the crisis deepened, however, and Democratic attacks on the Republican state administration increased, Republican editors and others attempted to divert attention from Michigan to the situation in Kansas or to heap the blame for the panic on the Buchanan administration in Washington. "The wound," a letter writer asserted in the *Advertiser,* "was produced by our Democratic party's policy in distributing the tariff, and by the popularity of 'FREE TRADE' deceiving the masses, and the country has been led to extravagance and disaster." The writer continued, "Let the country be enlightened on the subject and the present dominant political party, who are responsible for all, be held to strict account."[63]

Throughout 1857, Michigan Democrats, for their part, incessantly alleged that the state treasury was empty, "plundered by the Black Republicans." Of the expenses approved by the Bingham administration, the grant of aid to settlers in Kansas came under most frequent attack. "At the moment he [Bingham] sent it," the *Detroit Free Press* lectured, "there was no suffering in Kansas, but there was suffering in Michigan. There were hundreds of our own citizens . . . with no other prospect before them than famine." Despite

Republican claims to the contrary, by January 1858, Gov. Kinsley Bingham had to concede that, because of diminished revenues, the state treasurer would be unable to meet the state's current expenses or to redeem the bonds that fell due on or before January 1, 1859. "The State," the *Free Press* proclaimed, "is bankrupt!" Faced with this grim prospect, Bingham called a special session of the state legislature, which responded to the crisis by authorizing the governor to borrow $50,000 and the state treasurer to issue state stocks sufficient to redeem those falling due before the next meeting of the legislature in January 1859. Against this backdrop of looming economic and financial catastrophe and with state debt and taxes rising, the stage was clearly set for the upcoming fall elections.[64]

Though seemingly poised to inflict great damage upon their political enemies, Democrats found themselves partially paralyzed by a division within their own ranks, caused by the Buchanan administration's endorsement of the proslavery Lecompton constitution for Kansas in December 1857. Buchanan's action stung many state Democrats and produced a split. On one side was a small group of proadministration Democrats, led by Cornelius O'Flynn, the postmaster at Detroit and editor of the *Detroit Herald,* and Democratic editors in Battle Creek and Grand Rapids. On the other was a much larger group of Michigan Democrats, led by the state's Democratic U.S. senator Charles E. Stuart and the *Detroit Free Press,* supporting Stephen Douglas's stand in opposition to Lecompton. According to the Buchanan-supporting *Grand Rapids Enquirer and Herald,*

> The Lecompton Convention represents the actual settlers of Kansas, if the Territorial Legislature was the Legislature of Kansas. That Legislature, which has been recognized by Congress, by the Judiciary and by the President, authorized the Lecompton Convention. The Lecompton Convention was the creature of the Territorial Legislature and if the one was legal, so was the other. The members of the Lecompton Convention were elected by the actual settlers of Kansas. It is true that a mistaken and deluded faction in Kansas, who would rule or ruin, under the advice of Beecher, Greeley and company, did not vote. But their refusal to vote does not validate the legality of the Lecompton Convention.

The *Ann Arbor Michigan Argus,* representing the Douglas faction, argued, "We hesistate not to say that the President holds opinions contrary to those cherished by the mass of the Democratic party in the North and West. . . .

The question of slavery is not the only one in which the people of Kansas are interested. . . . The natural and inalienable rights, give the People—not a few of them gathered in convention convened—the power to regulate their own domestic concerns and create their own institutions." Echoing this sentiment was Sen. Charles Stuart. "Here is a people remonstrating . . . by 10,000 votes at the polls against having this constitution forced on them," he insisted in front of his Senate colleagues. "You say to force [it] on them is non-intervention! To leave these people . . . free to regulate [slavery] in their own way is intervention. . . . Could anything be more absurd?" As party infighting continued, some Michigan Democrats began to worry that, in the words of the *Cass County National Democrat,* their party would come out of the fight like the "Kilkenny cats," who had been all "used up but their tails."[65]

State Democrats naturally tried to avoid the Lecompton controversy in the early months of 1858 and to focus the attention of Michigan's voters upon the state's dismal economy, the recent Republican tax increase and concurrent escalation in appropriations, and the Bingham administration's empty treasury. The Democrats' attempts to smooth over intraparty differences were furthered by the passage of the so-called English Compromise bill in April 1858. "The Democratic party can reunite in this disposition of the Kansas question," the *Detroit Free Press* beamed, "and it will reunite if wise counsels and wise action prevail." To be sure that some semblance of harmony was restored within the party before its nominating convention, the Democratic State Central Committee postponed the party's state convention until September 2.[66]

For their part, state Republicans played the one card dealt them: the Lecompton controversy. This, of course, was not surprising, given the unifying role that the Free-Soil issue had played in the party ever since its inception in July 1854. Free-Soilism and all that it had come to symbolize was common ground for the party's disparate constituency. Accordingly, legislative Republicans took the opportunity afforded them by the special legislative session to pass a joint resolution instructing the state's senators and requesting its congressmen to "oppose the admission of Kansas into the Union under the Lecompton constitution or any constitution maintaining slavery therein." On the floor of the U.S. Senate, Zachariah Chandler continued the Republican assault. "When he [Buchanan] attempted to force a constitution on an unwilling people," the freshman senator insisted, "he was no longer James Buchanan, President, but James Buchanan, criminal. . . . Should he attempt it and blood be shed, he would be liable to impeachment and liable to be hanged as a murderer." The *Marshall Statesman* agreed, commenting, "By his recommendation of the passage of the Lecompton constitution he has violated the Pledge made by the convention which nominated him. By his reckless violation of that pledge he has proved himself to be a double faced, treacherous and weakminded man." In the Republican county and state conventions, resolutions were adopted condemning the Buchanan administration's endorsement of the Lecompton Constitution and lauding Michigan's congressional delegates for their devotion to the principles of Free-Soilism. At its August 19 state convention, the party nominated the former Whig Moses Wisner, an antislavery Pontiac lawyer who had been suggested as the party's nominee for attorney general at the 1854 Jackson convention, as its candidate for governor.[67]

As the state Democratic convention neared, the name of Michigan's Democratic senator, Charles E. Stuart of Kalamazoo, an outspoken critic of the Buchanan administration's handling of the Kansas situation, quickly surfaced as the favorite candidate for that party's gubernatorial nomination. "It is the impression," a Port Huron Democrat affirmed in a letter to former senator Alpheus Felch, "that he will command a larger vote than any other man for the reason that he is the least obnoctious [*sic*] to Black Republicans—and that all who are Douglas men will go for Stuart." "We care but little who the nominee may be," the *Jackson Patriot* commented, "provided he is acceptable to the *whole* Democracy of the State; and, on the contrary, any one who is in any degree obnoxious to any portion of the Democracy, ought not to be nominated, no matter who he may be, or what may have been his position before."[68]

At their September 2 convention, state Democrats gave their nomination to Stuart. Concurrently, they exerted additional energy to repair the still visible rift within their ranks. The party's platform included a resolution in favor of popular sovereignty and one that declared the party's confidence "in the ability, integrity, and patriotism of the administration of our venerable President, James Buchanan." The Lecompton issue was notably absent from the platform. Instead, the Democrats continued their strategy of attempting to maintain party unity by including a scathing attack upon Republican rule in the state. "The administration of our State affairs for the last four years," the convention insisted,

> meets with unqualified condemnation; that the money of the State has been squandered for partisan purposes; the taxes more than doubled; the treasury made bankrupt; that part of the state debt which should have been paid, renewed and continued for twenty years; the statute books filled with such crude and undigested legislation as to render null and void many important laws; the liberal

grants of swamp and railroad lands by Congress endangered, if not lost, by a deliberate violation of the trusts and conditions upon which they were donated; and generally that the affairs of our State have been managed with such reckless extravagance, such criminal negligence, such utter disregard of the good faith and credit of the State and the interest of the people, as to demand a complete and thorough reform.

Pleased with the results of the convention, the *Free Press* confidently boasted that "the ticket and the platform have perfectly united the whole party and have opened up the doors of the Democratic church to thousands who have been awaiting this opportunity to enter and take up their abode." United once more, Michigan's Democrats eagerly anticipated regaining control of the state.[69]

On November 2, however, they learned that they would have to wait a while longer, for Moses Wisner easily outpolled his Democratic opponent, 65,202 to 56,067. The Republicans also captured three of the state's four congressional districts outright and seized the fourth after successfully challenging and overturning the result in the First District, where the Republican incumbent, William Howard, had been defeated by only 75 votes. Nonetheless, there was, as historian Floyd Streeter remarked, a "noticeable dissatisfaction" with the Republican Party throughout the state. Indeed, Stuart polled 1,982 more votes than his Democratic predecessor had in 1856, while the total Republican vote declined by 6,200. In each of the state's congressional districts, the number of Republican votes cast also fell. In addition, Democrats gained four seats in the state senate, giving them a total of eight, and nine seats in the state house, raising their representation there to twenty-four.[70]

Tradition has it that the Republican decline of 1858 was caused by a such factors as internal squabbling over appointments and representation among the party's Whig, Free-Soil, and Democratic factions; the panic of 1857; and the party's marked increase in public expenditures and the rate of taxation. The *Free Press* interpreted the results to mean "that the people are sick of the continual hum-drum of the Republican declaimers upon the slavery question" and that Michiganians "were ready to banish the whole tribe of them from the political arena." That paper's Republican analogue, the *Advertiser,* blamed bad weather, overconfidence, and nonvoting.[71]

Yet another possible reason for the Republican decline in 1858 was a renewal of nativism in Michigan. Though the evidence for such a claim is impressionistic at best, the argument for nativist disaffection is plausible. In local elections in the spring of 1859, for example, "people's tickets" and other nonpartisan slates took the field as they had in 1854 and 1855, suggesting, as historian Ronald Formisano claimed, that "Know Nothingism, or some similar manifestation, still percolated through Michigan politics." Writing to a friend in the weeks following the November 1858 election, Farmington Republican Daniel Arnold claimed that the Republican electoral majority would have been "much larger in this State than it was if our Republican State Convention had fused as it might have done with the American party." Arnold continued, "The sympathies of the American party are nearly all with the Republican party on the subject of slavery, and if that party gives up its organization as I think they will be compelled to do for want of success, the Republican party will receive a large accession of strength." For the time being, however, such an outcome had been stymied; it seems that Republican efforts to embrace immigrant voters—efforts clearly revealed in the 1857 legislative session and made imperative by the growing number of immigrant voters and the recent panic—may have produced a mild nativist backlash. Events in late 1858 and early 1859 further substantiate that claim.[72]

In December 1858, the *Lansing State Republican* ran an editorial demanding the state legislature pass a voter-registration law. "Illegal voting, both by unnaturalized persons, and by actual residents of another country and subjects of another form of government," the paper protested, "has become an intolerable evil." Prompted, in part, by the disputed First District election, accusations flew in Detroit regarding widespread voter fraud and of an invasion of "Kanuck border ruffians" from Canada who voted in accordance with the wishes of the collector of Detroit, Cornelius O'Flynn. As the state legislators convened, they were greeted with some fifty petitions requesting a registration law. The newly elected governor, whose brother George was a vocal nativist, also pitched into the fray. The "great right of self-government and of electing our rulers by a majority of legal votes," Wisner pronounced in his address to the legislature, "is a right that should be sacredly guarded. Whoever seeks to carry an election by illegal votes, is an enemy to your liberties." A voter-registration law was needed to safeguard these liberties, Wisner concluded.[73]

On February 8, 1859, the Registry Bill, requiring all voters to register with local officials at least ten days before an election, passed the state senate by a vote of seventeen to fourteen. Four days later, the bill passed the house by a vote of forty-two to thirty-four. The acrimony created by the fight over this bill, which the *Free Press* labeled a "know-nothing measure," did not immediately dissipate. The former Democratic congressman from Wayne County, Alexander W. Buel, now representing that county in the state legislature, offered a substitute title for the bill: "a bill to violate the constitution of this State, and deprive the people of their constitutional rights at all general, special and municipal elections." A Republican member of the house then suggested adding the following: "and to prevent the manufacture of democrats on too short notice." Neither suggestion prevailed, and Governor Wisner signed the bill into law under its original name.[74]

After appeasing the nativists within their party's ranks, the Republican legislators quietly moved to offer their ethnic supporters an olive branch by reestablishing the post of immigration commissioner and appointing two Germans successively to the position. In addition, in spite of numerous pleas to pass a more stringent liquor law, the Republican-controlled body remained silent on the temperance issue. Further efforts to win over ethnic voters would be made in 1860 when the Republican State Central Committee appointed two Germans as delegates to the party's national convention in Chicago.[75]

Additional measures were undertaken by the Republicans in the 1859 legislature to shore up their party as well. One of the first matters to be addressed by the assembled legislators was the question of electing a new member of the U.S. Senate to replace the outgoing Charles Stuart. State Republicans had, of course, been discussing the issue for quite some time prior to the winter 1859 session. In fact, by January, many had already reached the same conclusion as A. H. Morrison of St. Joseph: Kinsley Bingham was the party's best choice. "How can we consistently as a party," Morrison had written Charles May in May 1858, "overlook the strong claims that the *democratic* branch have on us?" The party could not, and Bingham was handily elected to the Senate.[76]

The state legislature also took up the banking issue once more. Though the general banking law passed during the 1857 session had been approved by the voters in 1858, few entrepreneurs proved willing to risk their capital in the banking field, given the state constitution's provision requiring unlimited liability for stockholders. Accordingly, an amendment to the constitution was passed and then later accepted by the state's electorate in 1860, making stockholders liable "equally and ratably to the extent of their respective shares of stock."[77]

With their party crisis now, they hoped, behind them, Michigan Republicans once again pushed the Free-Soil issue into the limelight. "I agree with you," Zachariah Chandler wrote a fellow Republican in mid-December 1858, "that old party landmarks should be obliterated and a *unity* of action upon present issues substituted in their place. . . . This organization, based upon the old Washingtonian and Jeffersonian doctrines, so far as the slavery issue is concerned, will stand well." Another Michigan Republican, Joseph R. Williams, calmly reassured a worried Charles May in the immediate aftermath of the 1858 election, "I think you are mistaken in regard to any danger of ruin. Our movement is founded in a sentiment and conviction so deep and ineradicable that the majority will stand by it when every unquiet crisis comes." "At the next Presidential contest," Williams confidently declared, "it [the Republican party] will sweep like a tornado. There will be nothing before it." Williams's perspective was an important one because the success of Free-Soil principles would require victory at the national level. The federal government had to be rescued from the Slave Power and its Democratic allies. "I believe slavery is destined to remain within its present limits for some time to come," one Michigan Republican cheerily wrote in early 1859. "Kansas has been the great battlefield between the champions of Freedom and the minions of Slavery and as the former have been triumphant there, the future march of freedom will be onward and that of slavery a retrograde one." The correspondent concluded, "If the Republican party act wisely and remain united, I think we have a fair prospect of having a Republican President and Congress elected in 1860." With that goal in mind, throughout the remainder of 1859 and into the early portion of 1860, the eyes of the state's Republican citizenry remained steadfastly fixed upon the enemy identified by their party—the Slave Power. The necessity of defeating this power—which seemed increasingly aggressive in its blatant attempts to undermine freedom—and the necessity of maintaining party loyalty in order to achieve that paramount goal kept the party and its adherents in a state of constant preparation for the electoral struggle in 1860 and would dominate the party's political vision for the next six years.[78]

6

"We Know no Party Until the Contest Is Over"

Michigan Partisan Politics during the Civil War Era, 1860–1866

ON THE eve of the 1860 presidential election, Michigan and the nation at large stood at a political crossroads. In the previous decade, rapid social and economic transformations, ethnocultural debates, and the question of slavery's expansion into the territories negated the traditional partisan affiliations of Whigs and Democrats and created new political agendas. Two major political organizations emerged from the realignment of the 1850s: a weakened, increasingly southern-oriented national Democratic Party and a wholly northern Republican Party. By 1860, the Democratic Party in Michigan faced a grim future as a political minority, although this circumstance was largely unrecognized at the time. As previously discussed, in 1854, anti-Democratic forces had successfully fused under the banner of Republicanism. Unable to counter this coalition, the Michigan Democrats lost their long-held dominance in the state, managing to retain toeholds only in Detroit and the Upper Peninsula.[1]

Although ailing, Michigan's Democratic Party was nonetheless still very much alive. Indeed, as the 1860 election neared, Democratic partisans followed a time-honored strategy: they retrenched and rallied around traditional party tenets—states' rights, limited government, strict adherence to the Constitution and the law, and personal autonomy. Convinced that a strong, centralized government threatened individual liberty, Democrats believed that governmental noninterference was vital in preserving equal opportunity for all Americans. Independence for the individual mandated that institutions such as slavery remain subject to local custom and law to the extent that those local practices did not oppose or negate the Constitution. Confident in the appeal of their conservative principles and buoyed by minor Republican setbacks in recent elections, partisan Democrats hoped to save the nation from the tyranny and radicalism of their "Black" Republican opponents by winning the November 1860 election.[2]

Michigan Republicans also had their sights set on the upcoming election. Sure of continued electoral success in Michigan and hopeful that the nation would follow suit, Republicans anticipated ultimate victory for their Free-Soil principles. They adopted political antislavery as their tool to preserve the "free" status of the western territories and to prevent the North's enslavement at the hands of the Slave Power. Succinctly stated, Republicans believed that whoever controlled the nation's vast reserve of land, whether Free-Soilers or "slavocrats," would ultimately determine the fate of liberty in the United States. Hence, Republican ascendancy was deemed imperative for the nation's future growth and development and for restoring the Constitution to its original design, now threatened by Slave Power.[3]

Perceiving that the nation was at risk, voters of both parties focused intensely on the 1860 party nominating conventions. The *Detroit Free Press* made this point explicit in March 1860—well before delegates of either major party even assembled in their respective conventions. The paper claimed that "the real issue of the coming campaign has already been made up, and the conventions meeting in Charleston and Chicago can only reduce it in form and give it expression, but cannot change it. The contest is to be over the very existence of the Union itself, and the issue is Union or Disunion."[4]

Astute Republicans expressed interest in the Democratic convention. Although Republicans interpreted Stephen Douglas's apparent popularity among northern Democrats as further proof that their opposition to the extension of slavery was gaining ground in the North, the *Detroit Advertiser* derided the objective of the assemblage as the selection of a "standard bearer of the black flag of slavery during the coming campaign" and predicted the breakup of the convention, assuring readers that they were to witness "the last dying spasm of the slave Democracy." The prediction of fragmentation proved accurate, and the ruptured Democratic Party offered two nominees for the presidency, Stephen Douglas and John Breckinridge.[5]

Michigan Democrats had overwhelmingly favored Douglas. They considered him the party's only chance for victory over the Republicans and failed to recognize the depth of the South's aversion to him because of his opposition to the admission of Kansas under the Lecompton constitution. With the Democratic Party hopelessly sundered, Michigan Democrats continued to stand by Douglas and his popular sovereignty ideas. The *Detroit Free Press*, repudiating the southerners who had bolted the Democratic convention at Charleston and who provided the bulk of Breckinridge's support, asserted that Douglas's "conservatism" offered the only alternative to southern extremism and northern "Black Republicanism."[6]

The Democratic split seemed to provide Republicans with further proof of an "irrepressible" conflict of interest between freedom and slavery. Once again, the intrigue of slaveowners and slavery's supporters appeared to be playing out. Some Republicans saw the split as a plot on the part of southerners to provoke a disputed election, thereby throwing the election of the president into the House of Representatives, where southern interests would prevail. The *Advertiser*, exploiting both Republican loyalty and the republican suspicion of political parties, branded the convention a meeting of unprincipled office seekers divided not over issues concerning the nation but rather over matters "simply about men." Plainly stated, Republicans distinguished between their use of party to promote principles of public interest and their opponents' use of party for selfish gain.[7]

Before the May Republican convention in Chicago, Michigan partisans made known their preference for William Seward as the candidate for president. Jacob Howard, the Detroit attorney and future U.S. senator, pointed to the radical Seward as "the man worthy to receive this high honor [the nomination]. Never has an American statesman been truer to this great cause. Let us omit no manly effort to give success to our party, and to bring back the Constitution to its original principles and purposes."[8]

Michigan's Democrats also desired a Seward nomination in Chicago. According to the *Free Press*, Seward's "radicalism" (in other words, his and his party's perceived abolitionism and strident antisouthernism) would explicitly define the election as a choice between "Union and Disunion, peace or the irrepressible conflict." Michigan's preference, however, was not that of the Republican Party. Because of the Republicans' need to avoid the appearance of radicalism in order to win key states, Seward's bid failed, and the convention nominated the moderate Abraham Lincoln. After initially expressing outrage and denouncing "the politicians that slaughtered Governor Seward at Chicago," Michigan Republicans moved to embrace Lincoln. The *Lansing State*

Republican pledged to "bow to the will of the majority of the convention." The *Advertiser* also endorsed Lincoln, insisting that its allegiance did not belong to men but "to great principles and to great principles only." Meeting in convention in June, state Republicans voted their support for Lincoln and selected Austin Blair of Jackson as their candidate for governor.[9]

The *Free Press* also approved of Lincoln's nomination. From the Democrats' perspective, Lincoln was a good choice, the paper argued, because his nomination offended Michigan Republicans. More important, Douglas had previously defeated Lincoln in the Illinois senatorial election of 1858. Conversely, the former Michigan governor and secretary of the interior under Franklin Pierce, Democrat Robert McClelland, believed Lincoln more dangerous than Seward; he feared that Lincoln might be susceptible to control by radicals such as Horace Greeley, Charles Sumner, and Benjamin Wade.[10]

With the conventions over and the November election fast approaching, both parties intensified efforts to assure the victory of their candidates. Election campaigns in nineteenth-century America were highly partisan affairs, full of symbolism and latent meaning. Partisans organized numerous rallies, parades, pole raisings, and speeches to get out the vote. The intent of such political activity was not to convert opponents but to keep existing voting bases energized, to build party unity, and to convince supporters of the necessity of casting their ballots. In the process, political organizations hoped to bind together the best interest of party with that of nation. In addition, the competitive nature of antebellum Michigan elections buoyed partisans even in defeat, as the next election offered the chance for a reversal and the ascendancy of one's own party. The deep-seated conviction that their party represented the republic's best—perhaps its only—chance for salvation demanded that partisans seize the chance and strive to oust the "dangerous" opposition. This political culture would shape Michigan partisans' responses to the election of Lincoln and the secession of the Deep South.[11]

On November 6, 1860, the nation went to the polls, and Lincoln and the Republicans emerged victorious. In Michigan, the Republican victory was complete, with even the Democratic stronghold of Detroit giving majorities to Lincoln and Blair. Stunned by defeat, the state's Democrats rallied to their party standard. Responding to calls for party restructuring, the *Detroit Free Press* declared that none was necessary; the party needed simply "the most faithful adherence, in all circumstances and under all temptations, to its organization and principles." Indeed, the paper continued, if the Democrats followed this advice, victory was attainable in 1864. Faith in the American political process, party loyalty, and reliance on accepted principles shaped the northern Democratic responses to Lincoln's election. Democrats cleaved to their party, confident of its potential for unseating the Republicans in the next election.[12]

The threat of secession left Michigan's Democratic Party little time to lick its wounds. Uniting around party and principles, Democrats worked to garner nonpartisan support for the Union, vowing to "act with any and every man, of whatever party, faith or section, who is for the perpetuity of the Constitution and the Union." Labeling secession "inexcusable treason," the *Free Press* advised southerners against hasty action, reminding them that the Democratic Party retained control of the Supreme Court and Senate. Given time, McClelland wrote Alexander Stephens, Lincoln, too, would be forced by popular opinion to denounce the abolitionists and support a moderate policy. Following such a course, he continued, would destroy the Republican Party and ensure conservative success.[13]

State Democrats readily blamed Republicans for creating the secession crisis. McClelland believed that the basis for southern discontent was "the antislavery laws of the northern states passed within the last few years to embarrass the execution of the Fugitive Slave law and to hurl defiance at southern men and states." The *Free Press* concurred and demanded that Michigan repeal its personal liberty law. Indeed, many Democrats were convinced that the South feared Lincoln only for what they thought he represented—overt disregard for the Constitution and the rights of southerners. A political party willing to disregard the Constitution regarding fugitive slaves was, they believed, a party willing to ignore the Constitution's authority over other rights.[14]

Republicans refused to repeal the personal liberty law. Throughout the secession winter of 1860 and 1861, Michigan Republicans resisted all concessions to the South, in part because they operated on the basis of a fundamental misunderstanding of southern secessionist sentiment: believing the majority of southerners were devoted to the Union, they anticipated a popular upheaval denouncing secession and were determined to give secessionists no concessions or leverage. Sen. Zachariah Chandler, a noted radical, wrote Governor-elect Austin Blair, imploring him to "take high Union ground" in his upcoming inaugural address, "characterize secession as treason, and [pledge] all the resources of the state to maintain the Union as it is." Flint lumberman and future governor Henry Crapo urged, "No concessions, no more compromises, nor toleration or forbearance toward cessionists [*sic*]." Only strict adherence to party doctrine could save the nation.[15]

Attempts at compromise in the early months of 1861 met with similar Republican condemnation. Concessions were considered unacceptable and unnecessary. Truly, most Republicans agreed, "we have nothing to concede, compromise or apologize for." Dexter-area Republicans, incensed over the proposed compromise plan of John J. Crittenden, petitioned Michigan's congressional delegation, stating "that such action is a practical surrender of long cherished principles, of our most patient, earnest and honest efforts to restore our government to its first principles and practice, and that such action is demoralizing and destructive to us as a party, and calculated to augment the evils it seeks to avoid, by inviting still further aggressions of the slave power through such hasty and injudicious submission to its dictates." It was believed that concessions to the South would lead only to further demands on the North and to the demise of the Republicans as a party. Accordingly, Michigan declined Virginia's invitation to send delegates to a "peace convention" to be held February 4. When it appeared that the convention might effect some form of compromise, Chandler asked Governor Blair to send a delegation of "stiff backed men . . . as a matter of courtesy to our erring brethren," adding that, "without a little blood-letting this Union will not, in my estimation, be worth a rush."[16]

Not all Republicans agreed with the inflexible stand taken by the majority of their colleagues. The *Ann Arbor Journal* cautioned, "It does not seem worth while to plunge the nation into civil war, to assert an abstract principle [anti-slavery extension]. We have gained a noble Republican victory; let us secure its fruits by a wise and conservative policy. By a course of Radicalism, all may be lost." One Michigan Republican counseled Governor-elect Blair to undertake a "conciliatory but firm" position in regard to the South so that "no fuel might be added to the disunion flame." Despite such pleas, conservatism remained a minority position among Michigan Republicans.[17]

Democrats attacked the Republicans for their refusal to compromise, misconstruing their adherence to fundamental Republican principles as mere partisanship practiced at the expense of the nation. Berating Republican intransigence, the *Free Press* claimed, "It [the Republican party] has been ready enough to compromise difficulties in its party, but it has set its face against compromise of the difficulties which are hurrying the country to ruin. Party before country has been its rule of action." Democrats fervently believed that they alone were acting in the nation's behalf. In their role as nonpartisan patriots, they hoped to appeal to Americans, from both the North and the South, who, they were convinced, sought the preservation of the Union and the Constitution under conservative government. Encouraged by a growing conservatism in the nation, McClelland nonetheless feared that Republicans would thwart all efforts at compromise, concluding dolefully, "Unless some extraordinary change occurs they [Republicans] will not repeal the personal liberty laws, nor adopt any measure looking to anything else than coercion. It really sickens the heart to know that we are to be ruled by such a set of fanatics and madmen. I still believe the people are right, but we cannot touch them because there are no elections in time." As he saw it, the nation faced betrayal at the hands of self-serving politicians.[18]

As the crisis deepened, Michigan anxiously awaited Lincoln's inauguration. On March 4, 1861, the new president addressed the nation. Hoping to maintain the loyalty of the upper South, Lincoln proclaimed a policy of watchful waiting. Michigan Republicans were surprisingly taciturn about the inaugural. Undoubtedly, many shared the sentiments that Rev. George Tuthill of Pontiac expressed in his diary: "Great is the relief that the corrupt old Buchanan and southern administration has gone out forever." The *Ann Arbor Journal* approved of the address, writing that it "will command the general assent of the people of the North, with few exceptions."[19]

The *Detroit Free Press,* however, initially found Lincoln's address disturbing: the new president's vow to use the power of the federal government "to hold, occupy and possess the property and places belonging to the government" proved his determination to use coercion against the South. But after reconsidering the address, the journal claimed that the inaugural could also be perceived as an offer of compromise. Lincoln's ambiguity led the *Free Press* to beseech the president to clarify his position. McClelland shared the paper's perplexity. The Monroe lawyer wrote a friend, "Lincoln is neither for peace or war. He must compromise and back down or call Congress together and declare war to the end. He cannot collect duties—he has no army—he has no men around him equal to those he has to oppose." Democrats insisted that Lincoln make known his course of action and act decisively for compromise or war.[20]

The rush of events soon intensified demands for unambiguous action. Shortly after assuming office, Lincoln was apprised that the garrison at Fort Sumter (one of two forts in the seceded states still in federal hands), located at the entrance to Charleston harbor in South Carolina, was facing a desperate logistical situation. Dwindling supplies at the fort compelled Lincoln to choose between evacuating the post or risking a confrontation by resupplying it. Neither party had arrived at an internal consensus on the best course of action before Charleston's shore batteries ended the debate. Responding to the attack, Lincoln called for seventy-five thousand volunteers to put down the rebellion. The presidential summons drove four of the remaining eight slave states out of the Union. Civil war had begun, as had an uncertain period in Michigan partisan politics.[21]

The outbreak of civil war in the United States in April 1861 initiated a period of ambivalence among northerners concerning the necessity and desirability of sustaining party politics during a time of national crisis. Infused with traditional republican distrust of political organizations and a desire for northern unity, Democrats and Republicans advanced pleas of "no party" for the duration of the war. Coexisting with this antiparty sentiment, however, was a growing perception among the politically active that political parties represented not an evil but a positive force in safeguarding liberty and ensuring the survival of the Republic. Imbued as well with republican concerns for the nation's fate, most northerners found themselves unwilling and, more important, unable to discard partisanship.[22]

Accordingly, Democrats and Republicans clung tenaciously to partisan principles and the party structures erected in defense of these principles. Each group insisted that nonpartisanship occur according to its own dictates; failing that, each group maintained its partisan loyalties. These loyalties were strengthened by the crisis of civil war and the deep-seated conviction that the principles embodied by one's own party represented the last, best hope for the survival of the Republic and that opposition to a party rooted in such principles necessarily smacked of treasonable subversion of the American experiment. Although the two-party system in the North remained suspect, its survival did not impede the war effort as contemporaries often argued but rather invigorated it as each party eyed its opponent warily, never quite believing that the opposition could truly be loyal. This suspicion, in turn, fostered intraparty cooperation and a unity of purpose that furthered party principles.

Michigan partisans proved no exception to the northern rule. Calls for nonpartisanship echoed throughout the state following the shelling of Fort Sumter. Concurrently, ambivalence and questions of political propriety gave way to revitalized party struggle as Republicans and Democrats alike looked to their traditional party tenets in order to save the Republic. Throughout the period 1860 to 1865, both parties faced continuous political opposition, although Michigan's Democratic Party would never seriously threaten the supremacy of state Republicans. In spite of inferior numbers, however, the Democrats had a great, albeit unintended, impact on state politics. By maintaining their party organization and challenging Republicans for political office, they compelled Republicans to work together to preserve party unity. Forced harmony on basic party tenets and the war effort thus enabled Michigan Republicans to keep their opponents politically subordinate and to thwart Democratic efforts to create new conservative or regional political coalitions.

Michiganians of both parties were enraged by the bombardment of

Sumter: the national flag had been fired upon. Men rushed forward in response to Lincoln's call for troops, and the state mobilized to defend the federal government. The advent of war also initiated a period of ambivalence for political partisans, especially Michigan Democrats. There could be only two positions on the war: either for the government or against it. Michigan partisans of all stripes adopted the former stance early in the war. "The people without reference to party are united in the purpose to maintain the federal government let it cost what it may," Jacob Howard wrote to Governor Blair within a week of Sumter's fall. Henry Crapo echoed Howard's observation several days later, claiming that "as in the East so here [in Flint] all party lines are destroyed and the entire population are determined to break up the southern rebellion at any cost and sacrifice."[23]

As news of Sumter reached Michigan, Democrats agreed that the "anarchy" of disunion had to be speedily and convincingly dispelled. McClelland urged Lincoln to "make every concession consistent with honor but manfully insist on the unity of the whole country." The *Free Press* pledged that all Democrats and conservative men would do their duty and support the government in "the exercise of all its constitutional functions to preserve the Union," and in a large Union rally in Detroit on April 13, Democrat Charles Walker asked the citizens of Detroit, "irrespective of party," to put aside debate over the causes of the war and to sustain the government.[24]

But Democrats faced a dilemma. Patriotism dictated abandoning party affiliation, yet as the election campaign of 1860 had reiterated, partisan ties ran deep. It would be impossible to suspend party principles and suspicion of political opponents while those opponents held power. How, then, could Democrats support the war without sacrificing their party's tenets and organization? And conversely, how would partisans retain political affiliation without appearing disloyal? For Michigan's Democrats, the answer was obvious: partisans needed simply to stand by traditional party principles. As a result, they pursued an agenda analogous to that of the past—based on strict adherence to the Constitution and the laws, the integrity of the Union, limited central government, and protection of individual liberties.

Democrats presumed that these principles offered the best plan for saving the Union and that the majority of northerners (and southerners, for that matter) held such views. Thus, they understood themselves as nonpartisan purveyors of the general will. By contrast, the secession crisis and the Republican refusal to compromise convinced Democrats that their opponents were self-interested politicians who cared nothing for the nation. Democratic nonpartisanship was really nothing more than traditional party loyalty, but the fact that party supporters understood their actions to be nonpartisan meant that political cooperation, if it occurred, would occur only along Democratic lines and under Democratic control.

Within this framework, Michigan Democrats accepted Walker's Union rally plea but carefully qualified the extent of their nonpartisanship. The *Michigan Argus* stated that "we know no party until the contest is over, we sustain the Federal Government as the Government, and not as a Republican administration." The *Free Press* endorsed nonpartisanship but also promised "to hold up to scorn and detestation those party leaders who have purposely and maliciously conspired for the shedding of blood." The paper ruthlessly berated Republicans for refusing to adhere to the Constitution and enforce the Fugitive Slave Law and for rejecting efforts to compromise and avert war. Finally, the *Free Press* assured Democrats that support for the war was tied to one goal: the restoration of the Union. By no means would the paper support a war to end slavery.[25]

Like the Democrats, Republicans assumed that their own party's principles embodied those of most northerners and that they provided for the nation's welfare, and they felt the 1860 election reinforced these beliefs. Therefore, for partisans, pursuit of Republican policies through party organization simply represented nonpartisan behavior. Republicans thus linked criticism of the Lincoln administration, which was merely pursuing supposedly nonpartisan policies to restore the Union, with criticism of the American system of government.

Politically speaking, nonpartisanship was more acceptable to Michigan Republicans than it was to their Democratic opponents because the Republicans controlled the state and national governments. Furthermore, suspension of political rivalry would probably ensure Republican political control throughout the war. But Republican appeals for nonpartisanship were more than mere political maneuvering. As Ronald Formisano aptly demonstrated in his study of antebellum Michigan politics, the Republican Party contained a strong antiparty bias. To many Republicans, partisanship served merely as a means for promoting principles. As long as war continued, one issue stood paramount: the nation's survival. It was therefore natural for Republicans to demand and expect suspension of party loyalty. Still, Michigan's Radical Republican proclivities, coupled with an established tradition of political competition, ensured that partisanship would endure among Republicans as well.[26]

Indeed, Republican pleas for nonpartisan support for the war opened new lines of attack against the Democrats. Speaking in Lansing, D. C. Leach, editor of the *State Republican,* declared that "there will be but one party in the North, and that will be the Union party. If there is any other party it will be a Tory party." Democratic partisanship smacked of disloyalty. Leach's newspaper pronounced its intention to abandon, "at least to a great extent," partisan feelings but apparently believed that Lansing Democrats posed enough of a threat to warrant maintaining some degree of partisan watchfulness.[27]

In the months between Lincoln's call for troops and the local November elections, the trend of intense but masked partisan activity persisted. The apparent ambiguity of Lincoln's war plan disturbed Michigan Democrats. McClelland attacked the president's secrecy, demanding that he make his policy public and nurture Union sentiment in the South. Henry Ledyard, Lewis Cass's son-in-law and a Breckinridge supporter in 1860, labeled Lincoln "an ordinary man far beneath the necessities of his position" and lamented that "there is but little hope that we shall ever be a united people." The *State Republican* rebuked such criticism and urged Democrats to judge the president "by deeds, not by words."[28]

But words themselves—and battles over their utterance—emphasized and reinforced persistent partisanship. On April 15, the *Detroit Tribune* published an editorial demanding martial law in the North, "in order that all who do not sing the war tune may be choked off." The *Free Press* countered by reminding the *Tribune* of its recent attack upon southerners for their denial of free speech and of the many Whigs (now Republicans) who had opposed the Mexican War. In May 1861, Republicans in the state legislature attempted to pass a sedition law that was intended to silence Democratic opposition. Warning that "radicalism" was undermining the unity of the North, the *Free Press* denounced the Republicans. Radicals were pursuing party interests during a time of national crisis, and by so doing, they were forcing Democrats to maintain partisanship to protect the Republic.[29]

Further proof of insidious radical partisanship came to hand with the defeat of the federal forces at Bull Run on July 21. McClelland blamed the Lincoln administration for the defeat, claiming that the army had been sent forward against a superior force to satisfy the demands of the radicals. Some state Republicans agreed, citing Gen. Winfield Scott's opposition to the attack as proof that the army had been unprepared. But the *Free Press* concluded that Republican partisanship, in the form of politically appointed generals, and the Radicals' "On to Richmond" demands gave clear evidence of the real interest of the Lincoln administration—partisanship.[30]

Republicans mounted their counterattack, remaining silent on the failures of Lincoln's war plan and darkly warning that men who "interpose partisanship in the path of those pursuing the war effort, are enemies." The *Detroit Advertiser* went further in its accusations of disloyalty by claiming that it was "a matter of well authenticated history that years ago the Northern Democrats entered into a bargain with their haughty and overbearing leaders at the South, and agreed to rule the destinies of this nation for their common benefit."[31]

In September 1861, rumors spread through Michigan about the existence in the state of a secret organization, the Knights of the Golden Circle, intent upon overthrowing the government. That month, Detroit's Republican press linked a number of prominent Michigan Democrats (McClelland among them) to the organization, going so far to accuse former president Franklin Pierce (who was in Detroit to visit McClelland) of being a "prowling traitorous spy."[32]

By October, political interest began to focus on upcoming local elections and speculation over whether these contests would be partisan in nature. Throughout most of the state, the elections were to prove uneventful, with Democrats and Republicans uniting under the Union banner. In Detroit, however, the stronghold of Michigan's Democrats, the story was much different. Contending that "there is really no difference in opinion in this city on the subject of the duty and necessity of prosecuting the war," the *Free Press* expressed the hope that the upcoming local election would foreswear partisanship and "be between men." On October 8, Detroit Republicans extended an invitation to local Democrats to "unite without distinction of party in nominating municipal candidates." The following day, the *Free Press* noted that it was "plainly apparent that the mass of our people, comprising all parties, are indisposed to go into any party convention at this time." However, the paper went on to endorse the plan only as long as party organizations remained separate and intact. One local Democrat questioned Republican motives. In a letter to the *Free Press,* he argued that the Republican call for "no party" was simply a trap. He maintained that Republicans had adhered to partisanship since they had been elected in 1860 and were only calling for cooperation to destroy the Democratic Party and usurp the party's principles. As a result, Republican partisanship dictated that Democrats maintain their party.[33]

Apparently, most Detroit Democrats concurred with this opinion. On October 20, the call went out for Democrats to meet in a citywide convention four days later. The *Free Press* remained unconvinced of the necessity of the convention; recent Republican accusations of disloyalty could hardly have helped convince the paper of the propriety of the meeting. Yet it refused to denounce the gathering. On October 22, the Seventh Ward Democrats held

their caucus and passed a resolution expressing the belief that "the principles and policies of the Democratic party [are] those best calculated to
advance the interests and ensure the perpetuity of our glorious American
union." They added: "We will continue to adhere to them, confident that in so
doing we are manifesting our patriotism and our earnest desire for the good
and welfare of our country." Two days later, the city convention adopted a very
similar position and nominated a slate of candidates.[34]

Local Republicans were incensed by what they interpreted as the blatant
appeal to partisanship and labeled the Democrats who favored the convention a group of disgruntled office seekers. Detroit's November 1861 election
pitted the regular Democratic Party against the People's or Citizen's Party—
the result of the Republican offer of nonpartisan cooperation—with its slate
of four Republicans and four Democrats. The regular Democrats emerged
victorious, winning seven of eight offices. Aware that many Democrats had,
"out of patriotism," worked for and supported the People's Party, the editors
of the *Free Press* were astounded at the extent of the victory. They attributed it
to Republican refusals to abandon partisanship in pursuing the war and to
local Democrats' inability to abandon cherished principles and unite with
abolitionists. Republicans blamed the loss on the absence of the Republican
voters who had volunteered for service and on the chicanery of politicians.[35]

Detroit's election marked a new period in Michigan Civil War politics.
Nonpartisan cooperation would remain the ideal in the state, but for active
men of both parties, the crisis of war increasingly drove home the need to continue partisan activity to save the country. This belief led McClelland to write a
friend: "I agree with you in regard to the party. I am unwilling to yield the old
name, and cannot [yield] the principles. At all counts it is well to stick by the old
ship, until we are agreed the good of the country requires its abandonment."[36]

The year 1862 proved to be pivotal in Michigan. A series of unsuccessful
military campaigns, Republican war measures expanding the scope of government, traditional fears of governmental power, and increased Democratic
criticism of the Lincoln administration contributed to a sense of urgency
about the future of the nation, an urgency clearly reflected in the November
1862 elections.

The new year began with the war stretching onward, with no end in sight.
Disturbed by the course of war, Michigan Democrats approached the Democratic state convention in March. McClelland indicated to Franklin Pierce
that "our party is ready to meet the issue, to stand up manfully for the right,
and to battle abolitionism." He went on to add that "we are constantly gaining strength in numbers." Complaining that the object of the war had been

perverted, McClelland wrote that southerners believed that the radical principles of "subjugation and the absolute extinguishment of their favorite domestic institution" were the goal of the North. He urged that "union feeling"
in the South be promoted and that Lincoln advance "with the olive branch in
one hand and the sword in the other."[37]

With an eye on the upcoming November election, the state Democrats
gathered in Detroit on March 5 to rally the party faithful and to nominate
candidates for the spring election. On the day of the convention, the *Free
Press* reminded delegates to "re-assert the old faith" in whose "cardinal principles may be found the salvation of the country." Flavius Littlejohn of Allegan County reiterated that plea in his speech to the convention that day,
calling for support of the government and denouncing the twin evils of abolitionism and secessionism. While calling for a vigorous pursuit of the war, he
explained that the conflict was not a war "for the thraldom of the loyal citizens, nor a war for rendering sovereign states to menial provinces" but rather
was intended to restore "the old Constitution and the old Union of our fathers." Littlejohn relied on the most basic of republican images—despotic
use of government power—to impress his message upon the minds of the assembled delegates. Radicalism, not Lincoln, posed the greatest threat to the
nation. Convinced that Radicals were bent on usurping power in order to destroy the old Union and to interfere with the Constitution and local institutions, Littlejohn insisted that "party organizations must be resorted to and
party platforms adopted at least so far as to test the fealty of voters to the time
honored work of our fathers. There can be no middle ground in this question." Radicalism had to be defeated at the ballot box, and the republican
principles of the nation had to be upheld by voting Democratic.[38]

The convention ratified a series of resolutions denouncing abolitionism
and secessionism and criticizing the administration's conduct of the war. The
convention's actions reaffirmed the Democratic Party's stand as a loyal opposition, on guard against the abuse of power. McClelland agreed with the convention's resolutions and wrote, "Now is the time to maintain the doctrines
and principles of the democratic party without bending of the knee to fanaticism." Indeed, the role of the party was "not to dog the war but to press it as
rapidly as possible to a conclusion, stay the progress of . . . fanaticism, and
maintain the integrity of the union through the constitution."[39]

During the early months of 1862, state Republicans continued to press
their own political agenda. Troubled by recent signs of overt party competition, they increasingly suspected Democratic motives and actions. When Ann
Arbor Democrats met in convention in early March to nominate delegates to

the state convention, the city's *Michigan State News,* a Republican journal, grieved that when the bell "sounded the call to party politicians to make war upon the union feelings which up to that time had been predominant in our city, the sound fell like a death knell upon our . . . hearts, and crushed for the moment our high hopes of a glorious future." The Republican State Central Committee added fuel to the fire with a circular charging that Democratic Party leaders were "incapable of rising above the most groveling partisanship, or even of divesting themselves of sympathy with traitors!" The circular asked: "Who ever heard of a Republican traitor? Our ranks do not even contain an apologist for rebellion." At the same time, the controversy over the Knights of the Golden Circle came to a head with the publication in the *Detroit Tribune* of a letter detailing the order's activities in Michigan. The letter was actually a hoax, but it was reprinted throughout the state, convincing many Republicans of Democratic disloyalty. As a result of the letter, at least one Republican newspaper, the *Lansing State Republican,* urged Republican partisans to "let a straight Republican ticket be put in nomination in every city and township. Let us not stain the Republican banner by a union with the Dark Lantern Knights of the Golden Circle who aim at the overthrow of the government." Democratic opposition was acting to bind the Republican Party together in self-defense. The grave danger that threatened the nation necessitated loyalty to the Republican Party and its principles.[40]

Throughout the summer of 1862, Michigan intently watched events in the East as George B. McClellan led his Army of the Potomac up the peninsula toward Richmond. Democrats were quick to blame McClellan's lack of progress on inadequate support from the Lincoln administration and the Committee on the Conduct of the War (one of whose members was Zachariah Chandler). The committee, the *Detroit Free Press* charged, was trying to direct military affairs and conspiring to replace McClellan, intending to make him appear incompetent by denying him further reinforcements.[41]

Responding to the Democratic attacks, Michigan Republicans united around their party and called for a more determined war effort. Future governor Henry Baldwin wished that "instead of calling for 300,000 men, half a million had been called for." Henry Crapo told his son, "It is terrible, this war; and I fear for the result unless a more energetic and decided course is pursued in the prosecution of the war."[42]

Disenchanted with the war effort, Michigan Democrats hoped to build a conservative coalition to sweep the radicals from power in the fall elections and bring the war to a speedy end. Meeting in Detroit on September 15, the Democratic State Central Committee issued a call for a Union convention, proclaiming the convention open to all conservative and Union-loving men, particularly moderate Republicans. But by the time the convention convened on October 1, the war had taken a new turn. On September 22, Lincoln issued his Emancipation Proclamation; one week later, Congress approved his suspension of the writ of habeas corpus, an action taken immediately after the attack on Fort Sumter. These two moves seemed to prove the Democrats' worst fears: radicalism had permeated the entire government. The *Free Press* was livid and argued that Lincoln "demands that the whole nation worship at his partisan shrine, that large numbers of people shall shed their blood and sacrifice their property for an object which they loathe, not for the preservation of the constitution, but for, what they regard [as] its subversion." Democrats beseeched Lincoln to adhere to the Constitution and to reconsider his actions. McClelland acidly predicted: "It will not be long before he will have to follow the example of King Philip and employ a servant to tell him every morning, before he meets his devotees, that he is still a man and not God." Tyrannical government threatened the nation. The Constitution was dead, power had been usurped, a national draft imposed, local institutions disregarded, arbitrary arrests made, and free speech threatened. For Michigan's Democrats, a conservative coalition against radical despotism was imperative.[43]

Most Republicans in the state viewed recent events very differently. They stoutly defended the constitutionality of Lincoln's action under the president's power as commander in chief and lauded his blow against the Slave Power. Although the conservative *Michigan Journal* manifested lukewarm support for the seemingly "noble and patriotic" Union movement and counseled Republicans who rejected the movement at least to avoid nominating radical candidates, the Democratic appeal for a Union convention met with little positive response among moderate or radical Republicans. Henry Crapo could see nothing of value in the Union party and labeled it a group of "proslavery, rebel sympathizing democrats." In Ann Arbor, the *Michigan State News* commented that the Democrats of Michigan had "given abundant evidence that they want no union party except such a one as will destroy the Republican party"; Democrats had made nonpartisan union impossible. The paper therefore implored Republicans "to stand by that organization which stands by the government."[44]

Lincoln's Emancipation Proclamation drew virtually no criticism from Republicans in Michigan. If anything, it elicited fervent praise. The *State Republican* claimed that the proclamation gave "life not only to four millions of black bondsmen, but also to an entire nation of white freemen." The paper also asserted that the proclamation was entirely constitutional under the president's powers as commander in chief. This was certainly not the act of a tyrant but rather of a patriot, "a second savior of our country." Lincoln had acted wholly within his delegated authority and had struck a blow against the Slave Power and the rebels.[45]

Thus galvanized to stand behind their administration, Michigan Republicans held their convention in Detroit on September 25. The body passed resolutions in support of the war effort and in favor of Lincoln's proclamation. A further resolution also attempted to maintain the party's nonpartisan status by refusing to tender or accept political issues as long as the rebellion continued. As their candidate for governor, the convention renominated Austin Blair.[46]

On October 1, 1862, the People's State Union Party Convention met at Jackson. The delegates nominated a slate of candidates for the upcoming election, headed by Byron Stout, a Pontiac Republican, for governor, and endorsed a series of resolutions pledging support for the war and condemning the Lincoln administration for containing too many "ambitious partizan [sic] politicians and philanthropists." After attending the convention, McClelland wrote, "We are opposed to all innovations upon the permanent institutions of our country, for the reestablishment of the Union and Constitution (as it needs restoring), opposed to separation and everything that even tends to mar the symmetry of our beautiful fabric." One week later, state Democrats met in convention and endorsed the candidates and platform of the Union Party. The battle lines were drawn and the struggle initiated. Democrats had established themselves as a loyal opposition party safeguarding the nation and its citizens, and now the nation's fate lay with the voters.[47]

The month preceding the election was a period of intense partisanship and political interest. On October 3, the Republican State Central Committee issued a circular addressed to the Republicans of Michigan. Asserting the party's nonpartisan focus on the war, the circular reminded Republicans that to desert the party "is to take from the government its most efficient support." Therefore, the plea concluded, "in times of profound peace, an administration without a party, can hardly hope to succeed in a steady and wise policy. The complications of the present enormous civil war, render the destruction of the government almost certain, unless it be supported by the organized powers of the loyal people." The party's message was clear: the nation's survival dictated that Republicans remain loyal to the party and its principles; anything less was treason.[48]

State Democrats harangued the voters that only the Union ticket could ensure the "integrity and restoration of the union, and the inviolability of the

Constitution." The *Free Press* reminded its readers of the excesses of radicalism, insisting that "every household that is in mourning read the letter [Chandler's "bloodletting" letter of 1861], let every soldier who is maimed for life peruse it, and curse the man who had so little of humanity as to conceive it." The evening before the election, a large Union rally was held in Detroit. Reminding participants of the failures of the Republicans and of their party's selfish pursuit of spoils, Unionists implored the assembled citizens to use their ballots to end the Republicans' destruction of the Constitution.[49]

On November 4, 1862, Michigan's citizens went to the polls. The following day, the *Free Press* announced a great victory in Detroit. Statewide, Democrats had failed to capture the governorship but managed to elect one congressman in the Fifth District. With the election over, the *Free Press* noted, "We speak . . . as the organ of a party which is triumphant in the nation and we have only one rule, respect for all the rights guaranteed by the constitution and the laws." The paper clearly overstated the case. The Democrats gained thirty-eight congressmen nationally (almost all from the Midwest) but remained the minority party by twenty-seven members.[50]

Republicans, for the most part, remained quiet about the election. The Republican loss in Detroit prompted Chandler to comment to Charles T. Gorham of Marshall, "You have done nobly in Calhoun [County]. I wish I could say so much for Wayne, but here we have had secret conservatism, Democracy and the Devil to contend with and they were too much for us." The *Detroit Advertiser and Tribune* found solace in the fact that "notwithstanding the immense drain of Republicans by the war from this state," Michigan remained Republican. Three days later, the paper insisted that "the Republicans, being fairly outvoted at the polls [in Detroit] will now set the Democracy an example of toleration and obedience to law, that they sadly need."[51]

The election over, Michigan focused its attention on the senatorial contest to be decided in January. The *State Republican* claimed that the Republican victory on November 4 demonstrated "that the people want a radical man, who is in favor of the most energetic, the most speedy, and the most thorough measures. . . . They want Zachariah Chandler." The Union-Democratic coalition disagreed and endorsed James Joy, the conservative Detroit Republican and longtime associate of Chandler. Joy's appeal to conservative men stemmed from his belief that politicians, notably radicals, had disrupted the war effort. He was a "pure," nonpartisan, public-spirited man—and others like him were needed to restore virtue to the government and to give their support to the president, wrote a supporter. "If the country dear to us is to be saved at all," another backer wrote Joy, "it can be done only by telling the truth so plainly that the people will not only understand it but act upon it and crush out the demagogues who not only brought on this war but also those who will do all they can to carry it on and thus complete the ruin which other demagogues have begun." On January 5, 1863, a pamphlet written by Joy arrived at the state legislature. Joy did not question the loyalty of the radicals, only their actions, and he objected to the "intermeddling of a few men stepping out of their sphere, and controlling other departments of the government with which they are not charged."[52]

Chandler, meantime, gathered his forces for the struggle ahead. Head of the so-called Detroit Regency, he wielded great power in Michigan and was determined to maintain Republican hegemony in the face of a now unmasked threat to the nation—the Democrats. "I hate a northern traitor," Chandler wrote his wife in the days following the U.S. Senate election, "worse a thousand fold than I do a southern and would exterminate both." Joy, he continued, "will finally find body and soul in the lap of treason. McClelland-ism and treason are fast becoming synonimous [*sic*] terms and Joy has taken the first step. Well let him go. He is and always has been a coward. Still he has gone lower than I thought possible for him to go. He has proven false to principle, false to friendship, and *false everyway*." On January 8, the matter was put to the state legislature. Not surprisingly, the votes were cast entirely along party lines, with Republicans supporting Chandler and Democratic-Unionists favoring Joy. Chandler withstood the challenge and was reelected. Partisan competition helped to bind members of the state Republican Party together and to cause them to fall in behind Chandler.[53]

While a national orientation overwhelmingly dominated Michigan's political landscape between the years 1861 and 1865, the older political features that had shaped the state's antebellum political course occasionally manifested themselves during the war years. Banking, long a staple of political debate in Michigan, assumed renewed significance after the passage of the National Banking Act in 1863. State banks, many of which had only recently begun operations after the popular endorsement of the 1858 general banking law, wasted little time in taking advantage of the opportunities provided by the legislation. Six banks (two in Detroit and one each in Ann Arbor, Ypsilanti, Fenton, and Hillsdale) obtained charters in 1863 alone, thus marking the end of state-level debate over the issue.[54]

Of even greater long-term significance was the revival of railroad agitation. Despite federal largesse (in the form of land grants) and the concerted efforts of the 1857 state legislature (which distributed the federal land grants to prospective railroad builders), rail construction in Michigan had ground to a halt by 1862 due to the combined effects of the panic of 1857 and the crisis of the Civil War. Lacking additional land to distribute and constitutionally prohibited from granting direct aid yet eager to pursue new initiatives, the 1863 legislature turned to local aid as a means of furthering railroad development in Michigan and enacted two separate laws authorizing the residents of the cities of Saginaw and Jackson (or any township in Jackson County) to loan money to further railroad construction projects.

The precedent now set, the 1864 special legislative session (called by Governor Blair to legalize and regularize the haphazard system of local bounties that had been adopted to spur enlistment in the aftermath of the passage of a federal conscription act) and the 1865 regular session spawned an orgy of similar railroad-aid legislation. In all, eleven new acts were passed in 1864 and ten more in 1865. Not all Republican legislators were entirely comfortable with this new trend, however. Future governor Henry Crapo, serving his first term in the state senate in 1863 and 1864, considered such legislation "very mischievous," pledging as it did (by mere majority vote) the credit of towns and counties to private companies. Using his position as chair of the standing Committee on Corporations (and undoubtedly aware of the anti-railroad hostility of many of the party's rank and file), Crapo recognized that he could not defeat the various bills and worked to amend the proposed legislation to secure some protection for state taxpayers. His diligence paid off, and by a one-vote margin, a committee of the whole agreed that no bonds could be sold for less than par value and that the proceeds of bond sales would not be delivered to the railroad companies until construction had actually begun. By passing these local aid bills, the legislature unwittingly opened a Pandora's box: state politics would be agitated and Republican cohesion would be threatened for the next decade.[55]

In the war years, the Republican-dominated legislature also attempted to continue its support for the various Whiggish social institutions that it had championed during the party's prewar administration of the state. Gross expenditures for education, prisons, and asylums rose over the course of the war. Nonetheless, rampant inflation resulted in a real-dollar expenditure decrease of 15 percent in this area. The fiscal demands of the war (supplying state regiments, paying bounties, and so forth) drained the bulk of available funds from existing programs and required new revenue streams. Faced with acute fiscal need, Michigan increased its level of indebtedness and raised millage rates on property from 2.697 mills in 1861 to 3.734 mills by 1865. Revenues from specific taxes (those imposed on corporate entities), by contrast, actually fell during the war. One study of Michigan's wartime legislature

suggested that this fiscal evidence (coupled with the expanding banking network and its blatantly prorailroad sympathies) "tells a tale of growing neglect
of the old Jacksonian element of the Republican coalition." Though this neglect would come back to haunt the Republicans, these economic and social
concerns took a back seat in 1863 to the ongoing war, which continued to
threaten the very existence of the nation. For Republicans, such concerns
were also secondary to the Free-Soil crusade that the party initiated in 1854—
a crusade that seamlessly merged local concerns about the fate of freedom in
the face of sweeping socioeconomic transformation with fears of a tyrannical
Slave Power bent on the destruction of American freedom.[56]

Throughout the early months of 1863, Michigan Democrats escalated
their attacks on the Lincoln administration. As the Emancipation Proclamation went into effect, the *Free Press* cried, "No measure of this imbecile, malig-
nant and tyrannical administration can compare with this." Because of the
proclamation and the continuing arrests of Democrats in the North under
the suspension of the writ of habeas corpus, Democrats felt cornered, and
they struck back. Continuing to blame Republicans for the war's inception,
its maladministration, and its protraction, they now turned venomously on
Lincoln as well, accusing him of dishonesty in "masking his true identity"—
an identity only recently exposed through his "iron grasp of oppression."
Lincoln had become so corrupt with power, Michigan Democrats believed,
that he threatened to ride roughshod over the Constitution and individual
liberties. The president appeared to threaten everything that Democrats
cherished. At their state convention in February, Michigan Democrats
adopted a series of resolutions attacking emancipation, suspension of the
writ of habeas corpus, and "the flagrant and monstrous usurpations of the
administration and encroachments of abolitionism." They then eagerly
awaited the spring election and a vindication of Democratic principles. They
were disappointed.[57]

Republicans, convinced that the Democrats were out to undermine the
war effort, had responded in kind to the Democratic attacks, steadfastly defending Lincoln's actions and accusing Democrats, whom they derisively
labeled "copperheads" (a reference to the poisonous snake common
throughout the lower midwest), of being determined to sustain the Slave
Power in the government and of intending to make peace with the rebels
once elected. Chandler wrote to his wife that the greatest threat to the country came "from the traitors of the Northern Union men, conservative men
who did not want to hurt the rebels." The *State Republican* maintained that
Democratic criticism of the Lincoln administration had made a mockery of

the Union movement and went on to assert that "the lion's skin is now off, and the asses' ears stick out very prominently."[58]

While Michigan partisans grappled and jousted at home, the shooting war continued unabated throughout 1863 and into 1864. Mid-1863 victories at Gettysburg and Vicksburg seemed to have turned the tide against the Confederacy, but by May 1864, the Union army was still slugging it out with Robert E. Lee's Army of Virginia in the east and Joseph Johnston's Confederate force northwest of Atlanta. Casualty lists lengthened, yet the armies apparently stood hopelessly deadlocked. Democrats on the home front remained skeptical of the true intent of Lincoln's administration and scrutinized its every move, always ready to spring to the Republic's defense. Similarly, their Republican counterparts remained alert for Democratic treason, convinced that Democratic copperheads were intent on subverting the nation's war effort. Within this context, the politically active men of Michigan eagerly looked forward to the 1864 presidential election. To the victor in that election went the responsibility for determining not only how to end the war but also how to reconstruct the Union.

Prior to the opening of the national nominating conventions, Michigan Democrats vehemently expressed their dissatisfaction with the war. In an editorial entitled "When Will It End?" the *Michigan Argus* bemoaned the length of the war and its toll in human life. Now, claimed the writer, "the people of the United States are insulted with the demand that the imbecile administration of Abraham Lincoln shall be continued in power for another four years." The people had to realize that the Democratic Party was "the only true Union party [the only one] which is true to the Constitution." Once again, the line was drawn for the upcoming election.[59]

On May 31, a group of Radical Republicans also displayed their disapproval of Lincoln's handling of the war by meeting in convention in Cleveland and nominating John C. Frémont for president. Democrats were ecstatic over the developing split in the Republican Party. Elihu Pond of Ann Arbor, the editor of the *Michigan Argus,* recorded the convention's decision in his diary, happily noting, "The Republicans are hopping mad over Fremont's acceptance of the Cleveland nomination. Hope they will get madder, as an evidence of that the Gods may destroy them." Michigan Republicans, however, did not appear overly worried about Frémont. The *Lansing State Republican* labeled the convention a gathering of "ultra abolitionists," German supporters of Frémont, and "a species of war Democrats." The paper urged Frémont instead to stand by the decision of the impending Baltimore convention.[60]

Delegates to the regular Republican convention gathered in Baltimore on June 7. They renominated Lincoln and adopted a new name—the National Union Party. State Republicans heartily endorsed "Old Abe" and vowed to maintain Republican loyalty in Michigan. For their part, state Democrats were now convinced of the Republican Party's true aim: despotic government. Lincoln—the tyrant who had suspended the writ of habeas corpus, who had proclaimed southern slaves free in disregard of the Constitution, and who now desired the subjugation of the South through military force rather than the achievement of peace through negotiations—had been renominated. Amazed at the recent turn of events, Pond wrote in disbelief, "Old Abe was renominated at Baltimore yesterday, and the administration endorsed. The Republicans exclaim Glory to God. The people have lost all realization of their position and want a master."[61]

The Republican Party in Michigan set about nominating a slate of candidates for state and national office in convention on July 7. The convention unanimously supported Lincoln's candidacy and nominated Flint businessman Henry Crapo for governor. Noting that "our national existence, the interests of unborn millions, the hopes of Constitutional freedom throughout the world, all depend upon the utter annihilation of this nefarious Rebellion," the convention resolved that "unconditional surrender is the only terms to armed traitors." Not only did the fate of the nation hang in the balance but, more important, so, too, did the survival of the world's last hope for self-rule and republican government. With so much at risk and believing themselves to be the only defenders of the Republic, Republicans could easily combine charges of Democratic copperheadism and pleas for nonpartisanship. They hammered home the point time and time again throughout the latter half of 1864. Indeed, the *Bay City Press and Times* claimed that "Mr. Crapo will bear aloft the Republican standard side by side with that of the union—one and inseparable." The Republic and Republicans were considered by partisans as indistinguishable; attacks on one were attacks upon the other.[62]

In late August, Democrats met in convention in Chicago and effected a compromise between the two main wings of the Democratic Party: the "purists," or peace Democrats, and the "legitimists." Purists denounced the war as a Republican ploy to subjugate the South. The group remained wedded to Democratic principles and refused political cooperation that necessitated sacrifice of these principles. Legitimists, by contrast, demanded a vigorous pursuit of the war and remained open to compromise with the opposition, expressing a willingness to cooperate with conservatives in achieving their aims; Michigan's Democrats generally belonged to this latter class. To bind these two wings together, Democrats worked out a compromise at Chicago,

with the legitimists nominating George McClellan for president and the purists drawing up the party platform.[63]

The Democratic platform of 1864 denounced the Republican suppres-
sion of freedom of speech and the press, arbitrary arrests, and disregard for
states' rights. More important, the platform demanded that immediate efforts be made to cease hostilities, with the ultimate aim of holding a convention of states to restore the Union. In his letter of acceptance, McClellan
reversed this order and stated, "The Union is the one condition of peace—we
ask no more." Michigan Democrats endorsed McClellan's nomination in Detroit on September 1 and chose William Fenton as the party's candidate for
governor. Rejoicing over McClellan's nomination, Pond related that "great
enthusiasm prevails all through the country. The fires are burning and ought
to burn up the Lincoln administration root and branch." The campaign for
the presidency was in full swing.[64]

Inadvertently, the Democratic convention helped to end Republican divisions. As historian James McPherson contended, "Faced with a tangible
threat from a party half opposed to war and wholly opposed to emancipation,
radicals suddenly realized that Lincoln was their only alternative to disaster."
This realization resulted in the withdrawal of Frémont's candidacy on September 22. Democratic partisanship once again forced the divergent factions
of the Republican Party to work together for the party's—and the nation's—
survival.[65]

Republican electioneering began in earnest with the adjournment of
the Democratic convention in Chicago, and the Democrats' peace plank became the favorite target of Republican attacks. Comparing the northern copperheads with Jefferson Davis, the *Jonesville Independent* noted that: "Jeff Davis
says a state cannot be coerced. So say these Northern copperheads. Jeff says
you cannot stop a state from seceding; so say these Vallandighammers, Jeff
says state sovereignty is above the Constitution and the Government; so say
these peace yelpers. Jeff says leave us alone; so says George H. Pendleton,
candidate for Vice President. Jeff and his foreign coadjutors say vote for
McClellan and Pendleton; so say his Northern allies. Jeff says Lincoln is a tyrant; so say Northern disunionists." A vote for McClellan was considered a
vote for the South. Peace before union was unacceptable. Republicans had
to march forward and defeat treason in both the South and the North. Republicans were determined "to bury copperheadism under a loyal majority
that will astound and silence it forever."[66]

Crapo delivered a series of speeches throughout the state giving form to
just such ideas, comparing Democratic opposition with that of the Federalists

at the Hartford convention and insisting that he also was for peace—"peace through conquest." Rather than Republicans breeding tyranny, Crapo added, Democrats were the culprits. Democratic cries for peace only masked their desire to establish a southern-style aristocracy throughout the country. Crapo railed against Democrats for their charges that Republicans had caused the war. After all, a Democrat, James Buchanan, had been in office when the first states seceded and had done nothing. For these reasons and because "no less a question than the life or death of our nation, and the salvation or ruin of our country" was at stake, he urged Republicans to remain loyal to their party and do their part to save the Union.[67]

Republicans accused Michigan Democrats of endorsing peace at any cost, but the allegation was inaccurate. In fact, throughout the campaign, whenever Republicans mentioned "Peace Democrats," the examples they used were Democrats from outside Michigan—most notably, Clement Vallandigham of Ohio. Michigan's Democrats did desire peace but not without Union. For this reason, they emphasized the failure of the Lincoln administration to restore the Union and Lincoln's alleged widespread abuse of power. The *Free Press* warned that the reelection of Lincoln would bring "four years more of war, conscription, devastation, and outrages upon liberty." Also, during this campaign, Democrats relied heavily upon "Negrophobia" to stir the voters. For McClellan, the *Free Press* affirmed, "the Union is the one condition for peace"; for Lincoln, "the Negro is the only condition for peace." To Democrats and to most nineteenth-century Americans, blacks symbolized laziness, backwardness, ignorance, and chaos. Therefore, in a period in which Democrats perceived the nation's progress and vitality imperiled by civil war, tyrannical government, and disorder, the "Negro" became the ideal image for conveying all that was amiss in America. Lincoln, the Republican Party, and the Negro symbolized all that had gone wrong with the nation.[68]

Election day again found Michigan in the corner of Lincoln and the Republican Party. The Democrats agonized over their loss. Pond noted, "The people have gone mad. Hope that good may come of it, but can't see it." Taking heart in the increased number of Democratic votes cast compared to 1860, the *Free Press* reminded Republicans and its own Democratic readers that, although the Democratic Party had been beaten, it had not been subjugated. Rather, Democrats would "reunite and yet save the country," relying upon party principles that had "the immortality of truth and can never die." Democrats had once again served state Republicans notice that their actions were being scrutinized and that individual liberties were protected by the Democratic Party.[69]

The *State Republican* interpreted the election victory to mean that "the United States is to be one people. That the United States is to be a free people [and that the] war is to be prosecuted until the Rebels sue for peace." Most important of all, Lincoln's reelection ensured that the people "were determined to maintain a Democratic form of government at all hazards and at whatever cost." The people had upheld true republican principles and renounced disloyalty.[70]

As 1865 commenced, Michigan turned its attention eastward. Rumors of peace talks and news of Ulysses Grant's campaign around Petersburg filled the newspapers. The proposed Thirteenth Amendment to the Constitution, though, seems to have sparked little partisan debate in Michigan. Harriette Dilla, in her study of the state's politics in the postwar period, contended that "some" Democratic journals opposed the Thirteenth Amendment, fearful that the measure might usher in more objectionable steps. However, she added, once it was ratified, Democrats were "ready to defend it." This position, which might strike some as hypocritical, was entirely consistent with Democratic behavior throughout the war period and compatible with party ideology. While northern Democrats believed emancipation through presidential proclamation to be unconstitutional, they had no objection to emancipation accomplished through the constitutional process of amendment.[71]

Also notably absent from widespread partisan discussion was the question of Reconstruction. Understandably, with the war not yet over, many partisans of both parties did not care to speculate on the future. Nor did Republicans, for the sake of maintaining party unity, want to engage in large-scale debate on the Reconstruction issue, an issue almost guaranteed to pit the party's radical wing against its moderates. Yet the question of dealing with the southern states and of their proper relationship to the federal government had been a topic of controversy in Congress for the previous year. The *Free Press,* calling for a policy of mercy, implored Lincoln to uphold his pledge that the North would fight to preserve the Union and thus to return the southern states to their former position within the nation. A letter to Governor Crapo hinted at the Republicans' views on Reconstruction. It called for a reconstruction not only of the South but also of the entire United States in order to rid the Constitution and the laws of the taint of slavery. In other words, whereas the Union was nearly restored, the Constitution was not; consequently, the task fell to Republicans to destroy the legacy of the Slave Power and its hold on the Constitution.[72]

Lee's surrender on April 9 provided a temporary respite from partisan squabbling, as adherents of both parties toasted the Union army. The shared euphoria, however, was short-lived. The war's end and Lincoln's assassination brought the issue of Reconstruction to the fore. What were the best policies to pursue? Who would determine what measures to adopt? How would the new president, Andrew Johnson—purportedly a Republican but a late convert from the Democratic Party—respond to the nation's needs? Understandably, these questions fostered continued partisan conflict in Michigan—conflict that would replicate the pattern of partisanship exhibited throughout the course of the war.

While hoping that "good feeling and harmony" would prevail when President Johnson framed his plan of Reconstruction, Democratic newspaper editor Elihu Pond remained fearful that "vindictiveness is to take the place of conciliation, and the policy [of Reconstruction will] be prolonged." The *Lansing State Republican,* encouraged by Johnson's statement that "treason must be made infamous, and traitors impoverished," hoped that the new president would carry out a policy of punishing the rebels. The journal defined five classes of rebels and established separate punishments for each class, ranging from death for rebels who committed crimes against humanity to hard labor for the organizers of secession. The following month, the *State Republican* addressed the issue of who should be allowed to vote in the South; concluding that "the present generation of rebels should be disenfranchised [*sic*]," the paper demanded that freedmen be given the vote "to protect their own interests."[73]

On May 29, 1865, President Johnson put his Reconstruction plan into motion by issuing two proclamations. The first offered amnesty and the restoration of property (other than slaves) to those men who took an oath of allegiance to the government (excepting certain categories of Confederates). Johnson's second proclamation designated a provisional governor for North Carolina. In Michigan, the response to the proclamations was immediate. Pleased with them, Elihu Pond remarked that the president had squelched "the hopes of the negro suffrage party." He added that Johnson appeared "to be a states' rights man." The *Free Press* pronounced Johnson's amnesty plan "statesman like and manly" and one that assured the nation that "President Johnson has not forgotten all of his democracy, and that he is too old to change now."[74]

For the most part, Michigan Republicans also seemed amenable to the president's actions. The *Advertiser and Tribune* affirmed that the amnesty proclamation embodied "the best judgment of the masses in the state." Importantly, the journal continued, Johnson had not shown "undue leniency." Rather, his first proclamation fully recognized that treason had been committed and, in total, was "as merciful as it [was] dignified." Zachariah Chandler disagreed. In a June 12 speech in Detroit, he claimed that Johnson had acted unconstitutionally in appointing a provisional governor for North Carolina. "If there was no authority of law," Chandler roared to the assembled crowd, "then it required the combined action of the House of Representatives, the Senate, and the President before an officer could be legally appointed." The battle line was being drawn between Johnson's authority over Reconstruction and that of Congress.[75]

Summer and autumn passed with little cause for partisan dispute. Elihu Pond mused on the antics of the Radicals such as Chandler, who denounced Johnson's proclamations and insisted upon "Negro equity or no Union." However, he felt confident of the final outcome and added that the president should "let 'em [Radicals] rip." The *Free Press* agreed that the Radicals were bent on demanding Negro suffrage as a prerequisite for restoration of the Union. Condemning this sentiment, the paper asserted that the people "generally recognized the inherent right of the states to regulate suffrage for themselves" and would not allow the Radicals to "delay . . . the restoration of the Union on a firm and cordial fraternal basis." Black suffrage was to be left to the dictates of the individual states. Michigan Democrats affirmed their devotion to states' rights, proclaiming that the southern states had never legally withdrawn nor could they ever withdraw from the Union. Consequently, with the war over, the South's full rights had to be restored at once.[76]

By December, the nation anxiously anticipated the opening of Congress. The summer had witnessed the reorganization of the southern states under President Johnson's general plan of Reconstruction, which required the states to ratify the Thirteenth Amendment and repudiate both the southern war debt and secession. Johnson did not, however, insist upon black suffrage, preferring instead to leave the matter in the hands of the individual states. Not surprisingly, given their belief that they had been completely justified in seceding from the Union, the southern states responded to Johnson's offer of self-reconstruction in a manner that would prove to be very unpopular among northern Republicans. The southern states readily admitted that slavery was over, but they also enacted a series of "Black Codes" that kept the free black population in conditions of virtual servitude. Moreover, state constitutional conventions throughout the South waffled on repudiating the Confederate debt and on the question of the legitimacy of secession. Finally and perhaps most galling to many in the North numerous former Confederates, including Confederate vice president Alexander Stephens, were elected to represent the southern states in the upcoming session of Congress. It would now be up to the new Congress to determine whether President Johnson's plan of Reconstruction had succeeded or failed.[77]

A month earlier, in a speech in Lansing, Sen. Jacob Howard insisted that "we owe it to the loyal people of the North to exclude the representatives from the late rebellious states. The states in question are subjugated provinces, whose inhabitants are not loyal today, and only submitted to the Union's authorities because they were unable to resist." Michigan Radical Republicans were obviously not convinced that Reconstruction was over. The southern states, upon leaving the Union, had forfeited their rights under the Constitution; therefore, until a "republican" form of government had been restored to these states, they would exist in a quasi-territorial state. Although the Slave Power had been defeated militarily, it continued to exercise political power. Until that last tentacle of the slavocracy had been loosened, American liberty remained in peril.[78]

Johnson's ambiguous message to Congress on December 5 evoked an immediate response in Michigan. The *Detroit Advertiser and Tribune*, increasingly the mouthpiece of moderate state Republicans, commended the president on a job well done in avoiding placing "himself in a position to come into collision with Congress on the question of admitting the southern members." The *Free Press* rejoiced at Johnson's insistence upon a government grounded in the principle of states' rights, confident that he would therefore not allow congressional interference with state institutions. The following day, the paper announced an end to Reconstruction and "the perpetuity of the Union, and the sufficiency of the Constitution for its preservation." The paper's proclamation, however, proved premature. The southern delegates to Congress were denied their seats. The schism between Congress and Johnson had begun to show.[79]

Throughout the early portion of 1866, Michiganians eagerly looked toward Washington, watching intently the actions of the Thirty-ninth Congress and Andrew Johnson. "What is the prospect of Reconstruction," Charles T. Gorham asked of Congressman John Longyear, "which end of the Avenue is to yield? Not the east end I hope and so hopes every loyal man hereabouts so far as I can perceive." Bemoaning the developing division between Congress and the president, Gorham concluded, "Poor 'Andy' promises fair to fail us in our hour of trial." Another worried constituent expressed similar concerns and affirmed his support of Congress. "I see things look a little rough at Washington," Ephraim Longyear asserted, "whatever the opinion of the people of the North may be as to Negro suffrage, I am satisfied that they prefer to see those rebels hung than to see them members of Congress, there is no doubt the *People* are opposed to any such men running or helping to run this government."[80]

Johnson's veto of the Freedmen's Bureau Bill in February 1866, his Washington's birthday address just a few days later, and his subsequent veto of the Civil Rights Bill in March finalized the schism. Claiming that "every patriot and respecter of the Constitution" would endorse Johnson's veto of the Freedmen's Bureau Bill, the *Free Press* branded the measure "unconstitutional, inexpedient, and extravagant." Johnson had vindicated Democratic Party principles by his repudiation of the bill as "dangerous, despotic, and undemocratic." His second veto evoked even greater praise. The president, the *Free Press* gloated, had once again succeeded in thwarting the "disunionist" Congress in its attempt to "subvert the Government and liberties of the people." The paper then thanked Johnson for his "second resistance to tyranny and oppression, to violations of the Constitution, and to Negro equality." Michigan Democrats were clearly pleased with Johnson and his commitment to states' rights.[81]

State Republicans took quite another view of Johnson's actions. "We, in Michigan, who have sustained the government through the horrors and trials of the last five years," F. G. Russell declared in a letter to Congressman Longyear, "are disgusted with, and alarmed at the speech made by President Johnson on the 22d inst." "The people after five years of war," Russell continued, "do not now propose that all they gained by every sort of manly sacrifice shall be lost through the incapacity or treason of one man." On March 28, Congressman Longyear, a noted moderate, railed against Johnson for his Reconstruction policy in a speech at Lansing. He asserted that, though the rebel states had not left the Union, they had nevertheless destroyed state civil government as it had existed under the Constitution. Furthermore, Longyear argued, Johnson lacked constitutional authority to reconstruct the states, that power lying entirely with Congress. Therefore, the president had acted despotically in "exceeding" the Constitution. Longyear also deemed Johnson's veto of the Freedmen's Bureau Bill unnecessary. The congressman contended that if the president had simply stated his objections to the measure, "Congress would have endeavored to modify the bill to meet those objections." In closing, Longyear pleaded with the citizens of Michigan to support the nation's lawmakers in Congress. "The simple question now," the *White Pigeon Republican* bluntly told its readership, "is whether the Union shall be reconstructed for the benefit of Andrew Johnson or the American people." By his actions, which emanated from his Democratic principles, Andrew Johnson inadvertently united the various wings of the Republican Party and in so doing assured that the party would assume a united front in promoting its own plan of Reconstruction. Accurately assessing the situation, the *Advertiser and Tribune* reported that "a very striking feature of the political situation is the abandonment of President Johnson by all the conservative papers or independent papers of conservative tendencies." "We would it otherwise," the *Flint Wolverine Citizen* lamented, "but it would tend to no good to endeavor to disguise the fact that Andrew Johnson has opened a gulf between himself and the truly loyal citizens of this country."[82]

Traditionally, historians have blamed Republican insistence upon basic civil rights for freed blacks and Andrew Johnson's uncompromising commitment to restructuring contemporary political loyalties for the breach between the president and his party. The split between Johnson and the Thirty-ninth Congress, however, represented the inevitable conclusion of the partisan strife that was so evident prior to and during the war. Johnson, after all, had been a Democrat. Therefore, his Reconstruction policies were based upon Democratic presuppositions and were directed by a Democratic agenda. Indeed, Johnson's attempt to realign national politics did not represent a new initiative on the part of the president but simply replicated the efforts advanced by Democrats throughout the war. It was partisanship, not humanitarian or moral concerns for the freedmens' welfare, that alienated Johnson from the Republicans. Conversely, conditioned to see the machinations of a Slave Power actively impeding American freedom, Republicans all too quickly surmised that, although the power was defeated, its control of government had not yet been fully broken. Writing to his former lieutenant governor, Charles S. May, Austin Blair put the matter plainly, stating that "the contest is not yet over . . . the rebels have gained a point in the president." Republicans naturally concluded that it was up to the party faithful to redouble their efforts in battling this organized conspiracy.[83]

The veto of the Civil Rights Bill conclusively estranged Johnson from his party. Declaring "The Separation Complete," the *Lansing State Republican* assailed Johnson for thwarting Congress in its honest effort to protect the freedmen in the enjoyment of their rights. Republicans did all that they could to avoid the rupture, the journal continued, but Johnson's determination to carry out his policy, "right or wrong," left Republicans with no alternative. Johnson had gone further than any other president in the exercise of executive power. Constitutional government was on trial, and it was left to the people to support Congress in carrying out Reconstruction in a constitutional manner. Left unchecked, the *Grand Rapids Daily Eagle* warned, Johnson "would turn usurper and act a Cromwell." "The loyal people of the

North," one Republican reassured his representative in Washington, "are not to be moved. I believe every member of the present Congress who stood by his manhood and humanity and equal justice should be endorsed this fall by a return to the next Congress."[84]

The growing tension between Congress and the president led Gov. Henry Crapo to proclaim April 19 a day of fasting and prayer for the successful reconstruction of the Union. "After a glorious contest in the field of battle," his proclamation read,

> let us not vainly imagine that all danger is past. . . . It was indeed a mighty achievement to scatter to the wind the armed hosts of treason and rebellion which were arrayed against us. . . . But the work is not yet finished. We have a mightier victory still to achieve in the reconstruction of a united country. Now when our political skies are clouded by antagonism between the ruling powers at the capital of our Republic . . . let us seek . . . Divine aid to subdue our pride, to surrender our wills, to abandon our prejudices, and to reconstruct the Republic upon the broad principles of Right, Humanity, Justice, and Eternal Truth.[85]

Crapo's proclamation drew vitriolic criticism from Michigan Democrats. Referring to it as "Crapo-Politico-Religion," a gathering of Detroit Democrats resolved that the proclamation was "a direct attack on the President for the exercise of his constitutional powers, and an insult to the majority of the citizens of this state, who are his [Johnson's] supporters." The assembled political activists also issued a nonpartisan appeal to "friends of the president's policy" to attend a rally in Detroit on April 9. Again, as during the war, Michigan Democrats were offering a friendly hand to conservatives.[86]

Republicans castigated the Democrats for their blatantly partisan appeal. The *Detroit Daily Post,* a radical newspaper begun in 1866, invited all Republicans to attend the rally and "hear the Democrats howl and swear to slavery and oppression." Noting that "the peace of the Union, . . . the honor of the nation, . . . and the whole future of the Republic" hung in the balance, the paper asked its readership to support the proclamation. Of note is the tenor of the *Daily Post*'s article. The editorial implied that Republicans still had the duty to destroy slavery—if not the institution itself, then the vestiges of its legacy, which still constrained the Republic.[87]

On April 9, Congress overrode Johnson's veto of the Civil Rights Bill and three months later succeeded in doing the same for the Freedmen's Bureau

Bill. In the interim, the body, led by the Joint Committee on Reconstruction (one of whose members was Jacob Howard of Michigan), turned its attention to devising its own program of Reconstruction. The committee designed a plan that eventually became the Fourteenth Amendment. The *Advertiser and Tribune* recognized the plan for what it was, "a policy of cautious expediency . . . designed to carry more states than [it] could otherwise carry." Here was a compromise proposal that would allow for broad support among the various components of the Republican Party. "President Johnson makes, by his veto acts, a tyrant's power more patent," Republican activist David Bagley wrote in early May. By so doing, he concluded, "he is really educating the masses to a higher anti-slavery standard." Democrats, by contrast, viewed the plan with disgust. The abolitionists in their "Star Chamber" committee had unleashed their despotic wrath against the South. The *Free Press* took comfort in the fact that the plan would likely face defeat in Congress, as the various components of the proposed amendment would alienate different elements of the majority party and thus guarantee its failure.[88]

With the November election fast approaching, Reconstruction policy dominated discussion at the state nominating conventions. Early in July, the *Detroit Free Press* directed the Democrats' attention to the importance of the fall election. It warned the Radicals that "the appeals of the president, the clamors of the Democrats and of the conservative men" would ensure that their goal of "no Union without Negro suffrage" would never be realized. The *State Republican* responded in kind, claiming, "There is no hope in an open fight under the Democratic banner, tainted with Copperheadism as it is, and as it has been throughout the war." Again, divergent political views resulted in suspicion and charges of disloyalty against opponents.[89]

In response to congressional measures to gain control over Reconstruction, Andrew Johnson and his backers pursued a strategy followed by Democrats throughout the secession crisis and the Civil War—that is, they determined to appeal directly to the people for nonpartisan support of the president's plan of Reconstruction. In June, supporters of the president were asked to assemble on August 14 in Philadelphia to create the National Union Party. The *Free Press* believed the convention was a good idea and urged that "every conservative, be he Democratic or Republican, can and ought to respond to this call." The convention demonstrated, the *Free Press* alleged, that "the days of Radicalism are numbered, and that the sober, healthy second thought is about to preserve the Union and the Constitution." The paper went on to endorse the convention's demand for "the whole Union and the integrity of the Constitution." The state's Republican press, not surprisingly, saw things differently. The efforts of the Philadelphia convention, the *White Pigeon Republican* confidently asserted, was "not so much the founding of a new party as . . . the gathering together of the shattered fragments of the old hulk of the Democracy." The *Grand Rapids Weekly Eagle* disavowed the movement as a "copper Johnson" convention. Similarly, the *Pontiac Gazette* condemned the convention as "an unclean thing which no true Union man should touch or look upon for fear of pollution."[90]

As the National Union convention met in Philadelphia, Michiganians prepared for the fall campaign. Dismissing the National Union Party as a group of disgruntled office seekers and traitors, state Republicans met in convention at Detroit on August 30. There, the party endorsed the congressional plan of Reconstruction, formally repudiated President Johnson, and renominated Henry Crapo for governor. In addition, Michigan's Republicans punished Congressman Longyear for his decision to attend the National Union convention by replacing him on their party's ticket in the Third Congressional District with the more radical Austin Blair. Just six days later, on September 5, Michigan Democrats, under the banner of the National Union Party, also met in Detroit, nominating Alpheus Williams as their gubernatorial candidate.[91]

The issue in the campaign was clear from the start—control over Reconstruction and the fate of American freedom. As in the past, political opposition bound Michigan Republicans together. Crapo viciously attacked Johnson, claiming that he had betrayed his party and his country. Furthermore, he insisted, Johnson had circumvented Congress in establishing his Reconstruction plan and therefore had acted unconstitutionally. Crapo also made use of his party's successful prosecution of the war, urging voters to beware of copperhead ploys to return the rebels to power. Michigan Republicans once again went to the well of partisan loyalty. The party had successfully defeated the Slave Power's military force, but it had yet to defeat the slaveocracy's political arm. The struggle, in other words, was not over. The Constitution had not been restored to its original luster, and once again, southern rebels were working in tandem with northern copperheads to obstruct the Republican Party's final achievement of that end.[92]

For the Democrats as well, the issues remained startlingly familiar. Would the "unscrupulous," deceitful, tyrannical Radicals in Congress be allowed to determine the fate of liberty in the United States, or would the people stand by the Constitution? Democrats urged the people to vote with their traditional republican loyalties and to stand by the Union and President Johnson's noble acts. The nation's fate lay in the people's hands. Would they choose despotism or the Constitution and the Union?[93]

On November 7, despite an unprecedented presidential visit to the state on September 4 and 5, Michigan voters spoke out loudly in favor of congressional Reconstruction. The results of the election left little doubt about which side of the Reconstruction debate residents agreed with. Governor Crapo handily defeated his Democratic opponent, by 96,746 votes (59 percent of the total cast) to 67,708 votes (41 percent of the votes cast). Republicans similarly captured all six of the state's congressional seats, with an average margin of victory of 3,000 votes. In the state legislature, Democratic representation declined by four seats in the state house and five seats in the state senate. Moreover, even such traditionally Democratic counties as Monroe, Livingston, and Macomb succumbed to the Republican onslaught. The people of the state clearly expressed their demand that the remnants of the old Slave Power be swept away forever—Michigan had once again pledged its loyalty to the party that it had given birth to in 1854. With "the great battle" now fought and won, Republicans across the nation confidently drafted a more aggressive Reconstruction plan that they believed would finally succeed in dislodging the Slave Power from its lofty aerie and protect American liberty from further predation. State Democrats, by contrast, had suffered a terrible rebuke. Michiganians convincingly demonstrated their belief that the Constitution and the Union were still in danger and that further Reconstruction measures were necessary in order to protect their freedom. But once again, while tasting defeat, the Democrats responded as they had so many times in the past and as they would continue to respond in the future—they simply rallied around their principles and girded themselves for the next election, confident that those principles would eventually draw the state back into the Democratic fold.[94]

Relieved by the Republicans' overwhelming electoral victory, the *Macomb Monitor* joyfully proclaimed, "All over the country the outrageous policy of Andrew Johnson has been repudiated, and the triumph of Congress is supreme." With the nation now safely in the hands of the party of freedom and beyond the grasping designs of the Slave Power and its tools in Washington, Michigan Republicans were finally free, for the first time since 1855, to turn their attention inward and to assess the needs of their own state and its citizens. Unexpectedly, however, this new opportunity would prove to be extremely problematic for state Republicans, as their party's diffuse constituency—a constituency long held together by the perceived threat to American liberty posed by the Slave Power—quickly resumed traditional antebellum positions relative to state affairs. In the span of one year's time, this reinvigorated and persistent Jacksonian political culture would pose a serious challenge to Republican cohesiveness in Michigan.[95]

"I am Sick and Pained that our Republicans so Act"

The Fraying of the Republican Coalition

As the 1867 legislative session opened in Lansing, anticipation swept through Michigan. For the first time in roughly a decade, the state legislature would be able to divert its attention away from national concerns and devote a significant portion of its time to state affairs. Grateful for the opportunity afforded them, the Republicans, who dominated the body and were increasingly directed by the state's new commercial and industrial elite, immediately started to identify and address the state's most pressing needs. Among these, party elites determined, was the furtherance of Michigan's immersion into the cash nexus. But the Republican leadership soon came to curse their party's so-called good fortune. As in the years that came before and immediately after the party's political ascendancy in the state in 1854, Michigan's continuing evolution into a market-driven economy promptly emerged as the most salient issue in the minds of state residents. Just as rapidly, the state's old Jacksonian-era tensions between those who favored such an evolution and those who remained ambivalent about the change also resurfaced. Moreover, debate over state intervention in and encouragement of economic development sparked a protracted and intense philosophical dialogue between the party's older partisans, most of whom had arrived in Michigan without tangible resources but managed to succeed through personal initiative and individual enterprise, and those who arrived on the scene later and had come to view activist government and individual enterprise as inextricably bound together. Such tensions, in turn, frequently eroded and occasionally disrupted the Republicans' recently forged political coalition in the years that followed.[1]

At first blush, one might expect that the crisis of the Civil War, with its enormous monetary, material, and human demands, would have blunted Michigan's market revolution. Just the opposite, however, occurred. Throughout the war years and continuing on through the remainder of the decade, the state's commercial metamorphosis proceeded unabated; if anything, it may have even accelerated.

On the agricultural front, commercial farming made great strides as a result of the war. Enticed by rapidly climbing prices and an incessant demand for agricultural products and livestock and blessed with uninterrupted access to their traditional markets on the Atlantic seaboard, many Michigan farmers eagerly took the plunge into the world of commercial agriculture. Even in Michigan's remote Upper Peninsula, commercial farming gained ground during this period, in large part due to the efforts of the region's mining firms and their practice of contracting with farmers to feed their swelling labor force. Simultaneously, the enlistments of tens of thousands of Michigan men into the Union army and navy made additional labor a very scarce commodity in the state. As a result, more and more Michigan farmers turned to a profusion of mechanical devices to assist them in increasing their yields. Over the course of the decade between 1860 and 1870, the value of agricultural machinery more than doubled in Michigan, from $5,819,832 to $13,711,979. Similarly, the number of firms producing such implements in the state and the value of their products also increased, from 108 firms producing $684,913 worth of goods in 1860 to 164 firms producing $1,569,596 worth of goods in 1870. The net results of these trends were nothing short of phenomenal.[2]

Despite a considerable decrease in the size of the average farm in Michigan over the war decade and an overall decline in farm employment, the farmers nearly doubled their annual output of wheat during the 1860s, growing some 16,265,773 bushels (5.6 percent of the nation's total) by 1869. Other crops, such as corn, oats, potatoes, barley, rye, buckwheat, and hay, showed increases during the war years as well, as did a commodity intended solely for external sale—hops. Michigan farmers also warmed to the task of providing substitutes for southern cotton. During the war decade, Michigan's output of flax skyrocketed from 4,000 to 240,000 pounds. Of greater importance to the farmers of Michigan, however, was the production of wool. Between 1861 and 1864 alone, the state's wool producers nearly doubled their output, from 4,062,858 pounds to 7,249,934 pounds. Livestock farming produced similar advances. Between 1861 and February 1866, the total value of livestock in the state increased from $23,714,771 to $52,091,122. A final ingredient in Michigan's "agricultural revolution" was the introduction of the factory system in butter and cheese production, an innovation that "struck a body blow at traditional self-sufficiency of [the state's] farm units." By 1870, there were thirty dairy factories in operation throughout Michigan, and their annual output accounted for more than two-thirds of the state's cheese production.[3]

Similar advancements occurred in other sectors of the state's economy, many of which eclipsed the gains made in agriculture. Indeed, by 1870, farmers and farm laborers actually comprised a minority (46 percent) of the state's workforce (down from 52 percent in 1860). Perhaps the most pronounced growth of all took place in Michigan's emerging lumber industry. After a sharp decline in the industry in 1861, state lumbering firms experienced "eleven fat years" beginning in 1862. In 1860, some 926 sawmills operated in Michigan's Lower Peninsula. By decade's end, the number had jumped to 1,158 (the number leaped to nearly 1,600 mills over the next three years), and lumbering ranked as the state's leading industry. It employed over 20,000 workers (nearly 35 percent the total), with the value of its product totaling over $32 million. Additionally, the war decade ushered in a period of decline for Michigan's small lumber firms and marked the beginning of a trend toward larger, more efficient, and more heavily capitalized companies in the industry. The growth of lumbering was so rapid in Michigan that by 1870, the state could boast that it produced more lumber than any other state in the Union, a position it would hold until the turn of the twentieth century.[4]

The war decade also proved to be a boon to the state's mining regions. Rising demand for copper and iron ore and a chronic shortage of labor resulted in technical innovation and increased production throughout Michigan's mineral districts and enabled the state to become the leading copper supplier in the nation. In 1859, its copper production stood at approximately 9 million pounds. Ten years later, output reached 26,625,301 pounds and was valued at over $6 million. By the mid-1870s, one mine alone, the Calumet and Hecla, was producing over 20 million pounds (nearly 90 percent of the region's total) annually and employed 1,780 men. Similarly, the production of iron ore in the state jumped from under 100,000 tons in 1860 to over 1 million tons by the early 1870s.[5]

Analogous developments occurred in Michigan's manufacturing and mercantile economy, particularly in and around Detroit. From 1860 to 1870, the amount of capital invested in manufacturing establishments in Detroit increased by 256 percent, and the value of the city's industrial output rose by 303 percent. Moreover, the number of manufacturing plants operating in the state during this period rose by 174 percent, to 9,455. Overall, the value of the state's industrial product in 1870 stood at $123 million, an increase of over 376 percent from 1860.[6]

Precipitate economic transformation was accompanied by a host of associated societal changes as well. Michigan's population (continuing the pattern established before the war) swelled in the years after 1860, reaching 1,184,282 in 1870 (a 60 percent increase over 1860) and 1,636,937 in 1880. Much of this growth was the result of a continual influx of foreign-born immigrants. Thousands of Germans, Dutch, Canadians, Irish, Cornish, and Scandinavian settlers flooded into the state. While many were drawn by plentiful employment opportunities (many, in fact, had been recruited by state immigration agents and private recruiters hired by Michigan's chronically labor-short employers, especially during the war years), others chose the state because of its cheap and plentiful land. To even the casual observer, however, it was increasingly apparent that among this foreign-born element, there was a growing number of men and women of southern and eastern European origin. Though these new arrivals could be found throughout the state, more often than not they were drawn to and settled in those areas most closely associated with Michigan's emerging capitalist economy—the mining towns of the Upper Peninsula (of the 3,426 miners enumerated in the 1870 census, only 233 were natives), the lumber camps of the Saginaw and Muskegon River valleys (where the 1870 census indicated that approximately one-half of the lumbermen, raftsmen, and wood choppers were foreigners), and Detroit (by 1873, four-fifths of the city's schoolchildren were of foreign parentage). Foreign-language newspapers, unfamiliar and insular social and cultural institutions, alien dress, ethnic neighborhoods, and, in burgeoning numbers, non-Protestant religious institutions proliferated in these areas and others, perpetuating an underlying sense of suspicion and mistrust in the wider population and marking these new arrivals as unwitting symbols of the state's social and economic metamorphosis.[7]

In the mushrooming urban enclaves (Detroit, for instance, grew by 74 percent between 1860 and 1870), social stresses frequently produced worrisome conditions. Detroit's ethnic population packed the old residential neighborhoods between Jefferson Avenue and the riverfront, an area known to locals as the Potomac. Crime, prostitution, poverty, filth, and squalor rendered the area a slum where respectable citizens refused to go. Similar conditions prevailed in Detroit's small but growing African American community. Moreover, many of the city's working-class neighborhoods still bore the scars of Detroit's 1863 race riot (sparked by the alleged rape of two young girls, one of whom was white, by a black man) in which two African Americans were killed and much property destroyed. Statewide, alcohol consumption, seen as one of the most obvious signs of social decay by the Protestant majority, continued unabated (especially in the ethnic neighborhoods of Detroit) in spite of the previously discussed efforts to eradicate it. Faced with a perceived breakdown of order, Detroiters responded in 1873 by creating a professional police force for their city of 80,000.[8]

Perhaps the greatest harbinger of change in the state, however, was the railroad, which experienced a period of extraordinary expansion in Michigan in the years following the Civil War. In 1860, the state's railroad mileage stood at 779 miles. By 1870, that figure had more than doubled to 1,638 miles. Three factors contributed to this spectacular growth: the rising demands of the state's economy; an intense competition between the Michigan Central and the Michigan Southern Railroads, which resulted in the construction of feeder lines as both companies sought to control rail traffic in the state; and millions of dollars in assistance offered the state's railroad companies by local governments in the years after 1863.[9]

Not surprisingly, as had happened in the past, railroads and questions of their expansion offered a convenient and metaphorical battleground for a citizenry that was ambivalent about the changes that were transforming Michigan. The centrality of the railroad and its importance in the expansion of the marketplace shaped much of the legislative debate in 1867. "We are in the midst of an era of railroads," the Lansing correspondent for the *Detroit Daily Post* informed his readers, "and the Legislature may fairly be said to be afloat on a sea of railroad bills." A rival reporter for the *Detroit Advertiser and Tribune* echoed this sentiment when he wrote on March 9, "Today has been a carnival for railroads in the legislature. Trains have arrived and departed from nearly every nook and corner of Michigan. The 'iron horse' has broken loose or got the bits in his teeth, and the Legislature is making railroads and history at a pace likely to prove memorable. . . . There may be a grand railroad smash-up yet, but there are old and experienced engineers aboard the train, both in and out of the Legislature, and there are certainly fair prospects of success." These two correspondents' comments were on the mark. Unlike the three previous legislative sessions—in 1863, 1864 (a special session), and 1865—in which a mere handful of bills authorizing the granting of local credit for railroad construction had been passed, the 1867 session was inundated with such measures, including one seeking the legalization of an already consigned bond issue of $63,000. Indeed, as historian Martin Lewis contended, "nearly every member of the legislature [was actively involved] in a combination to secure the passage [of these bills]." The purpose in proposing so many local aid bills, the *Daily Post's* Lansing correspondent concluded, was to "increase the strength of the railroad interest in both Houses by furnishing every member a local reason for supporting the bond issuing scheme."[10]

This plethora of railroad initiatives led apprehensive Michiganians, such as Charles Mercer, a Hartland farmer, to voice their concerns. In a desperate letter of opposition to Governor Crapo, Mercer pleaded with the governor to use his "interference to put a stop to [the] sad state of affairs" in Michigan, which he labeled "railroads on the brain." "If sutch [sic] companies have a right to 10 or 20 percent of a man's farm," Mercer argued, "they have a right to the whole in fact." Pulling no punches, he concluded his letter by reminding Crapo that "this system strikes at the freehold system and destroys it entirely by loading property with sutch [sic] dets [sic] as are equal to the whole value of the property." If the aid bills passed, Mercer suggested, the Republican Free-Soil ideal, with its promise of autonomy and opportunity, would be repudiated. Another correspondent, J. R. Kellogg of Allegan, reminded Crapo that a similar aid scheme had been employed in the Black River country of New York and related that "it was melancholy to travel the region where these roads was [sic] located and an old citizen and friend pointed out to me farm after farm where the old early settlers are ruined sold out and left poor and not a rod of road completed." Concluding his letter, Kellogg stated, "I tremble for my beloved Michigan."[11]

Recuperating from a persistent bowel malady, Crapo closely and warily observed the progress of the numerous railroad bond bills. Convinced that those measures "should excite apprehension and alarm" and that they were "in conflict with the spirit and implication" of the state constitution, he rebuked the state legislature in a series of stinging vetoes, warning them that "no matter how desirable the end may be regarded which is sought to be secured by the legislation, nothing can compensate for the mischief and for the long catalogue of evils which . . . is sure to result in the future." "If it be so unwise a thing, on the part of the State at large, thus to engage in, or aid uncertain enterprises of this character," Crapo reasoned, "it must be vastly more unwise and perilous, for the feebler townships and cities, thus to involve themselves, and expose to serious hazards, their more limited credit." The

Flint Wolverine Citizen agreed with Crapo's assessment, adding that "these railroads, after having settled down to the earth just long enough to have swallowed the millions voted them by a victimized people, would again have taken wings from the loftiest embankments and gone to the uncertain regions whence the railway speculators draw their gorgeous conceptions."[12]

To his credit, Crapo astutely recognized the perilous waters into which his party was drifting. In a very revealing passage, he wrote his son, "I am but one branch of the Government and have my responsibilities and duties, and the Legislature are another branch occupying the same position with respect to the people; and both of us must go to the people for support. There is this difference, however. The members of the Legislature are acting in the interests of certain railroad cliques, and are laboring almost exclusively to promote their interest, whereas I stand upon the question as the guardian of the public interest." Republicans, Crapo cautioned, would be well advised to recall the difficulty faced by their party in its attempt to orchestrate a successful political fusion in 1854, to remember the concerns of its Jacksonian wing, and to tread very carefully among an uneasy citizenry conditioned to see abuse of power and threats to its freedom at every turn. Echoing the governor's apprehensions, Kellogg confided to Crapo, "[I am] sick and pained that our Republicans so act. I do believe it better and safer to have a legislature more equally represented, than to have one of so large a majority." "The time is not very distant," the editor of the *Wolverine Citizen* told his Republican readers, "when those of the party more interested in the perfect success of the principles it advocates than in the triumph of schemes for merely selfish aggrandizement, will recur to the railroad vetoes of Governor Crapo and thank him for the salvation of the party in this state."[13]

The ongoing debate over the desirability of Michigan's market revolution and its implications for the liberties of the residents rapidly spilled over into state's constitutional convention of 1867. Under the state constitution of 1850, the question of constitutional revision was to be put before Michigan voters every sixteen years. As required by law, the issue thus went before the electorate in 1866. Although Michiganians endorsed a new constitutional convention by a vote of 79,505 to 28,623, some 56,000 of the state voters who cast ballots in the election abstained from voting on the question. Clearly, residents viewed the question of who should control Reconstruction to be of far greater consequence than the question of constitutional revision. In the end, it is likely that a majority of those who did cast a vote on the issue voted in the affirmative because state Republicans, particularly Governor Crapo, had urged them to do so. That is, they may have simply concluded that because the old constitution of 1850 had been written by a Democratic convention, the state's new Republican majority deserved a chance to create its own governmental blueprint. Others may have simply welcomed the opportunity to correct flaws in the 1850 constitution, a document that the *Detroit Advertiser and Tribune* labeled "a crude and unsatisfactory performance, [which] has been amended no less than thirteen times." Still others may have hoped to alter the constitution to allow for municipal aid to railroad companies. What is clear, however, is that few state residents viewed the question of constitutional revision as the leading issue of the day. As the convention assembled, however, and its proceedings were made public, many Michiganians would change their minds about just how momentous this meeting really was.[14]

Unfortunately, no good history of Michigan's 1867 constitutional convention exists. But among those works that have examined the convention, one issue has traditionally received the lion's share of attention—the question of black suffrage. This emphasis, of course, comes as no great surprise, given the tendency to view Michigan's antebellum and wartime history as a moral crusade to end slavery in the Union. Moreover, accounts by contemporary observers, particularly the state press, tend to reinforce this perception. The emphasis on black suffrage as the most pressing concern among the convention delegates, however, is erroneous and thus distorts the convention's true significance. As in 1850, ethnocultural issues such as prohibition and black suffrage, though important, did not consume the bulk of the delegates' time. (The proposed state constitution included a provision guaranteeing black suffrage, whereas a prohibition proposal, which was also drafted by the convention, was submitted to state voters as a separate ballot referendum.) Rather, as had their counterparts in 1850, the delegates to the 1867 convention paid far more attention to questions relating to state government and economic development. The fact that contemporary political leaders often underscored the importance of black suffrage as the most salient concern of state voters suggests that they themselves were out of touch with the electorate and/or that they were unaware of just how vital questions such as the authorization of local aid to railroad corporations were to their own constituencies.[15]

Angered by their perceived betrayal at the hands of Governor Crapo and driven by the belief that their prodevelopment agenda truly represented the views of the majority of state residents (a belief reinforced for them by the election of a 75-to-25 Republican majority to the convention), Michigan's promarket Republicans saw the Lansing constitutional convention as a golden opportunity to create an environment conducive to the further expansion of market forces in the state. The key to promoting such an end, the party's delegates readily agreed, was to allow local governments to aid railroad development. "Experience has so clearly demonstrated the necessity and importance of railroads," William L. Stoughton, a St. Joseph County Republican, confidently asserted to his peers, "that it is no longer an open question. . . . They increase trade and commerce, afford easy and rapid transportation for persons and property, advance the value of land, and generally promote the prosperity of the country." To foster future railroad development, the convention incorporated a provision into the proposed constitution authorizing the legislature to empower any city or township (counties in the Upper Peninsula were also extended the same privilege) to provide aid to railroad corporations, not in excess of 10 percent of the assessed value of its property, upon the approval of a majority of its voters. And in a move clearly meant, at least in part, to further this end, the delegates also proposed, as a separate item to be incorporated into the proposed constitution with the assent of state voters, a proviso abandoning Michigan's biennial legislative sessions and replacing them with annual sessions. The rapid pace of change transforming the state and the need to give direction to such change required the constant attention of the state government.[16]

Yet not all of the Republican convention delegates agreed with the direction in which their party was moving. Perhaps the most vocal critic of his party's market-oriented agenda was John M. Lamb, a Lapeer County farmer and merchant. Lamb's enmity for the constitutional provision allowing for local aid to railroad corporations ran so deep that he refused to endorse the convention's proceedings and abstained from signing the proposed constitution because it included that provision. Lamb informed the convention delegates on August 17 that his constituents believed

that it is radically wrong to adopt such a measure as this as a matter of constitutional law. . . . They say that it is not right that the property of a man should be taken without his consent, by the vote of his neighbor, and placed under, what they term private control. They say further that, if measures of this kind may be adopted in reference to railroads, they may also be adopted with regard to mills; and if such measures are proper in regard to railroads and mills, then they may extend to toll-bridges; and if they extend to toll-bridges, then you may on the same principle, go one step further and tax a township for the support of a public house. I say for myself that we might by a very small strain go further and authorize townships to vote aid for the construction and running of churches, for although belonging to private corporations, the mill, the toll-bridge, the public house and the church may be regarded as public institutions in the same sense in which railroads are so regarded.

Decisions about whether to invest in railroads or any other type of private commercial venture should be left to the individual, he argued, and should not also encumber those who did not wish to expose themselves to such risks. As Lamb's comments suggest, the Republicans' aggressive, market-oriented agenda was beginning to raise some suspicions among the party's rank and file.[17]

Lamb's protest did not pass without comment in the Republican press. Indeed, the *Detroit Advertiser and Tribune* deemed his protest significant enough to devote an entire column to discussing its merits. Despite candidly admitting that the question of municipal aid to the railroads "has been one of the most exciting and absorbing issues ever presented to, or considered by, the people of our state," the paper nevertheless dismissed Lamb's opposition without fully responding to his criticism. "As the matter now stands," the *Advertiser and Tribune* reassured its readers, "it is difficult to conceive of any reasons why any elector should not wish to vote affirmatively upon the new Constitution as far as this feature is concerned."[18]

As previously discussed, both contemporaries and later generations alike ignored this important issue and its broader implications when discussing the debate surrounding the proposed constitution. With the convention's business barely settled in Lansing, the *Detroit Free Press* stridently proclaimed the Democratic Party's opposition to the document. State Democrats, the paper pronounced, "will not have any responsibility for negro suffrage on their consciences (if we must have it), to, in the future, disgrace their party."[19]

As the constitutional referendum approached in the spring of 1868, the debate continued along these lines. "Let ambitious Republicans beware," former congressman and chair of the Republican State Central Committee William Howard wrote to Charles May, adding, "I do not believe the Republican organization will elect any man constable who turns his back on this fundamental principle [equal suffrage]." "Let Copperheads howl as much as they please," he continued assuredly, "let them spell '*Nigger*' with three g's— we shall triumph." On March 18, the Republican state convention endorsed this position and openly called for the passage of the proposed constitution, avowing that "the Republicans of Michigan owe it to themselves, to the memory of the framers of the Declaration of Independence, and to the interests of free government everywhere, to secure by a triumphant majority the ratification of the proposed constitution, with its broad platform of equal and exact justice to all men, impartial suffrage and equality before the law." Similarly, the Democratic *Free Press*, in an editorial titled "Nineteen Reasons Why the New Constitution Should Be Defeated," listed the question of Negro suffrage as its first objection.[20]

On April 6, state voters soundly defeated the constitution by a vote of 110,582 to 71,729, a margin of 38,853 votes. The separate annual session and prohibition proposals also went down to defeat. The election results have usually been interpreted as a repudiation of equal suffrage. Historian David Katzman aptly summarized the prevailing wisdom by arguing that "prejudice proved stronger than reason." "Though impartial suffrage is not responsible for all of the majorities that have been rolled up against the Constitution," the *Detroit Advertiser and Tribune* asserted, "it is entitled to first consideration as one of the chief complication of maladies that proved fatal."[21]

Gleefully, the *Detroit Free Press* proclaimed the election result a repudiation of "Radicalism" in Michigan. Crediting Republican Reconstruction measures and the insistence upon Negro suffrage for their opponent's political reversal, the paper affirmed that the election results

evince the certainty that the people are reading and judging for themselves, being no longer blinded by prejudice, nor controlled by the party lash. There is no doubt of the intelligence of the people or, of their ability to judge between right and wrong, but there has been so overwhelming a confidence in the leadership of the party to which a majority of them have been attached that it boldly followed them long after Republicanism had been succeeded by Radicalism, and long after Radicalism had exceeded in its revolutionary acts anything Republicanism had ever dreamed of . . . because the Republican party had been in power during the conduct of, and glorious success of the war. . . . We conclude with the heartiest congratulations to the people of this State that a fearful political peril has been wisely met and overcome.[22]

Clearly, in a state as overwhelmingly Republican as Michigan was in 1868, the *Free Press* was correct in its assertion that party ties had loosened. But was it and others right in attributing this partisan drift to prejudice and opposition to black suffrage? The evidence suggests otherwise. In the days, weeks, and months preceding the spring election, widespread interest in the socioeconomic and political aspects of the proposed constitution—such as the questions of pay raises for state officials, annual legislative sessions, and the desirability of municipal aid to railroads—continued to be evident throughout the state. The *Free Press,* for example, opposed ratification of the new constitution because of its municipal aid provisions, which it deemed (in language harkening back to the party's antebellum heyday) "a violation of the right of property by taking it from individuals and giving it to the stock-holders of corporations." The paper complained bitterly that the document "relieves all stockholders from liability for obligations of the corporation." Republicans, too, focused on such issues. In a revealing statement, the Republican state convention concluded its endorsement of the new constitution by resolving "that this Constitution, in the opinion of this convention, is far better adapted to develop the resources of Michigan and advance the real interests of the people than our present Constitution." Similarly, the *Detroit Advertiser and Tribune* argued that a defeat for the new constitution would be "a damaging blow to the material prosperity of the state," an opinion that was, the paper maintained, endorsed by "the clear-headed, practical, and well-informed business men from all parts of the state" who comprised the bulk of the convention's delegates. In addition, besides painting their Democratic opponents as "anti-negro" and "anti-prohibition," Republicans also labeled them "anti-salary, and anti-railroad."[23]

Moreover, subsequent events in Michigan also indicate that the state's market revolution remained uppermost in the minds of the residents. In 1869 and 1870, the railroad issue once again surfaced as the predominant topic in state politics. Early in the legislative session of 1869, the General Railroad Aid Bill was approved by both houses of the Republican-dominated state assembly. The bill was quickly signed into law by the new Republican governor, Detroit merchant and banker Henry P. Baldwin. Under the aegis of this act, towns and cities throughout the state (and in some cases counties) were authorized to loan their credit (not to exceed 10 percent of assessed value of property, or 5 percent for Detroit) to railroad corporations and to levy taxes to aid these corporations, after first submitting the matter to the people. The law immediately spawned numerous aid schemes. The new wave of railroad aid mania led the *Monroe Commercial* to wryly note, "The towns along the lines of both the Toledo, Ypsilanti and Holly, and the Toledo, Ann Arbor and Northern Railroad are voting aid with gushing spontaneity. One would suppose the people were so over-burdened with money as to be at great loss what to do with it."[24]

In May 1870, a test case of the new law's constitutionality, *The People ex rel.*

Detroit and Howell Railroad Company v. Township Board of Salem, went before the justices of the state supreme court. In a three-to-one decision, the court determined that municipal aid to railroads was an unconstitutional use of tax revenues, which to be valid had to be used for public purposes. Justice Thomas M. Cooley delivered the most stinging rebuke. Setting up his position, he argued that "railroads are no longer public works, but private property; individuals and not the state own and control them for their own profit; the public may reap many and large benefits from them, and indeed are expected to do so, but only incidently and only as they might reap similar benefits from other modes of investing private capital." "When taxation is prostituted to objects in no way connected with the public interest or welfare," Cooley concluded, "it ceases to be taxation and becomes plunder." His bench mate, James V. Campbell concurred, adding that to tax citizens for the benefit of a private interest such as a railroad "can only rest on a foundation of absolute and irresponsible power to make favored classes and citizens, and make the whole body of tax-payers tributary to them." "No such power," Campbell stated, "can be tolerated in a republic." With its decision, the court destroyed aid worth over $7 million.[25]

Although lauding the court's action, the *Detroit Free Press* lamented that "all the bonds issued and sold of this character are utterly void." "This is a serious matter and places the State in a most unenviable position," the paper continued. But, it queried,

> at whose door does the blame lie? Most assuredly at the door of the Republican party, which has not only taught, but practiced, the dangerous doctrine that Constitutions can be overridden and trampled on with impunity by the legislative body. . . . If the people had sustained such an amendment we should have avoided our present humiliating position, but neither the Legislature nor Governor Baldwin were willing to go to the people, but attempted to do what is impossible without violating the Constitution.

The "effect of this decision upon both the credit and prosperity of the state," the *Detroit Advertiser and Tribune* agreed, "will be disastrous." What was needed to remedy the situation, the paper suggested, was an extra session of the state legislature so that new railroad aid legislation, in the form of a constitutional amendment, could be drafted and then submitted to the people of Michigan. On June 8, Governor Baldwin responded, issuing a call for an extra legislative session to convene on July 27.[26]

Undeterred by their recent setback and completely ignoring the warning sign given to them by voters in the referendum on the 1867 state constitution, Michigan's Republican legislative leaders plunged ahead with their unrelenting push to further the reach of the market in the state. In a flurry of activity, the extra session drafted three proposed constitutional amendments to be placed before the electorate in November (a fourth, extending the right of suffrage to the state's black males, was drafted during the earlier legislative session in 1869): one granting a salary increase to state officeholders; a second allowing township supervisors to borrow or raise through taxation up to $2,000 to repair and improve public buildings, highways, and bridges; and a third dealing with railroads. Interestingly, the suggested railroad amendment was broken down into three independent sections, each of which was to be voted on separately. The first two sections of the amendment were clearly regulatory in nature, authorizing the legislature to regulate passenger and freight rates and prohibit discrimination and forbidding the consolidation of parallel or competing lines. The third section of the amendment allowed municipalities to vote to pay their railroad aid indebtedness should they so desire.[27]

That state Republican leaders were increasingly out of touch with the desires of a large number of their constituents became all too clear by late 1870. At the Republican nominating convention for the Third Congressional District, the incumbent Austin Blair, the onetime darling of state anti-railroad/antimonopoly forces, narrowly avoided being passed over for renomination because of a widespread belief that, while in Congress, he had actively promoted measures friendly to railroad corporations (that is, he had voted in favor of land grants to railroads). Finding himself on the defensive, Blair clarified his position and reassured district Republicans by telling them, "I do not expect to vote for many, if for any, measures for land grants to railroads. Certainly an indiscriminate granting of public lands for railroad purposes will not get my support. As a rule I design to oppose them, but there are cases in which they are required by sound policy. They ought to be of national and not merely local importance to secure Congressional aid." Though Blair emerged victorious in the nominating convention, both he and his party had been served warning that many of the rank and file, uneasy about the direction in which their party was so swiftly moving, believed that their vision of the Republicans' mission (to preserve autonomy and the value of individual enterprise) was being betrayed.[28]

An even clearer articulation of that message was delivered by state Republicans in the November election. Though they managed to retain control of Michigan, their majorities were far smaller than those of 1868. Blair, for example, was reelected by a mere 1,468 votes and barely won his hometown of Jackson. The successful Republican congressional candidate in the Fifth District won by only 189 votes. In the Sixth District, the Republican incumbent, John A. Driggs, lost to Democratic challenger Jabez G. Sutherland.[29]

The vote on the constitutional amendments clearly revealed the growing discontent with Republican economic policies. Only one of the four proposed constitutional amendments—that providing for black suffrage—was ratified, by a vote of 54,105 to 50,098. The affirmation of black suffrage suggests that this issue, which successfully garnered a majority of votes cast in 1870, was not the cause of the defeat of the proposed state constitution of 1867, as so many have assumed. While it is true that some voters may have simply conceded the right to vote to blacks due to the ratification of the Fifteenth Amendment earlier in the year, it seems unlikely that so many would reverse their previous course, if indeed that had been the voters' primary reason for voting against the 1867 constitution. In short, opposition to black suffrage did not sink the constitution of 1867. What, then, did? The election of 1870 suggests that the blatantly promarket orientation of that document and its attempt to revise the political and economic axioms incorporated into the 1850 constitution were the primary reasons for its defeat. The salary amendment fell in a crushing defeat, 68,912 to 36,109. The amendment to increase the powers of township supervisors met a similar fate. In reference to the railroad question, only the first two sections of the amendment, those that established broader regulatory powers for the state, won voter approval, while the third section, the municipal aid section, was rejected by a vote of 78,453 to 50,078.[30]

As the election returns indicated, a significant number of Michigan's rank-and-file Republicans—men who had put aside divergent political, economic, and social views in 1854 to join in the party's crusade to preserve American freedom—seemingly found themselves in an unholy alliance by 1870. With freedom ostensibly safe and the Slave Power defeated, their leaders had determined to set a new political agenda for their party. The course that they set, however, proved to be a costly one, reviving long dormant fears among the more tradition-minded elements of their party and resulting in intraparty strife. In tandem with Michigan's Democratic voters, who embraced more conservative social and economic tendencies than those promoted by the Republican leadership, the state's disaffected Republican voters clearly expressed themselves on the question of the direction in which their party and their state were headed—they wanted none of it.[31]

Distraught over what had happened to his beloved party, Battle Creek resident B. F. Gram, writing in 1871, aptly summarized the sentiments of many state Republicans when he wrote, "Oh that some eagle would descend among these birds of night and carrion that now fatten on the body politic and fill the air with their ravenous and discordant notes." A few of these disgruntled Republicans, most especially those of Democratic antecedents, may have found solace within their former party and concurred with that party's state convention when it resolved in 1871 that "the class legislation of the Republican party, by which immense private fortunes are being consolidated in the hands of the few to the detriment of the many, the public domain wasted, monopolies created, and sections of the country fostered at the expense of the greater portion of the nation, deserves the reprehension of all advocates of equal rights for all men." The majority of this disaffected faction, however, whose partisan ties to the Republican Party proved too strong to be readily abandoned—whether due to their earlier Whig–Free-Soil antecedents, their adopted party's successful repression of southern treason, or the taint of disloyalty affixed to the Democrats—could not bring themselves to take such a drastic step and instead sought alternate means of expressing their discontent.[32]

The first concerted internal effort to organize and channel this discontent was the ill-fated "Liberal Republican" movement of 1872. Alienated by the corruption and unfettered probusiness attitudes of the Grant administration and disgusted by the direction of the state party and its dominance by Zachariah Chandler's political machine, a group of Michigan Republicans, led by the party stalwart and former war governor Austin Blair, broke with the party's leadership and donned the Liberal mantle. The Liberals had plenty to complain about by 1872. Jay Gould's failed effort to corner the gold market (with the assistance of Grant's brother-in-law, Abel Corwin) in 1869 and the emerging Credit Mobilier scandal (another blow to railroads) raised serious questions about Republican leadership nationally. Similarly, at the state level, a variety of problems put Michigan's Republicans in a bad light: the Chandler ring's defeat of the popular Blair's senatorial bid in 1871; the legislature's adoption that March—in total disregard of recent history—of a joint resolution recommending a constitutional amendment providing for the payment by counties, townships, and municipalities of all railroad bonds and other obligations previously negotiated; a proposed amendment to increase judicial salaries; and charges of corruption and eleven articles of impeachment leveled against the commissioner of the State Land Office, Republican Charles Edmonds. All of this led many state Republicans to concur with Austin Blair when he railed, "I am compelled to say that this administration as a whole is simply damnable." If they could convince state Democrats to join with them, the Liberals believed, victory would be theirs.[33]

Such a working coalition, however, was quickly rendered impractical by both the national and state Liberal Republican nominating conventions. At the national Liberal convention, held in Cincinnati on May 1, the delegates gave their fledgling organization's nomination to Horace Greeley, the outspoken editor of the *New York Tribune.* Greeley was considered by many as an eccentric with a long record of hostility to Democrats, and his nomination, though later endorsed by the Democratic Party, doomed any hope of establishing a broad-based coalition. State cooperation was further hindered by the two groups' decision to mutually nominate Blair as their candidate for governor. Though disgruntled Republicans had found a vehicle through which to voice their discontent, the new Liberal movement was anathema for most partisan Democrats. Despite their longing to oust the Republicans from power, the prospect of voting for Greeley and their suspicions of the former darling of the radical Republican wing, Austin Blair, convinced many state Democrats to simply stay home. The Liberal movement was handed a crushing defeat, validating Zachariah Chandler's campaign boast that "the people of Michigan are too thoroughly imbued with Republican principles to give them up for the husks of Democracy." Interestingly, however, the spirit of unrest did make its presence felt in the election, as the people of Michigan once again strongly voted down the proposed railroad bond amendment and the proposed salary increase.[34]

Despite the stinging rebuke, however, reform sentiment did not abate. On the contrary, shortly after the election, the actions of administration Republicans at both the federal and state levels raised more eyebrows. In March 1873, just before adjourning, Congress voted itself a $2,500 per year pay raise, retroactive for two years. At the state level, a similar pattern emerged when, on April 24, additional payments, totaling several thousand dollars, were voted to secretaries, clerks, sergeants at arms, firemen, and messengers of the legislature. Michigan's Republican-dominated legislature also once again pursued constitutional revision, this time authorizing the new governor, John Bagley (another Detroit businessman), to appoint an eighteen-member commission to revise the state constitution so that it would better "conform to the growth and development of the State and the advanced ideas of the people." The end product, completed in October, focused on taxation (particularly as it related to local aid to railroads), methods of fixing salaries (the issue was left in legislative hands), and annual legislative sessions.[35]

The state legislature, anticipating the end result of the commission's work, wasted little time in moving these "advanced ideas" forward. Hoping to allay the fears of antirailroad Michiganians so that they might approve of the document, the legislature enacted a regulatory measure that, among other things, sought to ensure that capital stock would be sufficient to cover the costs of constructing new lines. The legislation also outlined conditions under which railroads could acquire real estate and established passenger rates that could be charged (up to $.04 per mile in the Lower Peninsula and up to $.05 in the Upper Peninsula). In addition, the measure imposed a 2 percent tax on gross receipts not over $4,000 per mile of line and $.03 for any amount above that figure. The new law also created the office of Commissioner of Railroads for the State of Michigan. The commissioner, to be appointed by the governor, was to serve a term of two years and was given responsibility for compiling (based upon an examination of company records) and publishing an annual report outlining the operations of all state railroads and suggesting needed railroad legislation. To be eligible to serve, the nominee was to be entirely free of pecuniary interest in any railroad corporation. Given the purely advisory role of the commissioner, the lack of state regulation of freight rates, and the blatantly probusiness orientation of state Republican leaders, the measure apparently did little to ease the fears of those still uncertain about the desirability of ongoing economic transformation. Voicing that ambivalence, the *Detroit Free Press,* after reviewing the activities of the winter legislative session, commented, "The revelations of the past winter have shown that the necessity for overthrowing the party in power is greater than we thought last year."[36]

The year 1873 also brought a vivid reminder of the perils of the new economy to those residents of Michigan who remained leery of the Republican Party's boundless devotion to unfettered capitalism—a panic. Beginning in the fall of 1873, the United States entered a period of six hard years. The effects of the panic upon the people of Michigan were severe and helped to reinforce the fears many people had relative to the direction that the state was heading. Industrial activity flagged in Michigan, and unemployment mounted. Iron-ore production, tied as it was to the vitality of the nation's railroads, also plummeted. In Michigan, railroad construction ground to a halt, with a mere sixty miles being built in 1874. Even the rate of population growth in the state slowed after the onset of the depression, resulting in a steep decline in state revenues generated by land sales—from $230,000 in 1873 to less than $62,000 the next year. This decline, along with other factors, left the state facing a $170,000 budgetary shortfall. Among the hardest hit by the panic was Michigan's farming community. Already suffering after three years of falling prices, farmers witnessed a further erosion of their economic viability. Prices for commodities continued to fall throughout the decade, and the cash value per acre of principal crops declined from $17.53 in 1875 to $13.88 in 1878, one of the sharpest declines among the western states. Wheat prices fell from $1.17 per bushel in 1871 to a paltry $.77 per bushel by 1878. Moreover, the rate of indebtedness among Michigan farmers rose dramatically, with one report claiming that as of approximately 1879, an average of 50 percent of state farms were mortgaged, more than in any other state in the Great Lakes region.[37]

Caught in the panic's downward spiral, the residents of Michigan identified any number of causes for their troubles and expressed their mounting anxiety in myriad ways. Many Michigan farmers turned to the recently organized Patrons of Husbandry, or Grange, for support. A new arrival to the state as of 1872, the Grange experienced tremendous growth in the ensuing years (despite the previously mentioned Republican efforts to head off dissent), organizing 113 chapters in 1873 and reaching a peak membership of 33,196 members organized in 605 chapters throughout the state in 1875. Moreover, by late 1873, the state Grange began shifting away from its early social orientation and began serving as a mouthpiece and advocate for farmers' economic and political interests. By 1874, many within the movement had concluded that railroads' power and privilege were to blame for the farmers' plight. Accordingly, Grange representatives gathered in Kalamazoo in January to frame a platform demanding that the state legislators deliberate upon the proposed constitution during the extra session that was about to convene. Further, they were to consider drafting legislation to utilize the state's power to set and regulate railroad passenger and freight rates, to ensure the construction of necessary safety devices, and to restrict the issuance of railroad passes. Concurrently, the Michigan Grange also expended considerable energy building buyer and seller cooperatives for state farmers in an effort to assist them in obtaining necessary goods at a lower cost and to enable them to break the railroad's presumed control over the prices paid for their commodities.[38]

Other Michigan farmers pointed to the nation's tariff rates as the source of their woes. Forced to buy expensive manufactured items protected by the tariff while simultaneously selling their own produce in an unprotected market, they denounced the current tariff policy. George Yaple, a Mendon farmer and a future Greenback/Democratic congressman and Populist candidate for governor, gave voice to this belief when he argued that "the farmer is still under the curse of feudalism and kept under tribute to the manufacturer. The farmer is robbed under the plea of protection to home industries."

"If protection is such a good thing," Yaple implored, "why not extend its benefits to the farmers and to all classes?" "Government," he railed, "stands convicted by its class legislation of being a thief." State mining and lumbering firms, which benefited immensely from the tariff, encouraged their allies in Washington, especially the protariff chair of the Senate Committee on Commerce, Zachariah Chandler, to hold the line. Still other Michiganians attributed their worsening positions to the lack of circulating currency in the United States—a problem further exacerbated, inflationists believed, by the recent "Crime of '73," whereby Congress ended the minting of silver coin—and demanded an immediate inflation of the nation's currency. These inflationists, however, found relatively little support within the Republican Party; though not entirely of one voice on the subject, the Republicans generally agreed with their leader, Chandler, who openly denounced the inflation of the currency by a further issuance of greenbacks and advocated an immediate resumption of specie payment.[39]

Yet another point of contention for a large number of Michigan's hard-pressed residents was the state's recent pattern of extensive spending on social reforms—reforms that many in the state, especially Democrats and those of Democratic antecedents, eyed with much suspicion. In the years following the war, state expenditures for public education (where the values and requisite skills of the marketplace were disseminated), state prison and asylums, and other social institutions had risen dramatically. The state budget was greatly expanded by mandatory free public education; the appropriation of tax funds to support the state's fledgling university system beginning in 1867; the construction of a new prison; the expansion of the state insane asylum in Kalamazoo and the asylum for the deaf, dumb, and blind in Flint; the construction of a home for indigent and needy children in Coldwater; and numerous other social expenditures. Many believed that, given the current panic, the continuance of such high levels of expenditure would cripple the state. By trimming unnecessary spending and tapping into the state's surplus of $13,600,985, they argued, significant tax relief could be offered to residents, and their hard times could be alleviated.[40]

With the election of 1874 looming on the horizon, yet another effort was made to tap into this swirling wave of discontent and to offer a united front against the state's entrenched Republican leaders and their policies. Adopting a strategy designed to avoid a repeat of the 1872 debacle, Michigan's Liberal Republicans (taking the name National Reform Party) and state Democrats more closely coordinated their actions and drafted a slate of candidates for concurrent nomination, although the parties maintained their separate organizations. Both parties adopted vague platforms relative to the ongoing inflation question—the National Reformers calling for a return to a specie basis as "rapidly as shall be consistent with financial prosperity" and the Democrats issuing a pledge to use specie to bolster the sagging greenback. Further, both the National Reform Party and the state Democrats extended a hand to hard-pressed farmers by adopting the Grange's demand for further railroad regulation and taxation. Both parties also insisted upon a more equitable system of taxation, an economical administration of government, a tariff for revenue only, and an end to corruption and extravagance—"unexampled extravagance and corruption," as the Democrats phrased it—in both Washington and Lansing.[41]

State Republicans, fearful of the surging unrest in Michigan, fell back on a tried and true tactic—waving the bloody shirt—as a means of heading off disaffection. (Governor Bagley derisively called the Democratic Party "the party of the backward look" and labeled it "the apple tree of Appomattox.") Offering no apologies for their recent actions, Republicans instead renominated Bagley for a second term in office and challenged voters to conduct "a faithful scrutiny of [the party's] record through every vicissitude of war and peace, and the candid judgement of all men." The platform similarly bragged that state Republicans were to be lauded for their efforts to promote social legislation. More to the point, the party warned, there was "no reason to surrender the reins of power into the hands of a party whose last public service was to drag the country into civil war." On economic matters, however, the platform remained extremely vague and noncommittal. Greenbacks were cited as being far superior to any other circulating paper medium in the United States, yet the platform demanded specie resumption "as soon as possible."[42]

On election day, Michigan's Republican leaders were served warning that their actions had, indeed, become a source of concern for many of their partisans. In a stinging rebuke, the party narrowly managed to hold on to the governorship with a meager 50.46 percent of the votes cast. In just two years, the party's support had fallen over 10 percent. The Reform/Democratic opposition made similar gains in the state legislature, sending fourteen men to the state senate and forty-seven to the house, thereby reducing the Republicans' joint majority to a scant ten votes. Most disturbing of all to party leaders was the fact that the opposition emerged victorious in three of the state's nine congressional districts. Finally, the proposed constitution, embodying as it did the ideals of the new party leadership—ideals that had been hotly contested since 1867—was thoroughly denounced and repudiated by a vote of 124,039 to 39,285.[43]

Their spirits high as a result of their successes, the opposition forces set their sights on unseating the man who symbolized everything they had come to despise—Zachariah Chandler—in the senatorial contest of 1875. Chandler and his political machine made ready for the contest. Marshaling his forces, he easily captured a large majority of the Republican Party caucus vote on January 7. On January 19, the question went to the full legislature. Three days later, largely due to the efforts of a number of Allegan County farmers serving in the lower house, Chandler was defeated. Michigan had a new senator—state supreme court justice Isaac P. Christiancy, a former Democrat who was one of the majority in the antirailroad aid *Salem* decision and one of the primary architects behind the Republican coalition of 1854. Arguably, Christiancy's antebellum Democratic roots, his conservative views relative to economic change, his solid reputation for integrity, and his connection to the party's heralded antebellum past provided the opposition with a greater degree of comfort than Chandler could. Chandler's defeat, the *Ann Arbor Argus* crowed, marked the "beginning of the people's rule and the end of politicians."[44]

As the results of the 1874 election and the ousting of Chandler demonstrate, Michigan's Republican Party had clearly lost touch with a sizable portion of its constituent base. Repeated prodevelopment initiatives, an activist social and economic policy, the taint of corruption and indifference, and machine politics combined with a sharp economic downturn to spawn the largest mass disaffection the party had known in its brief, twenty-year history. Its leadership, dominated as it was by successful business elites, had forged too far ahead of some of the party faithful. Despite being bound tightly to their adopted party by shackles forged in the antebellum sectional crisis and the war that followed, these partisans could not ignore their own suspicions and fears about the emerging economic order—suspicions and fears that had, in 1854, prompted them to embrace the new party as the protector of individual rights, autonomy, and Free-Soilism. By the early 1870s, however, party leaders had seemingly abandoned that legacy and instead tilted in the direction of unfettered economic development, activist social policy, and corrupt spoilsmanship. "We must learn," Governor Bagley unabashedly asserted,

> that Government can not create money any more than it can create wheat—that it can not run banks, or railroads, or farms—it can not fix the price of labor, or furnish labor to the idle, or open its coffers to the empty-handed. . . . The idea that times are to be bettered by statute, that values can be fixed by law, that labor for the idle is to be furnished by Government, has poisoned the public mind to a dan-

gerous degree, and caused a large amount of misery. It has set hundreds of us waiting for something to turn up, when we ought to have been at work.

The panic now gripping their state and the nation, many logically concluded, was the obvious result of such beliefs. Accordingly, these anxious Republicans sought out or created an alliance of convenience with state Democrats, many of whom shared a similar frame of mind, and they now threatened to rend asunder the once unassailable Republican coalition.[45]

Confronted by this rude awakening, state Republicans quickly retrenched in order to ensure that the dissident surge would be short-lived. Bagley and the legislature soon moved to bind German voters (angry over the Republicans' continued flirtation with Prohibition) to the party, repealing the state's 1855 statute and putting in its stead a system of taxation and licensing. Party papers, such as the *Lansing State Republican,* lent their voices to the cause and denounced the "so-called 'reform' element" in the state legislature, accusing it of wasting valuable time. Meeting in convention in Grand Rapids on May 10, the Chandler machine also retrenched and adopted a new strategy. Determined to retain control over the party's national offices and build support for a later bid to return to the Senate, Chandler, now serving as secretary of the interior, relinquished some control over the forthcoming state nominations to the party's reform wing. With the way now cleared, state Republicans gave their nomination to "the People's candidate," Charles M. Croswell, an Adrian attorney with pro-Granger proclivities (he had also been among the most vocal supporters of Governor Crapo's veto of railroad aid legislation in 1867). The party platform, however, remained obtuse, offering a ringing tribute to the Republican nominations and avoiding any mention of the heated tariff or currency questions.[46]

The opposition elements in Michigan continued their pattern of cooperation while maintaining separate organizations. Early in 1876, however, a growing rift over the currency question threatened to disrupt the loose coalition. In late May, state Democrats met in convention in Lansing. There, two separate reports were presented from the Committee on Resolutions. The majority report reiterated the party platform of 1874, with its vague endorsement of hard money and a tariff for revenue only. A minority report, however, denounced "sixteen years of Republican rule," which, it claimed, had "entailed upon the country vast indebtedness, national and domestic." Further, the report asserted, the Specie Resumption Act (a measure passed by Congress in 1875 that set January 1, 1879, as the date when greenbacks, then redeemable in gold, would be withdrawn from circulation) was a "sharp leg-islative device in the unwarrantable interest of the creditor class, calculated to enrich the few and sacrifice the best interests of the country." The report demanded the repeal of both the Specie Resumption Act and the Mint Act of 1873, which had demonetized silver. In the end, the majority report, without mention of the tariff, was adopted by the convention. Yet the currency issue was clearly rising in prominence in the minds of state voters.[47]

Additional evidence of this growing trend was provided by the formal or-ganization of the Greenback, or Independent, Party in Michigan in the spring of 1876. Unflinchingly devoted to soft money and inflation (which had come under attack with the passage of the Specie Resumption Act in 1875), the Greenbackers organized their party in Jackson (the birthplace of Republicanism) on May 3, vowing, in language harkening back to the Free-Soil pleas of the Republicans, to defend the "efforts of the laboring class to improve their condition." The platform adopted by the fledgling organiza-tion demanded the repeal of the Resumption Act and declared it "the duty of Congress to so regulate the volume of currency that the rate of interest shall never be greater than the increase of wealth by productive labor."[48]

Confused about where to go, apostate Republicans, who had cooperated with Democrats in the past while never actually switching party allegiance, found themselves in a tough spot. Voting for Democratic candidates was not an option. Nor did the new political organization, the Greenback Party, which staunchly guarded its autonomous existence, hold much appeal. Many un-doubtedly accepted their own party's apparent contrition as real and felt com-fortable voting Republican again after sending party leaders a message. Others apparently remained confused and simply opted not to vote. In the end, the state Republican Party, relying upon its superior organization and the chaotic state of its opposition, handily won the fall contest by a margin of 16,500 over the combined vote of its opponents in the presidential contest and 14,300 in the gubernatorial race. Moreover, the party increased its majority in the state legislature from ten votes to sixty-four. It also won all but one of the state's con-gressional races. The opposition's short-lived success was over.[49]

The pragmatism of the Republican Party and its leadership had pro-duced the intended result. The lesson was obvious to all: if party organization could be maintained, future Republican success was assured. While steps were taken to do precisely that by the Chandler machine and by Chandler's shrewd successor, Detroit industrialist James McMillan, the party's fortunes remained uncertain in the state, for economic hardship and the raging cur-rency debate continually reminded voters of their long-standing ambivalence about socioeconomic change. Haranguing the government for what he deemed its active promotion of economic change, George Yaple captured the spirit of the discontented:

> If the government does more for me, it infringes on the rights of someone else. If it does more than that for me, it begins the unholy work of class legislation; and class legislation has ever been the bane of the world's progress, the greatest obstacle to the growth and prosperity of common people. It is always in the interest of the few, and against the rights of the many. It engenders a war of classes. It builds up caste and monopoly. It is the prime minister of every despotism; it is hostile to the genius of democracy.

In another speech, Yaple argued that "the centralization of wealth in a few hands means despotism and despotism is the mother of ignorance and slavery." "Every new invention," he boldly concluded, "art, science, and discovery ought to add something to the common wealth of the world."[50]

In 1878, the worst year of the ongoing depression, the Republicans narrowly retained control of the governorship, though the combined tally for the Greenback and Democratic gubernatorial candidates surpassed that for Governor Croswell by over 45,000 votes. Exuberant over the rising tide of disaffection, one state Greenbacker—the future gubernatorial candidate David Woodman—penned the following bit of doggerel:

> With good reasons to hope
> That we're going to succeed
> 'Gainst the sachems of avarice
> And stealth, and of greed
> And as helpers are needed
> At once to do battle,
> 'Gainst heroes who'd slay us
> As butchers do cattle—
> Don't skulk like those pig-tail
> Mongolian Tartars,
> Who hoard all their nickels
> And dimes and their quarters,
> Then scud as do panic-struck
> Thieves and deserters;
> When a little tall skirmishing,

Nerve and decision,
May send mammon's thugs
To the moon on a mission;
And with prudence and foresight,
And wise co-operation,
We can baffle hell's powers,
Then replenish the nation.

Four years later, in 1882, a fusion ticket put forth by the two parties, headed by Josiah Begole, a former Republican and soft-money congressman from Flint, succeeded in momentarily breaking the Republican stranglehold on Michigan, winning the governorship by a mere 5,000 votes. Though the Republicans captured the remaining state offices, the fusion ticket also captured six of the state's eleven congressional seats. While elated over the recent victory, one Greenbacker despairingly wrote a friend, "I tell you it is uphill work and the change will only come when the avarice of capital has so far overcome their judgment that they will rob the masses their assets so close that hunger forces them to defend themselves. As long as they only take the surpluses each year the fools will quietly submit."[51]

Such cautious hesitation proved warranted and fusion's success (and the continued allure of once hallowed Jacksonian paeans) proved fleeting, as Republicans recaptured the governorship in 1884. Indeed, despite the tireless efforts of its proponents, fusion, mired in older ideals of self-sufficiency and community rights, proved incapable of sustaining victory in the face of runaway industrial capitalism and the efforts of state Republican leaders to recast their party as the unabashed promoter of unfettered development. The Republican "redemption" was briefly interrupted again in 1890 when Democrat Edwin B. Winans, a farmer from Livingston County and recent member of Congress, defeated James M. Turner, a wealthy Lansing railroad man. But Republicans quickly recovered, nominating a farmer of their own, John T. Rich, and they regained control of the state. Despite such notable fluctuations and the onset of yet another economic downturn in 1893, the Republican Party held fast. Its partisan hemorrhage cauterized and its rump Jacksonian constituency shed, the party's metamorphosis was complete. Wedded to an unabashedly prodevelopment agenda, the party retained control of Michigan throughout the remainder of the nineteenth century and well into the next and thus paved the way for the state's phenomenal twentieth-century industrial growth. The tide had turned forever, and the ethic of the Jacksonian yeomanry had been rendered obsolete.[52]

NOTES

INTRODUCTION

1. The clearest articulation of the meaning of the term *free soil* remains Eric Foner, *Free Soil, Free Labor, Free Men: The Ideology of the Republican Party before the Civil War* (New York: Oxford University Press, 1970).

2. The development of the market economy in the United States during the first half of the nineteenth century has been the subject of a great deal of historical literature. Among the best works are W. Elliot Brownlee, *Dynamics of Ascent: A History of the American Economy*, 2nd ed. (New York: Alfred A. Knopf, 1988); Stuart W. Bruchey, *Enterprise: The Dynamic Economy of a Free People* (Cambridge, Mass.: Harvard University Press, 1990); Christopher Clark, *The Roots of Rural Capitalism: Western Massachusetts, 1780–1860* (Ithaca, N.Y.: Cornell University Press, 1991); Thomas C. Cochran, *Frontiers of Change: Early Industrialism in America* (New York: Oxford University Press, 1981); Peter D. McClelland, *Sowing Modernity: America's First Agricultural Revolution* (Ithaca, N.Y.: Cornell University Press, 1997); Douglass C. North, *The Economic Growth of the United States, 1790–1860* (Englewood Cliffs, N.J.: Prentice-Hall, 1961); Charles Sellers, *The Market Revolution: Jacksonian America, 1815–1846* (New York: Oxford University Press, 1991); and George R. Taylor, *The Transportation Revolution, 1815–1861* (New York: Holt, Reinhart and Winston, 1962).

3. Historians have long argued about the attitudes of antebellum Americans toward the changes wrought by the advent of the market economy. Many believe that Americans readily embraced the market and eagerly promoted its expansion; see, for example Jeremy Atack and Fred Bateman, "Self-Sufficiency and the Marketable Surplus in the Rural North," *Agricultural History* 58 (July 1984): 296–313; Andrew R. L. Cayton and Peter S. Onuf, *The Midwest and the Nation: Rethinking the History of an American Region* (Bloomington: Indiana University Press, 1990); Albert Fishlow, *American Railroads and the Transformation of the Antebellum Economy* (Cambridge, Mass.: Harvard University Press, 1965); William E. Gienapp, *The Origins of the Republican Party, 1852–1856* (New York: Oxford University Press, 1987), pp. 356–57; McClelland, *Sowing Modernity;* and Winifred Rothenberg, *From Market Place to Market Economy: The Transformation of Rural Massachusetts, 1750–1850* (Chicago: University of Chicago Press, 1992). A Michigan-specific example of this trend is Susan E. Gray, *The Yankee West: Community*

Life on the Michigan Frontier (Chapel Hill: University of North Carolina Press, 1996). Also see Steven C. Wilkshire, "Markets and Market Culture in the Early Settlement of Ionia County, Michigan," *Michigan Historical Review* 24 (Spring 1998): 1–22.

The weight of evidence, however, suggests otherwise. Americans appear to have been exceedingly ambivalent about the developing market economy and its accompanying social dislocation. In fact, even those who chose to participate in market production often did so not with the intent of becoming wealthy but rather to foster familial independence and autonomy. These feelings of ambivalence are well documented in Christopher Clark, "Rural America and the Transition to Capitalism," *Journal of the Early Republic* 16 (Summer 1996): 223–36; Steven Hahn and Jonathan Prude, eds., *The Countryside in the Age of Capitalist Transformation: Essays in the Social History of Rural America* (Chapel Hill: University of North Carolina Press, 1985); Dale R. Prentiss, "Economic Progress and Social Dissent in Michigan and Mississippi, 1837–1860" (Ph.D. diss., Stanford University, 1990); Sellers, *Market Revolution;* J. Mills Thornton III, *Politics and Power in a Slave Society: Alabama, 1800–1860* (Baton Rouge: Louisiana State University Press, 1978); idem, "The Ethic of Subsistence and the Origins of Southern Secession," *Tennessee Historical Quarterly* 48 (1989): 67–85; Harry L. Watson, *Liberty and Power: The Politics of Jacksonian America* (New York: Noonday Press, 1990); and Sean Wilentz, *Chants Democratic: New York City and the Rise of the American Working Class, 1788–1850* (New York: Oxford University Press, 1984).

4. The problems associated with cross-level inference are discussed in Christopher H. Achen and W. Phillips Shively, *Cross-Level Inference* (Chicago: University of Chicago Press, 1995), and Gary King, *A Solution to the Ecological Inference Problem: Reconstructing Individual Behavior from Aggregate Data* (Princeton, N.J.: Princeton University Press, 1997). The concept of moral economy is lucidly discussed in Edward P. Thompson, *The Making of the English Working Class* (New York: Pantheon Books, 1964).

5. An excellent synopsis of the literature on the importance of republicanism to antebellum Americans is Marc W. Kruman, "The Second American Party System and the Transformation of Revolutionary Republicanism," *Journal of the Early Republic* 12 (Winter 1992): 509–37. For similar sentiments, see Jean H. Baker, *Affairs of Party: The Political Culture of Northern Democrats in the Mid-Nineteenth Century* (Ithaca, N.Y.: Cornell University Press, 1983); Lacy K. Ford, *The Origins of Southern Radicalism: The South Carolina Upcountry, 1800–1860* (New York: Oxford University Press, 1988); Thornton, *Politics and Power;* Watson, *Liberty and Power;* and Major Wilson, "Republicanism and the Idea of Party in the Jacksonian Period," *Journal of the Early Republic* 8 (Winter 1988): 419–42.

The democratization of the American citizenry during the Jacksonian era is well documented in Sellers, *Market Revolution,* and Robert H. Wiebe, *The Opening of American Society: From the Adoption of the Constitution to the Eve of Disunion* (New York: Vintage Books, 1984). The importance of Andrew Jackson as a symbol for this new democratic age is described in John W. Ward, *Andrew Jackson, Symbol for an Age* (New York: Oxford University Press, 1955).

6. Lawrence F. Kohl, *The Politics of Individualism: Parties and the American Character*

in the Jacksonian Era (New York: Oxford University Press, 1989), p. 63; on the Democrats, see pp. 21–62. Kohl's book provides a particularly convincing portrayal of the frame of mind of the American polity during the Jacksonian era.

7. My understanding of the political culture of the Jacksonian era has been shaped by the following works: Daniel Walker Howe, *The Political Culture of the American Whigs* (Chicago: University of Chicago Press, 1979); Kohl, *The Politics of Individualism;* Thornton, *Politics and Power;* idem, "Ethic of Subsistence"; Watson, *Liberty and Power;* and Rush Welter, *The Mind of America, 1820–1860* (New York: Columbia University Press, 1975). The quote is from the *Detroit Free Press,* October 8, 1850.

8. Prime examples of this type of prodevelopment interpretation are Cayton and Onuf, *The Midwest and the Nation,* and McClelland, *Sowing Modernity.*

9. One of the most glaring examples of the tendency to see this economic transformation in static terms is Sellers, *Market Revolution.*

10. The ethnocultural interpretation is best exemplified by Ronald P. Formisano, *The Birth of Mass Political Parties: Michigan, 1827–1861* (Princeton, N.J.: Princeton University Press, 1971). The primary work on Michigan that emphasizes the importance of the slavery issue to the Republican cause is Benjamin F. Streeter, *Political Parties in Michigan 1837–1860: An Historical Study of Political Issues and Parties in Michigan from the Admission of the State to the Civil War* (Lansing: Michigan Historical Commission, 1918).

11. The most obvious examples of the continued relevancy of these tensions are the Greenbacker and Populist insurgencies.

CHAPTER 1

The quotation in this chapter's heading is from Benjamin F. Graves, "Isaac P. Christiancy," paper read before the Convention of Judges at Lansing, Michigan, December 27, 1900 (n.p., n.d.), p. 9, in Benjamin F. Graves Papers, 1815–1849, Michigan Historical Collections, Bentley Historical Library, University of Michigan, Ann Arbor.

1. John C. McCloskey, "Land Speculation in Michigan as Described in Mrs. Kirkland's *A New Home—Who'll Follow?*" *Michigan History* 42 (March 1958): 29. Michigan's explosive early growth is described in detail in Willis F. Dunbar, *Michigan: A History of the Wolverine State* (Grand Rapids, Mich.: William B. Eerdmans, 1970), pp. 261–85.

2. The devastating impact of the panic of 1837 upon Michigan is well documented in Dunbar, *Michigan,* pp. 261–85; George N. Fuller, *Michigan: A Centennial History of the State and Its People,* vol. 1 (Chicago: Lewis, 1939), pp. 86, 217, 255–57, and 264; and Henry M. Utley and Byron M. Cutcheon, eds., *Michigan as a Province, Territory and State, The Twenty-Sixth Member of the Federal Union,* vol. 3 (n.p.: Publishing Society of Michigan, 1906).

3. For a brief overview of Michigan's early politics, see James V. Campbell, *Outlines of the Political History of Michigan* (Detroit, Mich.: Schober, 1876); Dunbar, *Michigan;* and Prentiss, "Economic Progress and Social Dissent in Michigan and Mississippi, 1837–1860" (Ph.D. diss., Stanford University, 1990). Though dated, Benjamin F. Streeter,

Political Parties in Michigan, 1837–1860: An Historical Study of Political Issues and Parties in Michigan from the Admission of the State to the Civil War (Lansing: Michigan Historical Commission, 1918), properly emphasizes the importance of economic issues as a driving force in early Michigan politics and remains a solid narrative account of the period.

Two other important works on Michigan's early politics are Ronald P. Formisano, *The Birth of Mass Political Parties in Michigan, 1827–1861* (Princeton, N.J.: Princeton University Press, 1971), and John F. Reynolds, "Piety and Politics: Evangelism in the Michigan Legislature, 1837–1861," *Michigan History* 61 (1977): 323–52. Influenced by the "ethnocultural" school of historiography, Formisano contended that antebellum Michigan politics can be understood only within the context of competing ethnocultural agendas and tensions. Unfortunately, this belief led Formisano to disregard the pervasive legislative and popular debates over economic questions as irrelevant and unimportant. Reynolds's article tested Formisano's ethnocultural thesis and found it lacking. Reynolds, however, stopped short of offering an alternative interpretation of Michigan's political behavior.

4. Very little has been written about the Woodbridge administration in Michigan. Perhaps the fullest account of the Whig electoral victory and subsequent administration can be found in Formisano, *Birth of Mass Political Parties*, pp. 129–36, and Utley and Cutcheon, *Michigan as a Province*, vol. 3, pp. 170–71. A very brief account of the Woodbridge administration can be found in Dunbar, *Michigan*, p. 277. For further information on the Woodbridge administration, see William G. Shade, "Banks and Politics in Michigan, 1835–1845: A Reconsideration," *Michigan History* 57 (Spring 1973): 46; Streeter, *Political Parties in Michigan*, pp. 37–39; and Henry M. Utley, "The Wildcat Banking System in Michigan," *Michigan Pioneer and Historical Collections* 5 (1882): 209–22.

5. A number of historians have identified a particularly strong antiparty bias among Whigs, a bias that continually threatened partisan unity. At the core of this antiparty spirit was the Whig notion of freedom as liberation and success. Whigs believed in the organic unity of human society and were convinced that diversity and social inequality were a given. It followed, Whigs argued, that those who possessed superior skills and intelligence should be recognized for their talents and rewarded with honor, prestige, and wealth. It is not surprising, then, that American Whigs readily embraced the developing market economy and its promise of reward for talent and effort. Accordingly, party organization, with its emphasis on egalitarianism and majority rule, offended Whigs. In fact, they conceded that the only reason for organizing a political party was to protect their American liberty (as they understood it) so that individuals could rise as far as their efforts and talents would take them.

For similar expressions, see John Ashworth, *Agrarians and Aristocrats: Party Ideology in the United States, 1837–1846* (New York: Cambridge University Press, 1983); Formisano, *Birth of Mass Political Parties*, p. 77; Michael F. Holt, *The Rise and Fall of the American Whig Party: Jacksonian Politics and the Onset of the Civil War* (New York: Oxford University Press, 1999); Daniel Walker Howe, *The Political Culture of the American Whigs*

(Chicago: University of Chicago Press, 1979); Marc W. Kruman, "The Second American Party System and the Transformation of Revolutionary Republicanism," *Journal of the Early Republic* (Winter 1992): 522; and Major Wilson, "Republicanism and the Idea of Party in the Jacksonian Period," *Journal of the Early Republic* (Winter 1988): 428–29. It should be noted that many of these works also describe a strong evangelical/reform strain among Whigs. The devotion to an absolute code of morality also constrained Whig political behavior, as partisans often found themselves unwilling or unable to put aside personal principles for the sake of party unity.

6. Shade, "Banks and Politics," pp. 48–49.

7. Bruce A. Rubenstein and Lawrence E. Ziewacz, *Michigan: A History of the Great Lakes State*, 3rd ed. (Wheeling, Ill.: Harlan Davidson, 2002), pp. 76–77. For more on John S. Barry, see Dunbar, *Michigan*, pp. 280–81; H. H. Riley, "John S. Barry," *Michigan Pioneer and Historical Collections* 9 (1887): 227–33; Sue I. Silliman, "A Prince in Puddleford," *Michigan History* 13 (January 1929): 252–64; and Shade, "Banks and Politics," pp. 48–49. The Democrats managed to cut state expenditures by 67 percent during the 1840s (spending per capita fell from $7.72 in 1840 to $1.34 by 1850). Michigan's indebtedness similarly fell 66 percent between 1842 and 1850. Benjamin W. Bellows, "Politics and Michigan Fiscal Policy, 1837–1865" (honors thesis, University of Michigan, 1996), p. 20.

8. An excellent account of Michigan's ambitious internal improvements program, especially as it related to railroad construction, is Robert J. Parks, *Democracy's Railroads: Public Enterprise in Jacksonian Michigan* (Port Washington, N.Y.: Kennikat Press, 1972). Parks correctly pointed out that Michigan's railroads were not sold merely because of debt but rather, in part, because of the state's inability to meet the costs of improving them. On Alpheus Felch, see Herbert Randall, "Alpheus Felch: An Appreciation," *Michigan History* 10 (April 1926): 157–74.

9. Dunbar, *Michigan*, p. 319, Utley and Cutcheon, *Michigan as a Province*, vol. 3, p. 315.

10. Michigan's efforts to enact homestead exemption legislation are well documented in Lena London, "Homestead Exemption in the Michigan Constitutional Convention of 1850," *Michigan History* 37 (December 1953): 385–406. For a national perspective on the issue, see Paul Goodman, "The Emergence of Homestead Exemption in the United States: Accommodation and Resistance to the Market Revolution, 1840–1880," *Journal of American History* 80 (September 1993): 470–98.

11. The best account of the Wilmot controversy from a national perspective is Michael Morrison, *Slavery and the American West: The Eclipse of Manifest Destiny and the Coming of the Civil War* (Chapel Hill: University of North Carolina Press, 1997). Also useful are Chaplain Morrison, *Democratic Politics and Sectionalism: The Wilmot Controversy* (Chapel Hill: University of North Carolina Press, 1967); Eric Foner "The Wilmot Proviso Revisited," *Journal of American History* 56 (September 1969): 262–79; Michael F. Holt, *The Political Crisis of the 1850s* (New York: W. W. Norton, 1978); and David M. Potter, *The Impending Crisis, 1848–1861* (New York: Harper & Row, 1976).

On the disruptive effects of the Wilmot controversy upon Michigan Democrats, see Formisano, *Birth of Mass Political Parties,* pp. 208–9; Ronald E. Seavoy, "The Organization of the Republican Party in Michigan, 1846–1854," *The Old Northwest* 6 (Winter 1980): 344–50; and Streeter, *Political Parties in Michigan,* pp. 84–104.

12. See Formisano, *Birth of Mass Political Parties,* pp. 208–9; Seavoy, "The Organization of the Republican Party"; and Streeter, *Political Parties in Michigan,* pp. 84–104. For information on Lewis Cass and his attitudes about the proviso, see Willis F. Dunbar, *Lewis Cass* (Grand Rapids, Mich.: William B. Eerdmans, 1970), pp. 57–58; Willard C. Klunder, *Lewis Cass and the Politics of Moderation* (Kent, Ohio: Kent State University Press, 1996), pp. 162–64; Andrew C. McLaughlin, *Lewis Cass* (Boston: Houghton Mifflin, 1899), p. 233; and Frank B. Woodford, *Lewis Cass: The Last Jeffersonian* (New Brunswick, N.J.: Rutgers University Press, 1950), p. 245. Kinsley Bingham's stand on the proviso is detailed in William McDaid, "Kinsley S. Bingham and the Republican Ideology of Antislavery," *Michigan Historical Review* 16 (Fall 1990): 47–56.

13. See Dunbar, *Lewis Cass,* pp. 57–58; Klunder, *Lewis Cass,* pp. 167–70; McLaughlin, *Lewis Cass,* p. 233; and Woodford, *Lewis Cass,* p. 245; Lewis Cass to Alfred Nicholson, December 24, 1847, printed in *Washington Daily Union,* December 30, 1847. Historians have long disagreed over Cass's promotion of the principle of popular sovereignty and upon what effect, if any, his presidential aspirations had on shaping this and his subsequent political action. McLaughlin and Seavoy, on the one hand, contend that Cass's actions were motivated almost entirely by his desire to attain the presidency. Dunbar, Klunder, and Woodford, on the other hand, though not denying that Cass was eager to become president, contend that he was even more concerned with preserving the nation—an interpretation I believe closer to the truth. Cass was not, as some maintain, the architect of popular sovereignty. The idea was first put forth by Congressman Daniel Dickinson in 1846. Cass, however, was the first politician to put the idea before the American people. See Morrison, *Slavery and the American West,* p. 84.

14. The organization of the Michigan Free-Soil Party is described in Seavoy, "Republican Party in Michigan," pp. 347–50.

15. Ibid. Cass won Michigan with a vote of 30,687 (47.2 percent), while Taylor received 23,940 (36.8 percent) and Van Buren 10,389 (16 percent). See Streeter, *Political Parties in Michigan,* p. 100.

16. "Message of Epaphroditus Ransom to the Legislature of the State of Michigan," January 1, 1849, in George N. Fuller, ed., *Messages of the Governors of Michigan,* vol. 2 (Lansing: Michigan Historical Commission, 1926), pp. 130–31.

17. Dunbar, *Lewis Cass,* pp. 64–65; McDaid, "Kinsley S. Bingham," pp. 56–57; Reynolds, "Piety and Politics," p. 336; Streeter, *Political Parties in Michigan,* pp. 103–4; and Woodford, *Lewis Cass,* pp. 273–74.

18. The legislature elected in November 1849 was the same body that would decide who would succeed Cass in the U.S. Senate in 1851. A good account of the failed effort to create a Whig–Free-Soil coalition in Michigan is Seavoy, "Republican Party in Michigan," pp. 350–58. Also see Formisano, *Birth of Mass Political Parties,* p. 214.

19. Jacob M. Howard to Marsh Giddings, April 18, 1849, quoted in Seavoy, "Republican Party in Michigan," p. 351.

20. Seavoy, "Republican Party in Michigan," pp. 353–54.

21. Ibid., pp. 355–58.

22. Streeter, *Political Parties in Michigan*, pp. 108 and 154–55.

23. Cass's support for Clay's compromise proposal stemmed from two sources: Clay's inclusion of the principle of popular sovereignty as a basis for organizing newly created territories and Cass's deeply felt patriotism. See Dunbar, *Lewis Cass*, pp. 66–67; Klunder, *Lewis Cass*, pp. 240–51; McLaughlin, *Lewis Cass*, pp. 278–80; Streeter, *Political Parties in Michigan*, pp. 108–16; and Woodford, *Lewis Cass*, pp. 277–87. Detroit Democrats held a large meeting on March 20 and issued a set of resolutions calling for the rescinding of the resolutions. See *Detroit Free Press*, March 22, 1850. For a comprehensive account of Michigan's response to the Compromise of 1850, see Roger L. Rosentreter, "Michigan and the Compromise of 1850," *The Old Northwest* 6 (Summer 1980): 154–73.

24. *Grand Rapids Enquirer*, June 5, 1850; *Detroit Free Press*, April 8, 1850.

CHAPTER 2

The quotation in this chapter's heading is from "Comments of John D. Pierce," *Report of the Proceedings and Debates in the Convention to Revise the Constitution of the State of Michigan, 1850* (Lansing, Mich.: R. W. Ingals, State Printer, 1850), p. 658.

1. Frank E. Robson, "How Lansing Became the Capital," *Michigan Pioneer and Historical Collections* 11 (1887): 241.

2. *Detroit Daily Advertiser*, April 29, 1850. For a similar expression of this belief on the part of Michigan Whigs, see the *Grand River Eagle*, April 30, 1850. A particularly lucid discussion of the image of the statesman can be found in Major Wilson, "Republicanism and the Idea of Party in the Jacksonian Period," *Journal of the Early Republic* 8 (Winter 1988): 423–31.

3. *Detroit Advertiser*, May 6, 1850, and *Grand River Eagle*, April 30, 1850.

4. *Detroit Free Press*, April 15, 1850. MacLeod would be one of the delegates to the constitutional convention from the county of Mackinac. Always able to "give the correct rule, and whenever required, the reason on which the rule was founded" and possessing "distinct and well formed" ideas, MacLeod was remembered by one of his colleagues as "the most brilliant man of the one hundred of that convention." MacLeod, along with two others—C. P. Bush of Ingham County and E. J. Roberts of Houghton County—issued a signed protest against the completed constitution on the grounds that it exhibited a total distrust in the intelligence of the people. See Michigan Historical Commission, *Michigan Biographies: Including Members of Congress, Elective State Officers, Justices of the Supreme Court, Members of the Michigan Legislature, Board of Regents of the University of Michigan, State Board of Agriculture and State Board of Education*, vol. 2 (Lansing: Michigan Historical Commission, 1924), p. 63; Hezekiah G. Wells, "A Sketch of the Members of the Constitutional Conventions of 1835 and 1850," *Michigan*

Pioneer and Historical Collections 3 (1881): 40; and *Report of the Proceedings and Debates in the Convention to Revise the Constitution of the State of Michigan, 1850* (Lansing, Mich.: R. W. Ingals, 1850), pp. 918–19 [hereafter cited as *Report*]. For a breakdown of the convention delegates by party, see *Detroit Advertiser,* June 3, 1850.

5. Reprint of article from *Michigan State Journal* in the *Grand Rapids Enquirer,* April 17, 1850; Willis F. Dunbar, *Michigan: A History of the Wolverine State* (Grand Rapids, Mich.: William B. Eerdmans, 1970), p. 366. The most recent and most often cited historical work on Michigan's antebellum political history, Ronald Formisano's *Birth of Mass Political Parties,* slighted these trends. Convinced that ethnocultural factors divided the nation into "evangelical" and "liturgical" camps, Formisano contended that the organized political parties of the Jacksonian era were conduits for ethnocultural tensions and that partisan affiliation was determined almost solely on the basis of ethnocultural identification—"evangelicals" became Whigs and "liturgicals" Democrats. He argued that "alien voting could be considered the most salient electorate oriented issue dividing the parties in the convention of 1850" (Formisano, p. 101). In fact, such ethnocultural issues as prohibition and alien voting consumed very little time at the convention. While it is true that Formisano suggested that debtor exemption may also have been a primary concern for the members of the constitutional convention, he offered no thorough analysis of that issue. In short, because he believed that economic and political divisions between Whigs and Democrats were false dichotomies, his overall impression of the 1850 convention tended to be misleading and misrepresented the true significance of the document that emerged. See Ronald P. Formisano, *The Birth of Mass Political Parties in Michigan, 1827–1861* (Princeton, N.J.: Princeton University Press, 1971), pp. 98–101. My assertion that ethnocultural issues consumed very little time at the 1850 Michigan constitutional convention is based upon a thorough reading of the published proceedings. Of the roughly nine hundred pages of published debate, only a small number were devoted to such issues. Of far greater importance to the convention delegates, given the overwhelming number of pages devoted to such issues, were the political and economic concerns discussed elsewhere in this chapter. Formisano ignored the debate over political issues such as biennial sessions and the single-district system altogether.

6. *Detroit Free Press,* April 5, 1850. For further evidence of the desire on the part of Michiganians to adopt such reforms, see the Whig *Grand River Eagle,* April 30, 1850; *Detroit Daily Advertiser,* April 23, 1850 (also Whig); the Democratic *Grand Rapids Enquirer,* March 20, 1850; and the *Detroit Free Press,* April 8 and 22 and May 2 and 24, 1850.

7. *Detroit Advertiser,* April 23, 1850; *Detroit Free Press,* April 13, 1850; and *Grand Rapids Enquirer,* March 20, 1850. Also see *Detroit Free Press,* June 5, 1850.

8. *Detroit Free Press,* April 10, May 2 and 10, and June 12, 1850.

9. *Report,* pp. 33 and 45–46.

10. Article from the *Marshall Expounder* reprinted in *Detroit Free Press,* May 2, 1850; *Report,* pp. 115–17.

11. *Detroit Free Press,* April 8 and 17, 1850.

12. *Report,* pp. 117–18 and 351–52.

13. Ibid., pp. 348, 354.

14. *Grand Rapids Enquirer,* July 4, 1850; remarks of Alfred H. Hanscom, *Report,* p. 352.

15. Wells, "Sketch of the Members," p. 39; *Detroit Daily Advertiser,* June 13, 1850. See also *Detroit Daily Advertiser,* June 21 and July 30, 1850.

16. No fewer than five Whigs (Hezekiah G. Wells, Jonathan R. White, Nathan Pierce, Joseph R. Williams, and Henry T. Backus—the latter three, considered to be the leaders of the Whig delegation, were referred to by their Democratic opponents as the "triangle") spoke out in favor of the amendment, and every Whig delegate in attendance voted for its passage. See *Report,* pp. 348–55. Obviously, given the fact that this measure was adopted, not every Democrat at the convention agreed with Bagg. John P. Cook, a staunch Hillsdale County Jacksonian, for example, stated that he would not allow "our whig friends to take the lead" in promoting single districts. On the contrary, Cook asserted, the single-district system was "a democratic measure." See *Report,* p. 349.

17. *Detroit Free Press,* July 22 and August 15, 1850. For similar expressions, see *Detroit Free Press,* July 31 and August 8 and 12, 1850.

18. *Detroit Advertiser,* July, 29, 30, 31 and August 9 and 19, 1850. Also see *Cass County Advocate,* August 3, 1850; *Detroit Advertiser,* August 5 and 10, 1850; and *Grand River Eagle,* July 22 and 29, 1850.

19. *Report,* pp. 360, 363–64, 369. Previous debate on this issue occurred on June 17. See *Report,* pp. 119–23.

20. *Report,* p. 354. Impressions of the tension between residents of Detroit and the hinterlands are largely based upon perceptions gleaned from various sources. The only real evidence for this dichotomy at the convention can be found in the roll call vote on the single-district question for the senate. In this vote, two of the three delegates from western Wayne County (those who, not coincidentally, represented areas farthest from the Michigan Central Railroad)—a region that continuously stood in the shadow of the state's largest city and commercial entrepôt, Detroit—both voted in favor of the single-district system, while their counterparts from the city all voted in the negative. See *Report,* p. 355.

The same vote provides some evidence of the divisions surrounding the construction of the state's railroads. For example, Calvin Britain, a delegate from the Berrien County town of St. Joseph, also voted in favor of single districts for the senate, whereas the other delegate from the county, Jacob Beeson of Niles, did not. The town of St. Joseph had originally been slated as the western terminus for the Michigan Central Railroad. Once the railroad was sold to private investors in 1846, however, the company obtained a variance from the state legislature that allowed it to divert the railroad away from St. Joseph and toward the growing city of Chicago and to build in a southwesterly direction through the rival town of Niles and on into New Buffalo in the state's southwestern corner. It seems likely, therefore, that Britain's vote was cast in favor of single districts so as to weaken the power of the Michigan Central lobby and its eastern allies. The same could probably be said about the vote of Isaac W. Willard, the delegate from Van Buren County, whose hometown of Paw Paw had also been bypassed by the Michigan Central. On the history of the Michigan Central Railroad, its expansion, and the reactions of state citizens to it, see Edmund A. Calkins, "Railroads of Michigan since 1850," *Michigan History* 13 (January 1929): 5–25; Willis F. Dunbar, *All Aboard: A History of Railroads in Michigan* (Grand Rapids, Mich.: William B. Eerdmans, 1969); Charles Hirschfeld, *The Great Railroad Conspiracy: The Social History of a Railroad War* (East Lansing: Michigan State College Press, 1953); and Robert J. Parks, *Democracy's Railroads: Public Enterprise in Jacksonian Michigan* (Port Washington, N.Y.: Kenniat Press, 1972). For further information on Paw Paw's anger at being slighted by the Michigan Central, see Thomas D. Brock, "Paw Paw versus the Railroads," *Michigan History* 39 (June 1955): 129–82. In addition, three of the five Jackson County delegates (all of whom were Democrats), including Elisha S. Robinson of Grass Lake, voted for single districts, as did the two Democratic delegates from Kalamazoo County. These counties, as will be discussed later in this chapter, were the center of the organized attacks against the Michigan Central Railroad Company. See *Report*, p. 355.

My discussion of the "Fogy/Young America" tension is informed by Dale R. Prentiss, "Economic Progress and Social Dissent in Michigan and Mississippi, 1837–1860" (Ph.D. diss., Stanford University, 1990), pp. 116–58. Though accepting Prentiss's labels "Old Fogy" and "Young American," I believe that Prentiss overstated his case in describing these groups. He linked Fogyism with fear of economic development and hatred of territorial expansion. Yet Michigan's most well known Fogy, Lewis Cass, was an ardent expansionist, and many in the conservative Old Fogy clique of 1850, including Cass, had been instrumental in establishing and investing in Michigan's early banks and promoting the state's ambitious program of internal improvements. Certainly, there were many Fogies who closely approximated the ideal articulated by Prentiss, and clearly, many who accepted the titles of "Young Michigan," "Young Democracy," and so on unabashedly embraced economic change as being consistent with public virtue. Additionally, it should be stated that Prentiss backed away from a hard and fast dichotomy between the two groups by claiming that most citizens demonstrated both Fogy and Young American attitudes. Within the context of the Michigan constitutional convention of 1850, references to the "young democracy" seem to have been designed to evoke images related to sectional animosity and the political and economic dominance of the southeastern portion of the state.

21. *Grand Rapids Enquirer*, March 20 and July 4, 1850.

22. *Detroit Free Press*, June 15 and 17, 1850.

23. Ibid.

24. *Report*, pp. 31–33, 40.

25. *Revised Constitution*, 1850 Article 4, "Legislative Department," sections 2, 3, 20, and 25.

26. Ibid., section 45; idem, Article 15, "Corporations," section 1; idem, Article 14, "Finance and Taxation," sections 3 and 9. It should be noted that Article 14, section 9, did authorize the state to distribute land granted to it to promote internal improvements projects.

27. Henry M. Utley and Byron M. Cutcheon, eds., *Michigan as a Province, Territory and State: The Twenty-Sixth Member of the Federal Union,* vol. 3 (n.p.: Publishing Society of Michigan, 1906), p. 338.

28. James V. Campbell, *Outlines of the Political History of Michigan* (Detroit, Mich.: Schober, 1876), p. 535; *1850 Constitution,* Article 8, "State Officers," section 1; idem, Article 5, "Executive Department," sections 2 and 16.

29. *Grand Rapids Enquirer,* July 4, 1850.

30. *Grand River Eagle,* June 10 and August 5, 1850, and *Grand Rapids Enquirer,* June 12 and 19, 1850.

31. *Report,* p. 599.

32. For coverage of the Judiciary Committee's reports, see *Detroit Free Press,* June 19 and 24, 1850. The positive response to the committee's report can be found in *Detroit Free Press,* July 8, 1850.

33. *Report,* pp. 642–47.

34. Ibid., p. 622; for the vote on McClelland's compromise, see p. 725.

35. *Detroit Free Press,* August 6, 1850; *Grand Rapids Enquirer,* August 7, 1850; and *Pontiac Jacksonian,* August 14, 1850. See also *Grand River Eagle,* August 5, 1850.

36. *1850 Constitution,* Article 6, "Judicial Department," sections 2 and 6.

37. Idem, Article 14, "Finance and Taxation," sections 3 and 9. Neither of these sections elicited debate in convention.

38. *Report,* pp. 29, 31. McClelland supported banks for a very specific reason—because he believed they were a necessary means of providing the state with some control over its currency. This same qualified endorsement of banks was characteristic of other probank Democratic delegates as well. See, for example, the comments of Edward S. Moore of St. Joseph County in *Report,* p. 560. For information on McClelland's view on banks, see Ronald E. Seavoy, "Borrowed Laws to Speed Development: Michigan, 1835–1863," *Michigan History* 59 (Spring-Summer 1975): 60.

39. *Report,* pp. 559–60, 581, 698. Bagg's hostility was likely widely shared by many state residents. Caroline Kirkland, for instance, commented on Michigan's devastating experience with banks when she noted that "a stout farmer might hope to whip a wild cat or two; but once in the grasp of a 'wild cat bank,' his struggles were unavailing. Helpless ruin has been the consequence in numerous instances, and every day adds new names to the list. . . . The distress among the poorer class of farmers, which was the immediate consequence of . . . Bank failures, was indescribable. Those who have seen only a city panic, can form no idea of the extent of the severity of the sufferings on these occasions. And how many small farmers are there in Michigan who have not suffered from this cause?" Caroline M. Kirkland, *A New Home—Who'll Follow? Or Glimpses of Western Life* (New Brunswick, N.J.: Rutgers University Press, 1990), pp. 121–26.

40. *Detroit Advertiser,* January 24, 1850; Lawrence F. Kohl, *The Politics of Individualism: Parties and the American Character in the Jacksonian Era* (New York: Oxford University Press, 1989), p. 67; *Report,* p. 576; and *Detroit Advertiser,* July 31, 1850. For a similar example of the Whig response to the debate over banking, see *Detroit Advertiser,* August 3, 1850. It is important to note that the Whig delegates said virtually nothing in convention regarding the bank issue. Most likely, this lack of vocal Whig support for banks was meant to protect the probank proposition of Robert McClelland—although McClelland's plan was a far cry from the type of conspicuously probank article that the Whigs probably would have preferred—from being labeled a Whig provision, a label that would have doomed it among those antibank Democrats who supported McClelland's article as a means of allowing the citizens of Michigan to decide the issue. This interpretation is supported by the plea made by antibank Democrat Isaac Crary of Calhoun County. Crary pleaded with Hanscom to withdraw his proposition for fear that the convention's endorsement of an antibank position would endanger the new constitution, as he believed that the Whigs and those Democrats who favored banks would unite to defeat the constitution at the polls. See *Report,* p. 581.

41. *Report,* pp. 574–76, 692; for the vote on these measures, see p. 693.

42. McClelland certainly recognized the weakness of his position. In August, he wrote Alpheus Felch, who was then serving in the U.S. Senate, and told him "banking corporations will stand rather a poor chance. General laws for banking purposes must be submitted to the people which will induce their projectors to frame and guard them carefully, and they will then be open to the scrutiny and criticism of everyone and before they are sanctioned or rejected, if there are any defects in them, they will surely be pointed out." Robert McClelland to Alpheus Felch, August 27, 1850, "Correspondence, McClelland, Robert, 1844–1850," Box 4, Alpheus Felch Papers, 1806–1896, Michigan Historical Collections, Bentley Historical Library, University of Michigan, Ann Arbor. *1850 Constitution,* Article 14, "Corporations," sections 3, 4, 5, and 6. Also see Seavoy, "Borrowed Laws," pp. 60–61.

43. *Report,* pp. 587 and 734.

44. *Detroit Advertiser,* June 24 and July 31, 1850.

45. *1850 Constitution,* Article 15, "Corporations," sections 1, 7, 10, 11, and 12.

46. Paul Goodman, "The Emergence of Homestead Exemption in the United States: Accommodation and Resistance to the Market Revolution, 1840–1880," *Journal of American History* 80 (September 1993): 476. Goodman provided an excellent account of the popularity of homestead exemption in the nineteenth-century United States and persuasively argued that the homestead exemption movement exemplified the ambivalence of Americans toward the market revolution. On the one hand, homestead exemption, by protecting a set amount of property from creditors, sought to protect the independence and autonomy of the traditional family economy. On the other hand, by providing potential entrepreneurs with a guarantee that they would not lose everything they owned if their commercial ventures should fail, homestead exemption also sought to encourage participation in the market economy. See also Henry Far-

nam, *Chapters in the History of Social Legislation in the United States to 1860* (Washington, D.C.: Carnegie Institute of Washington, 1938).

47. Information on Pierce's early years is derived from Lena London, "Homestead Exemption in the Michigan Constitutional Convention of 1850," *Michigan History* 37 (December 1953): 389–90. See also *Michigan Biographies*, vol. 2, p. 194.

48. London, "Homestead Exemption," pp. 390–91.

49. Ibid., p. 395–96.

50. *Report*, pp. 658–59, 677. The *Free Press* denounced Backus's "boldfaced demagoguism" and accused Backus of having made his proposed amendment solely to make any homestead amendment so obnoxious that it would be defeated. See *Detroit Free Press*, August 2, 1850. A similar motion was later made by Whig delegate Nathan Pierce. See *Report*, p. 678.

51. *Report*, pp. 658–60. For similar sentiments, see the comments of delegates Jabez G. Sutherland—at twenty-four, the youngest delegate—and Calvin Britain in *Report*, pp. 677 and 669. *1850 Constitution*, Article 16, "Exemptions," sections 1, 2, 3, and 4.

52. *Detroit Free Press*, August 20 and September 3, 1850; *Grand Rapids Enquirer*, October 9, 1850; article from the *Adrian Watchtower* printed in the *Detroit Free Press*, September 7, 1850; article from the *Jackson American Citizen* in the *Detroit Free Press*, September 7, 1850; *Detroit Advertiser*, August 22, 1850.

53. *Report*, p. 588. See also p. 736.

54. Parks, *Democracy's Railroads*, pp. 3, 102, 104–5; William M. Fenton quoted in idem, p. 179.

55. On the expansion of the Michigan Central, see Dunbar, *Michigan*, pp. 314–17; Parks, *Democracy's Railroads*, pp. 251–52; and James A. Van Dyke, *Arguments in the Railroad Conspiracy Case: Entitled the People of the State of Michigan vs. Abel F. Fitch and Others. Tried before His Honor, Warner Wing, Presiding Judge of the Circuit Court for Wayne County, at the May Term, 1851, in the City of Detroit* (Detroit, Mich.: Duncklee, Wales, 1851), p. 13.

56. The most complete accounts of the events surrounding the Michigan Railroad Conspiracy are Charles Hirschfeld, *The Great Railroad Conspiracy: The Social History of a Railroad War* (East Lansing: Michigan State College Press, 1953), and Hirschfeld, "The Great Railroad Conspiracy." Michigan operated under an open-range system until 1851.

57. William Nowlin, *The Bark Covered House, or Back in the Woods Again* (Ann Arbor, Mich.: University Microfilms, 1966), pp. 31–34, 60–66, and 110. Caroline Kirkland, in her thinly fictionalized portrayal of life in frontier Pinkney, Michigan, noted the annual spring burning of local marshes to facilitate the growth of new grass for local ranging livestock. Kirkland, *A New Home—Who'll Follow?* p. 112. Cattle were known to be hardy animals requiring little direct attention and able, as Alan Taylor described them, to "endure the cold and find sustenance in the forests." Moreover, given their size, cattle were also better able to defend themselves against marauding carnivores than other livestock. Equally important, cattle, when tended by a few men, could walk themselves long

distances over primitive roads to get to market. On the advantages of cattle for pioneering families, see Alan Taylor, *William Cooper's Town: Power and Persuasion on the Frontier of the Early American Republic* (New York: Vintage Books, 1995), pp. 105–6.

58. Richard W. Judd, *Common Lands, Common People: The Origins of Conservation in Northern New England* (Cambridge, Mass.: Harvard University Press, 1997).

59. Most historians, even those who focus on the contested transition to the cultural values of capitalism, nonetheless seem to have generally accepted the standard historical trope that northern Yankee culture, which predominated in Michigan, was inherently favorable to capitalism. For example, see David Blanke, *Sowing Modernity: How Consumer Culture Took Root in the Rural Midwest* (Athens: Ohio University Press, 2000); Andrew R. L. Cayton and Peter S. Onuf, *The Midwest and the Nation: Rethinking the History of an American Region* (Bloomington: Indiana University Press, 1990); John Mack Faragher, *Sugar Creek: Life on the Illinois Prairie* (New Haven, Conn.: Yale University Press, 1990); Susan E. Gray, *The Yankee West: Community Life on the Michigan Frontier* (Chapel Hill: University of North Carolina Press, 1996); Peter D. McClelland, *Sowing Modernity: America's First Agricultural Revolution* (Ithaca, N.Y.: Cornell University Press, 1997); and Richard L. Power, *Planting Corn Belt Culture: The Impress of the Upland Southerner and Yankee in the Old Northwest* (Indianapolis: Indiana Historical Society, 1953). Three important exceptions to this rule are Christopher Clark, *The Roots of Rural Capitalism: Western Massachusetts, 1780–1860* (Ithaca, N.Y.: Cornell University Press, 1990); Charles Sellers, *The Market Revolution: Jacksonian America, 1815–1846* (New York: Oxford University Press, 1991); and Thomas S. Wermuth, *Rip Van Winkle's Neighbors: The Transformation of Rural Society in the Hudson River Valley, 1720–1850* (Albany: State University of New York Press, 2001). A more balanced examination of the issue with a Michigan focus can be found in Steven C. Wilkshire, "Markets and Market Culture in the Early Settlement of Ionia County, Michigan," *Michigan Historical Review* 24 (Spring 1998): 1–22. Gray, *Yankee West,* p. 15.

60. Shawn E. Kantor and J. Morgan Kousser, "Common Sense or Commonwealth? The Fence Law and Institutional Change in the Postbellum South," *Journal of Southern History* 59 (May 1993): 212–13. Accusations regarding the intentional slaughter of debilitated animals were frequent. See Hirschfeld, "Great Railroad Conspiracy," p. 100.

61. A good discussion of the promarket orientation of stock law proponents can be found in Hahn, *Roots of Southern Populism,* pp. 249–51. Also see Adams, "How Can a Poor Man Live?" pp. 97–98; Charles E. Brooks, *Frontier Settlement and Market Revolution: The Holland Land Purchase* (Ithaca, N.Y.: Cornell University Press, 1996), p. 99; Charles H. Danhof, "The Fencing Problem in the Eighteen-Fifties," *Agricultural History* 19 (1944): 169–70; Judd, *Common Lands, Common People,* pp. 40–47; and Nowlin, *Bark Covered House,* p. 44. Caroline Kirkland also alluded to the tensions surrounding the fencing controversy when she wrote, "bad fences, missing dogs, unruly cattle, pigs' ears, and women's tongues, are among the most prolific sources of litigation [in Pinkney]." Kirkland, p. 176.

62. Hirschfeld, "The Great Railroad Conspiracy," p. 100.

63. *Marshall Democratic Expounder,* June 25, 1849; Wayne K. Durrill, "Producing Poverty: Local Government and Economic Development in a New South County, 1874–1884," *Journal of American History* 71 (March 1985): 773.

64. Hirschfeld, "The Great Railroad Conspiracy," pp. 121–22.

65. Historians of mid-nineteenth-century Michigan have generally ignored episodes of antirailroad hostility other than the most pronounced example—that directed at the Michigan Central. See Dunbar, *All Aboard,* p. 76; *Detroit Free Press,* July 29, 1850.

66. Article from *Centreville Western Chronicle* printed in *Detroit Free Press,* January 24, 1850; *Detroit Free Press,* March 6, 21, and 25, 1850; for similar expressions from the Pontiac meeting, see *Detroit Free Press,* March 26, 1850.

67. Hirschfeld, "The Great Railroad Conspiracy," p. 127. Such regulatory legislation would not be enacted until the Republicans assumed power in 1855.

68. *Report,* pp. 734–35. For an analysis of the vote on the railroad exemption, see Prentiss, "Economic Progress and Social Dissent," pp. 44–46.

69. Hirschfeld, "The Great Railroad Conspiracy," p. 102.

70. Ibid., pp. 103–4. Brooks would get his test case in 1851. In the case of *Williams v. Michigan Central Railroad Company,* the Michigan Supreme Court upheld Brooks's contention that livestock lost to the railroads had, in actuality, trespassed on railroad property and that the railroad company thus had not been negligent in their death. Lothrop would later go on to become one of the lawyers representing the Michigan Central in its case against Fitch and the other railroad conspirators in 1851. *Jackson American Citizen,* September 24, 1851.

71. For details on the events of late 1850, see Hirschfeld, "The Great Railroad Conspiracy."

72. From the names included in various arrest lists published by state newspapers, I have been able to locate forty-two of these men in the 1850 federal census. The model used for the ensuing statistical analysis was derived from John W. Quist, "'The Great Majority of our Subscribers are Farmers': The Michigan Abolitionist Constituency of the 1840s," *Journal of the Early Republic* 14 (Fall 1994): 325–58.

73. U.S. Department of Commerce, Bureau of the Census, *The Seventh Census of the United States, 1850;* Quist, "Great Majority," pp. 342–54. On the history of antebellum fencing law, see R. Ben Brown, "The Southern Range: A Study in Nineteenth Century Law and Society" (Ph.D. diss., University of Michigan, 1993). It should be noted that many of the youngest "conspirators" were arrested alongside their fathers, and thus, although they may not have had as much direct experience with the ups and downs of the market as the older men, their response to the conflict with the Michigan Central might have been influenced by those who had.

74. U.S. Department of Commerce, *The Seventh Census.*

75. Ibid.; Quist, "Great Majority," pp. 342–54.

76. U.S. Department of Commerce, *The Seventh Census;* Quist, "Great Majority," pp. 342–54.

77. It is my contention that the market activities of some of these farmers, such as Ammi Filley, have been exaggerated. Though Filley did possess a great deal of property ($4,500) and produced 420 bushels of grain on his 280-acre farm, his main connection to the market seems to have been limited to supplying fresh game and fish for the Detroit market. This reliance upon extracted resources rather than the products of commercial farming suggests a more tentative connection to the cash nexus than one might otherwise assume. It also helps, in part, to account for his devotion to the cause of the open range. Fences and the end to communal range rights would undoubtedly have hindered Filley's ability to continue in this line of trade. William Nowlin similarly killed and dressed game (mainly deer) near his Dearborn home for the Detroit market, where they brought between $2.50 and $5.00 each. His participation, however, was not designed to increase personal wealth but rather was part of the family's effort to pay off a mortgage that, Nowlin wrote, "was like a cancer eating up your substance." Nowlin, *Bark Covered House*, p. 156. On Fitch's early exposure to the market, see Hirschfeld, "Great Railroad Conspiracy," p. 111. Burnett's opinions are well represented in the *Grass Lake Public Sentiment*, a newspaper that he published subsequent to his trial. See *Grass Lake Public Sentiment*, March 15, 1854. Abel F. Fitch to his wife Amanda, June 29, 1851, Abel F. Fitch Letters, 1851, Michigan Historical Collections, Bentley Historical Library, University of Michigan, Ann Arbor; for a similar expression of his belief that his liberties were in danger, see Fitch's letter of May 14, 1851.

78. The vote to adopt the constitution of 1850 stood at 36,169 in favor and 9,433 against. See *Report*, p. xlv.

CHAPTER 3

The quotation in this chapter's heading is from Anson de Puy Van Buren to "Friend" Martin, December 12, 1854, Anson de Puy Van Buren Papers, 1846–1885, "Correspondence 1851–1855," Box 1, Michigan Historical Collections, Bentley Historical Library, University of Michigan, Ann Arbor.

1. Alexis de Tocqueville, *Democracy in America* (New York: New American Library, 1956), p. 215; Charles Sellers, *The Market Revolution: Jacksonian America, 1815–1846* (New York: Oxford University Press, 1991).

2. Willis F. Dunbar, *Michigan: A History of the Wolverine State* (Grand Rapids, Mich.: William B. Eerdmans, 1970), p. 315. For other evidence of Michigan's frontier conditions, see Ralph Ely, "History of Gratiot County from 1850 to 1860," *Michigan Pioneer and Historical Collections* 2 (1877–1878): 264. W. B. Williams, "Personal Reminiscences," *Michigan Pioneer and Historical Collections* 22 (1893): 534. On Lansing in 1850, also see Sarah E. Dart, "Early Lansing," *Michigan Pioneer and Historical Collections* 28 (1897–1898): 172–79. Joe L. Norris, "The Country Merchant and Industrial Magnate," *Michigan History* 40 (September 1956): 332.

3. A. C. Glidden, "Pioneer Farming," *Michigan Pioneer and Historical Collections* 18 (1891): 422. Glidden's comment about the transitory nature of subsistence farmers is telling. Michigan in 1850 was populated, in large part, by recent arrivals from New

York State, many of whom, it stands to reason, left New York to escape the clutches of the market or simply to perpetuate for their families a pattern of family-oriented, self-provisioning farming in a region where land was both more plentiful and less expensive. This tendency is well documented in the literature. See, for example, Hal S. Barron, "Staying down on the Farm: Social Processes of Settled Rural Life in the Nineteenth-Century North," in Steven Hahn and Jonathan Prude, eds., *The Countryside in the Age of Capitalist Transformation: Essays in the Social History of Rural America* (Chapel Hill: University of North Carolina Press, 1985), pp. 331–37; Christopher Clark, *The Roots of Rural Capitalism: Western Massachusetts, 1780–1860* (Ithaca, N.Y.: Cornell University Press, 1990); John Mack Faragher, *Sugar Creek: Life on the Illinois Prairie* (New Haven, Conn.: Yale University Press, 1986); and James A. Henretta, "Families and Farms: Mentalité in Pre-industrial America," *William and Mary Quarterly* 35 (January 1978): 3–32. Not all historians acknowledge this desire for self-sufficiency. See, for example, Winifred Rothenberg, *From Market Place to Market Economy* (Chicago: University of Chicago Press, 1992). Indeed, one historian of antebellum Michigan went so far as to argue, incorrectly I believe, that "scholars have generally agreed that the initial goal of frontier development was the rapid commercialization of agricultural production. From the beginning of settlement, agricultural investment was strongly oriented toward market production"; Ronald E. Seavoy, "Borrowed Laws to Speed Development: Michigan, 1835–1860," *Michigan History* 59 (Spring-Summer 1975): 41. Bruce Rubenstein and Lawrence Ziewacz similarly contended that "while new settlers [in Michigan] were primarily agriculturalists, their interest was in growing cash crops of wheat and corn, not merely in subsistence farming"; Bruce A. Rubenstein and Lawrence E. Ziewacz, *Michigan: A History of the Great Lakes State*, 3rd ed. (Wheeling, Ill.: Harlan Davidson, 2002), p. 74. E. B. Hill, "Farm Management," *Michigan History* 22 (Summer 1938): 312; Ethel Hudson, "A Patriarch of Pioneering Days," *Michigan History* 37 (June 1953), pp. 146–47. For similar expressions of self-sufficiency, see Sarah E. Soper, "Reminiscence of Pioneer Life in Oakland County," *Michigan Pioneer and Historical Collections* 28 (1897–1898): 405. U.S. Department of Commerce, Bureau of Census, *The Seventh Census of the United States: An Appendix Embracing Notes upon the Tables of Each of the States, Etc.* (Washington, D.C.: Robert Armstrong, 1853), "Table XI.—Agriculture—Farm Implements, Stock, Products, Home Manufactures, &c.," Michigan, p. 907. For the number of farms in Michigan in 1850, see Hill "Farm Management," p. 314. Figures for 1829 were gleaned from Dale R. Prentiss, "Economic Progress and Social Dissent in Michigan and Mississippi, 1837–1860" (Ph.D. diss., Stanford University, 1990), p. 42.

4. A vast body of literature has investigated the meaning of "self-sufficiency" among antebellum American farmers. Among the best works are Clark, *Roots of Rural Capitalism;* Faragher, *Sugar Creek;* and Sellers, *The Market Revolution.* For evidence of cooperative activities among antebellum Michigan farmers, see Glidden, "Pioneer Farming," p. 422; Hudson, "A Patriarch of the Pioneering Days," pp. 148–49; Soper, "Reminiscence of Pioneer Life," p. 402; and Stanley B. Smith, "Notes on the Village of

Schoolcraft in the 1850's," *Michigan History* 40 (June 1956): 137–38. Mrs. Caroline Kirkland, *A New Home—Who'll Follow? Or Glimpses of Western Life,* 3rd ed. (New York: Charles S. Francis, 1841), p. 106.

5. For information on Michigan's water transportation, see Dunbar, *Michigan,* pp. 312–14, and Harvey J. Hollister, "Events in Grand Rapids from 1850 to 1860," *Michigan Pioneer and Historical Collections* 35 (1907): 650–51.

6. A good account of the events surrounding the building of the Sault Canal can be found in Dunbar, *Michigan,* pp. 305–9. Also see Ferris E. Lewis, *Michigan Yesterday and Today* (Hillsdale, Mich.: Hillsdale Educational, 1956), pp. 278–81. For information on the early attempts to obtain federal assistance in building the canal, see Clark F. Norton, "Early Movement for the St. Mary's Falls Ship Canal," *Michigan History* 39 (September 1955): 257–80. An interesting glimpse of the types of merchandise and the number of passengers using the canal is found in Philip P. Mason, ed., "The Operation of the Sault Canal, 1857," *Michigan History* 39 (March 1955): 69–71. Also see Alex Campbell, "The Upper Peninsula," *Michigan Pioneer and Historical Collections* 3 (1881): 258. A final improvement to the Great Lakes waterway worthy of note is the federally funded dredging of the St. Clair flats between Lakes St. Clair and Huron in 1858 and 1859. This project allowed ships of deeper draught to travel the lakes unimpeded. For further information, see Thomas D. Odle, "The Commercial Interests of the Great Lakes and the Campaign Issues of 1860," *Michigan History* 40 (March 1956): 1–23.

7. For figures on Michigan's railroad mileage from 1840 to 1859 and the state's ranking among its neighbors, see "Historical (Railroads)," James F. Joy Papers, 1834–1900, Box 7, Michigan Historical Collections, Bentley Historical Library, Ann Arbor. The 1860 figure was obtained from Dunbar, *Michigan,* pp. 314–15. Michigan's incomplete rail lines ironically became an asset because their routes could be adapted to meet new circumstances.

8. On the Michigan Central, see Edmund A. Calkins, "Railroads of Michigan since 1850," *Michigan History* 13 (Winter 1929): 6–7; Willis F. Dunbar, *All Aboard: A History of Railroads in Michigan* (Grand Rapids, Mich.: William B. Eerdmans, 1969); idem, *Michigan,* pp. 314–17; and Frank N. Elliott, "When the Railroad Was King," *Michigan History* 49 (December 1965): 296–97.

9. A good account of the activities of the Michigan Southern can be found in Dunbar, *Michigan,* p. 317. Also see Calkins, "Railroads of Michigan," pp. 6–7.

10. The active lobbying on behalf of the Michigan Central to block the Southern's attempt to divert its line southward is well documented in numerous letters in the Joy Papers, Bentley Historical Library. Similar letters can be found among the James F. Joy Papers, 1700–1869, Burton Historical Collection, Detroit Public Library, Detroit, Mich. Also see the James W. Gilbert Collection, Box 1, Clements Historical Library, University of Michigan, Ann Arbor.

11. Calkins, "Railroads of Michigan," pp. 5–6.

12. Information about the linking of Michigan's railroads with the East was derived from Dunbar, *All Aboard,* and idem, *Michigan,* pp. 316–18. The Great Western

Railway reached Windsor in 1854. The railroad suspension bridge between Buffalo and Fort Erie, however, was not completed until the following year. Data on the operations of the two railroads were gleaned from Calkins, "Railroads of Michigan," p. 7; Dunbar, *All Aboard,* p. 75; and idem, *Michigan,* pp. 315–17. In 1857, the Michigan Southern and the Michigan Central reached an arrangement whereby the two roads agreed to pool the freight and passenger business.

13. Dunbar, *All Aboard,* pp. 75–78, 92, 97, and idem, *Michigan,* p. 318. Other railroads were built in Michigan in the years before the Civil War; but for the most part, these roads, such as the Jackson and Palmyra, tended to link points along already existing lines. The larger railroad projects begun late in the decade, such as the Flint and Pere Marquette and the Amboy, Lansing and Grand Traverse Bay (both of which sought to connect the state's timber region with the outside world), were mainly the by-product of a large grant of land (almost 4 million acres) to the state by the federal government in 1856 and a similar state grant of recently received swamplands (over 1.6 million acres). These roads were still largely in the planning stage by 1860, primarily as the result of the financial difficulties surrounding the panic of 1857. For further information on these and other late-1850s railroads, see Calkins, "Railroads of Michigan," pp. 7–10; Dunbar, *All Aboard,* pp. 105–10; and Elliott, "When the Railroad Was King," pp. 304–11.

14. Ralph Waldo Emerson, *The Conduct of Life,* pt. 3, "Wealth," in Ernest Rhys, ed., *Emerson's Conduct of Life and Other Essays* (New York: E. P. Dutton, 1908), p. 192.

15. Dunbar, *Michigan,* pp. 319–20.

16. Ibid., p. 319. Also see Lewis, *Michigan Yesterday and Today,* pp. 220–21; Larry Massie, "Plows, Ships and Shovels: Economic Development in Michigan, 1836–1866," in Richard J. Hathaway, ed., *Michigan: Visions of Our Past* (East Lansing: Michigan State University Press, 1989), pp. 102–3; and Prentiss, "Economic Progress and Social Dissent," p. 64. In 1855, the general incorporation law was altered to allow the use of gravel rather than planks. See *Grand River Eagle,* March 4, 1850.

Though easily constructed and instrumental in expanding the scope of market activity in Michigan, plank roads were also noted for their rapid rate of deterioration and were notoriously rough. After a stagecoach trip over the Grand Rapids–Kalamazoo plank road, Mark Twain wrote that the trip would have been enjoyable had not "some unconscionable scoundrel now and then dropped a plank across the road." Another traveler along the same road, pioneer poet Asa Stoddard of Cooper, described a similar experience on the plank:

> Horses balking, drivers lashing,
> Wishing all plank roads in——
> And their owners with them flashing
> So it goes on the plank.
> Wagons creaking, groaning, cracking,
> Wrecks bestrewing either bank
> Jarring, jolting, jambing, dashing,

This is riding on the plank
Crocks and baskets rolling, smashing,
Helpless owners looking blank,
Eggs and butter mixing, mashing,
Cannot help it on the plank.

See Dunbar, *Michigan,* p. 320, and Asa H. Stoddard, *Miscellaneous Poems* (Kalamazoo, Mich.: C. G. Townsend, 1880), p. 8.

17. Dunbar, *Michigan,* pp. 320–21.

18. Milton M. Quaife and Sidney Glazer, *Michigan: From Primitive Wilderness to Industrial Commonwealth* (New York: Prentice-Hall, 1946), p. 185; Hill, "Farm Management," p. 312; Richard H. Sewell, "Michigan Farmers and the Civil War," *Michigan History* 44 (December 1960): 353; Jeremy Atack and Fred Bateman, "Self-Sufficiency and the Marketable Surplus in the Rural North, 1860," *Agricultural History* 58 (July 1984): 296. Although deliberately attempting to bias their results against finding a marketable surplus of food among northern farmers, Atack and Bateman demonstrated that by 1860, most northern farms were able not only to meet their own consumption needs but also to produce a surplus that had to be marketed. In fact, they concluded, "farms in the midwestern heartland were so productive that they had to seek more distant markets. The bulk and weight of this surplus was such that water or rail transportation was almost a sine qua non for the kind of agriculture which had evolved in the Midwest"; ibid., p. 313.

19. U.S. Department of Commerce, Bureau of Census, *Agriculture of the United States in 1860; Compiled from the Original Returns of the Eighth Census* (Washington, D.C.: Government Printing Office, 1864), "Recapitulation, 1850–1860," pp. 184–87 and 222. Massie, "Plows, Ships and Shovels," p. 109; Gary M. Walton, "River Transportation and the Old Northwest Territory," in David C. Klingaman and Richard K. Vedder, eds., *Essays on the Economy of the Old Northwest* (Athens: Ohio University Press, 1987), p. 229.

20. U.S. Department of Commerce, *Agriculture of the United States*; Prentiss, "Economic Progress and Social Dissent," p. 62; Robert McClelland to Alpheus Felch, April 13, 1854, "McClelland, Robert 1851–55," Box 4, Alpheus Felch Papers, 1806–1896, Michigan Historical Collections, Bentley Historical Library, University of Michigan, Ann Arbor. Also see Seavoy, "Borrowed Laws," p. 39.

21. Preston Mitchell to Peter Mitchell, June 12, 1852, "Mitchell-Strong Family Correspondence, 1836–1925," Michigan Historical Collections, Bentley Historical Library, University of Michigan, Ann Arbor; *Kalamazoo Gazette,* January 3, 1851.

22. "Circular and Replies thereto Pertaining to the Resources of Michigan," *Michigan Pioneer and Historical Collections* 12 (1887): 381–406; "Message of Andrew Parsons to the Legislature of the State of Michigan," January 3, 1855, in George N. Fuller, ed., *Messages of the Governors of Michigan,* vol. 2 (Lansing: Michigan Historical Commission, 1926), p. 272.

23. Henry M. Utley and Byron M. Cutcheon, eds., *Michigan as a Province, Territory*

and State: The Twenty-Sixth Member of the Federal Union, vol. 3 (n.p.: Publishing Society of Michigan, 1906), p. 332. Michigan's copper fields proved extremely beguiling because of the availability of masses of pure copper in commercial quantities. Angus Murdoch, *Boom Copper: The Story of the First U.S. Mining Boom* (New York: MacMillan, 1943), p. 112; Larry Lankton, *Cradle to Grave: Life, Work, and Death at the Lake Superior Copper Mines* (New York: Oxford University Press, 1991), p. 9. The Cliff Mine would go on to pay a return of 200 percent to its investors by 1871. William B. Gates, *Michigan Copper and Boston Dollars: An Economic History of the Copper Mining Industry* (Cambridge, Mass.: Harvard University Press, 1954), p. 6. For further information on the early years of Michigan's copper mines, see Lew A. Chase, "Early Copper Mining in Michigan," *Michigan History* 29 (January–March 1945): 22–30; idem, "Early Days of Michigan Mining," *Michigan History* 29 (April–June 1945): 166–79; idem, "Michigan Copper Mines," *Michigan History* 29 (October–December 1945): 479–88; Robert E. Clarke, "Notes from the Copper Region," *Harper's New Monthly Magazine* 4 (March 1853): 433–48; idem, "Notes from the Copper Region," *Harper's New Monthly Magazine* 4 (April 1853): 577–88; John H. Forster, "Life in the Copper Mines of Lake Superior," *Michigan Pioneer and Historical Collections* 11 (1887): 175–86; Charles K. Hyde, "From 'Subterranean Lotteries' to Orderly Investment: Michigan Copper and Eastern Dollars, 1841–1865," *Mid-America: An Historical Review* 66 (January 1984): 3–20; David J. Krause, *The Making of a Mining District: Keweenaw Native Copper 1500–1870* (Detroit, Mich.: Wayne State University Press, 1992); and G. M. Steele, "Down in a Copper Mine," *Michigan History* 40 (June 1956): 227–35.

24. Gates, *Michigan Copper,* pp. 13, 197, 203, and 208. Arthur W. Thurner, *Calumet Copper and People: History of a Michigan Mining Community, 1864–1970* (Hancock, Mich.: The Book Concern, 1974), pp. 66–67. Copper's primary uses in antebellum America included sheathing for wooden ships, roofing material, and pots and pans. Alloyed with zinc to make brass or with tin to make bronze, copper went into buttons, candlesticks, machinery bearings, weapons, and hardware. See Lankton, *Cradle to Grave,* p. 8. Interestingly, Michigan's copper proved to be of such purity that it often exceeded the needs of domestic manufacturers, so that, between 1855 and 1861, some 30 to 80 percent of the state's annual copper output was shipped abroad. See Gates, *Michigan Copper,* p. 10.

25. Utley and Cutcheon, *Michigan as a Province,* p. 333; Massie, "Plows, Ships and Shovels," p. 107; Dunbar, *Michigan,* p. 305. For further information on Michigan's early iron mines, see Herbert Brinks, "The Effects of the Civil War in 1861 on Michigan Lumbering and Mining Industries," *Michigan History* 44 (March 1960): 101–7; Campbell, "The Upper Peninsula," p. 255; Dunbar, *Michigan,* pp. 302–5; and Alvah L. Sawyer, *A History of the Northern Peninsula of Michigan and Its People: Its Mining, Lumber and Agricultural Industries,* vol. 1 (Chicago: Lewis, 1911).

26. John Van Oosten, "Michigan's Commercial Fisheries of the Great Lakes," *Michigan History* 22 (Winter 1938): 109. Campbell, "The Upper Peninsula," p. 249, and Dunbar, *Michigan,* pp. 310–11.

27. Leroy Barnett, "Haulin' Ash: 100 Years of Making Potash," *Michigan History* (January-February 2002): 16–21.

28. Barbara E. Benson, *Logs and Lumber: The Development of the Lumber Industry in Michigan's Lower Peninsula, 1837–1870* (Mt. Pleasant: Clarke Historical Library, Central Michigan University, 1989), p. 8.

29. Ibid., pp. 62–64 and 163–66. Those counties designated as "lumber counties" are: Allegan, Genesee, Huron, Tuscola, Sanilac, Kent, Lapeer, Michilimackinac, Montcalm, Ottawa, Saginaw, St. Clair, and Wayne. The number of mills for 1854 and the corresponding production figures for that year are incomplete, and therefore, as Benson suggested, the expansion of the industry from 1850 to 1854 was probably significantly greater than indicated. Dunbar, *Michigan,* pp. 295 and 310; U.S. Department of Commerce, Bureau of Census, *Manufactures of the United States in 1860; Compiled from the Original Returns of the Eighth Census* (Washington, D.C.: Government Printing Office, 1865), p. 275.

30. Benson, *Logs and Lumber,* pp. 11–12 and 122–23. Michigan's rail links to Chicago, the Michigan Central and the Michigan Southern, actually carried little of the state's lumber to that city. Rather, the bulk of Michigan lumber reached market via water, down one of the state's many rivers to a sawmill located near the river's mouth and from there along the Great Lakes to Chicago or some other market. The real influence of the railroad on lumbering during the 1850s was that it enabled Michigan pine to reach the prairies after it reached Chicago. The railroad would come to play a much larger role in the marketing of Michigan's lumber resources after the Civil War.

31. Ibid., pp. XIV, 11–12, and 121–25. Among the most important supplementary industries that developed as a result of lumbering were the log-booming companies, woodenware and shingle factories, and, after the state legislature's passage of a bill granting a bounty of $.10 per bushel in 1859, the manufacture of salt. The next year, the Saginaw Valley produced 10,727 barrels of salt. On the importance of the salt industry, which relied upon waste wood and sawdust for fuel, to lumber producers, see James V. Campbell, *Outlines of the Political History of Michigan* (Detroit, Mich.: Schober, 1876), pp. 573–74; Jeremy W. Kilar, *Michigan's Lumbertowns: Lumbermen and Laborers in Saginaw, Bay City, and Muskegon, 1870–1905* (Detroit, Mich.: Wayne State University Press, 1990), pp. 40 and 55–58; Quaife and Glazer, *Michigan,* p. 236; and William H. Sweet, "A Brief History of Saginaw County," *Michigan Pioneer and Historical Collections* 28 (1897–1898): 499–500.

For more information on Michigan lumbering, see Bruce Catton, *Michigan: A Bicentennial History* (New York: W. W. Norton, 1976), pp. 128–47; Ormond S. Danford, "The Social and Economic Effects of Lumbering on Michigan, 1835–1890," *Michigan History* 26 (Summer 1942): 346–64; Dunbar, *Michigan,* pp. 295–96; Theodore J. Karamanski, *Deep Woods Frontier: A History of Logging in Northern Michigan* (Detroit, Mich.: Wayne State University Press, 1989); Kilar, *Michigan's Lumbertowns;* Lewis, *Michigan Yesterday and Today,* pp. 252–65; and Martin D. Lewis, *Lumberman from Flint: The Michigan Career of Henry H. Crapo, 1855–1869* (Detroit, Mich.: Wayne State University Press, 1958).

32. Prentiss, "Economic Progress and Social Dissent," pp. 69–70; Dunbar, *Michigan*, p. 460; U.S. Department of Commerce, Bureau of Census, *Population of the United States in 1860; Compiled from the Original Returns of the Eighth Census* (Washington, D.C.: Government Printing Office, 1864), "Occupations," p. 249.

33. Melvin G. Holli, ed., *Detroit* (New York: New Viewpoints, 1976), p. 275; George W. Stark, *City of Destiny: The Story of Detroit* (Detroit, Mich.: Arnold-Powers, 1943), pp. 325, 346–47, and 361; Dunbar, *All Aboard*, p. 100; Lankton, *Cradle to Grave*, p. 12; William Stocking, "Industrial Detroit: Fifty Years of Industrial Progress," *Michigan History* 10 (October 1926): 609–16; and Frank B. Woodford and Arthur M. Woodford, *All Our Yesterdays: A Brief History of Detroit* (Detroit, Mich.: Wayne State University Press, 1969), pp. 201–11.

Other Michigan cities also experienced the first pangs of industrial birth during the 1850s. George Gale moved his successful agricultural implement factory from Hillsdale to Albion during this decade. Kalamazoo became home to a number of small iron foundries and machine shops. The Upper Peninsula town of Hancock became the site of the Copper Country's first copper smelter, and stamp mills became common throughout the region. Finally, the furniture industry in Grand Rapids also got its start during this period and by 1858 was already "shipping out approximately $40,000 worth of furniture by wagon or steamboat to Lake Michigan and from there by boat to Chicago and Milwaukee" and later, to New York and Ohio via the Great Lakes and Erie Canal. By 1860, Grand Rapids could boast nine furniture manufacturing firms, employing fifty-three workers. See Francis X. Blouin Jr., "Not Just Automobiles: Contributions of Michigan to the National Economy," in Hathaway, *Michigan*, pp. 157–59; Dunbar, *Michigan*, pp. 463 and 466; and Massie, "Plows, Ships and Shovels," pp. 107–8.

34. Alexandra U. McCoy, "A New Power Structure: Wealth before and after the Civil War," in Wilma W. Henrickson, ed., *Detroit Perspectives: Crossroads and Turning Points* (Detroit, Mich.: Wayne State University Press, 1991), pp. 172–89; Norris, "Country Merchant," pp. 333–34. Also see "Commercial Detroit," *Hunt's Merchants' Magazine* 16 (April 1860): 422–34. There were those in Detroit who, although grateful for the city's commercial success, regretted the primitive state of the city's industry. For example, see the *Detroit Advertiser*, February 18, 1860.

35. "Message of Andrew Parsons to the Legislature of the State of Michigan," January 3, 1855, in Fuller, *Messages of the Governors*, vol. 2, p. 267; Dunbar, *Michigan*, p. 745; Prentiss, "Economic Progress and Social Dissent," pp. 132–33 and 219; U.S. Department of Commerce, *Population of the United States in 1860*, "Population of Cities, Towns, &c.," pp. 237–47.

36. JoEllen M. Vinyard, *The Irish on the Urban Frontier: Nineteenth Century Detroit* (New York: Arno Press, 1976), pp. 70 and 137; John C. Schneider, *Detroit and the Problem of Order, 1830–1880: A Geography of Crime, Riot and Policing* (Lincoln: University of Nebraska Press, 1980), p. 37. Further evidence of the mobility of frontier populations is contained in Don Harrison Doyle, *The Social Order of a Frontier Community:*

Jacksonville, Illinois, 1825–1870 (Urbana: University of Illinois Press, 1978), and Faragher, *Sugar Creek,* pp. 50–60.

37. Ronald P. Formisano, *The Birth of Mass Political Parties: Michigan, 1827–1861* (Princeton, N.J.: Princeton University Press, 1971), pp. 17 and 98. It should be noted that by 1855, Detroit's immigrant population outnumbered its native-born population. See Tyler Anbinder, *Nativism and Slavery: The Northern Know Nothings and the Politics of the 1850s* (New York: Oxford University Press, 1992), p. 9. C. Warren Vander Hill, *Settling the Great Lakes Frontier: Immigration to Michigan, 1837–1924* (Lansing: Michigan Historical Commission, 1970), p. 16, and Dunbar, *Michigan,* p. 288. Michigan's 1860 population also included 25,743 English, 36,482 Canadians, and 5,705 Scots. Among the best works on Michigan's antebellum immigrants are Dunbar, *Michigan,* pp. 288–94; James Fisher, "Michigan's Cornish People," *Michigan History* 29 (July-September 1945): 377–85; Formisano, *Birth of Mass Political Parties;* George P. Graff, *The People of Michigan* (Lansing, Mich.: State Library Services, 1974); Frederic H. Hayes, *Michigan Catholicism in the Era of the Civil War* (Lansing, Mich.: Civil War Centennial Observance Commission, 1965); Gordon W. Kirk and Carolyn T. Kirk, "Migration, Mobility and the Transformation of the Occupational Structure in an Immigrant Community: Holland, Michigan, 1850–1880," *Journal of Social History* 7 (Fall 1973): 142–64; Henry S. Lucas, *Netherlanders in America: Dutch Immigration to the United States and Canada, 1789–1950* (Ann Arbor: University of Michigan Press, 1955); John Rowe, *The Hard Rock Men: Cornish Immigrants and the North American Mining Frontier* (Liverpool, England: University of Liverpool Press, 1974); JoEllen Vinyard, "Inland Urban Immigrants: The Detroit Irish, 1850," *Michigan History* 57 (Summer 1973): 121–39; and idem, *Irish on the Urban Frontier.*

38. Formisano, *Birth of Mass Political Parties;* Hayes, *Michigan Catholicism;* and Leslie Woodcock Tentler, *Seasons of Grace: A History of the Catholic Archdiocese of Detroit* (Detroit, Mich.: Wayne State University Press, 1990), p. 21; Vinyard, *Irish on the Urban Frontier,* pp. 113–15.

39. U.S. Department of Commerce, *The Seventh Census of the United States,* "Table I. Population by Counties," p. 886; Dunbar, *Michigan,* p. 288; and David M. Katzman, *Before the Ghetto: Black Detroit in the Nineteenth Century* (Urbana: University of Illinois Press, 1973), pp. 26–27 and 62. Cass County's thriving black community began when a North Carolina planter purchased land there for his manumitted slaves. Blacks were also drawn to the area by the existence of a Quaker settlement. See Justin L. Kestenbaum, "Modernizing Michigan: Political and Social Trends," in Hathaway, *Michigan,* p. 123.

40. Francis W. Shearman to Robert McClelland, June 20, 1853, Francis W. Shearman Papers, 1817–1874, Michigan Historical Collections, Bentley Historical Library, University of Michigan, Ann Arbor, and William S. Brown to Alpheus Felch, September 12, 1853, "July–December 1853," Box 1, Alpheus Felch Papers, 1806–1926, Michigan Historical Collections, Bentley Historical Library, University of Michigan, Ann Arbor.

41. Anson de Puy Van Buren to "Friend" Martin, December 12, 1854, Anson de

Puy Van Buren Papers, 1846–1885, "Correspondence, 1851–1855, Box 1, Michigan Historical Collections, Bentley Historical Library, University of Michigan, Ann Arbor.

42. Quaife and Glazer, *Michigan*, p. 185; Prentiss, "Economic Progress and Social Dissent," pp. 133–36; Schneider, *Detroit and the Problem of Order*, p. 69. Michigan also built its first asylum for the insane at Kalamazoo during the same decade. See Utley and Cutcheon, *Michigan as a Province*, vol. 1, p. 389.

43. *Hillsdale Gazette*, August 22, 1850; A. R. Morgan to Fred A. Staring, January 12, 1856, C. F. Leneweaker Papers, 1833–1857, Michigan Historical Collections, Bentley Historical Library, University of Michigan, Ann Arbor; *Grass Lake Public Sentiment*, March 1, 1853. It is interesting to note the editor's use of the term *competence*. As historian Virginia Anderson demonstrated in her work on the Puritan migration to New England, the idea of competence was at the core of Puritan society. Competency, Anderson argued, entailed the pursuit of a "modest prosperity that would sustain a family's economic independence." This notion of economic self-sufficiency is precisely the image that the editor hoped to conjure in the minds of his readers. See Virginia DeJohn Anderson, *New England's Generation: The Great Migration and the Formation of Society and Culture in the Seventeenth Century* (New York: Cambridge University Press, 1991), p. 9. John M. Norton, "Early Pioneer Life in Oakland County," *Michigan Pioneer and Historical Collections* 26 (1894–1895): 263.

44. Robert McClelland to Alpheus Felch, September 10, 1853, Felch Papers, 1806–1926, "McClelland, Robert 1851–1855," Box 4; *Centreville Western Chronicle*, August 8, 1850; *Hillsdale Gazette*, February 7, 1850; Anson de Puy Van Buren to Major Wildy, December 6, 1858, Van Buren Papers, 1846–1885, "Correspondence, 1856–1858," Box 1. Many similar expressions can be found in Van Buren's journal. For example, see Anson de Puy Van Buren Journal, February 17, 1855, Van Buren Papers, 1846–1885, Box 1.

45. Preston Mitchell to Peter Mitchell, June 12, 1852, "Mitchell-Strong Correspondence, 1836–1925," vol. 1; "Description of the Grand River Valley," [1855], John Ball Papers, 1815–1883, Clarke Historical Library, Central Michigan University, Mt. Pleasant, Mich.; Journal entry of March 24, 1854, Fred B. Porter Journals, Michigan Historical Collections, Bentley Historical Library, University of Michigan, Ann Arbor; *Detroit Tribune*, July 24, 1858. Detroit's bustle led the daughter of future state supreme court justice James V. Campbell to comment to a friend, "I don't know whether people run about so everywhere, but they certainly keep pretty constantly in motion here." Elizabeth Campbell to Mary Barstow, James V. Campbell Papers, 1830–1941, "Family Correspondence, 1850s," Box 1, Michigan Historical Collections, Bentley Historical Library, University of Michigan, Ann Arbor.

For other positive affirmations of the changes sweeping midcentury Michigan, see Enos Goodrich, "Trials of Pioneer Business Men," *Michigan Pioneer and Historical Collections* 28 (1897–1898): 126–27; *Grand River Eagle*, April 30 and June 24, 1850; *Hillsdale Gazette*, November 28, 1850; and Preston Mitchell to Peter Mitchell, June 3, 1851, "Mitchell-Strong Correspondence, 1836–1925," vol. 1.

46. James V. Campbell to Cornelia, August 6, 1853, Campbell Papers, 1830–1941, "Family Correspondence, 1850s," Box 1. My understanding of Christiancy's attitudes toward the market are derived from no one source but rather are based upon impressions gleaned from a close reading of Christiancy's correspondence. See Isaac P. Christiancy Papers, 1840–1883, Michigan Historical Collections, Bentley Historical Library, University of Michigan, Ann Arbor. *Albion Weekly Review*, March 3, 1860. Other examples of this belief are numerous. For example, see *Niles Express*, August 15, 1850, and *Grand River Eagle*, August 12, 1851.

47. Susan E. Bloomberg et al., "A Census Probe into Nineteenth-Century Family History: Southern Michigan, 1850–1880," *Journal of Social History* 5 (Fall 1971): pp. 25–45. The best work on reform activities in antebellum Michigan is John W. Quist, *Restless Visionaries: The Social Roots of Antebellum Reform in Alabama and Michigan* (Baton Rouge: Louisiana State University Press, 1998). On the Beaver Island Mormon community, see Dunbar, *Michigan*, pp. 354–55.

CHAPTER 4

The quotation in this chapter's heading is from Elizabeth E. Stuart to her son, February 26, 1853, in Helen Stuart Mackay-Smith Marlatt, ed. *Stuart Letters of Robert and Elizabeth Sullivan Stuart and Their Children, 1819–1864*, vol. 1 (privately printed, 1961), p. 481.

1. On the meeting "under the oaks," see Malcolm Moos, *The Republicans: A History of Their Party* (New York: Random House, 1956), pp. 9–14. A particularly glaring example of the tendency to downplay Michigan's role in the birth of the Republican Party is found in William E. Gienapp, *The Origins of the Republican Party, 1852–1856* (New York: Oxford University Press, 1987), p. 106. "That Michigan took the lead in the movement to form a northern party," Gienapp contended, "was entirely an *accident of timing* [emphasis added]." Also see David M. Potter, *The Impending Crisis, 1848–1861* (New York: Harper Torchbooks, 1976), p. 248. Some works go so far as to omit Michigan altogether. For example, see Tyler Anbinder, *Nativism and Slavery: The Northern Know-Nothings and the Politics of the 1850s* (New York: Oxford University Press, 1992), and Michael F. Holt, *The Political Crisis of the 1850s* (New York: W.W. Norton, 1978).

2. Harry L. Watson, *Liberty and Power: The Politics of Jacksonian America* (New York: Noonday Press, 1990), pp. 14–15. For a similar interpretation, see Daniel Feller, "Politics and Society: Toward a Jacksonian Synthesis," *Journal of the Early Republic* 10 (Summer 1990): 135–62; Lawrence F. Kohl, *The Politics of Individualism: Parties and the American Character in the Jacksonian Era* (New York: Oxford University Press, 1989); Charles Sellers, *The Market Revolution: Jacksonian America, 1815–1846* (New York: Oxford University Press, 1991); and J. Mills Thornton III, *Politics and Power in a Slave Society: Alabama, 1800–1860* (Baton Rouge: Louisiana State University Press, 1978). The debate over the degree to which conflict or consensus shaped the political culture of the Jacksonian era is nicely summarized in "A Symposium on Charles Sellers, *The Market Revolution: Jacksonian America, 1815–1846*," *Journal of the Early Republic* 12 (Winter

1992): 458–64. The literature on republicanism and its influence on Jacksonian politics is extremely rich. Among the best works are Marc W. Kruman, "The Second American Party System and the Transformation of Revolutionary Republicanism," *Journal of the Early Republic* 12 (Winter 1992): 502–37; Thornton, *Politics and Power;* Watson, *Liberty and Power;* and Major Wilson, "Republicanism and the Idea of Party in the Jacksonian Period," *Journal of the Early Republic* 8 (Winter 1988): 419–42.

3. Sellers, *Market Revolution,* p. 297. On Michigan's transformation into a market society during the 1850s, see Dale R. Prentiss, "Economic Progress and Social Dissent in Michigan and Mississippi, 1837–1860" (Ph.D. diss., Stanford University, 1990). On Alabama, see Thornton, *Politics and Power.* Many historians have demonstrated the continued transition of various parts of the United States into market-oriented societies well beyond the Civil War. Among the best such studies are Carl N. Degler, *The Age of the Economic Revolution, 1876–1900* (Glenview, Ill.: Scott, Foresman, 1967); Lawrence Goodwyn, *The Populist Moment: A Short History of the Agrarian Revolt in America* (New York: Oxford University Press, 1978); and Steven Hahn, *The Roots of Southern Populism: Yeoman Farmers and the Transformation of the Georgia Upcountry, 1850–1890* (New York: Oxford University Press, 1983).

4. Anbinder, *Nativism and Slavery;* Gienapp, *Origins of the Republican Party;* and Holt, *Political Crisis of the 1850s.* Notable exceptions to this trend are Lacy K. Ford, *Origins of Southern Radicalism: The South Carolina Upcountry, 1800–1860* (New York: Oxford University Press, 1988), and Thornton, *Politics and Power.*

5. Asa Whitney to Alpheus Felch, February 2, 1852, Alpheus Felch Papers, 1806–1896, Box 4, "Wa–Wh," Michigan Historical Collections, Bentley Historical Library, University of Michigan, Ann Arbor; E. M. Mason to C. F. Leneweaker, February 27, 1856, C. F. Leneweaker Papers, 1833–1857, Michigan Historical Collections, Bentley Historical Library, University of Michigan, Ann Arbor.

6. E. M. Mason to C. F. Leneweaker, February 27, 1856, Leneweaker Papers; Abner Pratt to Henry C. Waldron, October 29, 1852, Henry Clay Waldron Papers, Box 1, "Correspondence 1850–1853," University Archives and Historical Collections, Michigan State University, East Lansing. For a similar expression of disgust with the current state of politics, see William Woodbridge to Robert McClelland, October 24, 1853, Robert McClelland Papers, 1833–1857, "1853," Burton Historical Collection, Detroit Public Library, Detroit, Mich.

7. One cannot overstate the importance of state and local issues in the process of party decomposition, collapse, and realignment. Indeed, state and local issues often shook partisans free from their traditional political moorings, thus making it easier for these disaffected voters to ease their way into new political alliances. On the importance of local issues in bringing about the political crisis of the 1850s, see Gienapp, *Origins of the Republican Party,* pp. 7–8.

8. None of the standard works on Michigan's antebellum political history pays much attention to this extremely important political issue. For example, see Willis F. Dunbar, *Michigan: A History of the Wolverine State* (Grand Rapids, Mich.: William B.

Eerdmans, 1970); Floyd B. Streeter, *Political Parties in Michigan, 1837–1860* (Lansing: Michigan Historical Commission, 1918); and John F. Reynolds, "Piety and Politics: Evangelism in the Michigan Legislature, 1837–1861," *Michigan History* 61 (Winter 1977): 323–52. At best, the issue garners a very brief mention. See Ronald P. Formisano, *The Birth of Mass Political Parties, Michigan, 1827–1861* (Princeton, N.J.: Princeton University Press, 1971), p. 253, and Ronald E. Seavoy, "The Organization of the Republican Party in Michigan, 1846–1854," *The Old Northwest* 6 (1980): 367, 370.

9. *Williams v. Michigan Central Railroad Company*, 2 Mich. 259. Edward Williams, the owner of the unfortunate horses killed on that Dearborn bridge, was typical of his fellow defenders of traditional rights. Born in New York State in 1794, Williams, his wife, Rebecka (born 1804), and his son, William (age eighteen in 1850), migrated to Michigan sometime between 1832 and 1836. Two additional children, a daughter, Saphara (born in 1836), and a son, Barney (born in 1839), rounded out the Williams household. Together, the family worked an eighty-acre farm, valued at a mere $252 in 1850, in the S1/2, NE1/4 of section 32, Town 3S, R 9E in Wayne County. The Williams family fell far short of the mean wealth ($1,048) attributed to state farmers as a whole and even further behind their Wayne County peers, whose farm values averaged $1,850.96. The family, in brief, seems to have either missed out or chosen to opt out of the state's expanding commercial system. The 1850 census provides further evidence of the family's distance from the modernizing trends of the day—whereas an average of 69.9 percent of Michigan's children between the ages of five and nineteen were reported to have attended school (the place where skills necessary to succeed in an emerging commercial world would be taught) in the previous year, none of the Williams children did so. Nonetheless, rather than responding to the loss of his property and the affront to traditional rights posed by the Michigan Central's refusal to compensate him fully for his deceased free-ranging livestock in a personal manner, as his neighbors farther west were doing, Williams turned to the courts. U.S. Department of Commerce, Bureau of the Census, *The Seventh Census of the United States, 1850;* Edward Williams Papers, 1838–1878, Michigan Historical Collections, Bentley Historical Library, University of Michigan.

10. *Williams v. Michigan Central Railroad Company*, 2 Mich. 299, 304. Also see R. Ben Brown, "The Southern Range: A Study in Nineteenth Century Law and Society" (Ph.D. diss., University of Michigan, 1993). It is important to note that this decision was quite exceptional in antebellum America. Only Michigan and Wisconsin among the states of the Old Northwest took the position that ranging stock were trespassing. Even among the older northern states, only Massachusetts, Rhode Island, Vermont, New Hampshire, and New Jersey had legally closed the range. The law in Pennsylvania and New York was in dispute. All of the remaining states in the Union were open-range states. Brown, "The Southern Range," pp. 106–75. The general transformation toward prodevelopment, promarket law is brilliantly described in Morton J. Horwitz, *The Transformation of American Law 1780–1861* (Cambridge, Mass.: Harvard University Press, 1977).

11. *Williams v. Michigan Central Railroad Company*, 2 Mich. 262; Charles Hirschfeld, "The Great Railroad Conspiracy," *Michigan History* 36 (June 1952): 124. Indeed, one resident implicitly alleged that recourse through the state courts was futile when he complained in a letter to a state newspaper that "Railroad gold bought [the] decision." See *Michigan Argus*, July 16, 1851. Pratt's opinion had been anticipated by John Pierce the previous year and had led Pierce to suggest including railroad corporations in his proposed thirty-year limitation on corporate charters at the state constitutional convention in 1850. See Chapter 1.

12. Elizabeth S. Stuart to Kate Stuart, June 18, 1851, in Helen Stuart Mackay-Smith Marlatt, ed., *Stuart Letters of Robert and Elizabeth Sullivan Stuart and Their Children, 1819–1864*, vol. 1 (privately printed, 1961), p. 205. Hirschfeld, "The Great Railroad Conspiracy," pp. 173–74. Also see *Jackson American Citizen*, August 27 and September 3, 1851. The prosecution also recognized the effect that Fitch's death was likely to have upon public opinion. James Joy, legal counsel for the Michigan Central, warned Superintendent John W. Brooks against allowing anybody connected with the railroad to make "injudicious remarks" about the deceased. See Hirschfeld, "The Great Railroad Conspiracy," p. 174. It was widely, though incorrectly, reported that Fitch had been poisoned while in jail, and such reports undoubtedly added to the shift in public opinion. See D. H. Pease to S. A. Keeney, September 28, 1851, D. H. Pease Papers, 1851, Michigan Historical Collections, Bentley Historical Library, University of Michigan, Ann Arbor.

13. *Jackson American Citizen*, August 27 and September 3, 1851; *Detroit Tribune*, August 15 and 25, 1851, quoted in Hirschfeld, "The Great Railroad Conspiracy," p. 176. For similar reservations about the guilt of the conspirators, see *Michigan Christian Herald*, August 28, 1851. On the Whig/Free-Soil reaction to the conspiracy trial, see Prentiss, "Economic Progress and Social Dissent," p. 60.

14. *Jackson American Citizen*, September 3, 1851.

15. Details of the meeting can be found in *Jackson American Citizen*, September 3, 1851.

16. *Jackson American Citizen*, September 17, 1851. The issue of the Jackson Branch, as the proposed line between Jackson and Adrian was called, had become a political hot potato earlier in the year, during the winter legislative session. Traveling to Lansing to attend the session, Amos Root, a Free-Soil Whig merchant from Jackson, and Abel Fitch demanded that the Michigan Southern live up to the terms of its original charter and complete the Jackson Branch. The Southern, however, had little interest in building this spur line. But the company was locked in a struggle with the Michigan Central to be the first to push through to Chicago. To do so, the Southern would need a variance of its charter. Accordingly, John Stryker, the head of the Michigan Southern lobby, held out the promise of completing the Jackson Branch in order to get the support of Jackson County for his own bill to allow the Southern to leave the state of Michigan to reach Chicago. Stryker, however, proved unable to muster the necessary two-thirds vote for his proposed amendment to the Southern's charter. He then switched gears and promoted the passage of a general railroad incorporation

law that would need only a majority to pass and would thus afford the Michigan Southern another means of connecting to lines in Indiana. The Jackson County foes of the Michigan Central eagerly threw their support behind this new proposal. In the end, however, James Joy and the Michigan Central lobby managed once again to defeat their rivals. For an excellent summary of this legislative struggle, see Hirschfeld, "The Great Railroad Conspiracy," pp. 127–28. Much information can also be obtained from the James F. Joy Papers, 1834–1900, Michigan Historical Collections, Bentley Historical Library, University of Michigan, Ann Arbor.

17. James A. Van Dyke, *Argument in the Railroad Conspiracy Case; Entitled the People of the State of Michigan vs. Abel F. Fitch and Others, Tried before His Honor, Warner Wing, Presiding Judge, of the Circuit Court for the County of Wayne, at the May Term, 1851, in the City of Detroit* (Detroit, Mich.: Duncklee, Wales, 1851), p. 6.

18. "Closing Argument of William Seward," quoted in Hirschfeld, "The Great Railroad Conspiracy," p. 183; *Detroit Tribune,* September 16, 1851.

19. Van Dyke, *Argument in the Railroad Conspiracy Case,* pp. 13 and 130.

20. G. R. Lilibridge, *Report of the Conspiracy Trial, in the Wayne County Circuit Court, Michigan. Hon. Warner Wing, Presiding, on the Five Indictments of the Grand Jury for the County of Wayne, Setting forth a Conspiracy for Burning the Freight Depot of the Michigan Central Railroad Company, and for Other Offences, Named in the Said Indictment* (Detroit: printed for the publisher at the *Tribune* office, 1851), p. 295.

21. *Jackson American Citizen,* October 15, 1851; *Jonesville Telegraph,* October 15, 1851.

22. Hirschfeld, "The Great Railroad Conspiracy," p. 203. Also see *Jackson American Citizen,* November 12, 1851, and Isaac P. Christiancy to Thomas M. Cooley, October 23, 1851, Thomas M. Cooley Papers, 1850–1898, Box 1, "Correspondence, 1851," Michigan Historical Collections, Bentley Historical Library, University of Michigan, Ann Arbor. In his letter, Christiancy noted in reference to the railroad issue that "it will be an evil day for Michigan when such matters are brought into politics and control elections."

23. Hirschfeld, "The Great Railroad Conspiracy," p. 201. Blair dropped the charges against Phelps on the grounds that the indictment was technically deficient. In a letter to James Joy dated March 22, 1853, McNaughton wrote that Blair's support was critical. "He has great weight with the people," McNaughton affirmed, "[and] from his character and position can do more, probably, than almost any other man to quiet or inflame the public mind on the subject." Blair, however, could not be bought, McNaughton continued, because "his ambition far exceeds his avarice and he is honest. Satisfy him a thing is right and you have gone far to get his cooperation. Add to this that it is also popular, the thing is done." Austin Blair would go on to play a critical role in the formation of the Republican Party and would become governor of the state in 1861. See Moses A. McNaughton to James F. Joy, March 22, 1853, Box 10, "Michigan Central, 1853," Joy Papers.

24. Elizabeth E. Stuart to her son, September 6, 1852, in Stuart Mackay-Smith Marlatt, ed., *Stuart Letters,* vol. 1, p. 402; *Jackson American Citizen,* October 6, 1852. Stuart

addressed an individual letter to McClelland requesting the pardon of Erastus Champlin. David Stuart to the Governor of the State of Michigan, June 15, 1852, Box 15, "1852," Joy Papers. For a detailed description of the campaign in Jackson County, see Hirschfeld, "The Great Railroad Conspiracy," pp. 203–4. Again, Jackson County's ticket splitting in the 1852 election is suggestive of the extent to which traditional partisan ties had already been eroded.

25. *Grass Lake Public Sentiment*, February 1, March 13, and June 1, 1853. Rhetoric of this sort permeates the newspaper and can be found in every issue. In actuality, Burnett's translation of the Michigan state mottos are both inaccurate. *Tuebor* means "I will defend," and *Si Quaeris Peninsulam Amoenam Circumspice* translates as "If you seek a pleasant peninsula, look about you."

26. For a detailed discussion of the movement to gain pardons for the Michigan Central "conspirators," see Hirschfeld, "The Great Railroad Conspiracy," pp. 203–7; Moses A. McNaughton to James F. Joy, February 23, 1853, Box 10, "Michigan Central 1853," Joy Papers; James F. Joy to unknown, January 8, 1853, Box 10, "Michigan Central (Conspiracy Case)," Joy Papers; Hirschfeld, "The Great Railroad Conspiracy," p. 205.

27. Hirschfeld, "The Great Railroad Conspiracy," pp. 205–6, and *Jackson American Citizen*, March 9, 1853. In support of the pardons, McClelland cited the favorable report of James Joy, the recommendation of David Stuart and prominent citizens of Jackson County, the petitions of over twenty-five hundred citizens, and good behavior. The remaining "conspirators" would be released in fairly rapid order, though the two men who received the longest sentences, Ammi Filley and Orlando Williams, would have to wait until 1855, when they received pardons from the state's first Republican governor, Kinsley S. Bingham.

28. Hirschfeld, "The Great Railroad Conspiracy," pp. 127, 208.

29. The best account of the competition between the two lines is ibid., pp. 210–11; Joseph R. Williams to James F. Joy, January 18, 1853, Box 10, "Michigan Central 1853," Joy Papers.

30. Hirschfeld, "The Great Railroad Conspiracy," pp. 125–26.

31. *Grand Rapids Enquirer*, January 8 and 12, 1853. The prospects that such a law would pass appeared quite good in early January 1853. C. C. Jackson, the owner of the *Detroit Free Press* and a staunch ally of the Michigan Central, warned James Joy that the bill would become law, largely because of McClelland's support. Jackson attributed McClelland's support of the bill to his impending appointment to Franklin Pierce's cabinet, an appointment that allowed him to act "too independent[ly]." See C. C. Jackson to James Joy, January 18, 1853, Box 10, "Michigan Central 1853," Joy Papers.

32. *Detroit Free Press*, January 23, 1853; Hirschfeld, "The Great Railroad Conspiracy," pp. 208–11 and 214. Also see C. C. Jackson to James Joy, January 20, 1853, Box 10, "Michigan Central 1853," Joy Papers.

33. Accounts of these meetings can be found in *Jackson American Citizen*, February 2 and 9, 1853; *Detroit Free Press*, February 2 and 11, 1853; and *Grand Rapids Enquirer*, March 2, 1853. A great deal of newspaper space was devoted to debating the merits of

the law. Examples of this discussion are too numerous to cite. A prime example is found in a series of articles published in the *Free Press* on January 25, 26, and 28, 1853. In the main, the *Free Press* argued that the passage of a general railroad law and the construction of the proposed line between Detroit and Monroe would greatly harm Detroit by siphoning its trade and diverting it to Toledo. *Jackson American Citizen*, February 2, 1853; *Grass Lake Public Sentiment*, February 1, 1853; and *Saginaw Spirit of the Times*, March 17, 1853. On the bill's death, see *Grand Rapids Enquirer*, February 9, 1853. There seems to have been some sectional animosity created by the debate over the bill as well. The southwestern Michigan sheet *Branch County Journal*, for example, argued that the Detroit press, which, with the exception of the *Tribune*, generally opposed the bill, "acted as they believed the best interests of the city required." *Branch County Journal* quoted in the *Saginaw Spirit of the Times*, March 3, 1853. Similar beliefs are hinted at in numerous articles in other outstate papers as well. See, for example, *Grand Rapids Enquirer*, January 19 and 26, February 2, and March 2, 1853; *Jackson American Citizen*, February 9 and September 21, 1853.

34. The best account of the Michigan Southern's decision to complete the Jackson Branch is Hirschfeld, "The Great Railroad Conspiracy," pp. 208–9.

35. *Jackson American Citizen*, August 17, 1853.

36. *Jackson American Citizen*, August 24, 1853. For a brief summary of the meeting, see Hirschfeld, "The Great Railroad Conspiracy," pp. 209–10.

37. Hirschfeld, "The Great Railroad Conspiracy," p. 210. Section five of the Michigan Central charter specified that "no railroad or railroads from the eastern or southern boundary of the state shall be built, constructed, or maintained, by or under any law of this state, any portion of which shall approach westwardly from Wayne County, within five miles of the line said railroad is designated in this act, without the consent of said company." Quoted in *Grand Rapids Enquirer*, January 26, 1853. For more on Judge Douglass's decision, see *Jackson American Citizen*, November 30, 1853.

38. S. M. Johnson to James F. Joy, May 4, 1853, Box 10, "Michigan Central 1853," Joy Papers. *Jackson American Citizen*, December 14, 1853. For accounts of some of these meetings, see *Grand Rapids Enquirer*, March 2 and June 1, 1853; *Grass Lake Public Sentiment*, July 1, 1853; and *Jackson American Citizen*, August 24, 1853.

39. On the December meeting at Jackson, see *Detroit Free Press*, December 30, 1853; *Grand Rapids Enquirer*, January 4, 1854; and *Jackson American Citizen*, January 4, 1854. The meeting was attended by individuals of all political stripes. It is important to note that a number of individuals who would play a critical role in the formation of the Republican Party in Michigan in just six months' time (William Howard, Austin Blair, and Isaac Christiancy, to name but a few) were in attendance at the meeting and assumed an active role. Hirschfeld, "The Great Railroad Conspiracy," p. 214.

40. Unlike the antirailroad/antimonopoly crusade in antebellum Michigan, nativism's role in state politics has received a great deal more attention from historians. See Formisano, *Birth of Mass Political Parties*; Frederic H. Hayes, *Michigan Catholicism in the Era of the Civil War* (Lansing: Michigan Civil War Centennial Observance Commis-

sion, 1965); George Paré, *The Catholic Church in Detroit, 1701–1888* (Detroit, Mich.: Wayne State University Press, 1951), pp. 463–67; Streeter, *Political Parties in Michigan;* and Leslie Woodcock Tentler, *Seasons of Grace: A History of the Catholic Archdiocese of Detroit* (Detroit, Mich.: Wayne State University Press, 1990), pp. 87–90 and 104–6.

41. Hayes, *Michigan Catholicism,* pp. 1, 6, and 10; Melvin G. Holli, ed., *Detroit* (New York: New Viewpoints, 1976), pp. 269–70; and Tentler, *Seasons of Grace,* p. 21.

42. An excellent summary of the nativist line of thinking in reference to the Catholic population can be found in Anbinder, *Nativism and Slavery,* pp. 103–26. For a more personal insight into anti-Catholicism, see the letters of Elizabeth E. Stuart in Stuart Mackay-Smith Marlatt, ed., *Stuart Letters,* vol. 1. For a good example of the Protestant belief in the superstitious nature of Catholicism, see Elizabeth E. Stuart to Kate Stuart Baker, April 6, 1852, pp. 304–5. Because of the Whig Party's orientation toward individual effort and the unleashing of individual potential and the predominance of evangelical Protestants within the organization's ranks, nativism proved popular among many partisan Whigs. On Whigs and nativism, see Formisano, *Birth of Mass Political Parties;* Michael F. Holt, *The Rise and Fall of the American Whig Party: Jacksonian Politics and the Onset of the Civil War* (New York: Oxford University Press, 1999); and Daniel Walker Howe, *The Political Culture of the American Whigs* (Chicago: University of Chicago Press, 1979).

43. Formisano, *Birth of Mass Political Parties,* pp. 195–205 and 220–21. Chandler was not the only Whig candidate to pursue the ethnic vote in 1852. The presidential campaign of that year is often noted for the Whigs' attempt to bury nativism and to court immigrant votes. It should be noted that nativism did rear its head for a short period of time in 1850 at the state constitutional convention. As the convention debated the franchise article in the proposed state constitution, the question of alien suffrage came to the fore. Despite a conservative effort, led primarily by the handful of Whigs and Free-Soilers at the convention, to eliminate alien voting from the constitution, Michigan retained its liberal voting requirements. By a vote of fifty-nine to thirty-one, the franchise was given to all white male citizens over twenty-one years of age, to every white inhabitant entitled to vote in 1835, to every white inhabitant resident on January 1, 1850, and to white male inhabitants over the age of twenty-one who had resided in the state for at least two and one-half years and who had declared their intention to become citizens. Ronald Formisano mistakenly suggested that the alien suffrage question was one of the more salient issues dividing convention delegates; Formisano, *Birth of Mass Political Parties,* pp. 99–101. As indicated earlier, my research indicates that the convention spent relatively little time debating such issues.

44. Ibid., p. 222; *Detroit Free Press,* January 5, 1853. Formisano's account of this affair, though it places too much emphasis upon such ethnocultural tensions as the critical factor leading to the destruction of the Jacksonian party system and creation of the Republican Party, still remains the most complete.

45. On Lefevere's motives in opposing the proposed measures, see Formisano, *Birth of Mass Political Parties,* pp. 222–23, and *Detroit Free Press,* January 5, 1853. For

proof of Lefevere's conviction that Catholics were a majority in Detroit, see Tentler, *Seasons of Grace*, p. 88. The argument that the proposed improvement measures were antirepublican was largely ignored by Formisano. Such claims, however, are very important and demonstrate that even seemingly innocuous political debates, such as the debate over these proposed city improvements, could assume a much more ominous meaning for antebellum Americans. For a particularly lucid discussion of republicanism among the antebellum American working class, see Bruce Levine, *Half Slave and Half Free: The Roots of the Civil War* (New York: Hill and Wang, 1992), and Sean Wilentz, *Chants Democratic: New York City and the Rise of the American Working Class* (New York: Oxford University Press, 1984).

46. The details of the January 5 meeting can be gleaned from *Detroit Free Press*, January 7, 1853; Formisano, *Birth of Mass Political Parties*, p. 223; *Michigan Christian Herald*, January 13, 1853; and Paré, *The Catholic Church in Detroit*, p. 463. Elizabeth E. Stuart to her son, January 12, 1853, in Stuart Mackay-Smith Marlatt, ed., *Stuart Letters*, vol. 1, pp. 450–51.

47. *Detroit Free Press*, January 10, 1853. The public school question aroused a great deal of interest and was the subject of numerous articles and letters to various Detroit newspapers. See, for example, *Detroit Free Press*, January 5, 11, 12, February 28, and March 1, 1853. The school issue disappeared from the paper in late January and early February, as the state legislature turned its attention to the general railroad law. Similar anti-Catholic articles appeared in Detroit's other newspapers throughout the early months of 1853. Tentler, *Seasons of Grace*, pp. 86–87. Tentler persuasively argued that it was Lefevere's desire to provide a proper education to the Catholic poor that provided the motivation for his effort in 1853 to obtain public funding for church schools.

48. *Detroit Free Press*, January 10–12, 15, 19, February 25, and March 6, 1853; Elizabeth E. Stuart to her son, February 26, 1853, in Stuart Mackay-Smith Marlatt, ed., *Stuart Letters*, vol. 1, p. 482. Petition quoted in Paré, *The Catholic Church in Detroit*, pp. 464–66. On Lefevere's lobbying, see Formisano, *Birth of Mass Political Parties*, pp. 223–24, and Tentler, *Seasons of Grace*, p. 88.

49. Elizabeth E. Stuart to Kate Stuart Baker, January 23, 1853, in Stuart Mackay-Smith Marlatt, ed., *Stuart Letters*, vol. 1, p. 459. "Remonstrance of Elders and Deacons of the First Presbyterian Church of Detroit," quoted in Paré, *The Catholic Church in Detroit*, p. 466. The *Michigan Christian Herald*, a Baptist newspaper published in Detroit, also berated Lefevere and his allies for lobbying "with all the blandness of the most practiced courtesans"; *Michigan Christian Herald*, January 27, 1853. Detroit's two Whig newspapers, the *Advertiser* and especially the *Tribune*, both joined the fray and vehemently denounced the bishop and his compatriots. See, for example, the *Detroit Advertiser*, March 9, 1853; *Detroit Tribune*, March 12, 1853; and Formisano, *Birth of Mass Political Parties*, p. 225. Unfortunately, extant copies of the *Tribune* for this period are very rare. However, it is important to note that once again, the *Tribune*, inclined toward Free-Soilism, took the lead in attempting to broaden the Whig Party's appeal by

endorsing a popular cause. A particularly lucid discussion of the importance attached to the common school system can be found in Gienapp, *Origins of the Republican Party,* p. 61.

50. Details on the legislative debate can be found in Paré, *The Catholic Church in Detroit,* pp. 466–67. Both the majority and minority reports of the Committee on Education are printed in *Detroit Free Press,* February 7, 1853.

51. Elizabeth E. Stuart to Kate Stuart Baker, January 26, 1853, in Stuart Mackay-Smith Marlatt, ed., *Stuart Letters,* vol. 1, p. 462.

52. *Detroit Free Press,* February 24, 1853; Elizabeth E. Stuart to her son, February 26, 1853, in Stuart Mackay-Smith Marlatt, ed., *Stuart Letters,* vol. 1, p. 481. Rumors also circulated in Detroit in the weeks before the charter election that city Catholics were arming themselves and that Irish residents of the city had threatened to burn the homes of the editors of the anti-Catholic *Detroit Tribune.* See *Detroit Free Press,* March 7, 1853, and Elizabeth E. Stuart to her son, March 3, 1853, in Stuart Mackay-Smith Marlatt, ed., *Stuart Letters,* vol. 1, p. 482. Both the regular and independent tickets nominated John H. Harmon as their candidate for mayor. The remainder of the tickets were composed of different nominees.

53. *Detroit Free Press,* February 25, 26 and March 6, 1853; Elizabeth E. Stuart to her son, March 3, 1853, in Stuart Mackay-Smith Marlatt, ed., *Stuart Letters,* vol. 1, p. 482.

54. Formisano, *Birth of Mass Political Parties,* p. 225; *Detroit Free Press,* March 8, 1853. The *Free Press* also claimed that every Whig in the city had voted the independent ticket. Elizabeth E. Stuart to her son, March 12, 1853, in Stuart Mackay-Smith Marlatt, ed., *Stuart Letters,* vol. 1, p. 491. Leslie Tentler noted that even some Detroit Catholics voted against the regular ticket, possibly because Lefevere had alienated them by his strident and much publicized campaign against the public schools. See Tentler, *Seasons of Grace,* p. 89.

55. Elizabeth E. Stuart to Kate Stuart Baker, undated but included in March 1853 correspondence in Stuart Mackay-Smith Marlatt, ed., *Stuart Letters,* vol. 1, pp. 494 and 496.

56. *Coldwater Sentinel,* January 7 and March 13, 1853; *Grand Rapids Enquirer,* February 23 and March 9, 1853; *Jackson American Citizen,* March 13, 1853; and *Pontiac Gazette,* March 5 and 12, 1853; Formisano, *Birth of Mass Political Parties,* pp. 228–29. Although he downplayed the importance of such issues as the antirailroad/antimonopoly movement, Formisano nevertheless was correct when he surmised that "if Independency or Know Nothingism were not afoot [in outstate elections in the spring of 1853] one thing seems clear: strong currents were affecting voters in both parties to act independently of party loyalty."

57. *Detroit Catholic Vindicator,* April 30, 1853; *Grand Rapids Enquirer,* March 9, 1853.

58. The motivations of Michigan's protemperance advocates are fully described in John Fitzgibbon, "King Alcohol: His Rise, Reign and Fall in Michigan," *Michigan History* 4 (October 1918): 737–78; Formisano, *Birth of Mass Political Parties,* pp. 63, 78,

126, 157, 116–20, and 229–33; John W. Quist, *"Restless Visionaries: The Social Roots of Antebellum Reform in Alabama and Michigan* (Baton Rouge: Louisiana State University Press, 1998), pp. 235–302; Peter D. Slavcheff, "The Temperate Republic: Liquor Control in Michigan, 1800–1860" (Ph.D. diss., Wayne State University, 1987); Floyd B. Streeter, "History of Prohibition Legislation in Michigan," *Michigan History* 2 (April 1918): 289–99; Bruce Tap, "'The Evils of Intemperance are Universally Conceded': The Temperance Debate in Early Grand Rapids," *Michigan Historical Review* 19 (Spring 1993): 17–45; and N. Gordon Thomas, *The Millennial Impulse in Michigan, 1830–1860: The Second Coming in the Third New England* (Lewiston, N.Y.: Edwin Mellen Press, 1989), pp. 92–111. Lyman Beecher speech to the Detroit Temperance Society, as quoted in Thomas, *The Millennial Impulse,* p. 99. The figures on consumption of alcohol were taken from Sellers, *The Market Revolution,* p. 259. Also see W. J. Rorabaugh, *The Alcoholic Republic: An American Tradition* (New York: Oxford University Press, 1979), and John C. Schneider, *Detroit and the Problem of Order, 1830–1880: A Geography of Crime, Riot, and Policing* (Lincoln: University of Nebraska Press, 1980), p. 41.

59. For an excellent account of the ambiguous results of the 1845 local option law as it related to Washtenaw County, see Quist, *Restless Visionaries,* pp. 254–60.

60. Formisano, *Birth of Mass Political Parties,* p. 230, and Reynolds, "Piety and Politics," p. 331. A good discussion of this confusion can be found in Tap, "Evils of Intemperance," pp. 25–26.

61. *Jackson American Citizen,* August 24 and December 8, 1852; *Grand Rapids Enquirer,* December 22, 1852, and January 12, 1853. The Free-Soil sheet *Michigan Free Democrat* urged its readers to send the state's "rum-seeking politicians to a remediless political grave" and to put "men into our legislative halls whose pleasure it will be to subserve the interests of their country"; *Michigan Free Democrat,* December 29, 1852.

62. Formisano, *Birth of Mass Political Parties,* p. 230, and *Grand Rapids Enquirer,* January 26, 1853. The motives of those who sought to undermine the bill are briefly discussed in Clark F. Norton, "Early Michigan Supreme Court Decisions on the Liquor Question," *Michigan History* 28 (January–March 1944): 46–47; *Detroit Free Press,* February 11 and 15, 1853; *Jackson American Citizen,* February 16, 1853.

63. Formisano, *Birth of Mass Political Parties,* p. 230. Discussion of the act's constitutionality can be found in *Coldwater Sentinel,* February 25, 1853, and *Detroit Free Press,* February 11 and 15, 1853. Select committees in both the state senate and state house raised similar concerns. See Norton, "Michigan Supreme Court Decisions," p. 47. Not everyone agreed that the act as passed was unconstitutional. For example, see *Grand Rapids Enquirer,* February 16, 1853.

64. On the bipartisan support for the law, see Formisano, *Birth of Mass Political Parties,* pp. 230–31. Many supporters of the law believed that an overwhelming victory at the polls would convince "muddy headed politicians" of the constitutionality of the law. *Grass Lake Public Sentiment,* April 1 and June 15, 1853; *Detroit Free Press,* May 25, 1853; and *Grand Rapids Enquirer,* May 4, 1853.

65. See Formisano, *Birth of Mass Political Parties,* p. 230, and Tap, "Evils of Intem-

perance," p. 33. Formisano, for instance, cited only one newspaper, the *Pontiac Gazette,* to back up his claim that "newspapers, whether hostile or sympathetic, Democrat or Whig, discussed little else that spring." Formisano and Tap clearly overstated their case. The general railroad law and railroad matters, for example, garnered a great deal of attention from the state press, especially in outstate areas, throughout the spring of 1853. See *Grand Rapids Enquirer,* March 16 and 22, May 11, and June 1, 1853; *Grass Lake Public Sentiment,* March 1 and 15, April 1, May 2, June 1 and 15, 1853; and *Jackson American Citizen,* March 9, 1853. Even the state's new tax law often attracted more attention than the upcoming Maine Law election. For example, see *Grand Rapids Enquirer,* March 22 and 30 and May 4 and 18, 1853. While it is true that the editor of the *Detroit Free Press,* Wilbur F. Storey, devoted a great deal of space to a discussion of the merits of the Maine Law, one must keep in mind that Storey opposed the law's passage—he referred to it as "crude and undigested . . . impracticable and of doubtful morality"—and therefore probably felt compelled to make his case at length, in the light of obvious public support for such a measure. Nevertheless, even the *Free Press* did not focus exclusively upon the prohibition issue. See *Detroit Free Press,* March 24–26, 1853. Elizabeth E. Stuart to her son, February 12, 1853, in Stuart Mackay-Smith Marlatt, ed., *Stuart Letters,* vol. 1, p. 472.

66. *Detroit Free Press,* November 6, 1852; Formisano, *Birth of Mass Political Parties,* pp. 231, 235, and 273; Quist, *Restless Visionaries,* pp. 267–69; Tap, "Evils of Intemperance," p. 33.

67. Formisano, *Birth of Mass Political Parties,* p. 231; Norton, "Early Michigan Supreme Court Decisions," pp. 47–48; Quist, *Restless Visionaries,* p. 270; and Tap, "Evils of Intemperance," p. 34.

68. *People v. Collins,* 3 Mich. 343; Quist, *Restless Visionaries,* p. 270. An excellent account of the court's actions in reference to the state's Maine Law is Norton, "Early Michigan Supreme Court Decisions," pp. 48–61. Norton argued that the main reason for the contradictory decisions in the three cases involving the state's Maine Law could be attributed to the illness and subsequent absence of Justice Copeland from the latter two cases, an absence that gave the protemperance justices a one-vote majority. "Questions reserved" was, according to Norton, a common practice in which "the inferior courts reserv[ed] legal questions for the opinion of the supreme court, with the final judgments being entered in the courts below in accordance with instructions from the appellate tribunal." Because the state lacked the authority to appeal a criminal case in which a circuit judge declared a law unconstitutional and discharged the defendant, this lower court decision would not be subject to the review of the supreme court; Norton, "Early Michigan Supreme Court Decisions," p. 57. *Adrian Watchtower,* February 7, 1854; Formisano, *Birth of Mass Political Parties,* p. 233.

69. This traditional interpretation is best represented in Streeter, *Political Parties in Michigan.* Also see Martha M. Bigelow, "The Political Services of William Alanson Howard," *Michigan History* 42 (March 1958): 1–23; Dunbar, *Michigan,* pp. 418–20; Jean Joy L. Fennimore, "Austin Blair: Political Idealist, 1845–1860," *Michigan History*

48 (June 1964): 130–66; Wilmer C. Harris, *Public Life of Zachariah Chandler, 1851–1875* (Lansing, Mich.: State Historical Commission, 1917); Justin L. Kestenbaum, "Modernizing Michigan, 1836–1866: Political and Social Trends," in Richard J. Hathaway, ed., *Michigan: Visions of Our Past* (East Lansing: Michigan State University Press, 1989), pp. 124–26; Ferris E. Lewis, *Michigan: Yesterday and Today* (Hillsdale, Mich.: Hillsdale Educational, 1956), pp. 239–41; Larry B. Massie, *Voyages into Michigan's Past* (Au Train, Mich.: Avery Color Studios, 1988), pp. 93–111; Malcolm Moos, *The Republicans: A History of Their Party* (New York: Random House, 1954), pp. 8–15; Milo M. Quaife and Sidney Glazer, *Michigan: From Primitive Wilderness to Industrial Commonwealth* (New York: Prentice-Hall, 1948), pp. 196–208; Ronald E. Seavoy, "The Organization of the Republican Party in Michigan, 1846–1854," *The Old Northwest* 6 (Winter 1980–1981): 343–76; Henry M. Utley and Byron M. Cutcheon, *Michigan as a Province, Territory and State, the Twenty-Sixth Member of the Federal Union*, vol. 4 (n.p.: Publishing Society of Michigan, 1906), pp. 355–65 and 373; A. D. P. Van Buren, "Michigan in Her Pioneer Politics, Michigan in Our National Politics, and Michigan in the Presidential Campaign of 1856," *Michigan Pioneer and Historical Collections* 17 (1890): 238–95. William Gienapp argued that the Northern Whig Party was particularly hard hit by the loss of traditional issues in the early 1850s—especially nativism and antislavery, both of which were abandoned by the party in 1852—because these issues traditionally attracted key constituencies to the Whig cause; Gienapp, *Origins of the Republican Party*, p. 35. Tyler Anbinder contended that part of the Know-Nothings' appeal to former Whigs was the party's success in linking nativism and antislavery; Anbinder, *Nativism and Slavery*.

70. John W. Quist, "'The Great Majority of our Subscribers are Farmers': The Michigan Abolitionist Constituency of the 1840s," *Journal of the Early Republic* 14 (Fall 1994): 331, and idem, *Restless Visionaries*, pp. 395–403. There are, however, two notable exceptions to the general trend: Ronald Formisano's *Birth of Mass Political Parties* and Ronald E. Seavoy's partial response to Formisano, "The Organization of the Republican Party in Michigan." Unfortunately, both of these works suffer from other shortcomings. In brief, both works miss the full complexity of Republican fusion in Michigan. Neither work offers the reader a comprehensive portrait of the complicated and nuanced process by which this new political movement came into being. For instance, although he clearly distinguished between abolitionism and antislavery, Seavoy continued in the traditional vein by relying completely upon antislavery as the driving force behind the formation of the Republican Party. Formisano, too, recognized the abolitionist/antislavery distinction, and he correctly emphasized antisouthern hostility as taking precedence over abolitionism within the ranks of the Republican faithful. At the same time, however, Formisano tended to downplay the role of antisouthernism as a contributing factor in the creation of the new Republican coalition. Instead, he chose to stress the importance of such ethnocultural issues as nativism and temperance within the Republican movement. This emphasis led Seavoy to criticize Formisano's approach, though for the wrong reasons; Seavoy argued that "Formisano

. . . strongly overstates the effects of local issues on Michigan election results from 1848 to 1854."

Clearly, there is a kernel of truth in both of these works. Antislavery/antisouthernism did assume great importance for Michigan's antebellum voters, particularly in 1854. Still, a total reliance upon antislavery as the pivotal force in Michigan politics, as proposed by Ronald Seavoy, is fatally flawed. The introduction of many so-called local issues such as nativism, temperance, and antirailroad/antimonopoly sentiment in the years preceding 1854 laid the groundwork for the state's ensuing political realignment, not antislavery. That is not to say, however, that Formisano's account of Michigan politics is any less flawed. Formisano clearly missed the importance of the ongoing debate over the market revolution as a force in Michigan politics. And, as mentioned, he did not give antisouthernism its due, either. Moreover, both Seavoy and Formisano failed to take into account two things: the persistence of the Jacksonian political culture in the 1850s despite the decomposition of the second party system and the broader environment of economic, cultural, and social change that characterized Michigan in the early 1850s. This environment and this political culture provided the lens through which Michiganians viewed contemporary problems and thus gave all of the issues mentioned here their immediacy. By expanding the study of antebellum Michigan politics to include the contextual background within which the issues of the day unfolded, we are able to appreciate that such issues as railroads, antislavery, temperance, and nativism represented much more than mere local questions. They embodied debates about nothing less than the fate of liberty in the United States. Formisano, *Birth of Mass Political Parties*; Seavoy, "The Organization of the Republican Party," pp. 371–72.

71. The clearest articulation of these ideals is found in Eric Foner, *Free Soil, Free Labor, Free Men: The Ideology of the Republican Party before the Civil War* (New York: Oxford University Press, 1970). Also see Gienapp, *Origins of the Republican Party*, and Holt, *Political Crisis*, pp. 184–213. James G. Birney to Horace Mann, July 29, 1850, in Dwight L. Dumond, ed., *Letters of James Gillespie Birney, 1831–1857*, vol. 2 (Gloucester, Mass.: Peter Smith, 1938), pp. 1137–38; *Michigan Free Democrat*, December 29, 1852.

72. Eric Foner, *Free Soil, Free Labor, Free Men: The Ideology of the Republican Party before the Civil War*, 2d ed. (New York: Oxford University Press, 1995), pp. IX–X and 11–39.

73. *Washtenaw Whig*, June 20, 1849; *Congressional Globe*, 31st Congress, 1st sess. (Washington: John C. Rives, 1850), p. 734; William A. Howard quoted in Bigelow, "William Alanson Howard," p. 7. On Bingham's Free-Soil ideals, see William McDaid, "Kinsley S. Bingham and the Republican Ideology of Antislavery, 1847–1855," *Michigan Historical Review* 16 (Fall 1990): 43–74. The strength of Free-Soil principles in the state's agricultural sector is readily apparent. See *Michigan Free Democrat*, December 29, 1852; Quist, "The Great Majority of Our Subscribers are Farmers," and Seavoy, "Organization of the Republican Party," p. 343.

74. *Detroit Daily Democrat*, May 24, 1854; *Pontiac Gazette*, March 11, 1854; and *Jackson American Citizen*, March 4, 1854. Also see *Detroit Advertiser*, February 20, 1854. The hue and cry against the bill is most thoroughly described in Streeter, *Political Parties in*

Michigan, pp. 183–86. Not all of these meetings came off without a hitch. The diarist Fred B. Porter noted that Detroit's Democrats attempted to thwart the June 7 meeting by carrying off the key to the city hall and turning off the gas. Porter triumphantly noted, however, that "the lock was broken and the gas turned on again," and the meeting, which was very full, proceeded; Fred B. Porter Journals, 1848–1854, "Second," entry of June 8, 1854, Michigan Historical Collections, Bentley Historical Library, University of Michigan, Ann Arbor.

75. On the continuing debate over the railroads see *Detroit Free Press,* January 12, 1854; *Grand Rapids Enquirer,* January 4 and 11, February 15 and 25, and May 31, 1854; *Grass Lake Public Sentiment,* February 15, April 1, May 15, and July 1, 1854; *Jackson American Citizen,* January 4, 1854; and Fred B. Porter Journal entry of February 6, 1854, Porter Journals, "Second." The continued interest in temperance is detailed in Formisano, *Birth of Mass Political Parties,* pp. 233, 235. Also see *Grass Lake Public Sentiment,* April 1 and July 15, 1854. Howard's speech on the Jesuits is described in *Detroit Advertiser,* March 2, 1854, and Fred Porter Journal entry of February 28, 1854, Porter Journals, "Second." Elizabeth E. Stuart to her son, June 1, 1854, in Stuart Mackay-Smith Marlatt, ed., *Stuart Letters,* vol. 2, p. 615.

76. A. D. P. Van Buren to "Friend" Martin, Anson de Puy Van Buren Papers; *Niles Republican,* April 8, 1854; Asa Whitney to Alpheus Felch, Alpheus Felch Papers.

CHAPTER 5

The quotation in this chapter's heading is from the speech delivered by Zachariah Chandler to the Jackson Republican convention, July 6, 1854, quoted in Milton Milo Quaife and Sidney Glazer, *Michigan: From Primitive Wilderness to Industrial Commonwealth* (New York: Prentice-Hall, 1948), p. 204.

1. *Lapeer County Democrat* quoted in *Grass Lake Public Sentiment,* May 15, 1854; undated and untitled essay on political parties and Republican government, "Correspondence, Undated," Box 1, Kinsley S. Bingham Papers, 1815–1920, Michigan Historical Collections, Bentley Historical Library, University of Michigan, Ann Arbor.

2. It was only very late in the Detroit campaign that a half-hearted effort was launched to associate the independent candidate for mayor, Oliver Hyde, with opposition to the Kansas-Nebraska Act. Even Detroit's Free-Soil paper, the *Michigan Free Democrat,* chose to emphasize "temperance and reform" over the issue of slavery's extension. See Ronald P. Formisano, *The Birth of Mass Political Parties: Michigan, 1827–1861* (Princeton, N.J.: Princeton University Press, 1971), pp. 235–38, and *Grand Rapids Enquirer,* April 5, 1854.

3. The best account of the political strategy of Michigan Free-Soilers is Ronald E. Seavoy, "The Organization of the Republican Party in Michigan, 1846–1854," *The Old Northwest* 6 (Winter 1980): 344–50.

4. On the reaction of Michigan Democrats to the Kansas-Nebraska Act, see Willard C. Klunder, *Lewis Cass and the Politics of Moderation* (Kent, Ohio: Kent State University Press, 1996), pp. 264–71; Andrew C. McLaughlin, *Lewis Cass* (Boston and New

York: Houghton Mifflin, 1899), pp. 297–300; and Frank B. Woodford, *Lewis Cass: The Last Jeffersonian* (New Brunswick, N.J.: Rutgers University Press, 1950), pp. 298–305.

5. The various Free-Soil attitudes are covered in more detail in Seavoy, "Organization of the Republican Party," pp. 362–66, and A. D. P. Van Buren, "Michigan in Her Pioneer Politics, Michigan in Our National Politics, and Michigan in the Presidential Campaign of 1856," *Michigan Pioneer and Historical Collections* 17 (1890): 262–64. Letter of Isaac P. Christiancy to Frank A. Flower, April 11, 1884, quoted in Van Buren, "Michigan in Her Pioneer Politics," p. 263.

6. A detailed discussion of the February 21 meeting can be found in Seavoy, "Organization of the Republican Party," p. 363. See also Floyd B. Streeter, *Political Parties in Michigan, 1837–1860* (Lansing: Michigan Historical Commission, 1916), p. 187, and William Stocking, "Little Journeys in Journalism: Michigan Press Influence on Party Formation," *Michigan History* 11 (1927): 210–11. Joseph Warren's argument in favor of the creation of an independent fusion movement, nearly identical to that of Christiancy, is well documented in Stocking, "Michigan Press Influence," p. 210. It seems quite likely that these Whig editors and other prominent Whigs such as James Joy, Zachariah Chandler, William Howard, and Jacob Howard believed that an independent fusion party was the only way to ensure that their partisans would acquiesce in disbanding their own party organization. Moreover, it would force into the party ranks those conservatives who were hesitant to take such a step and who sought to avoid a Free-Soil platform in their current party, by leaving them with no other option but to vote for the new organization. See Seavoy, "Organization of the Republican Party," pp. 364–65.

7. Seavoy, "Organization of the Republican Party," pp. 363–64; Charles Hirschfeld, "The Great Railroad Conspiracy," *Michigan History* 36 (June 1952): 215.

8. *Pontiac Gazette*, March 11, 1854; *Marshall Statesman*, June 7, 1854.

9. Seavoy, "Organization of the Republican Party," p. 365; Van Buren, "Michigan in Her Pioneer Politics," p. 263; Zachariah Chandler to James F. Joy, May 30, 1854, "James F. Joy 1852–55," Box 4, James F. Joy Papers, 1834–1900, Michigan Historical Collections, Bentley Historical Library, University of Michigan, Ann Arbor.

10. Seavoy, "Organization of the Republican Party," p. 365; Van Buren, "Michigan in Her Pioneer Politics," pp. 263–64; Zachariah Chandler to James F. Joy, June 2, 1854, "June–December 1854," Box 15, Joy Papers. According to Chandler, the agreed upon Free-Soil principles were: a promise of no new slave states, repeal of the Kansas-Nebraska Act, repeal of the Fugitive Slave Act, and an end to slavery in the District of Columbia. Isaac P. Christiancy to Frank A. Flowers, April 11, 1884, in Van Buren, "Michigan in Her Pioneer Politics," p. 364.

11. "Call to the First Republican Convention," in Isaac P. Christiancy Papers, 1840–1883, Michigan Historical Collections, Bentley Historical Library, University of Michigan, Ann Arbor.

12. *Detroit Tribune*, undated, 1854, quoted in Stocking, "Michigan Press Influence," p. 209; *Kalamazoo Telegraph*, undated, 1854, quoted in ibid., p. 211. See also *Jackson American Citizen*, June 14, 1854. Van Buren, "Michigan in Her Pioneer Politics," p. 265.

13. "Resolutions Adopted by the Free Democratic Party in Convention, June 21, 1854," Christiancy Papers; Van Buren, "Michigan in Her Pioneer Politics," p. 264.

14. Accounts of this traditional portrayal of the Republican convention as a grass-roots movement are too numerous to cite. Typical among them are: Jean Joy L. Fennimore, "Austin Blair: Political Idealist, 1845–1860," *Michigan History* 48 (June 1964): 147–48; Larry B. Massie, *Voyages into Michigan's Past* (Au Train, Mich.: Avery Color Studios, 1988), pp. 93–96; and Streeter, *Political Parties in Michigan*, p. 147. Seavoy, "Organization of the Republican Party," p. 366.

15. *Grass Lake Public Sentiment*, July 1, 1854.

16. The Jackson republican convention is minutely described in a number of works. Among the most helpful brief accounts are *Detroit Post and Tribune, Zachariah Chandler: An Outline Sketch of His Life and Public Service* (Detroit, Mich.: Post and Tribune Company 1880), pp. 89–118; Moos, *The Republicans*, pp. 9–11; Seavoy, "Organization of the Republican Party," pp. 367–68; and Streeter, *Political Parties in Michigan*, pp. 191–93. No published biography of Jacob Howard exists. My discussion of his varied political interests is based upon earlier portions of this work. On Howard's decision to withdraw from the Michigan Railroad Conspiracy case, see Hirschfeld, "The Great Railroad Conspiracy," p. 179.

17. Milton Milo Quaife and Sidney Glazer, *Michigan: From Primitive Wilderness to Industrial Commonwealth* (New York: Prentice-Hall, 1948), p. 204.

18. Arthur M. Schlesinger, Jr., ed., *History of U.S. Political Parties*, vol. 2, *1860–1910* (New York: Chelsea House, 1973), pp. 1185–88.

19. Ibid., p. 1188; Hirschfeld, "The Great Railroad Conspiracy," p. 215. State Democrats included a similar railroad law provision in their platform just two months later. Also see Dale R. Prentiss, "Economic Progress and Social Dissent in Michigan and Mississippi, 1837–1860" (Ph.D. diss., Stanford University, 1990), pp. 64–66, and Ronald E. Seavoy, "Borrowed Laws to Speed Development: Michigan, 1835–1860," *Michigan History* 59 (1975): 64. Prentiss correctly noted that advocacy of a general railroad law was necessary for Republicans if they hoped to win over the state's small farmers and laborers. Seavoy, "Organization of the Republican Party," p. 367.

20. The evidence that antirailroad/antimonopoly forces were mollified is largely impressionistic. The *Grass Lake Public Sentiment*, for one, felt confident enough that its agenda had been finally pushed onto the political stage to cease publication in August 1854.

21. Massie, *Voyages into Michigan's Past*, pp. 95–96; Seavoy, "Organization of the Republican Party," p. 368; and Formisano, *Birth of Mass Political Parties*, p. 243. The complete Republican ticket can be found in any number of state newspapers. See, for example, the *Jackson American Citizen*, July 7, 1854. The preponderance of former Whigs and Democrats on the slate was intentional, the purpose being to cement the loyalties of these former party men to the new fusion organization. This strategy was clearly endorsed by the Free Democrats who, Isaac Christiancy wrote in 1884, had reached an understanding prior to the Jackson convention "that they should remain

in the background and not be pressed for prominent positions either as officers of the convention or as candidates for nomination; but that these should be taken mainly from those who had left the democratic and whig parties to join our movement"; Van Buren, "Michigan in Her Pioneer Politics," p. 265.

22. *Hillsdale Standard, Constantine Mercury,* and *Marshall Statesman,* all undated, quoted in *Jackson American Citizen,* July 26, 1854.

23. *Detroit Advertiser,* July 8, 1854. Similar sentiments were expressed in the columns of the *Adrian Expositor,* July 21, 1854. *Grand Rapids Enquirer,* August 9, 1854. On the conservative Whig response to the Jackson convention, see Streeter, *Political Parties in Michigan,* pp. 193–97.

24. The details surrounding the Whig convention can be found in Martha M. Bigelow, "The Political Services of William Alanson Howard," *Michigan History* 42 (March 1958): 8, and Streeter, *Political Parties in Michigan,* pp. 195–97. Ironically, even before the Whig state convention met, the chair of the Whig State Central Committee, William Howard, had already been nominated by both the Whig and Republican Parties (both of which held their district conventions on September 20) as a candidate for the U.S. House of Representatives in Michigan's Third District.

25. On Whig conversions to the Democratic Party, see *Jackson American Citizen,* July 26, 1854. The best accounts of Michigan's Know-Nothing activities are Formisano, *Birth of Mass Political Parties,* pp. 248–53, and Streeter, *Political Parties in Michigan,* pp. 178–82. See also *Detroit Advertiser,* September 6, 1854. *Detroit Advertiser,* December 11, 1854. The *Advertiser* remained primarily a Know-Nothing sheet until it changed hands in July 1855, after which it converted to the Republican Party. Formisano, *Birth of Mass Political Parties,* p. 249; *Grand Rapids Enquirer,* November 1, 1854; and *Niles Republican,* October 28, 1854. Equating Republicans with Know-Nothings became a common Democratic tactic as the election neared. See *Detroit Free Press,* November, 3, 4, and 7, 1854, and *Grand Rapids Enquirer,* October 25 and November 1, 1854.

26. Robert McClelland to Alpheus Felch, July 14, 1854, "McClelland, Robert, 1851–55," Box 4, Alpheus Felch Papers, 1806–1896, Michigan Historical Collections, Bentley Historical Library, University of Michigan, Ann Arbor. For similar sentiments before the Jackson convention, see Robert McClelland to Alpheus Felch, April 13, 1854, "McClelland, Robert, 1851–55," Box 4, Felch Papers.

27. *Grand Rapids Enquirer,* July 5, 1854. Lewis Cass's response to the rising tide of hostility to the Kansas-Nebraska Act is found in Willis F. Dunbar, *Lewis Cass* (Grand Rapids, Mich.: William B. Eerdmans, 1970), pp. 72–73; Klunder, *Lewis Cass,* pp. 268–71; McLaughlin, *Lewis Cass,* pp. 297–300; and Frank B. Woodford, *Lewis Cass: The Last Jeffersonian,* pp. 298–305. Lewis Cass to J. H. Cleveland, June 4, 1854, quoted in McLaughlin, *Lewis Cass,* p. 299.

28. *Detroit Free Press,* August 15, 1854; *Detroit Free Press* quoted in *Grand Rapids Enquirer,* September 27, 1854; and *Grand Rapids Enquirer,* September 20, 1854.

29. Streeter, *Political Parties in Michigan,* p. 197, and *Grand Rapids Enquirer,* September 20, 1854.

30. *Jackson American Citizen,* November 1, 1854, and *Detroit Daily Democrat,* October 31, 1854.

31. *Detroit Free Press,* November 7, 1854, and *Grand Rapids Enquirer,* November 1, 1854.

32. Formisano, *Birth of Mass Political Parties,* p. 251, and Streeter, *Political Parties in Michigan,* pp. 197–200. Streeter mistakenly attributed support for the Republican Party among the state's small farmers to their New England/New Yorker roots and their ingrained hostility to slavery. Prentiss, "Economic Progress and Social Dissent," p. 218; Robert McClelland to Alpheus Felch, February 19, 1855, "McClelland, Robert, 1851–55," Box 4, Felch Papers.

33. "Message of Kinsley Bingham to the Legislature of the State of Michigan," January 4, 1855, in George N. Fuller, ed., *Messages of the Governors of Michigan,* vol. 2 (Lansing: Michigan Historical Commission, 1926), p. 287.

34. Ibid., pp. 283–86 and 289–92. For Republican reaction to the inaugural, see *Jackson American Citizen,* January 10, 1855.

35. Isaac P. Christiancy to Kinsley Bingham, January 26, 1855, Executive Department, RG-44, Box 141, Folder 8, State Archives of Michigan, Lansing. In his inaugural, Governor Bingham had expressed similar concerns, warning against the "malign and corrupting influences" of lobbyists; "Message of Kinsley Bingham," January 4, 1855, in Fuller, ed., *Messages of Governors,* vol. 2, pp. 300–301. George A. Coe to Kinsley Bingham, December 4, 1854, Executive Department, RG-44, Box 134, Folder 9, State Archives of Michigan; William [illegible] to Kinsley Bingham, December 16, 1854, Executive Department, RG-44, Box 141, Folder 8, State Archives of Michigan.

36. The best account of the debate over the proposed general railroad law is Hirschfeld, "The Great Railroad Conspiracy," pp. 216–17. See also George Porter to James F. Joy, January 12, 1855 [misdated typed copy listed as December 12, 1855], "Sep–Dec, 1855," Box 16, Joy Papers. W. Tracy Howe to Kinsley Bingham, February 1, 1855, Executive Department, RG-44, Box 191, Folder 16, State Archives of Michigan; Ronald E. Seavoy, "Borrowed Laws to Speed Development: Michigan, 1835–1863," *Michigan History* 59 (Spring-Summer 1975): 64–65.

37. Seavoy, "Borrowed Laws," p. 65; Hirschfeld, "The Great Railroad Conspiracy," p. 217; Benjamin W. Bellows, "Politics and Michigan Fiscal Policy, 1837–1865" (honors thesis, University of Michigan, 1996), p. 35.

38. My claim of widespread temperance support for the Republican ticket is based upon similar claims made by Streeter, *Political Parties in Michigan,* p. 201, and idem, "History of Prohibition Legislation in Michigan," *Michigan History* 2 (April 1918): 298.

39. Formisano, *Birth of Mass Political Parties,* pp. 256–57.

40. Seavoy, "Borrowed Laws," p. 66. Interest in the banking issue had never fully subsided after 1850–1851 and, in fact, occasionally showed itself during the election campaign in 1854. For example, see *Grand Rapids Enquirer,* September 6, 1854. Not surprisingly, given their emphasis upon ethnocultural factors and slavery, respectively,

both Ronald Formisano and Floyd Streeter (the authors of the two most cited works on Michigan politics in this era) chose to disregard such debates as the ones surrounding the general railroad law and the banking bill. Both men saw such debates, although potentially popular, as mere sideshows involving inconsequential matters. For example, in relation to the general railroad law, Formisano said the following: "Prosperity and rising expectations created great faith in the benefits it would bestow, but significant increases in capital investment in railroads did not immediately follow." Formisano's conclusion is debatable, but more important, he missed the broader significance of such issues to the people of Michigan. Mid-nineteenth-century Michiganians did not look at the debate over the general railroad law in purely economic terms. Rather, they thought more in terms of protecting and expanding freedom and equal rights in a rapidly changing world. In short, these issues reveal an ongoing attempt to come to grips with the changes related to Michigan's market revolution. Formisano, *Birth of Mass Political Parties,* p. 256. Ronald Seavoy argued that the general railroad law had an immediate and profound economic impact on Michigan; Seavoy, "Borrowed Laws," p. 65.

41. Streeter, *Political Parties in Michigan,* pp. 202–3; Fennimore, "Austin Blair," p. 154.

42. The best account of the 1855 American convention is Tyler Anbinder, *Nativism and Slavery: The Northern Know Nothings and the Politics of the 1850s* (New York: Oxford University Press, 1992), pp. 206–12. Also see Formisano, *Birth of Mass Political Parties,* pp. 263–64. Historians focusing upon the antebellum era have devoted a great deal of attention to the relationship between the Republican and American Parties. In his seminal work *The Political Crisis of the 1850s,* Michael Holt portrayed the two organizations as competitors vying to replace the Whig Party as the opposition to the Democrats. William Gienapp, by contrast, presented the Know-Nothing Party as a transitional home for former Whigs on the path to becoming Republicans. In his account of antebellum Michigan, Ronald Formisano in effect synthesized these two arguments by arguing that Know-Nothingism existed independently of Republicanism, competing for a time but ultimately serving as a merely temporary home for the state's old-line Whig faction before final uniting with the Republican Party. To prove his point, Formisano made much of the spring 1855 elections in the state, elections that revealed Know-Nothingism at high tide in Michigan. Know-Nothings experienced some success in local elections in early 1855, but Formisano made far too much of the party's influence upon state politics. As Floyd Streeter had shown in his earlier account of Michigan politics, the Know-Nothing Party was comparatively weak and short-lived in the state. Even Formisano was forced to concede that the party offered few, if any, candidates of its own; instead, it generally, although not exclusively, worked in tandem with local Republican organizations. In fact, the Know-Nothing influence in Michigan appears to have been quite limited, and that limited influence ebbed even further in the aftermath of the American Party convention in mid-1855. Holt, *Political Crisis of the 1850s,* pp. 164–69; Gienapp, *Origins of the Republican Party;* Streeter, *Political Parties in Michigan,* p. 180; Formisano, *Birth of Mass Political Parties,* pp. 249–63.

43. "Call of the Republican State Central Committee," August 1, 1855, quoted in Fennimore, "Austin Blair," p. 156; *Kalamazoo Telegraph,* September 13, 1855.

44. An excellent account of the North's response to the attack on Charles Sumner can be found in David H. Donald, *Charles Sumner and the Coming of the Civil War* (New York: Fawcett Columbine, 1960), pp. 288–311. H. J. Alvord to George Hill, March 6, 1856, George Hill Papers, 1846–1866, Michigan Historical Collections, Bentley Historical Library, University of Michigan, Ann Arbor; Jacob M. Howard to Robert McClelland, March 7, 1856, "1856, Jan–June," Jacob M. Howard Papers, 1796–1879, Burton Historical Collection, Detroit Public Library, Detroit, Mich.; Seymour B. Treadwell to Kinsley Bingham, June 2, 1856, Executive Department, RG-44, Box 134, Folder 6, State Archives of Michigan; Egbert St. Nichols to Henry C. Waldron, May 27, 1856, Henry Clay Waldron Papers, University Archives and Historical Collections, Michigan State University, East Lansing.; Speech of Zachariah Chandler, May 30, 1856, quoted in *Detroit Post and Tribune, Zachariah Chandler,* p. 120; Austin Blair to A. J. McCall, April 7, 1856, quoted in Fennimore, "Austin Blair," p. 158.

45. Fennimore, "Austin Blair," pp. 158–59.

46. Speech of Zachariah Chandler delivered at Kalamazoo on August 27, 1856, quoted in *Detroit Post and Tribune, Zachariah Chandler,* pp. 122–23; Jacob M. Howard to Dr. Samuel Niles, June 17, 1856, Howard Papers.

47. Van Buren, "Michigan in Her Pioneer Politics," pp. 278, 282; Lewis Cass to John P. Cook, July 4, 1856, John Potter Cook Papers, 1856–1878, Michigan Historical Collections, Bentley Historical Library, University of Michigan, Ann Arbor.

48. Willis F. Dunbar, *Michigan: A History of the Wolverine State* (Grand Rapids, Mich.: William B. Eerdmans, 1970), p. 364; Fennimore, "Austin Blair," p. 160; Formisano, *Birth of Mass Political Parties,* p. 273; Streeter, *Political Parties in Michigan,* pp. 205–6; W. Hastings to George Hill, November 14, 1856, George Hill Papers.

49. *Detroit Post and Tribune, Zachariah Chandler,* pp. 123–25; Henry C. Waldron to Charles S. May, January 11, 1857, "1856–1859," Charles S. May Papers, 1833–1899, Burton Historical Collection, Detroit Public Library, Detroit, Mich.; *Marshall Statesman,* January 14, 1857.

50. "Message of Kinsley Bingham to the Legislature of the State of Michigan," January 7, 1857, in Fuller, ed., *Messages of Governors,* vol. 2, pp. 302–21.

51. *Detroit Free Press,* January 7, 22, and 31, February 11, 1857.

52. On the 1856 federal land grant and the 1857 state railroad law, see Edmund A. Calkins, "Railroads of Michigan since 1850," *Michigan History* 13 (January 1929): 7–8, and Willis F. Dunbar, *All Aboard: A History of Railroads in Michigan* (Grand Rapids, Mich.: William B. Eerdmans, 1969), pp. 107–10. In reality, the law accomplished very little in the short run. Railroad construction came to a virtual standstill with the panic of 1857 and the onset of the Civil War in 1861 and did not begin again in earnest until after the war.

53. "Message of Kinsley Bingham to the Legislature of the State of Michigan," January 7, 1857, in Fuller, ed., *Messages of Governors,* vol. 2, pp. 315–16. Isaac P. Chris-

tiancy to Kinsley Bingham, January 19, 1857, Executive Department, RG-44, Box 141, Folder 8, State Archives of Michigan.

54. *Detroit Free Press*, January 20, 1857.

55. A brief account of the 1857 banking bill can be found in Seavoy, "Borrowed Laws," pp. 66–67.

56. "Message of Kinsley Bingham to the Legislature of the State of Michigan," January 7, 1857, in Fuller, ed., *Messages of Governors*, vol. 2, pp. 317–21.

57. *Detroit Free Press*, January 18, 1857; "Joint Resolution Respecting Slavery in the Territories," February 4, 1857, and "Joint Resolution Instructing Our Senators and Representatives in Congress in Relation to the Affairs of Kansas," February 10, 1857, in Zachariah Chandler Papers, 1854–1879, Reel 1, Michigan Historical Collections, Bentley Historical Library, University of Michigan, Ann Arbor; Streeter, *Political Parties in Michigan*, p. 263.

58. *Detroit Free Press*, January 14, 18, and 30, 1857.

59. Ibid., February 15, 1857; Bellows, ""Politics and Michigan Fiscal Policy," p. 38; Streeter, *Political Parties in Michigan*, pp. 262–63. It should also be noted that state indebtedness (though constitutionally limited to $50,000) also increased by 20 percent between 1857 and 1860 due to the effects of deflation.

60. *Detroit Free Press*, January 20, 1857.

61. Formisano, *Birth of Mass Political Parties*, pp. 272, 303–4; John F. Reynolds, "Piety and Politics: Evangelism in the Michigan Legislature, 1837–1861," *Michigan History* 61 (1977): 333; William Seyfferdt to his parents, undated, quoted in Streeter, *Political Parties in Michigan*, pp. 176–77. Also see *Detroit Free Press*, February 18, 1857.

62. *Port Huron Observer*, undated, quoted in *Detroit Free Press*, May 2, 1857; *Kalamazoo Gazette*, October 17, 1857; Elizabeth E. Stuart to her son, May 28, 1857, in Stuart Mackay-Smith Marlatt, ed., *Stuart Letters of Robert and Elizabeth Sullivan Stuart and Their Children, 1819–1864*, vol. 2 (privately printed, 1961), p. 794; *Grand Rapids Enquirer and Herald*, October 9, 1857; *Detroit Advertiser*, October 20 and 21, 1857. The best account of the panic of 1857 in Michigan is Streeter, *Political Parties in Michigan*, pp. 257–61.

63. *Detroit Advertiser*, August 29 and October 6, 1857. For mention of Kansas see, *Detroit Advertiser*, September 11, 26, and 28 and October 1 and 5, 1857.

64. *Detroit Free Press*, September 14, November 21, 1857, and January 13, 1858; Streeter, *Political Parties in Michigan*, p. 264.

65. *Grand Rapids Enquirer and Herald* quoted in *Grand Rapids Eagle*, December 2, 1857; *Ann Arbor Michigan Argus*, December 11, 1857; speech of Sen. Charles E. Stuart quoted in Anne McCain, "Charles Edward Stuart of Kalamazoo," *Michigan History* 44 (September 1960): 332; *Cass County National Democrat* quoted in *Detroit Advertiser*, December 28, 1857.

66. Numerous examples of Democratic criticism of the Bingham administration can be cited for the early months of 1858. For example, see *Detroit Free Press*, January 13 and 16, 1858; *Grand Rapids Enquirer and Herald*, January 22 and February 3 and 6,

1858. For later examples, see *Detroit Free Press,* September 1 and 3 and October 21, 1858. *Detroit Free Press,* May 1, 1858; Streeter, *Political Parties in Michigan,* pp. 278–79. Despite the Democratic Party's hope, the English Bill did not please every Michigan Democrat. In a letter to former senator Alpheus Felch, one disgruntled Port Huron Democrat wrote, "I happen to be *one* of the firmest anti-Lecompton men in this section and one of the *few* who do not accept the English amendment as a *fair* settlement—or in fact, as any settlement of the Kansas difficulties." H. P. Vrooman to Alpheus Felch, August 27, 1858, Box 2, "1857–58," Felch Papers.

67. "Joint Resolution of the Michigan Legislature" quoted in Streeter, *Political Parties in Michigan,* pp. 273–74. Speech of Zachariah Chandler of March 12, 1858, quoted in Wilmer C. Harris, *Public Life of Zachariah Chandler, 1851–1875* (Lansing: Michigan Historical Commission, 1917), p. 45; *Marshall Statesman,* March 11, 1858; *Detroit Advertiser,* August 20, 1858. Attorney General Jacob M. Howard, a man who seemed to appeal to all of the party's disparate factions, was the only incumbent renominated by the convention.

68. H. P. Vrooman to Alpheus Felch, July 15, 1858, Box 2, "1857–58," Felch Papers; *Jackson Patriot,* undated, quoted in *Detroit Advertiser,* August 6, 1858.

69. *Detroit Free Press,* September 3 and 14, 1858.

70. Streeter, *Political Parties in Michigan,* pp. 267–68.

71. The traditional interpretation is best represented by Streeter, *Political Parties in Michigan,* p. 254. *Detroit Free Press,* November 11, 1858; *Detroit Advertiser,* November 4 and 5, 1858.

72. Formisano, *Birth of Mass Political Parties,* p. 284; Daniel Arnold to Nathan Pierce, January 14, 1859, "Papers, 1851–1862," Box 1, Nathan Pierce Papers, 1790–1862, Michigan Historical Collections, Bentley Historical Library, University of Michigan, Ann Arbor.

73. *Lansing State Republican,* December 7, 1858; *Detroit Free Press,* March 22–27, 1859. Although testimony revealed that both sides in the disputed election used strong-arm tactics, Howard was awarded the seat by the Republican-controlled Congress. See Bigelow, "Political Services of William Alanson Howard," p. 13; "Message of Moses Wisner to the Legislature of the State of Michigan," January 5, 1859, in Fuller, ed., *Messages of Governors,* vol. 2, p. 363.

74. *Detroit Free Press,* January 11, 1859; Formisano, *Birth of Mass Political Parties,* p. 286.

75. Formisano, *Birth of Mass Political Parties,* p. 300.

76. A. H. Morrison to Charles May, May 20, 1858, "1856–1859," Charles S. May Papers; *Detroit Free Press,* January 11, 1859.

77. Seavoy, "Borrowed Laws," p. 67.

78. Zachariah Chandler to John Clark, December 18, 1858, Reel 1, Chandler Papers; *Detroit Free Press,* February 8, 1859; Joseph R. Williams to Charles May, November 12, 1858, "Letters from Joseph R. Williams, 1853–1861," May Papers; Daniel Arnold to Nathan Pierce, January 14, 1859, "Papers, 1851–1862," Box 1, Pierce Papers. In

furtherance of the goal of agitating the Free-Soil issue, the state legislature, prodded by fears that the Supreme Court's *Dred Scott* decision might result in Michigan becoming a slave state, even debated a bill to outlaw slavery in the state.

CHAPTER 6

The quotation in this chapter's heading is from *Ann Arbor Michigan Argus*, April 19, 1861.

1. Perhaps the best account of the destruction of the Second American Party system and its subsequent realignment is Michael F. Holt, *The Political Crisis of the 1850's* (New York: W.W. Norton, 1978). Although I do not agree with the author's complete reliance upon ethnocultural factors in restructuring Michigan's antebellum party system, the best description of antebellum Michigan politics remains Ronald P. Formisano, *The Birth of Mass Political Parties: Michigan 1827–1861* (Princeton, N.J.: Princeton University Press, 1971).

2. For good descriptions of Democratic ideology, see Jean H. Baker, *Affairs of Party: The Political Culture of Northern Democrats in the Mid-Nineteenth Century* (Ithaca, N.Y.: Cornell University Press, 1984); Formisano, *Mass Political Parties;* and Joel H. Silbey, *The Shrine of Party: Congressional Voting Behavior, 1841–1852* (Pittsburgh, Pa.: University of Pittsburgh Press, 1967).

3. On Republican Party ideology, see Eric Foner, *Free Soil, Free Labor, Free Men: The Ideology of the Republican Party before the Civil War* (New York: Oxford University Press, 1970); William E. Gienapp, *The Origins of the Republican Party, 1852–1856* (New York: Oxford University Press, 1987); and Holt, *Political Crisis of the 1850s,* pp. 184–213.

4. *Detroit Free Press,* March 2, 1860.

5. Republicans pointed to Douglas's opposition to the admission of Kansas to the Union under the proslavery Lecompton constitution and to his so-called Freeport Doctrine as evidence of his proclivities against slavery's extension. *Detroit Advertiser,* April 24, 1860. An excellent account of the Democratic split of 1860 can be found in Roy F. Nichols, *The Disruption of American Democracy* (New York: MacMillan, 1948).

6. For evidence of the strong Democratic approval of Douglas in Michigan, see *Detroit Free Press,* April 8, 1860; William D. Phillips to Alpheus Felch, March 29, 1860, Alpheus Felch Papers, "Correspondence 1860–1870," Michigan Historical Collections, Bentley Historical Library, University of Michigan, Ann Arbor; and L. M. Johnson to Alpheus Felch, Felch Papers, "Correspondence 1860–1870." After the Charleston debacle, the *Free Press* went out of its way to prove that Douglas still appealed to southerners, quoting extensively from southern newspapers that were favorable to his candidacy. See *Detroit Free Press,* May 13 and 20 and June 26, 1860.

7. *Detroit Advertiser,* May 1 and 5, 1860. For further proof of this sentiment ,see letter of Jacob M. Howard in the *Detroit Advertiser,* April 28, 1860.

8. Jacob M. Howard to R. Hosmer, quoted in Harriette M. Dilla, *Politics of Michigan, 1865–1878* (New York: Columbia University Press, 1912), p. 22. For additional expressions of Michigan Republicans' support for Seward, see *Detroit Advertiser,* April

11, 1860, and "Resolutions of the Wayne County Republican Convention" in *Detroit Advertiser,* April 13, 1860. The republican image of the statesman was both a commonly held conception in the contemporary political culture, regardless of party, and a useful political image. The nation's interest required the election of statesmen and the defeat of politicians. Examples of this image are too numerous to note. For illustrations from the preelection period of 1860, see *Detroit Advertiser,* April 11, 1860, and Henry H. Crapo to William W. Crapo, April 5 and April 20, 1860, Henry H. Crapo Papers, Box 2, Michigan Historical Collections, Bentley Historical Library, University of Michigan, Ann Arbor.

9. *Detroit Free Press,* March 2, 1860; *Detroit Advertiser,* May 21, 1860. For additional commentary on Seward's defeat and Michigan Republicans' disappointment, see George M. Tuthill Diary, May 19, 1860, Michigan Historical Collections, Bentley Historical Library, University of Michigan, Ann Arbor. *Lansing State Republican,* May 23, 1860; *Detroit Advertiser,* May 19 and June 8, 1860.

10. *Detroit Free Press,* May 19, 1860; Robert McClelland to J. D. B. DeBow, July 22, 1860, Robert McClelland Letterbook, Box 2, Burton Historical Collection, Detroit Public Library, Detroit, Mich.

11. As early as July 1860, young Republicans organized a Detroit band of "wide awakes," with differing ranks and uniforms worn by each member. Such groups reinforced party loyalty and infused members with a sense of serving as soldiers in the cause (both the party's and the nation's) and as champions of truth. This explains the importance of the torch in "wide awake" activities, symbolizing the party's enlightened and unblemished principles. Marching under banners proclaiming "We Are Republicans Because We Think for Ourselves," wide awakes took part in parades and political events throughout the months preceding the election. Michigan Democrats organized their own such associations, forming a Young Men's Douglas Club in Detroit and constructing a Democratic Club House. Local ward assemblies sponsored pole raisings, culminating in the unfurling of partisan banners emblazoned with party symbols: Douglas, the American eagle, and the motto "Union." For party supporters, the pole represented the strength of the party, its ascendant political position, and its unbending devotion to party principles. The banner's intent was obvious—to reinforce the vital psychological link between the election of Douglas and the survival of the American Republic. On Republican activities, see *Detroit Advertiser,* July 2 and September 5, 1860, and George M. Tuthill Diary, August 11, 14 and September 4, 1860. For Democratic campaigning, see *Detroit Free Press,* July 22 and 29, 1860. A fine analysis of the symbolism incorporated into the pole-raising ceremony is found in Baker, *Affairs of Party,* pp. 297–98.

12. Lincoln received 88,481 votes in Michigan, or 57 percent of those cast. Douglas managed only 65,057, or 42 percent. The remaining two candidates (Breckinridge and John Bell) obtained a total of 1,220 votes (Breckinridge–805, Bell–415). In addition, all four of the state's congressional seats went to Republicans, with margins of victory ranging from a high of 20 percent to a low of 5.5 percent. In the race for the governorship, Austin Blair garnered 87,780 votes, or nearly 57 percent, while

his opponent, John Barry, tallied only 67,053, or 43 percent. In the city of Detroit, Lincoln received 4,407 votes to Douglas's 3,893. Bell obtained 118 and Breckinridge 65. In the race for governor, Austin Blair tallied 4,406 votes to Barry's 4,046. In the state house of representatives, Republicans captured a hundred seats to the Democrats' twenty-five. In the state senate, Republicans dominated as well, holding thirty seats compared to only two for state Democrats. See Congressional Quarterly, Inc., *Congressional Quarterly's Guide to U.S. Elections*, 2nd ed. (Washington, D.C.: Congressional Quarterly, 1985); *Detroit Free Press*, November 14, 1860; Dilla, *Politics of Michigan*, p. 27; and *Detroit Free Press*, November 10, 1860. My understanding of the strength of party systems has been shaped by Richard Hofstadter, *The Idea of a Party System: The Rise of Legitimate Opposition in the United States, 1780–1840* (Berkeley: University of California Press, 1972) and Holt, *Political Crisis*.

13. *Detroit Free Press*, November 13 and 16, 1860; Robert McClelland to Alexander Stephens, November 21, 1860, McClelland Letterbook, Box 2.

14. Robert McClelland to J. S. Wilson, November 12, 1860, McClelland Letterbook, Box 2; *Detroit Free Press*, November 19 and December 1, 1860.

15. For an example of Republican misunderstanding of secessionist sentiment, see *Lansing State Republican*, November 7, 1860; Zachariah Chandler to Austin Blair, December 19, 1860, Austin Blair Papers, 1860, "Correspondence A–C," Burton Historical Collection, Detroit Public Library, Detroit, Mich.; Henry H. Crapo to William Crapo, November 25, 1860, Crapo Papers, Box 2.

16. Letter of Henry Waldron quoted in Wilmer C. Harris, *Public Life of Zachariah Chandler, 1851–1875* (Lansing: Michigan Historical Commission, 1917), p. 53; Petition 1861 Concerning Crittenden Amendment, Rice Abner Beal Papers, Box 1, Michigan Historical Collections, Bentley Historical Library, University of Michigan, Ann Arbor; Zachariah Chandler to Austin Blair, February 11, 1861, Blair Papers, 1861 "Correspondence A–C." For further proof of the feared impact of compromise on the Republican Party, see Fernando C. Beaman to Henry Waldron, January 21, 1861, quoted in Sister Mary K. George, *Zachariah Chandler: A Political Biography* (East Lansing: Michigan State University Press, 1969), p. 34.

17. *Ann Arbor Journal*, January 23, 1861, quoted in George S. May, "Ann Arbor and the Coming of the Civil War," *Michigan History* 36 (September 1952): 246; J. J. Skeirritt to Austin Blair, December 20, 1860, Blair Papers, 1860 "Correspondence S."

18. *Detroit Free Press*, April 11, 1861; Robert McClelland to Jefferson Davis, December 14, 1860, McClelland Letterbook, Box 2; Robert McClelland to Moses Kelly, February 1, 1861, McClelland Letterbook, Box 2.

19. George Tuthill Diary, March 4, 1861; *Ann Arbor Journal*, March 6, 1861, quoted in May, "Ann Arbor and the Civil War," p. 247.

20. *Detroit Free Press*, March 7 and 8, 1861; Robert McClelland to Robert Pritchette, March 19, 1861, McClelland Letterbook, Box 2.

21. For evidence of the confusion reigning within both parties as to the proper course for Lincoln to pursue in regard to Fort Sumter, see *Ann Arbor Michigan Argus*,

March 22, 1861, quoted in May, "Ann Arbor and the Civil War," p. 248; *Detroit Free Press,* March 14, 1861; *Lansing State Republican,* March 27, 1861.

22. My use of the term *partisan* simply refers to a firm adherent to a political party and its ideology. Republicanism, for mid-nineteenth-century American northern males, is best described as an overriding belief in a harmony of interests throughout the nation. Citizens were to act for the good of the community without greed or selfishness. Fear of power, especially governmental power, in the form of tyranny or anarchy, dominated republican thought, as power impeded the liberties of citizens and disrupted equality of opportunity. Hence, contemporaries viewed political parties in contradictory ways: in the negative sense of an organized group of self-serving individuals and, increasingly common, as defenders from abuse of governmental power and protectors of individual liberties. My understanding of republican ideology is derived from a number of varied sources. Among the best for the nineteenth century are Baker, *Affairs of Party;* Steven Hahn, *The Roots of Southern Populism: Yeomen Farmers and the Transformation of the Georgia Upcountry, 1850–1890* (New York: Oxford University Press, 1983); Holt, *Political Crisis of the 1850's;* and J. Mills Thornton III, *Politics and Power in a Slave Society: Alabama, 1800–1860* (Baton Rouge: Louisiana State University Press, 1978).

23. Jacob M. Howard to Austin Blair, April 20, 1861, Jacob M. Howard Letterbook 1861, Burton Historical Collection, Detroit Public Library, Detroit, Mich.; Henry H. Crapo to William W. Crapo, April 25, 1861, Crapo Papers, Box 3.

24. Robert McClelland to W. Murphy, May 5, 1861, McClelland Letterbook, Box 2; *Detroit Free Press,* April 14 and 16, 1861.

25. *Ann Arbor Michigan Argus,* April 19, 1861; *Detroit Free Press,* April 19 and 24, 1861.

26. I refer to Michigan as a Radical Republican state for the following reasons: the state's loyal support of Seward in the 1860 Republican convention; the overwhelming vote for Lincoln in 1860 (Lincoln achieved a larger margin of victory in Michigan than in any other Midwestern state with the exception of Minnesota); and the political character of the state's elected officials—newly elected Governor Blair was a borderline Radical, as was Sen. Kinsley S. Bingham, and Sen. Zachariah Chandler was unquestionably radical, as was Bingham's replacement, Jacob M. Howard. Furthermore, Michigan's approach to the secession crisis speaks to the appeal of hard-line Republicanism in the state. Formisano, *Mass Political Parties,* p. 264; Foner, *Free Soil, Free Labor,* pp. 103–48.

27. *Lansing State Republican,* April 19 and May 1, 1861.

28. Robert McClelland to W. W. Seaton, July 15, 1861, McClelland Letterbook, Box 2; Henry Ledyard to C. C. Trowbridge, June 6, 1861, Charles C. Trowbridge Letterbook 1860–1862, Burton Historical Collection, Detroit Public Library, Detroit, Mich.; *Lansing State Republican,* July 10, 1861.

29. *Detroit Tribune,* April 15, 1861; *Detroit Free Press,* April 15 and June 7, 1861. The June 7 issue of the paper triumphantly announced the law's defeat.

30. Robert McClelland to W. Shauley [?], July 23, 1861, McClelland Letterbook, Box 2; for examples, see *Lansing State Republican,* July 24, 1861, and George Tuthill Diary, July 28, 1861; *Detroit Free Press,* July 21 and August 1, 1861.

31. *Lansing State Republican,* July 10, 1861; *Detroit Advertiser,* July 22, 1861.

32. *Detroit Tribune,* undated, quoted in Frank L. Klement, "The Hopkins Hoax and Golden Circle Rumors in Michigan: 1861–1862," *Michigan History* 47 (March 1963): 4. James McPherson contended that the Knights of the Golden Circle, an organization begun in 1850 to promote "southern" interests in the Caribbean, began to fade in the North in 1863 after it was linked to Confederate attempts to subvert the northern war effort. This linkage is the key to understanding the mind-set of Michigan Republicans who had never acknowledged the Democratic Party's legitimacy as a loyal opposition. See James M. McPherson, *Battle Cry of Freedom: The Civil War Era* (New York: Oxford University Press, 1988), pp. 599 and 762–63. Historians have often viewed Republican accusations of disloyalty as merely an electoral ploy. I would argue, however, that charges of disloyalty were genuinely believed. Bull Run proved to the North that the war was not to be won quickly and that final victory would require great effort and sacrifice. Thus, continued partisan rivalry and attacks upon the Lincoln administration intensified Republican suspicions of Democratic motives. Naturally, accusations of disloyalty most often accompanied election campaigns, as it was during these periods that Democratic criticism of the Republicans was most common. The campaigns, however, were the occasion, not the cause, of the accusations.

33. *Detroit Free Press,* October 3, 1861; *Detroit Advertiser,* October 8, 1861; *Detroit Free Press,* October 9 and 19, 1861.

34. *Detroit Free Press,* October 20 and 23, 1861.

35. *Detroit Advertiser,* October 21, 1861; *Detroit Free Press,* November 6 and 7, 1861. Detroit Democrats garnered a total of 679 more votes than did their opponents. *Detroit Advertiser,* November 7, 1861.

36. Robert McClelland to John Tull, November 16, 1861, McClelland Letterbook, Box 2.

37. Robert McClelland to Franklin Pierce, January 15, 1862, McClelland Letterbook, Box 2; Robert McClelland to Thomas Blackwell, January 7, 1862, McClelland Letterbook, Box 2.

38. *Detroit Free Press,* March 5, 1862; speech of Flavius Littlejohn given at the Democratic state convention in Detroit, March 5, 1862, Flavius Littlejohn Papers, Michigan Historical Collections, Bentley Historical Library, University of Michigan, Ann Arbor.

39. *Detroit Free Press,* March 6, 1862. A set of draft resolutions is located in "Correspondence 1862," Box 2, Robert McClelland Papers. These resolutions differ little from those printed in the *Free Press.* Robert McClelland to Robert Pritchette, April 1 and 12, 1862, McClelland Letterbook, Box 2.

40. *Ann Arbor Michigan State News,* March 4, 1862, quoted in George S. May, "Politics in Ann Arbor during the Civil War," *Michigan History* 37 (March 1953): 56; Circular from the Republican State Central Committee, March 22, 1862, quoted in May, "Politics in Ann Arbor," p. 57; *Detroit Tribune,* March 18, 1862. Although disagreeing with the author's contention that charges of disloyalty were used simply for political

gain, I would still consider the following work to be a good account of the Golden Circle scare: Frank L. Klement, "The Hopkins Hoax and Golden Circle Rumors in Michigan: 1861–1862," *Michigan History* 47 (March 1963): 1–14. For further information on alleged Knights of the Golden Circle activities, see *Lansing State Republican*, April 4, 1862; *Detroit Tribune*, March 29, April 3 and 12, 1862; and *Detroit Advertiser*, April 1, 1862; *Lansing State Republican*, April 2, 1862.

41. *Detroit Free Press*, June 18 and July 30, 1862.

42. H. P. Baldwin to James F. Joy, July 14, 1862, James F. Joy Papers, 1700–1869, "Correspondence 1862 January–July," Burton Historical Collection, Detroit Public Library, Detroit, Mich.; Henry H. Crapo to William W. Crapo, July 18, 1862, Crapo Papers, Box 3.

43. Robert McClelland to L. Peabody, September 15, 1862, McClelland Letterbook, Box 2. Interestingly, Michigan's Union movement of 1862 was initiated by Democrats. For the Midwest, this situation was unique. All of the other states in the region also ran Union tickets that year; however, these parties had been assembled under Republican auspices. *Detroit Free Press*, September 28, 1862; Robert McClelland to J. Kennedy, November 17, 1862, McClelland Letterbook, Box 2.

44. *Ann Arbor Michigan Journal*, September 10, 1862, quoted in May, "Politics in Ann Arbor," p. 59; Henry H. Crapo to William W. Crapo, November 10, 1862, Crapo Papers, Box 3; *Ann Arbor Michigan State News*, September 9, 1862, quoted in May, "Politics in Ann Arbor," p. 58.

45. *Lansing State Republican*, October 1, 1862. See also *Detroit Advertiser and Tribune*, September 24, 1862.

46. Paul A. Randall, "Gubernatorial Platforms for the Political Parties of Michigan 1834–1864" (master's thesis, Wayne State University, 1937), p. 145.

47. *Ann Arbor Michigan Journal*, October 1, 1862, quoted in May, "Politics in Ann Arbor," p. 59; Robert McClelland to Joseph Miller, October 6, 1862, McClelland Letterbook, Box 2; Randall, "Gubernatorial Platforms," p. 148.

48. Circular of the Republican State Central Committee, October 3, 1862, Crapo Papers, Box 5. For an expression of similar sentiment, see *Detroit Advertiser and Tribune*, October 29, 1862.

49. *Detroit Free Press*, October 12 and November 2, 1862. Because of constant references to Chandler's "bloodletting" letter and others like it, most historians of Michigan's 1862 election have perceived Chandler's reelection to the Senate as the primary issue of the campaign. Although Chandler did have many political enemies, especially in outstate Michigan, I am convinced that the issue was not Chandler himself but rather what he stood for: radicalism. See Harris, *Public Life*, and George, *Chandler; Detroit Free Press*, November 3, 1862.

50. Republican Austin Blair was reelected to the governorship. He received 68,716 votes, or 52.5 percent, to his opponent Byron Stout's 62,102, or 47.5 percent. The total number of votes cast, 130,818, was 15 percent lower than the number cast in 1860. Blair's vote total was 23,940 lower than it had been four years before, for a loss

of 22 percent. Stout received 4,951 fewer votes than his Democratic counterpart, John Barry, in 1860, for a loss of 7 percent. In the congressional races, Michigan elected five Republicans and one Democrat. The margins of victory for the Republicans ranged from a high of 16 percent to a low of .8 percent. The Democratic-Union margin of victory in the Fifth Congressional District was also .8 percent. In Detroit, the Democratic majority increased from 679 in 1861 to 775 in 1862. In the state legislature, Republicans maintained 63 seats in the House, down from 100 in 1860, while the Democrat-Unionists held 37 seats, up 25 from 1860. In the state senate, Republicans held 18 seats, down from 30 in 1860, to the Democrats' 14, up from 2 in 1860. See *Congressional Quarterly, U.S. Elections*, pp. 509 and 776; *Detroit Advertiser and Tribune*, November 6, 1862, and Dilla, *Politics of Michigan*, p. 27. *Detroit Free Press*, November 8, 1862; *Congressional Quarterly, U.S. Elections*, p. 117.

 51. Zachariah Chandler to Charles T. Gorham, November 9, 1862, quoted in Harris, *Political Life*, p. 67; *Detroit Advertiser and Tribune*, November 5 and 8, 1862.

 52. *Lansing State Republican*, December 3, 1862; A. T. Hall to James F. Joy, December 20, 1862, Joy Papers, 1862 "Correspondence July–December"; Junius Hatch to James F. Joy, January 17, 1863, "1862–63," Box 16, James F. Joy Papers [Burton], 1834–1900, Michigan Historical Collections, Bentley Historical Library, University of Michigan, Ann Arbor. For other examples of this antiradical sentiment, see Joseph E. Beebe to Sons, January 1, 1862, Joseph Beebe Papers, Michigan Historical Collections, Bentley Historical Library, University of Michigan, Ann Arbor, and E. S. Moore to James F. Joy, January 15, 1863, Joy Papers, 1863, "Correspondence January–June." It is interesting to note that, although the total number of letters of support for Joy's candidacy in either set of the Joy collections is very small, most of these came from the southwestern part of the state. Possibly, this area's conservatism derives from the composition of its population. Unlike the vast majority of the state, which was settled by emigrants from New York and New England, this region was populated by settlers from Ohio and Indiana, states that remained much more conservative during the war. "Address to the Legislature," pamphlet by James F. Joy, printed in full in the *Detroit Free Press*, January 10, 1863.

 53. On the 1863 Senate race and the Detroit Regency, see George, *Chandler*, and Harris, *Political Life*, pp. 63–69. I have been unable to locate any good information on the Detroit Regency, but the power it wielded in the state Republican organization was immense. Both of Michigan's senators, Chandler and Jacob Howard, were from Detroit, as was the head of the Republican State Central Committee, William Howard. It is likely that the Regency was radical in politics. Democrats occasionally alluded to the rivalry between the Regency and outstate Republicans, but they did little to take advantage of this animosity. Most likely, there was little Democrats could have hoped to achieve in an alliance with outstate Republicans anyway, as these individuals also tended to be radical or at least moderate. For example, see Martin D. Lewis, *Lumberman from Flint: The Michigan Career of Henry H. Crapo, 1855–1869* (Detroit, Mich.: Wayne State University Press, 1958), pp. 141–76. Zachariah Chandler to his wife, February 22,

1863, Reel 1, Zachariah Chandler Papers, 1854–1879, Michigan Historical Collections, Bentley Historical Library, University of Michigan, Ann Arbor. On the senatorial vote in the state legislature, see Harris, *Public Life*, p. 69, and Henry H. Crapo to William W. Crapo, January 9, 1863, Crapo Papers, Box 3.

54. Willis F. Dunbar, *Michigan: A History of the Wolverine State* (Grand Rapids, Mich.: William B. Eerdmans, 1970), p. 388.

55. Idem, *All Aboard! A History of Railroads in Michigan* (Grand Rapids, Mich.: William B. Eerdmans, 1969), p. 130; Lewis, *Lumberman from Flint*, pp. 142–44.

56. Benjamin W. Bellows, "Politics and Michigan Fiscal Policy, 1837–1865" (honors thesis, University of Michigan, 1996), pp. 53–64.

57. *Detroit Free Press*, January 14, 1863; a detailed account of the convention can be found in John J. Prichett, "Michigan Democracy in the Civil War," *Michigan History* 11 (January 1927): 92–110.

58. *Lansing State Republican*, February 11 and March 4 and 25, 1863; Zachariah Chandler to his Wife, February 22, 1863, quoted in George, *Chandler*, p. 100.

59. *Ann Arbor Michigan Argus*, May, 27, 1864.

60. Elihu Pond Diary, June 6, 1864, Pond Family Papers, Box 7, Michigan Historical Collections, Bentley Historical Library, University of Michigan, Ann Arbor; *Lansing State Republican*, June 8, 1864.

61. *Lansing State Republican*, June 15, 1864; Pond Diary, June 9, 1864, Pond Family Papers, Box 7.

62. Crapo's handling of the railroad aid issue in the 1864 special session is alleged to have garnered the attention of state Republicans and to have resulted in his nomination as governor later that year. See Lewis, *Lumberman from Flint*, p. 144. Randall, "Gubernatorial Platforms," p. 151; *Bay City Press and Times*, July [?], 1864, Crapo Papers, Box 5, also see *Cass County Republican*, June 9, 1864, Crapo Papers, Box 5.

63. Joel H. Silbey, *A Respectable Minority: The Democratic Party in the Civil War Era, 1860–1868* (New York: W. W. Norton, 1977). I would speculate that Michigan's legitimist approach to Democratic politics derived from two sources. First, Michigan, unlike the areas of strongest purist influence (the southern parts of Ohio, Indiana, and Illinois), was settled by New Yorkers and people from New England, while purist regions tended to be settled by southerners, who would understandably have closer ties to the Confederacy. Second, Michigan Democrats may have been motivated by the need to cooperate with conservative Republicans in order to mount any type of successful challenge to the state's strong Republican Party.

64. "The Platforms," 1864, Crapo Papers, Box 5; George B. McClellan, letter of acceptance to Chicago convention, quoted in James B. McPherson, *Ordeal by Fire: The Civil War and Reconstruction* (New York: Alfred A. Knopf, 1982), p. 441; Pond Diary, August 31, 1864, Pond Family Papers, Box 7.

65. McPherson, *Ordeal by Fire*, p. 441.

66. *Jonesville Independent*, October 27, 1864, Crapo Papers, Box 5; *Flint Wolverine Citizen*, October [?], 1864, Crapo Papers, Box 5.

67. "Papers Concerning Campaign, 1864," Crapo Papers, Box 5.

68. *Detroit Free Press,* November 7 and 8, 1864; Baker, *Affairs of Party,* pp. 212–58.

69. Lincoln received 91,133 votes in Michigan, or 55 percent of the ballots cast. McClellan received 74,146, or 45 percent. The total vote was 165,279, 6 percent larger than that in 1860. Lincoln's vote increased 3 percent over his 1860 total, while McClellan's vote total was 12 percent higher than Douglas's in 1860. In the governor's race, Henry Crapo was elected with a total of 91,353, or 55 percent, to William Fenton's 74,293, or 45 percent. All six representatives elected to congress were National Unionists, with the largest margin of victory being 20 percent and the smallest 3 percent. See Congressional Quarterly, *U.S. Elections,* pp. 336, 509, and 769; Pond Diary, November 9, 1864, Pond Family Papers, Box 7; *Detroit Free Press,* November 10, 1864.

70. *Lansing State Republican,* November 16, 1864; John L. Marble to C. S. Beal, November 18, 1864, Rice A. Beal Papers, Michigan Historical Collections, Bentley Historical Library, University of Michigan, Ann Arbor.

71. Dilla, *Politics of Michigan,* p. 40. James McPherson pointed out that, although most Democrats objected to the passage of the Thirteenth Amendment, a small number had, by 1865, come to recognize the inevitability of such a measure and thus strove to distance their party from its ties to slavery. It may be that Michigan's Democrats, who for so long (longer than any other state Democratic Party) had butted heads with antislavery sentiment in the guise of the Republican Party, chose this point in time to shift to new ground. At the very least, it can be said that even if most Michigan Democrats opposed the Thirteenth Amendment, the fact that it was approved via constitutional means left them little choice (given their party's belief in strict adherence to the Constitution) other than to accept emancipation as the law of the land. McPherson, *Battle Cry of Freedom,* p. 839.

72. *Detroit Free Press,* April 10, 1865; Silas Hawley to Henry H. Crapo, February 4, 1865, Crapo Papers, Box 3.

73. Pond Diary, April 16, 1865, Pond Family Papers, Box 7; Jeremy W. Kilar, "Andrew Johnson 'Swings' through Michigan: Community Response to a Presidential Crusade," *The Old Northwest* 3 (September 1977): 252; *Lansing State Republican,* April 19 and May 31, 1865.

74. McPherson, *Ordeal by Fire,* p. 498; Pond Diary, May 30, 1865, Pond Family Papers, Box 7; *Detroit Free Press,* May 29, 1865.

75. *Detroit Advertiser and Tribune,* June 6, 1865; see also *Lansing State Republican,* June 7, 1865; Zachariah Chandler's speech at Detroit, June 12, 1865, quoted in Dilla, *Politics of Michigan,* pp. 45–46.

76. Pond Diary, June 1, 1866, Pond Family Papers, Box 7; *Detroit Free Press,* June 14 and 20, 1865.

77. On Andrew Johnson's plan of Reconstruction, see Dan T. Carter, *When the War Was Over: The Failure of Self-Reconstruction in the South, 1865–1867* (Baton Rouge: Louisiana State University Press, 1985); Eric Foner, *Reconstruction: America's Unfinished Revolution, 1863–1877* (New York: Harper & Row, 1988), pp. 176–227; Eric L. McKitrick,

Andrew Johnson and Reconstruction (Chicago: University of Chicago Press, 1960); McPherson, *Ordeal by Fire*, pp. 493–512; and Michael Perman, *Emancipation and Reconstruction, 1862–1879* (Arlington Heights, Ill.: Harlan Davidson, 1987), pp. 30–38. Northerners, of course, did not comprehend that in the southern mind, men such as Alexander Stephens and Jefferson Davis were Unionists. That is, they were men that remained loyal to the United States until their states seceded from the Union. Out and out Union men, the type of individuals that the North expected to be elected to office, were very few in the South and were considered traitors to their states. Thus, by electing men such as Stephens to office, southerners were really attempting to placate northerners and not to inflame them.

78. Speech of Jacob M. Howard, delivered at Lansing, Michigan, November 24, 1865, quoted in Dilla, *Politics in Michigan*, p. 48.

79. *Detroit Advertiser and Tribune,* December 6, 1865; *Detroit Free Press,* December 6 and 7, 1865.

80. Charles T. Gorham to John W. Longyear, February 16, 1866, "Correspondence, Feb 14–23, 1866," Box 1, John W. Longyear Papers, 1846–1875, Michigan Historical Collections, Bentley Historical Library, University of Michigan, Ann Arbor; Ephraim Longyear to John W. Longyear, February 16, 1866, "Correspondence, Feb 14–23, 1866," Box 1, Longyear Papers.

81. *Detroit Free Press,* February 21 and March 26, 1866.

82. F. G. Russell to John W. Longyear, February 24, 1866, "Correspondence, Feb 24–29, 1866," Box 1, Longyear Papers; *Lansing State Republican,* March 28, 1866. For similar expressions, see Hulbert S. Shank to John W. Longyear, February 26, 1866, "Correspondence, Feb 24–29;" and S. W. Fowler to John W. Longyear, "Correspondence, Mar 1–15, 1866," Box 1, Longyear Papers; *White Pigeon Republican,* February 12, 1866; *Detroit Advertiser and Tribune,* April 11, 1866. For a lucid discussion of the political ramifications of Johnson's vetoes on the various wings of the Republican Party, see Kenneth M. Stampp, *The Era of Reconstruction* (New York: Vintage Books, 1965), pp. 83–118. *Flint Wolverine Citizen,* February 24, 1866, quoted in Jeremy W. Kilar, "'The Blood-Rugged Issue Is Impeachment or Anarchy.' Michigan and the Impeachment of Andrew Johnson," *The Old Northwest* 6 (Fall 1980): 248.

83. For examples of such an interpretation, see Lawanda and John H. Cox, *Politics, Principle, and Prejudice, 1865–1866: Dilemma of Reconstruction America* (London: Free Press of Glencoe Collier-MacMillan, 1963); McKitrick, *Andrew Johnson and Reconstruction;* and Austin Blair to Charles S. May, May 12, 1866, "1860–1869," Charles S. May Papers, 1830–1901, Michigan Historical Collections, Bentley Historical Library, University of Michigan, Ann Arbor. Both Blair and May would become disillusioned by the Republican Party in the early 1870s and join the so-called liberal disaffection from the party.

84. *Lansing State Republican,* April 4, 1866; *Grand Rapids Daily Eagle,* July 1, 1866; Sullivan M. Cutcheon to John W. Longyear, March 16, 1866, "Correspondence, Mar 16–20, 1866, Box 1, Longyear Papers. Also see *Detroit Daily Post,* March 17, 1866.

85. *Ann Arbor Michigan Argus,* April 13, 1866.

86. *Detroit Daily Post,* April 6, 1866, Crapo Papers, Box 5; *Detroit Free Press,* April 9, 1866.

87. *Detroit Daily Post,* April 6, 1866, Crapo Papers, Box 5; see also *Detroit Advertiser and Tribune,* April 7, 1866.

88. *Detroit Advertiser and Tribune,* May 1, 1866; David M. Bagley to John W. Longyear, May 2, 1866, "Correspondence, May 1–13, 1866," Box 1, Longyear Papers; *Detroit Free Press,* May 3, 1866.

89. *Detroit Free Press,* July 6, 1866; *Lansing State Republican,* July 18, 1866.

90. For a succinct discussion of the National Union movement, See McPherson, *Ordeal by Fire,* pp. 518–20. *Detroit Free Press,* August 1, 1866. James Joy, the Union candidate for the Senate in 1863, attended this conference, as did sitting Republican congressman John W. Longyear. *Detroit Free Press,* August 10 and 16, 1866; *White Pigeon Republican,* July 17, 1866; *Grand Rapids Weekly Eagle,* July 26, 1866; and *Pontiac Gazette,* July 13, 1866, quoted in *Detroit Advertiser and Tribune,* July 25, 1866.

91. Good examples of this attitude toward the Philadelphia convention are found in the *Lansing State Republican,* August 22, 1866, and *Detroit Advertiser and Tribune,* July 19, 1866. Accounts of the parties' conventions can be found in *Detroit Advertiser and Tribune,* August 31, 1866, and *Detroit Free Press,* September 6, 1866.

92. "Notes on Campaign 1866," Crapo Papers, Box 5; "Circular of the Republican State Central Committee," September 20, 1866, Crapo Papers, Box 5; see also speech of Henry Crapo in *Lansing State Republican,* September 5, 1866.

93. *Detroit Free Press,* November 5 and 6, 1866.

94. See Congressional Quarterly, *U.S. Elections,* pp. 509 and 772; Dilla, *Politics of Michigan,* pp. 68–72; Kilar, "Andrew Johnson 'Swings' through Michigan," pp 266–69.

95. *Macomb Monitor,* November 9, 1866.

CHAPTER 7

The quotation in this chapter's heading is from J. R. Kellogg to Henry H. Crapo, March 4, 1867, "Correspondence, March, 1867," Box 3, Henry H. Crapo Papers, 1830–1910, Michigan Historical Collections, Bentley Historical Library, University of Michigan, Ann Arbor.

1. An excellent discussion of the philosophical devotion to individual enterprise and personal experiences shared by many within the ranks of the antebellum and wartime Republican Party can be found in George M. Blackburn, "Michigan: Quickening Government in a Developing State," in James C. Mohr, ed., *Radical Republicans in the North: State Politics during Reconstruction* (Baltimore, Md.: Johns Hopkins University Press, 1976), pp. 121–22.

2. Larry Lankton, *Beyond the Boundaries: Life and Landscape at the Lake Superior Copper Mines, 1840–1875* (New York: Oxford University Press, 1997), p. 72; Richard H. Sewell, "Michigan Farmers and the Civil War," *Michigan History* 44 (December 1960): 355–58. Sewell also noted that the number of working oxen, which proved to be too

slow for the new agricultural implements, declined by 40 percent between 1860 and 1870 in the state. See also Joseph J. Marks, ed., *Effects of the Civil War on Farming in Michigan* (Lansing: Michigan Civil War Centennial Observance Commission, 1965). A more general discussion of the impact of the Civil War upon northern agriculture is Wayne D. Rasmussen, "The Civil War: A Catalyst of Agricultural Revolution," *Agricultural History* 39 (October 1965): 187–95.

3. Sewell, "Michigan Farmers," pp. 360–70. The tremendous growth in Michigan's agricultural output during the war years is even more noteworthy when compared to the experiences of other states in the Old Northwest. In Ohio and Wisconsin, for example, overall crop yields remained roughly equivalent to their prewar levels. Such a level of production is, of course, significant given the loss of manpower in these states. In Michigan, however, as previously noted, production of most crops nearly doubled despite similar losses in manpower. See Rasmussen, "The Civil War: A Catalyst of Agricultural Revolution," pp. 189–90.

4. Ibid., p. 360; Barbara E. Benson, *Logs and Lumber: The Development of the Lumber Industry in Michigan's Lower Peninsula, 1837–1870* (Mt. Pleasant, Mich.: Clarke Historical Library, Central Michigan University, 1989), pp. 144–66; Jeremy W. Kilar, *Michigan's Lumbertowns: Lumbermen and Laborers in Saginaw, Bay City, and Muskegon, 1870–1905* (Detroit: Wayne State University Press, 1990), p. 53; Milton M. Quaife and Sidney Glazer, *Michigan: From Primitive Wilderness to Industrial Commonwealth* (New York: Prentice-Hall, 1946), p. 219.

5. Willis F. Dunbar, *Michigan: A History of the Wolverine State* (Grand Rapids, Mich.: William B. Eerdmans, 1970), pp. 425 and 460; Alvah L. Sawyer, *A History of the Northern Peninsula of Michigan and Its People: Its Mining, Lumber and Agricultural Industries*, vol. 1 (Chicago: Lewis, 1911), pp. 280–82; Lankton, *Beyond the Boundaries*, p. 205.

6. JoEllen M. Vinyard, *The Irish on the Urban Frontier: Nineteenth Century Detroit* (New York: Arno Press, 1976), p. 127; Harriette M. Dilla, *Politics of Michigan, 1865–1878* (New York: Columbia University Press, 1912), p. 239. The figure for the state's 1860 manufacturing output can be found in Chapter 2. In 1864, the firm of R. G. Dunn and Company counted 5,934 business houses in the state, with an aggregate wealth of $83,943,000. *Detroit Advertiser and Tribune*, January, 9, 1865.

7. Bruce A. Rubenstein and Lawrence E. Ziewacz, *Michigan: A History of the Wolverine State*, 3rd ed. (Wheeling, Ill.: Harlan Davidson, 2002), pp. 116, 134–42; Dunbar, *Michigan*, pp. 426–29; Dilla, *Politics of Michigan*, pp. 237–38; Robert Conot, *American Odyssey* (Detroit, Mich.: Wayne State University Press, 1986), p. 77.

8. Conot, *American Odyssey*, p. 78; Quaife and Glazer, *Michigan*, pp. 258–59. The best accounts of the Detroit riot of 1863 are drawn from period newspapers. It is important to note that both the Democratic and Republican presses in the city blamed immigrants for much of the violence (the Democrats blamed the Germans—who voted Republican—and the Republicans the Irish—who voted Democratic). See *Detroit Free Press*, March 7, 1863, and *Detroit Advertiser and Tribune*, March 7, 1863.

9. Quaife and Glazer, *Michigan*, p. 243; Willis F. Dunbar, *All Aboard: A History of*

Railroads in Michigan (Grand Rapids, Mich.: William B. Eerdmans, 1969), pp. 129–30 and 139; *Detroit Daily Post,* March 23, 1867.

10. *Detroit Daily Post,* January 16 and February 13, 1867; *Detroit Advertiser and Tribune,* March 12, 1867; Martin D. Lewis, *Lumberman from Flint: The Michigan Career of Henry H. Crapo, 1855–1869* (Detroit, Mich.: Wayne State University Press, 1958), p. 213. Kalamazoo and Portage Townships were responsible for the $63,000 bond issue. Regarding the ambivalence of Michiganians toward the railroad in the postwar years, see Dunbar, *All Aboard,* p. 250.

11. Charles H. Mercer to Henry H. Crapo, January 15, 1867, "Correspondence, January, 1867," Box 3, Henry H. Crapo Papers, 1830–1910, Michigan Historical Collections, Bentley Historical Library, University of Michigan, Ann Arbor; J.R. Kellogg to Henry H. Crapo, March 4, 1867, "Correspondence, March 1867," Box 3, Crapo Papers. Similar concerns can be found in "Petition of the Citizens of Green Oak to Governor Crapo" [1867], "Correspondence, March, 1867," Box 3, Crapo Papers, and *Flint Wolverine Citizen,* March 30, 1867.

12. Governor Crapo's veto messages of February 5 and 25, 1867, quoted in Lewis, *Lumberman from Flint,* pp. 214 and 217; *Flint Wolverine Citizen,* April 27, 1867. Efforts to override the governor's vetoes failed (with the exception of the Kalamazoo and Portage bill). Crapo had signed a number of similar bills into law during the 1865 legislative session. When asked about his course of action, he explained that he had been "governed more by a deference to the practice of my predecessors, and the views of the then Legislature, than my own judgment. If I erred at that time, it was because I distrusted my own convictions too much to act in direct opposition to the opinions entertained by the majority of the Legislature." Quoted in Lewis, *Lumberman from Flint,* p. 219. Crapo's animus toward these measures might also have stemmed from the fact that he (along with others) had earlier raised (without any such aid) the necessary private capital for the construction of a rail line between Flint and Holly, on the Detroit and Milwaukee.

13. Henry H. Crapo to son, February 11, 1867, "Correspondence, February 1867," Box 3, Crapo Papers. A similar expression can be found in Henry H. Crapo to James F. Joy, March 5, 1867, "1867," Box 1, James F. Joy Papers, 1834–1900, Michigan Historical Collections, Bentley Historical Library, University of Michigan, Ann Arbor. *Flint Wolverine Citizen,* April 27, 1867. In a letter to his son, Crapo made the same point: "I am now regarded as having saved the Republican party in this state." Henry H. Crapo to William Crapo, March 17, 1867, "Correspondence, March, 1867," Box 3, Crapo Papers. For further information on the railroad debate and the legislature of 1867, see Dilla, *Politics of Michigan,* pp. 74–75; Dunbar, *All Aboard,* pp. 131–32; Arvid Larson, "The Railroad Aid Decision," unpublished student paper, 1950, "Larson, Arvid," Box 3, University of Michigan Department of History—Student Papers; and Richard O'Dell, "Governor Crapo's Vetoes of Michigan Railroad Legislation," unpublished student paper, 1941, "O'Dell, Richard," Box 4, University of Michigan Department of History—Student Papers. In all, Crapo vetoed thirty-three railroad aid bills. Only one of

these bills, which legalized bonds already issued for the construction of the Kalamazoo and Schoolcraft Railroad, passed over the governor's veto. J. R. Kellogg to Henry H. Crapo, March 4, 1867, "Correspondence, March, 1867," Box 3, Crapo Papers.

14. Dilla, *Politics of Michigan*, p. 70; *Detroit Advertiser and Tribune*, May 15, 1867.

15. For examples of this "traditional" approach, see Dilla, *Politics of Michigan*, esp. pp. 78–80, and David M. Katzman, *Before the Ghetto: Black Detroit in the Nineteenth Century* (Urbana: University of Illinois Press, 1973), pp. 36–37. Numerous contemporary examples of this trend exist. See, for example, *Detroit Advertiser and Tribune*, April 8, 1868, and William A. Howard to Charles S. May, February 20, 1868, "1860–69," Charles S. May Papers, 1830–1901, Michigan Historical Collections, Bentley Historical Library, University of Michigan, Ann Arbor. State Democrats tended to emphasize the issue of black suffrage in conjunction with the Radicals' desire to expand governmental power. See *Detroit Free Press*, March 28, 1867, and February 23, 1868. Dilla, *Politics of Michigan*, pp. 81–82.

Even the most cursory examination of the index for the *Proceedings* of the 1867 convention demonstrates that economic questions (that is, local aid to railroad corporations) and state government attracted far more of the convention's attention than did black suffrage or Prohibition. Moreover, the question of black suffrage, although introduced into the convention on May 21, was not brought up for debate until late in the session, while railroad aid, annual sessions, pay raises for state officials, and Prohibition were debated much earlier in the proceedings. Additionally, debate over the issue of alien voting was nonexistent at the convention, suggesting that the need for ethnic votes was too strong for even the nativists within Republican ranks to offer at least a symbolic challenge to the practice. *Report of the Debates and Proceedings of the Constitutional Convention of the State of Michigan, Convened at the City of Lansing, Wednesday, May 15th, 1867* (Lansing, Mich.: John A. Kerr, 1867) [hereafter cited as *Report*].

16. The composition of the 1867 constitutional convention also suggests a more market-oriented outlook for its members. Unlike the 1850 convention, in which forty-eight of the hundred delegates were farmers, the bulk of the 1867 convention was made up of members of the commercial classes (thirty-seven lawyers and one law student, eleven merchants, four physicians, two clergymen, two bankers, two lumbermen, two printers, one register of deeds, and one furniture dealer). Only twenty-eight of its members were classified as farmers. See *Report*, vol. 1, pp. 452–53. Remarks of William S. Stoughton in *Report*, vol. 2, p. 140; see *1867 Proposed Constitution*, Article 5, "Legislative," section 27; *Detroit Advertiser and Tribune*, August 24, 1867.

17. *Detroit Advertiser and Tribune*, August 24, 1867; comments of John M. Lamb in *Report*, vol. 2, p. 925.

18. *Detroit Advertiser and Tribune*, August 26, 1867.

19. *Detroit Free Press*, August 23, 1867; also see Katzman, *Before the Ghetto*, pp 36–37.

20. William A. Howard to Charles May, February 20, 1868, "1860–1869," May Papers; *Detroit Advertiser and Tribune*, March 19, 1868; *Detroit Free Press*, March 29, 1868.

21. Dilla, *Politics of Michigan*, pp. 90–91; Katzman, *Before the Ghetto*, p. 37; *Detroit Advertiser and Tribune*, April 8, 1868.

22. *Detroit Free Press*, April 9, 1868.

23. *Detroit Free Press*, March 29, 1868; *Detroit Advertiser and Tribune*, March 19 and 20, 1868; *Michigan Argus*, March 13, 1868. Even Harriette Dilla in her study of Michigan's Reconstruction-era politics—despite her attempt to imply that black suffrage was the primary reason for the 1867 constitution's defeat—conceded that "whether the rejection of the proposed constitution was due, then, to partisan feeling, aversion to the negro, or opposition to railroad aid, it is impossible to decide." Dilla, *Politics of Michigan*, p. 92.

24. Dunbar, *All Aboard!*, pp. 132–33; Dilla, *Politics of Michigan*, pp. 108–9; *Monroe Commercial*, March 10, 1870.

25. Dilla, *Politics of Michigan*, pp. 108–9; Thomas M. Cooley and James V. Campbell quoted in Cara Shelly, "Republican Benchmark: The Michigan Supreme Court, 1858–1875" (seminar paper for History 700, University of Michigan), pp. 88–89. The U.S. Supreme Court, in the case of *Moses Taylor v. City of Ypsilanti* (1882), later validated the claims of the bondholders impacted by the decision.

26. *Detroit Free Press*, May 27, 1870; *Detroit Advertiser and Tribune*, May 27, 1870; Dilla, *Politics of Michigan*, p. 110.

27. Dilla, *Politics of Michigan*, pp. 110 and 118–19.

28. Ibid., p. 114; *Jackson Daily Citizen*, September 5, 1870.

29. Dilla, *Politics of Michigan*, pp 119–23.

30. Ibid.

31. Harriette Dilla also recognized this "change . . . in the popular mind." But, because she misinterpreted the party's origins, she mistakenly identified it as a sudden turnaround and completely missed its earlier manifestation, in 1867. Dilla, *Politics of Michigan*, p. 121.

32. B. F. Gram to Thomas M. Cooley, March 24, 1871, "Jan–Apr 1871," Box 1, Thomas M. Cooley Papers, 1850–1898, Michigan Historical Collections, Bentley Historical Library, University of Michigan, Ann Arbor; *Detroit Free Press*, February 22, 1871.

33. Dilla, *Politics of Michigan*, pp. 130–32; *Detroit Free Press*, July 11, 1873.

34. Dilla, *Politics of Michigan*, pp. 144–45; Zachariah Chandler to Charles Gorham, July 1872, quoted in Wilmer C. Haris, *Public Life of Zachariah Chandler, 1851–1875* (Lansing: Michigan Historical Commission, 1917), pp. 121–22. Democrats also made a play for German voters in 1872 by pledging to support temperance (which would make permissible the consumption of beer) and not Prohibition. Though the plan failed, Republicans were concerned about possible German disaffection. Rubenstein and Ziewacz, *Michigan*, p. 125.

35. The justices of the Supreme Court and the president were also voted raises. The congressional raise would later be repealed, while the others mentioned were allowed to stand. George B. Tindall and David E. Shi, *America: A Narrative History*, 4th

ed., vol. 1 (New York: W. W. Norton, 1996), pp. 787–88; Dilla, *Politics of Michigan*, pp. 148–50; *Detroit Free Press*, March 4, 1874.

36. Dunbar, *All Aboard!* pp. 251–52; Russell D. Kilborn, "The Michigan Railroad Commission," *Michigan History* 3 (1919): 447; *Detroit Free Press*, March 6, 1873.

37. Dunbar, *Michigan*, pp. 425 and 460; Dilla, *Politics of Michigan*, pp. 233 and 248; Quaife and Glazer, *Michigan*, pp. 250–51; Richard M. Doolen, "The National Greenback Party in Michigan Politics, 1876–88," *Michigan History* 47 (June 1963): 170; "Western Farm Mortgages," n.d. but probably circa 1879–1880, located in "Scrapbook," David Woodman Papers, Michigan Historical Collection, Bentley Historical Library, University of Michigan, Ann Arbor.

38. For a brief overview of Grange activities in Michigan, see Dilla, *Politics of Michigan*, pp. 153–54; Quaife and Glazer, *Michigan*, p. 246; and Bruce Rubenstein and Larry Ziewacz, "Michigan in the Gilded Age: Politics and Society, 1866–1900s," in Richard J. Hathawy, ed., *Michigan: Visions of Our Past* (East Lansing: Michigan State University Press, 1989), p. 144.

39. Speech of George L. Yaple, delivered October 16, 1877, in Scrapbook 1, George L. Yaple Scrapbooks, 1881–1940, Michigan Historical Collections, Bentley Historical Library, University of Michigan, Ann Arbor. Chandler served as chair of the senate committee from 1861 to 1875. On tariffs and inflation, see Doolen, "National Greenback Party"; Dunbar, *Michigan*, pp. 445–47; and Harris, *Zachariah Chandler*, pp. 123–24.

40. The best account of this tension is Blackburn, "Michigan." See also Dilla, *Politics of Michigan*, p. 169, and Benjamin W. Bellows, "Politics and Michigan Fiscal Policy, 1837–1865" (honors thesis, University of Michigan, 1996), pp. 72–75.

41. Dilla, *Politics of Michigan*, pp. 155–71.

42. Handwritten outline of undated speech, in "Newspaper Clippings of Letters and Speeches," Box 1, John J. Bagley Papers, 1830–1900, Michigan Historical Collection, Bentley Historical Library, University of Michigan, Ann Arbor; *Detroit Daily Post*, September 4, 1874.

43. Dilla, *Politics of Michigan*, pp. 171–72.

44. On the 1875 senatorial contest, see Dilla, *Politics of Michigan*, pp. 174–79; Harris, *Zachariah Chandler*, p. 128; and *Ann Arbor Argus*, Jan 22, 1875.

45. Undated speech of Governor John J. Bagley, "Newspaper Clippings of Letters and Speeches," Box 1, Bagley Papers.

46. Rubenstein and Ziewacz, *Michigan*, p. 125; *Lansing State Republican*, March 26, 1875; Dilla, *Politics of Michigan*, pp. 189–94.

47. Dilla, *Politics of Michigan*, p. 196.

48. Greenback Party state platform quoted in *Hastings Republican*, May 8, 1876. On the Greenback movement, see also Doolen, "National Greenback Party," and Donald C. Swift and Lawrence E. Ziewacz, "The Election of 1882: A Republican Analysis," *Journal of the Great Lakes History Conference* 1 (1976): 12–26.

49. Dilla, *Politics of Michigan*, pp. 202–3.

50. Speech of George L. Yaple, delivered October 16, 1877, in Scrapbook 1,

Yaple Scrapbooks; Speech of George L. Yaple, delivered July 4, 1881, in Scrapbook 1, Yaple Scrapbooks.

51. "The Anti-Third Termer," "Scrapbook," Woodman Papers; N. C. Putnam to Charles F. Bates, March 1, 1883, "Correspondence–Greenback Party," Box 1, Charles F. Bates Papers, 1861–1888, Michigan Historical Collection, Bentley Historical Library, University of Michigan, Ann Arbor.

52. A brief overview of late-nineteenth-century Michigan politics can be found in Dunbar, *Michigan*, pp. 381–92. Some might argue that the famous Progressive reformer Hazen Pingree's two terms as governor from 1897 to 1900 represent yet another example of the Republicans' vulnerability in Michigan. I would argue, however, that Pingree was advanced as a candidate by the McMillan-controlled party leadership, which was most interested in promoting William McKinley's presidential candidacy and thus saw Pingree's Progressivism as a useful means of undermining pro-Bryan sentiment in the state. Republicans would not lose another gubernatorial race in Michigan until 1913.

BIBLIOGRAPHY

BOOKS

Ambrosius, Lloyd E., ed. *A Crisis in Republicanism: American Politics in the Civil War Era.* Lincoln: University of Nebraska Press, 1990.

Anbinder, Tyler. *Nativism and Slavery: The Northern Know Nothings and the Politics of the 1850s.* New York: Oxford University Press, 1992.

Ashworth, John. *Agrarians and Aristocrats: Party Ideology in the United States, 1837–1846.* New York: Cambridge University Press, 1983.

Atack, Jeremy, and Fred Bateman. *To Their Own Soil: Agriculture in the Antebellum North.* Ames: Iowa State University Press, 1987.

Baker, Jean H. *Affairs of Party: The Political Culture of Northern Democrats in the Mid-Nineteenth Century.* Ithaca, N.Y.: Cornell University Press, 1984.

Bald, F. Clever. *Michigan in Four Centuries.* New York: Harper, 1961.

Baxter, Albert. *History of the City of Grand Rapids, Michigan.* New York: Munsell, 1891.

Belknap, Charles E. *The Yesterdays of Grand Rapids.* Grand Rapids, Mich.: Dean-Hicks, 1922.

Benedict, C. Harry. *Red Metal: The Calumet and Hecla Story.* Ann Arbor: University of Michigan Press, 1952.

Benson, Barbara E. *Logs and Lumber: The Development of the Lumber Industry in Michigan's Lower Peninsula, 1837–1870.* Mt. Pleasant: Clarke Historical Library, Central Michigan University, 1989.

Blue, Frederick J. *The Free Soilers: Third Party Politics, 1848–1854.* Urbana: University of Illinois Press, 1973.

Bogue, Allan G. *The Earnest Men: Republicans of the Civil War Senate.* Ithaca, N.Y.: Cornell University Press, 1981.

———. *The Congressman's Civil War.* Cambridge: Cambridge University Press, 1989.

Bowen, A. W., and Company. *City of Grand Rapids and Kent County, Michigan, Containing Biographical Sketches of Prominent and Representative Citizens.* Logansport, Ind.: Wilson, Humphreys, 1900.

Brownlee, W. Elliot. *Dynamics of Ascent: A History of the American Economy.* 2nd ed. New York: Alfred A. Knopf, 1988.

Bruchey, Stuart W. *Enterprise: The Dynamic Economy of a Free People.* Cambridge, Mass.: Harvard University Press, 1990.

Burton, Clarence M., ed. *The City of Detroit, Michigan, 1701–1922.* 5 vols. Detroit, Mich.: S. J. Clarke, 1922.

———. *Compendium of History and Biography of the City of Detroit and Wayne County, Michigan.* Chicago: Henry Taylor, 1909.

Campbell, James V. *Outlines of the Political History of Michigan.* Detroit, Mich.: Schober, 1876.

Carter, Dan T. *When the War Was Over: The Failure of Self-Reconstruction in the South, 1865–67.* Baton Rouge: Louisiana State University Press, 1985.

Catlin, George B. *The Story of Detroit.* Detroit, Mich.: Detroit News, 1923.

Catton, Bruce. *Michigan: A History.* New York: W. W. Norton, 1976.

Cayton, Andrew R. L., and Peter S. Onuf. *The Midwest and the Nation: Rethinking the History of an American Region.* Bloomington: Indiana University Press, 1990.

Chapman, Charles C., and Company. *History of Kent County, Michigan.* Chicago: Charles C. Chapman, 1881.

Chaput, Donald. *The Cliff: America's First Copper Mine.* Kalamazoo, Mich.: Sequoia Press, 1971.

Chase, Lew Allen. *Rural Michigan.* New York: Macmillan, 1922.

Clark, Christopher. *The Roots of Rural Capitalism: Western Massachusetts, 1790–1860.* Ithaca, N.Y.: Cornell University Press, 1991.

Cochran, Thomas C. *Frontiers of Change: Early Industrialization in the United States.* New York: Oxford University Press, 1981.

Common Council of the City of Detroit. *Journal of the Proceedings of the Common Council of the City of Detroit.* Detroit, Mich.: Detroit Free Press Steam Book and Job Printing, 1837–1878.

Conot, Robert. *American Odyssey.* Detroit, Mich.: Wayne State University Press, 1986.

Cox, Lawanda, and John H. Cox. *Politics, Principle, and Prejudice, 1865–1866: Dilemma of Reconstruction America.* London: Free Press of Glencoe Collier-MacMillan, 1963.

Crapo, Henry Howland, II. *The Story of Henry Howland Crapo, 1804–1869.* Boston: Privately published, 1933.

Cross, Whitney R. *The Burned-Over District: A Social and Intellectual History of Enthusiastic Religion in Western New York, 1800–1850.* Ithaca, N.Y.: Cornell University Press, 1950.

Degler, Carl N. *The Age of the Economic Revolution, 1876–1900.* Glenview, Ill.: Scott, Foresman, 1967.

Dell, Christopher. *Lincoln and the War Democrats: The Grand Erosion of Conservative Tradition.* Rutherford, N.J.: Fairleigh Dickinson University Press, 1975.

Detroit Post and Tribune. *Zachariah Chandler: An Outline Sketch of His Life and Public Services.* Detroit, Mich.: Post and Tribune, 1880.

Dilla, Harriette M. *Politics of Michigan, 1865–1878.* New York: Columbia University Press, 1912.

Donald, David. *Charles Sumner and the Coming of the Civil War*. New York: Fawcett Columbine, 1960.

Dumond, Dwight L., ed., *Letters of James Gillespie Birney, 1831–1857*. Vol. 1. Gloucester, Mass.: Peter Smith, 1938.

Dunbar, Willis F. *All Aboard! A History of Railroads in Michigan*. Grand Rapids, Mich.: William B. Eerdmans, 1969.

———. *Lewis Cass*. Grand Rapids, Mich.: William B. Eerdmans, 1970.

———. *Michigan: A History of the Wolverine State*. Grand Rapids, Mich.: William B. Eerdmans, 1970.

Faragher, John Mack. *Sugar Creek: Life on the Illinois Prairie*. New Haven, Conn.: Yale University Press, 1990.

Farmer, Silas. *History of Detroit and Wayne County and Early Michigan: A Chronological Cyclopedia of the Past and Present*. 3rd ed. Detroit, Mich.: Silas Farmer, 1884.

Fehrenbacher, Don E. *The Dred Scott Case: Its Significance in American Law and Politics*. New York: Oxford University Press, 1978.

Fisher, Ernest B., ed. *Grand Rapids and Kent County Michigan: Historical Account of their Progress from First Settlement to the Present Time*. Vols. 1 and 2. Chicago: Robert O. Law, 1918.

Fishlow, Albert. *American Railroads and the Transformation of the Ante-bellum Economy*. Harvard Economic Studies. Vol. 77. Cambridge, Mass.: Harvard University Press, 1965.

Fite, Emerson D. *Social and Economic Conditions in the North during the Civil War*. New York: Ungar, 1963.

Foner, Eric. *Free Soil, Free Labor, Free Men: The Ideology of the Republican Party before the Civil War*. New York: Oxford University Press, 1970.

———. *Politics and Ideology in the Age of the Civil War*. New York: Oxford University Press, 1980.

———. *Nothing but Freedom: Emancipation and Its Legacy*. Baton Rouge: Louisiana State University Press, 1983.

———. *Reconstruction: America's Unfinished Revolution, 1863–1877*. New York: Harper & Row, 1988.

Ford, Lacy K. *The Origins of Southern Radicalism: The South Carolina Upcountry, 1800–1860*. New York: Oxford University Press, 1988.

Formisano, Ronald P. *The Birth of Mass Political Parties: Michigan, 1827–1861*. Princeton, N.J.: Princeton University Press, 1971.

Franklin, John, H. *Reconstruction: After the Civil War*. Chicago: University of Chicago Press, 1961.

Fredrickson, George M. *The Inner Civil War: Northern Intellectuals and the Crisis of the Union*. New York: Harper & Row, 1965.

Freitag, Alfred. *Detroit in the Civil War*. Detroit, Mich.: Wayne State University Press, 1951.

Fuller, George N. *Economic and Social Beginnings of Michigan: A Study of the Settlement of the Lower Peninsula during the Territorial Period, 1805–1837.* Lansing: Michigan Historical Commission, 1916.

Fuller, George N., ed. *Messages of the Governors of Michigan.* Lansing, Mich.: State Historical Commission, 1926.

———. *Michigan: A Centennial History of the State and Its People.* 5 vols. Chicago: Lewis, 1939.

Gates, Paul W. *Agriculture and the Civil War.* New York: Alfred A. Knopf, 1965.

Gates, William B. *Michigan Copper and Boston Dollars: An Economic History of the Copper Mining Industry.* Cambridge, Mass.: Harvard University Press, 1954.

George, Sister Mary Karl. *Zachariah Chandler: A Political Biography.* East Lansing: Michigan State University Press, 1969.

Gienapp, William E. *The Origins of the Republican Party, 1852–1856.* New York: Oxford University Press, 1987.

Goodrich, Calvin. *The First Michigan Frontier.* Ann Arbor: University of Michigan Press, 1940.

Goodwyn, Lawrence. *The Populist Moment: A Short History of Agrarian Revolt in America.* New York: Oxford University Press, 1978.

Goss, Dwight. *History of Grand Rapids and Its Industries.* 2 vols. Chicago: C. F. Cooper, 1906.

Graff, George P. *The People of Michigan.* Lansing, Mich.: State Library Services, 1974.

Gray, Susan E. *The Yankee West: Community Life on the Michigan Frontier.* Chapel Hill: University of North Carolina Press, 1996.

Gray, Wood. *The Hidden Civil War: The Story of the Copperheads.* New York: Viking Press, 1942.

Hahn, Steven. *The Roots of Southern Populism: Yeoman Farmers and the Transformation of the Georgia Upcountry, 1850–1890.* New York: Oxford University Press, 1983.

Hahn, Steven, and Jonathan Prude, eds. *The Countryside in the Age of Capitalist Transformation: Essays in the Social History of Rural America.* Chapel Hill: University of North Carolina Press, 1985.

Hamilton, Holman. *Prologue to Conflict: The Crisis and Compromise of 1850.* Lexington: University of Kentucky Press, 1964.

Hammond, Bray. *Sovereignty and an Empty Purse: Banks and Politics in the Civil War Congress.* Princeton, N.J.: Princeton University Press, 1970.

Harris, Wilmer C. *Public Life of Zachariah Chandler, 1851–1875.* Lansing: Michigan Historical Commission, 1917.

Hathaway, Richard J., ed. *Michigan: Visions of Our Past.* East Lansing: Michigan State University Press, 1989.

Hawes, George W. *Michigan State Gazetteer and Business Directory for 1860.* Detroit, Mich.: F. Raymond, 1859.

Hayes, Frederic H. *Michigan Catholicism in the Era of the Civil War.* Lansing, Mich.: Civil War Centennial Observance Commission, 1965.

Henrickson, Wilma W. *Detroit Perspectives: Crossroads and Turning Points.* Detroit, Mich.: Wayne State University Press, 1991.

Hess, Earl. *Liberty, Virtue, and Progress.* New York: New York University Press, 1988.

Hesseltine, William B. *Lincoln and the War Governors.* New York: Alfred A. Knopf, 1948.

Higgs, Robert. *The Transformation of the American Economy, 1865–1914: An Essay in Interpretation.* New York: John Wiley & Sons, 1971.

Hirschfeld, Charles. *The Great Railroad Conspiracy: The Social History of a Railroad War.* East Lansing: Michigan State College Press, 1953.

Hofstadter, Richard. *The Idea of a Party System: The Rise of Legitimate Opposition in the United States, 1780–1840.* Berkeley: University of California Press, 1972.

Holli, Melvin G., ed. *Detroit.* New York: New Viewpoints, 1976.

Holt, Michael F. *The Political Crisis of the 1850's.* New York: W. W. Norton, 1978.

———. *The Rise and Fall of the American Whig Party: Jacksonian Politics and the Onset of the Civil War.* New York: Oxford University Press, 1999.

Howe, Daniel Walker. *The Political Culture of the American Whigs.* Chicago: University of Chicago Press, 1979.

Johnson, Paul E. *A Shopkeeper's Millennium: Society and Revivals in Rochester, New York: 1815–1837.* New York: Hill and Wang, 1978.

Karamanski, Theodore J. *Deep Woods Frontier: A History of Logging in Northern Michigan.* Detroit, Mich.: Wayne State University Press, 1989.

Katzman, David M. *Before the Ghetto: Black Detroit in the Nineteenth Century.* Urbana: University of Illinois Press, 1973.

Kestenbaum, Justin L., ed. *The Making of Michigan, 1820–1860: A Pioneer Anthology.* Detroit, Mich.: Wayne State University Press, 1990.

Kilar, Jeremy W. *Michigan's Lumbertowns: Lumbermen and Laborers in Saginaw, Bay City, and Muskegon, 1870–1905.* Detroit, Mich.: Wayne State University Press, 1990.

Kirk, Gordon, W., Jr. *The Promise of American Life: Social Mobility in a Nineteenth-Century Immigrant Community: Holland Michigan, 1847–1894.* Philadelphia: American Philosophical Society, 1978.

Kirkland, Caroline. *A New Home—Who'll Follow? Or Glimpses of Western Life.* 3rd ed. New York: Charles S. Francis, 1841.

Klement, Frank L. *The Copperheads in the Middle West.* Chicago: University of Chicago Press, 1960.

Kleppner, Paul. *The Cross of Culture: A Social Analysis of Midwestern Politics, 1850–1900.* New York: Free Press, 1970.

———. *The Third Electoral System, 1853–1892.* Chapel Hill: University of North Carolina Press, 1979.

Klingaman, David C., and Richard K. Vedder, eds. *Essays in Nineteenth Century Economic History: The Old Northwest.* Athens: Ohio University Press, 1975.

Klunder, Willard C. *Lewis Cass and the Politics of Moderation.* Kent, Ohio: Kent State University Press, 1996.

Kohl, Lawrence F. *The Politics of Individualism: Parties and the American Character in the Jacksonian Era.* New York: Oxford University Press, 1989.

Krause, David J. *The Making of a Mining District: Keweenaw Native Copper 1500–1870.* Detroit, Mich.: Wayne State University Press, 1992.

Lankton, Larry. *Cradle to Grave: Life, Work, and Death at the Lake Superior Copper Mines.* New York: Oxford University Press, 1991.

———. *Beyond the Boundaries: Life and Landscape at the Lake Superior Copper Mines, 1840–1875.* New York: Oxford University Press, 1997.

Lanman, Charles. *The Red Book of Michigan History: A Civil, Military and Biographical History.* Detroit, Mich.: E. B. Smith, 1871.

Larson, John L. *Internal Improvement: National Works and the Promise of Popular Government in the Early United States.* Chapel Hill: University of North Carolina Press, 2001.

Leeson, Michael A. *History of Saginaw County, Michigan.* Chicago: C. C. Chapman, 1881.

Levine, Bruce. *Half Slave and Half Free: The Roots of the Civil War.* New York: Hill and Wang, 1992.

Lewis, Ferris E. *Michigan Yesterday and Today.* Hillsdale, Mich.: Hillsdale, 1956.

Lewis, Martin Deming. *Lumberman from Flint: The Michigan Career of Henry H. Crapo, 1855–1869.* Detroit, Mich.: Wayne State University Press, 1958.

Lilibridge, G. R. *Report of the Conspiracy Trial, in the Wayne County Circuit Court, Michigan, Hon. Warner Wing, Presiding, on Five Indictments of the Grand Jury for the County of Wayne, Setting forth a Conspiracy for Burning the Freight Depot of the Michigan Central Rail Road Company, and for Other Offences, Named in Said Indictments.* Detroit, Mich.: *Detroit Tribune,* 1851.

Lydens, Z. Z., ed. *The Story of Grand Rapids.* Grand Rapids, Mich.: Kregel, 1966.

McKitrick, Eric L. *Andrew Johnson and Reconstruction.* Chicago: University of Chicago Press, 1960.

McLaughlin, Andrew C. *Lewis Cass.* Boston and New York: Houghton Mifflin, 1899.

McLaughlin, Doris B. *Michigan Labor: A Brief History from 1818 to the Present.* Ann Arbor, Mich.: Institute of Labor and Industrial Relations, 1970.

McPherson, James M. *Ordeal by Fire: The Civil War and Reconstruction.* New York: Alfred A. Knopf, 1982.

Madison, James H., ed. *Heartland: Comparative Histories of the Midwestern States.* Bloomington: Indiana University Press, 1988.

Maizlish, Stephen E., and John J. Kushma, eds. *Essays on American Antebellum Politics.* College Station: Published for the University of Texas at Arlington by Texas A & M University Press, 1982.

Malin, James C. *The Nebraska Question, 1852–1854.* Lawrence: University of Kansas Press, 1953.

Marks, Joseph J., ed. *Effects of the Civil War on Farming in Michigan.* Lansing: Michigan Civil War Centennial Observance Commission, 1965.

Mason, Philip P., ed. *Copper Country Journal.* Detroit, Mich.: Wayne State University Press, 1991.

Mason, Philip P., and Paul J. Pentecost. *From Bull Run to Appomattox: Michigan's Role in the Civil War*. Detroit, Mich.: Wayne State University Press, 1961.

May, George S. *Michigan and the Civil War Years, 1860–1866*. Lansing: Michigan Civil War Centennial Observance Commission, 1964.

Maybee, Roland H. *Michigan's White Pine Era, 1840–1900*. Lansing: Michigan Historical Commission, 1960.

Michigan Historical Commission. *Michigan Biographies: Including Members of Congress, Elective State Officers, Justices of the Supreme Court, Members of the Michigan Legislature, Board of Regents of the University of Michigan, State Board of Agriculture and State Board of Education*. Lansing: Michigan Historical Commission, 1924.

———. *Governors of the Territory and State of Michigan*. Lansing: Michigan Historical Commission, 1928.

Mills, James Cooke. *History of Saginaw County Michigan*. Saginaw, Mich.: Seemann and Peters, 1918.

Milton, George Fort. *Lincoln and the Fifth Column*. New York: Vanguard Press, 1942.

Mohr, James C., ed. *Radical Republicans in the North: State Politics during Reconstruction*. Baltimore, Md.: Johns Hopkins University Press, 1976.

Moos, Malcolm. *The Republicans: A History of Their Party*. New York: Random House, 1956.

Morrison, Chaplain. *Democratic Politics and Sectionalism: The Wilmot Proviso Controversy*. Chapel Hill: University of North Carolina Press, 1967.

Morrison, Michael. *Slavery and the American West: The Eclipse of Manifest Destiny and the Coming of the Civil War*. Chapel Hill: University of North Carolina Press, 1997.

Murdoch, Angus. *Boom Copper: The Story of the First U.S. Mining Boom*. New York: Macmillan, 1943.

Nichols, Roy F. *The Disruption of American Democracy*. New York: Macmillan, 1948.

North, Douglass C. *The Economic Growth of the United States, 1790–1860*. Englewood Cliffs, N.J.: Prentice Hall, 1961.

Paludan, Phillip Shaw. *"A Peoples Contest:" The Union and Civil War, 1861–1865*. New York: Harper & Row, 1988.

Paré, George. *The Catholic Church in Detroit, 1701–1888*. Detroit, Mich.: Wayne State University Press, 1951.

Parks, Robert J. *Democracy's Railroads: Public Enterprise in Jacksonian Michigan*. Port Washington, N.Y.: Kennikat Press, 1972.

Perman, Michael. *Emancipation and Reconstruction, 1862–1879*. Arlington Heights, Ill.: Harlan Davidson, 1987.

Potter, David M. *Lincoln and His Party in the Secession Crisis*. New Haven, Conn.: Yale University Press, 1942.

———. *The Impending Crisis, 1848–1861*. New York: Harper & Row, 1976.

Pound, Arthur. *Detroit: Dynamic City*. New York: D. Appleton Century, 1940.

Power, Richard L. *Planting Corn Belt Culture: The Impress of the Upland Southerner and Yankee in the Old Northwest*. Indianapolis: Indiana Historical Society, 1953.

Powers, Perry F. *A History of the Northern Peninsula of Michigan and Its People.* 3 vols. Chicago: Lewis, 1912.

Quaife, Milton M., and Sidney Glazer. *Michigan: From Primitive Wilderness to Industrial Commonwealth.* New York: Prentice-Hall, 1946.

Quill, J. Michael. *Prelude to the Radicals: The North and Reconstruction in 1865.* Washington, D.C.: University Press of America, 1980.

Quist, John W. *Restless Visionaries: The Social Roots of Antebellum Reform in Alabama and Michigan.* Baton Rouge: Louisiana State University Press, 1998.

Rawley, James A. *Race and Politics: "Bleeding Kansas" and the Coming of the Civil War.* Philadelphia: J. B. Lippincott, 1969.

———. *The Politics of Union: Northern Politics during the Civil War.* Lincoln: University of Nebraska Press, 1974.

———, ed. *Lincoln and Civil War Politics.* Huntington, N.Y.: R. E. Krieger, 1969.

Report of the Debates and Proceedings of the Constitutional Convention of the State of Michigan, Convened at the City of Lansing, Wednesday, May 15th, 1867. Lansing, Mich.: John A. Kerr, 1867.

Report of the Proceedings and Debates in the Convention to Revise the Constitution of the State of Michigan, 1850. Lansing, Mich.: R. W. Ingals, 1850.

Reports of the Cases Argued and Determined in the Supreme Court of the State of Michigan. Vol. 2. Chicago: Callaghan, 1880.

Rorabaugh, W. J. *The Alcoholic Republic: An American Tradition.* New York: Oxford University Press, 1979.

Rothenberg, Winifred. *From Market Place to Market Economy: The Transformation of Rural Massachusetts, 1750–1850.* Chicago: University of Chicago Press, 1992.

Rothman, David J. *The Discovery of the Asylum: Social Disorder in the New Republic.* Glenview, Ill.: Scott, Foresman, 1971.

Rowe, John. *The Hard Rock Men: Cornish Immigrants and the North American Mining Frontier.* Liverpool, England: University of Liverpool Press, 1974.

Rubenstein, Bruce A., and Lawrence E. Ziewacz. *Michigan: A History of the Great Lakes State.* 3rd ed. Wheeling, Ill.: Harlan Davidson, 2002.

Sawyer, Alvah L. *A History of the Northern Peninsula of Michigan and Its People: Its Mining, Lumber and Agricultural Industries.* Vols. 1–3. Chicago: Lewis, 1911.

Schlesinger, Arthur M., Jr., ed. *History of U. S. Political Parties.* Vol. 2. New York: Chelsea House, 1973.

Schneider, John C. *Detroit and the Problem of Order, 1830–1880: A Geography of Crime, Riot and Policing.* Lincoln: University of Nebraska Press, 1980.

Sellers, Charles. *The Market Revolution: Jacksonian America 1815–1846.* New York: Oxford University Press, 1991.

Sewell, Richard H. *Ballots for Freedom: Antislavery Politics in the United States, 1837–1860.* New York: Oxford University Press, 1976.

———. *A House Divided: Sectionalism and Civil War, 1848–1865.* Baltimore, Md.: Johns Hopkins University Press, 1988.

Shade, William. *Banks or No Banks: The Money Issue in Western Politics, 1832–1865*. Detroit, Mich.: Wayne State University Press, 1972.

Silbey, Joel H. *The Shrine of Party: Congressional Voting Behavior, 1841–1852*. Pittsburgh, Pa.: University of Pittsburgh Press, 1967.

———. *A Respectable Minority: The Democratic Party in the Civil War Era, 1860–1868*. New York: W. W. Norton, 1977.

———. *The Partisan Imperative: The Dynamics of American Politics before the Civil War*. New York: Oxford University Press, 1985.

Sprague, Dean. *Freedom under Lincoln*. Boston: Houghton Mifflin, 1965.

Stampp, Kenneth M. *And the War Came: The North and the Secession Crisis, 1860–1861*. Baton Rouge: Louisiana State University Press, 1950.

———. *The Era of Reconstruction, 1865–1877*. New York: Vintage Books, 1965.

———. *America in 1857: A Nation on the Brink*. New York: Oxford University Press, 1990.

Stark, George W. *City of Destiny: The Story of Detroit*. Detroit, Mich.: Arnold-Powers, 1943.

Stewart, James B. *Holy Warriors: The Abolitionists and American Slavery*. New York: Hill and Wang, 1976.

Streeter, Benjamin F. *Political Parties in Michigan, 1837–1860: An Historical Study of Political Issues and Parties in Michigan from the Admission of the State to the Civil War*. Lansing: Michigan Historical Commission, 1918.

Stuart Mackay-Smith Marlatt, Helen, ed. *Stuart Letters of Robert and Elizabeth Sullivan Stuart and Their Children, 1819–1864*. Privately printed, 1961.

Taylor, George R. *The Transportation Revolution, 1815–1861*. New York: Holt, Reinhart and Winston, 1962.

Tentler, Leslie Woodcock. *Seasons of Grace: A History of the Catholic Archdiocese of Detroit*. Detroit, Mich.: Wayne State University Press, 1990.

Thomas, N. Gordon. *The Millennial Impulse in Michigan, 1830–1860: The Second Coming in the Third New England*. Lewiston, N.Y.: Edwin Mellen Press, 1989.

Thornton, J. Mills. *Politics and Power in a Slave Society: Alabama, 1800–1861*. Baton Rouge: Louisiana State University Press, 1978.

Thurner, Arthur W. *Calumet Copper and People: History of a Michigan Mining Community, 1864–1970*. Hancock, Mich.: The Book Concern, 1974.

Tocqueville, Alexis de. *Democracy in America*. New York: New American Library, 1956.

Trefousse, Hans. *The Radical Republicans*. New York: Alfred A. Knopf, 1969.

Tuttle, Charles R. *General History of the State of Michigan with Biographical Sketches*. Detroit, Mich.: R. D. S. Tyler, 1873.

———. *History of Grand Rapids with Biographical Sketches*. Grand Rapids, Mich.: Tuttle and Cooney, 1874.

Tyler, Alice F. *Freedom's Ferment: Phases of American Social History from the Colonial Period to the Outbreak of the Civil War*. Minneapolis: University of Minnesota Press, 1944.

Utley, Henry M., and Byron M. Cutcheon, eds. *Michigan as a Province, Territory and*

State, the Twenty-Sixth Member of the Federal Union. Vols. 3 and 4. N.p.: Publishing Society of Michigan, 1906.

Vander Hill, C. Warren. *Settling the Great Lakes Frontier: Immigration to Michigan, 1837–1924.* Lansing: Michigan Historical Commission, 1970.

Van Dyke, James A. *Argument in the Railroad Conspiracy Case; Entitled the People of Michigan vs. Abel F. Fitch and Others, Tried before His Honor, Warner Wing, Presiding Judge, of the Circuit Court for the County of Wayne, at the May Term, 1851, in the City of Detroit.* Detroit, Mich.: Duncklee, Wales, 1851.

Vatter, Harold G. *The Drive to Industrial Maturity: The U.S. Economy, 1865–1914.* Westport, Conn.: Greenwood Press, 1975.

Vinovskis, Maris A., ed. *Toward a Social History of the American Civil War.* Cambridge: Cambridge University Press, 1990.

Vinyard, JoEllen M. *The Irish on the Urban Frontier: Nineteenth Century Detroit.* New York: Arno Press, 1976.

Voegeli, V. Jacques. *Free but Not Equal: The Midwest and the Negro during the Civil War.* Chicago: University of Chicago Press, 1967.

Wallace, Anthony F. C. *Rockdale: The Growth of an American Village in the Early Industrial Revolution.* New York: W. W. Norton, 1972.

Walters, Ronald G. *American Reformers, 1815–1860.* New York: Hill and Wang, 1978.

Ward, John W. *Andrew Jackson, Symbol for an Age.* New York: Oxford University Press, 1955.

Watson, Henry L. *Liberty and Power: The Politics of Jacksonian America.* New York: Noonday Press, 1990.

Welter, Rush. *The Mind of America, 1820–1860.* New York: Columbia University Press, 1975.

Wermuth, Thomas S. *Rip Van Winkle's Neighbors: The Transformation of Rural Society in the Hudson River Valley, 1720–1850.* Albany: State University Press of New York, 2001.

Whitaker, James W., ed. *Farming in the Midwest, 1840–1900.* Washington, D.C.: Agricultural History Society, 1974.

Wiebe, Robert H. *The Opening of American Society: From the Adoption of the Constitution to the Eve of Disunion.* New York: Vintage Books, 1984.

Wilentz, Sean. *Chants Democratic: New York City and the Rise of the American Working Class, 1788–1850.* New York: Oxford University Press, 1984.

Williams, Frederick D. *Michigan Soldiers in the Civil War.* Lansing: Bureau of Michigan History, Michigan Department of State, 1994.

Williams, T. Harry. *Lincoln and the Radicals.* Madison: University of Wisconsin Press, 1941.

Woodford, Frank B. *Lewis Cass: The Last Jeffersonian.* New Brunswick, N.J.: Rutgers University Press, 1950.

———. *Father Abraham's Children: Michigan Episodes in the Civil War.* Detroit, Mich.: Wayne State University Press, 1961.

———, and Arthur M. Woodford. *All Our Yesterdays: A Brief History of Detroit.* Detroit, Mich.: Wayne State University Press, 1969.

Zornow, William F. *Lincoln and the Party Divided.* Norman: University of Oklahoma Press, 1954.

ARTICLES

Abrams, Ray H. "Copperhead Newspapers and the Negro." *Journal of Negro History* 20 (1935): 131–52.

Atack, Jeremy, and Fred Bateman. "Self-Sufficiency and the Origins of the Marketable Surplus in the Rural North, 1860." *Agricultural History* 58 (1984): 296–313.

Baker, Jean H. "A Loyal Opposition: Northern Democrats in the Thirty-Seventh Congress." *Civil War History* 25 (1979): 139–55.

Belding, George A. "Thunder in the Forest." *Michigan History* 33 (March 1949): 30–42.

Bigelow, Martha. "The Political Services of William Alanson Howard." *Michigan History* 42 (March 1958): 1–23.

Blackburn, George M. "Letters to the Front: A Distaff View of the Civil War." *Michigan History* 49 (March 1965): 53–67.

Blackburn, George M., and Sherman L. Richards Jr. "A Democratic History of the West: Manistee County Michigan, 1860." *Journal of American History* 57 (December 1970): 600–618.

Bloomberg, Susan E., Mary Frank Fox, Robert M. Warner, and Sam Bass Warner Jr. "A Census Probe into Nineteenth-Century Family History: Southern Michigan, 1850–1880." *Journal of Social History* 5 (Fall 1971): 26–45.

Brinks, Herbert. "The Effect of the Civil War in 1861 on Michigan Lumbering and Mining Industries." *Michigan History* 44 (March 1960): 101–7.

Brock, Thomas D. "Paw Paw versus the Railroads." *Michigan History* 39 (June 1955): 130–31.

Burkland, Carl E. "A Country Store a Century Ago." *Michigan History* 40 (September 1956): 309–16.

Calkins, Edmund A. "Railroads of Michigan since 1850." *Michigan History* 13 (January 1929): 5–25.

Catlin, George B. "Little Journeys in Journalism: Wilbur F. Storey." *Michigan History* 10 (October 1926): 515–33.

———. "Adventures in Journalism: Detroit Newspapers since 1850." *Michigan History* 29 (July–September 1945): 343–76.

Chase, L. A. "Early Copper Mining in Michigan." *Michigan History* 29 (1945): 22–30.

———. "Early Days of Michigan Mining." *Michigan History* 29 (1945): 166–79.

———. "Michigan Copper Mines." *Michigan History* 29 (1945): 479–88.

Collier, T. Maxwell. "William H. Seward in the Campaign of 1860, with Special Reference to Michigan." *Michigan History* 19 (Winter 1935): 91–106.

Crawford, Riley C. "Memoir of Hon. Henry Fralick." *Michigan Pioneer and Historical Collections* 18 (1891): 318–21.

Curry, Leonard P. "Congressional Democrats, 1861–1863." *Civil War History* 12 (1966): 213–29.

Curry, Richard O. "The Union as It Was: A Critique of the Recent Interpretations of
    the Copperheads." *Civil War History* 13 (1967): 25–39.
Danford, Ormond S. "The Social and Economic Effects of Lumbering on Michigan,
    1835–1890." *Michigan History* 26 (Summer 1942): 346–64.
Dart, Sarah E. "Early Lansing." *Michigan Pioneer and Historical Collections* 28 (1897–
    1898): 172–79.
Dondero, George A. "Lincoln in Kalamazoo, 1856." *Michigan History* 41 (March
    1957): 61–66.
Doolen, Richard M. "The National Greenback Party in Michigan Politics, 1876–88,"
    Michigan History 47 (June 1963): 161–83.
Dunbar, Willis F. "Year of Decision on Michigan's Education Policy: 1855." *Michigan
    History* 39 (December 1955): 445–60.
Easterlin, Richard A. "Population Change and Farm Settlement in the Northern
    United States." *Journal of Economic History* 36 (March 1976): 45–83.
Egnal, Marc. "The Beards Were Right: Parties in the North, 1840–1860." *Civil War
    History* 47 (March 2001): 30–56.
Elliott, Frank N. "When the Railroad Was King." *Michigan History* 49 (December
    1965): 289–343.
Ely, Ralph. "History of Gratiot County from 1850 to 1860." *Michigan Pioneer and His-
    torical Collections* 22 (1893): 264.
Feller, Daniel. "Politics and Society: Toward a Jacksonian Synthesis." *Journal of the
    Early Republic* 10 (Summer 1990): 135–62.
Fennimore, Jean Joy L. "Austin Blair: Political Idealist, 1845–1860." *Michigan History*
    48 (June 1964): 130–66.
———. "Austin Blair: Civil War Governor, 1861–1862." *Michigan History* 49 (Sep-
    tember 1965): 193–227.
———. "Austin Blair: Civil War Governor, 1863–64." *Michigan History* 49 (Decem-
    ber 1965): 344–69.
Fisher, James. "Michigan's Cornish People." *Michigan History* 29 (1945): 377–85.
Fitzgibbon, John. "King Alcohol: His Rise, Reign and Fall in Michigan." *Michigan
    History* 2 (October 1918): 737–79.
Foner, Eric. "The Wilmot Proviso Revisited." *Journal of American History* 56 (1969):
    262–79.
Forster, John H. "Life in the Copper Mines of Lake Superior." *Michigan Pioneer and
    Historical Collections* 11 (1887): 175–86.
———. "War Times in the Copper Mines." *Michigan Pioneer and Historical Collections*
    18 (1891): 375–82.
Gilbert, John. "The Great Conspiracy." *Michigan Pioneer and Historical Collections* 31
    (1901): 232–37.
Gilbert, Thomas D. "Development of Western Michigan." *Michigan Pioneer and His-
    torical Collections* 17 (1890): 319–25.

Glazer, Sidney. "The Michigan Labor Movement." *Michigan History* 29 (January-March 1945): 73–84.

Glidden, A.C. "Pioneer Farming." *Michigan Pioneer and Historical Collections* 18 (1891): 418–22.

Goodman, Paul. "The Emergence of Homestead Exemption in the United States: Accommodation and Resistance to the Market Revolution, 1840–1880." *Journal of American History* 80 (September 1993): 470–98.

Goodrich, Enos. "Trials of Pioneer Business Men." *Michigan Pioneer and Historical Collections* 28 (1897–1898): 126–27.

Greenalch, James. "Civil War Letters." *Michigan History* 44 (June 1960): 192–240.

Haigh, Henry A. "Lansing in the Good Old Seventies." *Michigan History* 13 (January 1929): 99–112.

Henretta, James A. "Families and Farms: Mentalité in Pre-industrial America." *William and Mary Quarterly* 35 (January 1978): 3–32.

Hershock, Martin J. "Copperheads and Radicals: Michigan Partisan Politics during the Civil War Era, 1860–1865." *Michigan Historical Review* 18 (Spring 1992): 28–69.

———. "To Shield a Bleeding Humanity: Conflict and Consensus in Mid-Nineteenth Century Michigan Political Culture." *Mid-America* 77 (Winter 1995): 33–50b.

Hill, E. B. "Farm Management." *Michigan History* 22 (Summer 1938): 311–25.

Hirschfeld, Charles. "The Great Railroad Conspiracy." *Michigan History* 36 (June 1952): 97–219.

Hollister, Harvey J. "Events in Grand Rapids from 1850 to 1860." *Michigan Pioneer and Historical Collections* 35 (1907): 643–61.

Hudson, Ethel. "A Patriarch of the Pioneering Days." *Michigan History* 37 (June 1953): 145–51.

Hyde, Charles K. "From 'Subterranean Lotteries' to Orderly Investment: Michigan Copper and Eastern Dollars, 1841–1865." *Mid-America* 66 (January 1984): 3–20.

Johnson, Ludwell H. "Lincoln's Solution to the Problem of Peace Terms, 1864–1865." *Journal of Southern History* 34 (1968): 576–86.

Kantor, Shawn E., and J. Morgan Kousser. "Common Sense or Commonwealth? The Fence Law and Institutional Change in the Postbellum South." *Journal of Southern History* 59 (May 1993): 212–13.

Kilar, Jeremy W. "Andrew Johnson 'Swings' through Michigan: Community Response to a Presidential Crusade." *The Old Northwest* 3 (September 1977): 251–73.

———. "'The Blood-Rugged Issue is Impeachment or Anarchy': Michigan and the Impeachment and Trial of Andrew Johnson." *The Old Northwest* 6 (Fall 1980): 245–69.

Kilborn, Russell D. "The Michigan Railroad Commission," *Michigan History* 3 (1919): 445–72.

Kirk, Gordon W., and Carolyn T. Kirk. "Migration, Mobility and the Transformation of the Occupational Structure in an Immigrant Community: Holland, Michigan, 1850–80." *Journal of Social History* 7 (Fall 1973): 142–64.

Klement, Frank L. "Economic Aspects of Middle Western Copperheadism." *Historian* 14 (1951): 27–44.

———. "The Hopkins Hoax and Golden Circle Rumors in Michigan: 1861–1862." *Michigan History* 47 (March 1963): 1–14.

Kruman, Marc W. "The Second American Party System and the Transformation of Revolutionary Republicanism." *Journal of the Early Republic* 12 (Winter 1992): 509–37.

Kulikoff, Allan. "The Transition to Capitalism in Rural America." *William and Mary Quarterly* 46 (January 1989): 120–44.

Lankton, Larry, and Jack K. Martin. "Technological Advance, Organizational Structure, and Underground Fatalities in the Upper Michigan Copper Mines, 1860–1929." *Technology and Culture* 28 (January 1987): 42–66.

Leech, Carl A. "Lumbering Days," *Michigan History* 18 (Spring 1934): 135–42.

London, Lena. "Homestead Exemption in the Michigan Constitutional Convention of 1850." *Michigan History* 37 (December 1953): 385–406.

McCain, Anne. "Charles Edward Stuart of Kalamazoo." *Michigan History* 44 (September 1960): 324–35.

McCann, William., ed. "A Trip to the Mining Country of Lake Superior." *Michigan History* 40 (June 1956): 227–26.

McCloskey, John C. "Back-Country Folkways in Mrs. Kirkland's *A New Home—Who'll Follow?*" *Michigan History* 40 (September 1956): 297–308.

———. "Land Speculation in Michigan as Described in Mrs. Kirkland's *A New Home—Who'll Follow?*" *Michigan History* 42 (March 1958): 26–34.

McCutcheon, O. E. "President Andrew Johnson at Albion." *Michigan History* 3 (October 1919): 530–39.

———. "Recollections of Zachariah Chandler." *Michigan History* 5 (January-April 1921): 140–49.

McDaid, William. "Kinsley S. Bingham and the Republican Ideology of Antislavery, 1847–1855." *Michigan Historical Review* 16 (Fall 1990): 43–74.

Mason, Phillip P., ed. "The Operation of the Sault Canal, 1857." *Michigan History* 39 (March 1955): 69–70.

———. "Apologia of a Republican Office Seeker." *Michigan History* 41 (March 1957): 76–90.

May, George S. "Ann Arbor and the Coming of the Civil War." *Michigan History* 36 (September 1952): 241–59.

———. "Politics in Ann Arbor during the Civil War." *Michigan History* 37 (March 1953): 53–73.

Merrill, Michael. "Cash Is Good to Eat: Self-Sufficiency and Exchange in the Rural Economy of the United States." *Radical History Review* 4 (Winter 1977): 42–73.

Moore, Charles. "A Sketch of the Life of Sullivan M. Cutcheon with Particular Reference to Michigan Political History during the War of Rebellion." *Michigan Pioneer and Historical Collections* 30 (1903): 99–108.

Norris, Joseph L. "Country Merchant—Industrial Magnate." *Michigan History* 40 (September 1956): 328–44.

Norton, Clark F. "Early Michigan Supreme Court Decisions on the Liquor Question." *Michigan History* 28 (January-March 1944): 41–66.

———. "Early Movement for the St. Mary's Ship Canal." *Michigan History* 39 (September 1955): 257–80.

Norton, John M. "Early Pioneer Life in Oakland County." *Michigan Pioneer and Historical Collections* 26 (1894–1895): 262.

Odle, Thomas D. "The Commercial Interests of the Great Lakes and the Campaign Issues of 1860." *Michigan History* 40 (March 1956): 1–23.

Prichett, John B. "Michigan Democracy in the Civil War." *Michigan History* 11 (January 1927): 92–110.

Quist, John W. "'The Great Majority of Our Subscribers are Farmers': The Michigan Abolitionist Constituency of the 1840s." *Journal of the Early Republic* 14 (Fall 1994): 325–58.

Randall, Herbert. "Alpheus Felch: An Appreciation." *Michigan History* 10 (April 1926): 157–74.

Rasmussen, Wayne D. "The Civil War: A Catalyst of Agricultural Revolution." *Agricultural History* 39 (October 1965): 187–96.

Reynolds, John F. "Piety and Politics: Evangelism in the Michigan Legislature, 1837–1861." *Michigan History* 61 (1977): 323–52.

Riley, H. H. "John S. Barry." *Michigan Pioneer and Historical Collections* 11 (1887): 227–33.

Robinson, O. W. "Recollections of Civil War Conditions in the Copper Country." *Michigan History* 3 (October 1919): 598–609.

Robson, Frank E. "How Lansing Became the Capital." *Michigan Pioneer and Historical Collections* 11 (1887): 237.

Rosentreter, Roger L. "Michigan and the Compromise of 1850." *The Old Northwest* 6 (Summer 1980): 154–73.

Ross, G. Alexander. "Fertility Change on the Michigan Frontier: Saginaw County, 1840–1850." *Michigan Historical Review* 12 (1986): 69–86.

———. "Delaying the Fertility Decline: German Women in Saginaw County, Michigan, 1850–1880." *Journal of Family History* 14 (Summer 1989): 157–70.

Russel, Robert R. "The Issues in the Congressional Struggle over the Kansas-Nebraska Bill, 1854." *Journal of Southern History* 29 (1963): 187–210.

Scheiber, Harry N. "Economic Change in the Civil War Era: An Analysis of Recent Studies." *Civil War History* 11 (1965): 396–411.

Schneider, John C. "Public Order and the Geography of the City: Crime, Violence and the Police in Detroit, 1845–1875." *Journal of Urban History* 4 (1978): 183–208.

Seavoy, Ronald E. "Borrowed Laws to Speed Development: Michigan, 1835–1860." *Michigan History* 59 (1975): 39–68.

———. "The Organization of the Republican Party in Michigan, 1846–1854." *The Old Northwest* 6 (1980): 343–76.

Sewell, Richard H. "Michigan Farmers and the Civil War." *Michigan History* 44 (December 1960): 353–74.

Shade, William G. " Banks and Politics in Michigan, 1835–1845: A Reconsideration." *Michigan History* 57 (March 1973): 28–52.

Shelly, Cara. "Republican Benchmark: The Michigan Supreme Court, 1858–1875." *Mid-America* 77 (Spring-Summer 1995): 93–119.

Silbey, Joel. "The Civil War Synthesis in American Political History." *Civil War History* 10 (1964): 130–40.

Silliman, Sue Imogene. "A Prince in Puddleford." *Michigan History* 13 (January 1929): 252–64.

Smith, Stanley B. "Notes on the Village of Schoolcraft in the 1850's." *Michigan History* 40 (June 1956): 129–51.

Soper, Sarah E. "Reminiscence of Pioneer Life in Oakland County." *Michigan Pioneer and Historical Collection* 28 (1897–98): 399.

Starr, Stephen Z. "Was There a Northwest Conspiracy?" *Filson Club Historical Quarterly* 38 (1964): 323–39.

Steele, G. M. "Down in a Copper Mine." *Michigan History* 40 (June 1956): 227–35.

Steele, William H. "Frontier Life in the Lake Superior Region." *Michigan History* 13 (July 1929): 398–420.

Stocking, William. "Industrial Detroit: Fifty Years of Industrial Progress." *Michigan History* 10 (October 1926): 609–16.

———. "Little Journeys in Journalism: Michigan Press Influence on Party Formation." *Michigan History* 11 (June 1927): 208–13.

Streeter, Floyd B. "History of Prohibition Legislation in Michigan." *Michigan History* 2 (April 1918): 289–308.

Swift, Donald C., and Lawrence E. Ziewacz. "The Election of 1882: A Republican Analysis." *Journal of the Great Lakes History Conference* 1 (1976): 12–26.

Taber, Morris C. "New England's Influence in Southeastern Michigan." *Michigan History* 45 (1961): 305–36.

Tap, Bruce. "'The Evils of Intemperance are Universally Conceded:' The Temperance Debate in Early Grand Rapids." *Michigan Historical Review* 19 (Spring 1993): 17–45.

Thornton, J. Mills. "The Ethic of Subsistence and the Origins of Southern Secession." *Tennessee Historical Quarterly* 48 (1989): 67–85.

Utley, Henry M. "The Wildcat Banking System in Michigan." *Michigan Pioneer and Historical Collections* 5 (1882): 209–22.

Van Buren, A. D. P. "Sketches, Reminiscences, and Anecdotes of the Old Members of the Calhoun and Kalamazoo County Bars." *Michigan Pioneer and Historical Collections* 11 (1887): 271–318.

———. "Michigan in Her Pioneer Politics, Michigan in Our National Politics, and Michigan in the Campaign of 1856." *Michigan Pioneer and Historical Collections* 17 (1890): 238–94.

———. "Memoir of Judge Isaac Peckham Christiancy." *Michigan Pioneer and Historical Collections* 18 (1891): 333–40.

Van Oosten, John. "Michigan's Commercial Fisheries of the Great Lakes." *Michigan History* 22 (Winter 1938): 107.

Vinyard, Jo Ellen. "Inland Urban Immigrants: The Detroit Irish, 1850." *Michigan History* 57 (1973): 121–39.

Walsh, Justin E. "Radically and Thoroughly Democratic: Wilbur F. Storey and the *Detroit Free Press*, 1853 to 1861." *Michigan History* 47 (September 1963): 193–225.

Warren, Louis A. "Lincoln's Eloquence in Kalamazoo, 1856." *Michigan History* 41 (March 1957): 67–75.

Wells, Hezekiah G. "A Sketch of the Members of the Constitutional Conventions of 1835 and 1850." *Michigan Pioneer and Historical Collections* 3 (1881): 37–40.

Wesley, Norton. "Methodist Episcopal Church in Michigan and the Politics of Slavery, 1850–1860." *Michigan History* 48 (1964): 192–213.

Wilkshire, Steven C. "Markets and Market Culture in the Early Settlement of Ionia County, Michigan," *Michigan Historical Review* 24 (Spring 1998): 1–22.

Williams, Frederick D. "Robert McClelland and the Secession Crisis." *Michigan History* 43 (June 1959): 155–64.

———. "Michigan Soldiers in the Civil War." *Michigan History* 44 (March 1960): 1–35.

Wilson, Charles R. "McClellan's Changing Views on the Peace Plank." *American Historical Review* 38 (1933): 498–505.

Wilson, Major. "Republicanism and the Idea of Party in the Jacksonian Period." *Journal of the Early Republic* 8 (Winter 1988): 419–42.

Woodman, Elias S. "Reminiscences of the Constitutional Convention of 1850." *Michigan Pioneer and Historical Collections* 17 (1890): 345–50.

NEWSPAPERS

Advertiser, Detroit, Michigan, 1850–1862

Advertiser and Tribune, Detroit, Michigan, 1862–1867

American Citizen, Jackson, Michigan, 1850–1867

Cass County Advocate, Cassopolis, Michigan, 1850

Catholic Vindicator, Detroit, Michigan, 1853–1857

Courier, Saginaw, Michigan, 1859–1866

Daily Democrat, Detroit, Michigan, 1850–1854

Daily Enquirer and Herald, Grand Rapids, Michigan, 1857–1861

Daily Enterprise, East Saginaw, Michigan, 1866–1867

Daily Post, Detroit, Michigan, 1866–1867

Democrat, Grand Rapids, Michigan, 1865–1867

Democratic Expounder, Marshall, Michigan, 1849–1850

Eagle, Grand Rapids, Michigan, 1850–1867

Eaton Democrat, Eaton Rapids, Michigan, 1850

Enquirer, Grand Rapids, Michigan, 1850–1862

Expositor, Adrian, Michigan, 1854

Express, Niles, Michigan, 1850

Free Democrat, Ann Arbor, Michigan, 1850–1854

Free Press, Detroit, Michigan, 1850–1867

Gazette, Hillsdale, Michigan, 1850

Gazette, Pontiac, Michigan, 1852–1854

Grand River Eagle, Grand Rapids, Michigan, 1850–1852

Jacksonian, Pontiac, Michigan, 1850

Lake Superior Mining Journal, Copper Harbor, Michigan, 1846–1848; Sault Ste.
    Marie, Michigan, 1848–1855; Marquette, Michigan, 1858–1860, 1865–1867

Macomb Gazette, Mt. Clemens, Michigan, 1850

Macomb Monitor, Mt. Clemens, Michigan, 1866

Michigan Christian Herald, Detroit, Michigan, 1851

Michigan Free Democrat, Detroit, Michigan, 1852–1855

Michigan State Journal, Lansing, Michigan, 1850

Northern Islander, St. James, Michigan, 1852–1856

Peninsular Freeman, Detroit, Michigan, 1851

Public Sentiment, Grass Lake, Michigan, 1852–1854

Republican, Niles, Michigan, 1854

Republican, White Pigeon, Michigan, 1866

Saginaw Enterprise, East Saginaw, Michigan, 1853–1867

Sentinel, Coldwater, Michigan, 1853

Shiawassee Democrat and Owosso Argus, Owosso, Michigan, 1850

Spirit of the Times, Saginaw, Michigan, 1850–1854

State Republican, Lansing, Michigan, 1855–1867

Statesman, Marshall, Michigan, 1854

Telegraph, Jonesville, Michigan, 1851

Telegraph, Kalamazoo, Michigan, 1854–1855

Tribune, Detroit, Michigan, 1850–1860 (weekly), 1861–1862 (daily)

Washtenaw Whig, Ann Arbor, Michigan, 1849

Watchtower, Adrian, Michigan, 1853–1854

Weekly Review, Albion, Michigan, 1860

Western Chronicle, Centreville, Michigan, 1850

THESES AND DISSERTATIONS

Applegate, Margaret J. "The *Detroit Free Press* during the Civil War." Master's thesis,
    Wayne State University, 1938.

Barton, Richard Harvey. "The Agrarian Revolt in Michigan, 1865–1920." Ph.D.
    diss., Michigan State University, 1958.

Brink, Alice M. "The Drama of Detroit from Its Inception to 1870." Master's thesis,
    Wayne State University, 1937.

Brown, Henry D. "Early Organization of the Republican Party." Ph.D. diss., University of Michigan, 1958.

Brown, R. Ben. "The Southern Range: A Study in Nineteenth Century Law and Society." Ph.D. diss., University of Michigan, 1993.

Cavanagh, Helen M. "Antislavery Sentiment and Politics in the Northwest, 1844–1860." Ph.D. diss., University of Chicago, 1938.

Christianson, Paul A. "The Public Life of Kinsley Scott Bingham: The First Republican Governor of Michigan." Master's thesis, Wayne State University, 1938.

Cole, Bruce M. "The Dissolution of the Whig Party in the Northwest." Ph.D. diss., University of Chicago, 1952.

Dickinson, John N. "The Canal at Sault Sainte Marie: Inception, Operation, and Canal Grant Lands." Ph.D. diss., University of Wisconsin, 1968.

Engelman, Larry D. "Prohibition in Michigan." Ph.D. diss., University of Michigan, 1971.

Everson, Hillary J. "Monroe and the Civil War Years, 1850–1865." Master's thesis, Wayne State University, 1950.

Fisher, Dorothy. "Personnel of Political Parties in Wayne County from 1848 to 1878." Master's thesis, Wayne State University, 1935.

Harris, Robert C. "Austin Blair of Michigan: A Political Biography." Ph.D. diss., Michigan State University, 1969.

Helfman, Harold M. "A Study of Penal, Reformatory, and Correctional Institutions in Michigan, 1839–1889." Ph.D. diss., University of Michigan, 1947.

Herdman, Gerald George. "The Impact of the Civil War on Calhoun County, Michigan." Ph.D. diss., University of Maryland, 1972.

Heyda, Marie. "The Urban Dimension and the Midwestern Frontier: A Study of Democracy at Ypsilanti, Michigan 1825–1858." Ph.D. diss., University of Michigan, 1968.

Holderreid, Elsa. "Public Life of Jacob Merritt Howard." Master's thesis, Wayne State University, 1950.

Jacobi, Robert H. "The Life of Zachariah Chandler." Ph.D. diss., University of Wisconsin, 1952.

Joseph, Rodney H. "The Michigan Press and the Coming of the Civil War, 1859–1861." Ph.D. diss., Michigan State University, 1972.

McCoy, Alexandra. "Political Affiliations of American Economic Elites: Wayne County, Michigan, 1844, 1860 as a Test Case." Ph.D. diss., Wayne State University, 1965.

Messner, Vivian T. "The Public Life of Austin Blair, War Governor of Michigan (1863–1894)." Master's thesis, Wayne State University, 1937.

Morrow, Curtis H. "Politico-Military Secret Societies of the Northwest during the Civil War." Ph.D. diss., Clark University, 1941.

Ndukwu, Maurice Dickson. "Anti-slavery in Michigan: A Study of Its Origin, Development and Expression from the Territorial Period to 1860." Ph.D. diss., Michigan State University, 1979.

Prentiss, Dale R. "Economic Progress and Social Dissent in Michigan and Mississippi, 1837–1860." Ph.D. diss., Stanford University, 1990.

Puffer, Raymond L. "The Michigan Agricultural Frontier: Southeastern Region, 1820–1860." Ph.D. diss., University of New Mexico, 1976.

Randall, Paul A. "Gubernatorial Platforms for the Political Parties of Michigan, 1834–1864." Master's thesis, Wayne State University, 1937.

Reid, Helen. "Michigan and the Policy of Free Homesteads, 1845–1862." Master's thesis, Wayne State University, 1937.

Renfrew, W. Andrew. "Copperheads, Confederates, and Conspiracies on the Detroit-Canadian Border." Master's thesis, Wayne State University, 1952.

Reynolds, John F. "Piety and Evangelicalism in the Michigan House, 1838–1860." Master's thesis, Michigan State University, 1974.

Rockway, Robert A. "History of Prohibition in Michigan." Ph.D. diss., University of Michigan, 1967.

Ryskamp, Henry. "The Dutch in Western Michigan." Ph.D. diss., University of Michigan, 1965.

Shapiro, Madeleine S. "Michigan Public Opinion, the Mexican War, and the Wilmot Proviso: Legislative Resolutions as Opinion Indicators." Master's thesis, Wayne State University, 1964.

Shirigian, John. "Zachariah Chandler: His Economic Policies and Practices in the United States Senate, 1857–1875." Master's thesis, Wayne State University, 1953.

Skavery, Stanley. "A Case Study of the Irish of Detroit, 1850–1880." Ed.D. diss., University of Michigan, 1986.

Slavcheff, Peter D. "The Temperate Republic: Liquor Control in Michigan, 1800–1860." Ph.D. diss., Wayne State University, 1987.

Smith, Earl O. "The Public Life of Austin Blair, War-Governor of Michigan, 1845–1863." Master's thesis, Wayne State University, 1934.

Steck, Douglas E. "The Liberal Reform Movement in Michigan Politics, 1870–1876." Ph.D. diss., Michigan State University, 1975.

Stevens, Walter W. "A Study of Lewis Cass and His United States Senate Speeches on Popular Sovereignty." Ph.D. diss., University of Michigan, 1959.

Thomas, Sister M. Evangeline. "Nativism in the Old Northwest, 1850–1860." Ph.D. diss., Catholic University, 1936.

Volpe, Vernon L. "Forlorn Hope of Freedom: The Liberty Party in the Old Northwest, 1838–1848." Ph.D. diss., University of Nebraska, 1984.

Walsh, Justin E. "To Print the News and Raise Hell: A Biography of Wilbur E. Storey." Ph.D. diss., Indiana University, 1964.

Warsh, Louis, P. "Zachariah Chandler: Merchant as Politician." Ph.D. diss., University of California, 1952.

Welch, Gerald D. "William Woodbridge (1780–1860): A Biography." Ph.D. diss., University of Denver, 1970.

Wilson, Benjamin C. "Michigan's Ante-bellum Black Haven: Cass County, 1835–1870." Ph.D. diss., Michigan State University, 1975.

PRIMARY SOURCES

Michigan Historical Collections, Bentley Historical Library, University of Michigan, Ann Arbor

Peter R. Adams Papers, 1826–1883

Rice Aner Beal Papers, 1843–1883

Joseph E. Beebe Papers, 1847–1871

Kinsley Scott Bingham Papers, 1815–1920

Austin Blair Papers, 1861–1863 and 1882

Buck Family Papers, 1851–1928

James V. Campbell Papers, 1830–1941

Candler Family Papers, 1794–1864

Zachariah Chandler Papers, 1854–1879

Isaac Peckham Christiancy Papers, 1840–1883

Clarke-DeLand Family Papers, 1830–1919

John Potter Cook Papers, 1856–1878

Thomas M. Cooley Papers, 1850–1898

Henry H. Crapo Papers, 1830–1910

DeLand Family Papers, 1842–1913

Dennis Family Papers, 1832–1863

Alpheus Felch Papers, 1806–1896

Abel Fitch Letters, 1851

Fox Family Papers, 1863–1866

James Fraser Letters, 1841–1861

George Germain Hill Papers, 1842–1852

Benjamin F. Graves Papers, 1815–1949

George D. Hill Papers, 1846–1866 and 1870–1876

William A. Howard Papers, 1856–1880

James F. Joy Papers, 1834–1900

Curtis F. Leneweaker Papers, 1833–1857

Flavius Littlejohn Papers, ca. 1862–1875

John W. Longyear Papers, 1846–1875

Robert McClelland Notebooks, 1861–1864

Charles S. May Papers, 1830–1901

Mitchell-Strong Family Correspondence, 1836–1925

Valorous R. Paine Papers, 1845–1865

D. H. Pease Letter, 1851

Darius Pierce Papers, 1810–1901

Nathan Pierce Papers, 1790–1862

Pond Family (Ann Arbor) Papers, 1864–1866

Fred B. Porter Journals, 1848–1854
Nathan Power Papers, 1826–1873
David Pratt (Family) Papers, 1836–1863
Joseph Rickey Papers, 1850–1863
Francis Shearman Papers, 1817–1874
Seth K. Shetterly Papers, 1829–1934
Oliver L. Spaulding Papers, 1861–1921
Thomas Stevenson Papers, 1856–1909
Student Papers, Department of History, University of Michigan
George M. Tuthill Diaries, 1847–1885
Anson de Puy Van Buren Papers, 1845–1885
Henry Clay Waldron Papers, 1865–1909
Williams Family [Owosso] Papers, 1838–1953
Jeremiah D. Williams (Family) Papers, 1808–1904
Warner Wing Papers, 1837–1878
David Woodman Scrapbook, 1877–1902
David O. Woodruff Papers, 1836–1883
William L. Clements Library, Ann Arbor, Michigan
James Birney Papers, 1816–1857
Lewis Cass Papers. 1774–1921
James W. Gilbert Collection, 1862
Lucius Lyon Papers, 1812–1852
Michigan Collection, 1761–1947
Burton Historical Collection, Detroit Public Library, Detroit, Michigan
John Barry Papers, 1847–1851
Kinsley Scott Bingham Correspondence, 1855–1861
Austin Blair Papers, 1838–1921
Buel Family Papers, 1832–1910
Lewis Cass Correspondence and Papers, 1780–1907
Henry H. Crapo Papers, 1853–1888
Alpheus Felch Papers, 1823–1897
Jacob M. Howard Collection, 1860–1865
James F. Joy Papers, 1700–1869
Robert McClelland Letterbook, 1833–1862
Charles S. May Papers, 1833–1899
Charles C. Trowbridge Collection
University Archives and Historical Collections, Michigan State University, East Lansing
Town Family Papers, 1830–1932, 1850–1876
Henry Clay Waldron Papers
State Archives of Michigan, Lansing
Executive Department Records, Record Group 44
Clarke Historical Library, Central Michigan University, Mt. Pleasant

John Ball Papers, 1815–1883
James Bartlett Letter, 1862
F. H. Cuming Letters, 1849–1850
Charles Henry Curtis Papers, 1854–1900
James S. Fisher Diary, 1850
Henrie B. Flager Letter, 1860
Abraham Wendel Papers, 1818–1874
Government Documents
U.S. Department of Commerce, Bureau of the Census, *The Seventh Census of the United States, 1850.*
U.S. Department of Commerce, Bureau of the Census, *The Eighth Census of the United States, 1860.*

BIBLIOGRAPHICAL AIDS

Brown, Ida C. *Michigan Men in the Civil War.* Ann Arbor: Michigan Historical Collections Bulletin no. 27, September 1977.

Ellis, Helen H. *Michigan in the Civil War: A Guide to the Material in Detroit Newspapers, 1861–1866.* Lansing: Michigan Civil War Centennial Observance Commission, 1965.

Hathaway, Richard. *Dissertations and Theses in Michigan History.* Lansing: Michigan History Division, Michigan Department of State, 1974.

Library of Michigan. *Michigan Newspapers on Microfilm.* Lansing: Michigan State Library, 1986.

May, George S., ed. *Michigan Civil War History: An Annotated Bibliography.* Detroit, Mich.: Wayne State University Press, 1961.

Michigan Historical Commission. *Michigan County Histories: A Bibliography.* Lansing: Michigan Department of Education, State Library Services, 1978.

Sprenger, Bernice Cox, ed. *Guide to the Manuscripts in the Burton Historical Collection.* Detroit, Mich.: Detroit Public Library, 1985.

INDEX

abolitionism, 112; criticized by Democrats, 171; distinguished from antislavery, 112; and Republican Party, 160. *See also* antislavery; Free-Soilism; slavery

Adrian, MI, 58, 68, 85, 96–97, 247n16

Adrian Watchtower, 38, 111

African Americans, 70, 197, 242n39. *See also* black codes; black suffrage

agriculture: and Civil War, 194–95; commercial, x, 40, 61–62; and fencing laws, 42; mechanization of, 194; post–Civil War crisis, 211; subsistence, x, 41–43, 53–55, 61, 71, 74, 235n3; wool trade, 36, 195. *See also* liberty; livestock; market economy; market revolution; open-range grazing; republicanism

Alabama, 78

Albany, NY, 67

Albion, MI, 115, 241n33

Albion Weekly Review, 74

Allegan County, MI, 214, 240n29

Alvord, H. J., 141

Amboy, Lansing, and Grand Traverse Bay Railroad, 237n13

American Party. *See* Know-Nothings

Anbinder, Tyler, 78–79, 256n69

Anderson, Virginia, 243n43

Ann Arbor, MI, 7–8, 43, 48, 68–69, 114, 119, 176

Ann Arbor American, 99

Ann Arbor Journal, 163–64

Ann Arbor Michigan Argus, 151–52, 167, 179, 214

Ann Arbor Michigan State News, 172–73

antiparty sentiment, 19–20

antirailroad hostility, 39–51, 81–97, 177, 214; and federal land grant of 1856, 145–46; impact on elections of 1851–52, 88–90; nonpartisan nature of, 120; and Patrons of Husbandry, 211, 213; in post–Civil War era, 198–207, 281n23; role in Republican fusion, 120, 123, 127, 129; and second American party system, 257n70. *See also* general railroad incorporation law; Great Railroad Conspiracy; Michigan Central Railroad Company

antislavery, xv; distinguished from abolitionism, 112; and historiography, 111; Know-Nothings and, 256n69; in politics, 79, 111–16; in Republican Party ideology, 112–15, 136. *See also* abolitionism; Free-Soilism; Free-Soil Party; liberty; Liberty Party; Slave Power; slavery

Army of the Potomac, 172

Arnold, Daniel, 155

ash trade, 65

Atack, Jeremy, 238n18

Atlanta, GA, 179

Backus, Henry T., 37, 227n16

Bagg, B. Rush, 110

Bagg, Joseph, 18, 20–21, 30–31, 229n39

Bagley, David, 190

Bagley, John, 209, 213–15

Baldwin, Henry P., 172, 204